P9-CSA-767

Shaping Sanctuary

Proclaiming God's Grace in an Inclusive Church

compiled and edited by
Kelly Turney

published in cooperation with the Welcoming Church Movement

Reconciling Congregation Program

Liturgies in this book may be reprinted for use in local church worship service, provided the following notice is included:

From *Shaping Sanctuary: Proclaiming God's Grace in an Inclusive Church*, edited by Kelly Turney. Copyright ©2000 by Reconciling Congregation Program. Reprinted by permission.

Copyright and reprint instruction for musical resources are included at the bottom of each hymn.

Scripture quotations are from the New Revised Standard Version of the Bible, copyright ©1989 by the Division of Christian Education of the National Council of the Churches of Christ in the U.S.A., and are used by permission. Adaptations may have been made for the sake of inclusive language.

Additional acknowledgment of sources may be found at the back of the book. We are grateful to the many publishers and authors who have given permission to include their work. Every effort has been made to determine the ownership of all texts and to make proper arrangements for their use. We will gladly correct in future editions any oversight or error that is brought to our attention.

Book design by Jan Graves

Artwork © by Jan Richardson

The Best Supper, cover; Change the World, p. 14; Moon Dance, p. 266; Mother Root, p. 88; The Quilter, p. 72; Redemption, p. 140; The Water-Bearer, p. 54

Printed in the United States of America

Library of Congress Cataloging-in-Publication Data

Shaping sanctuary : proclaiming God's grace in an inclusive church / compiled and edited by Kelly Turney. — 1st ed.
    p. cm.
    Includes bibliographical references and index.
    ISBN 0-9701568-0-4 (pbk. : alk. paper)
    1. Worship programs.   2. Gays—Religious life.
    3. Homosexuality—Religious aspects—Christianity.
    I. Turney, Kelly, 1965– .
BV199.G39S53 2000
    264'.0086'64—dc21   00-010237

Contents

Chapter 5

Chapter 6

Chapter 7

Chapter 8

Introduction

*T*he charged quality of her voice stays with me still.
Sitting across the table from me was a mother with a
story of pain, anger and heartbreak. She told of ten
agonizing years separated from her gay son as she tried to
follow the church's teaching about homosexuality. She was
advised by one pastor to turn her back on her son and his
sin until he repented. Another told her to "love the sinner but
hate the sin." She tried to hate one while loving the other
but "it all got mixed up" she said. Her son, always a deeply
religious boy growing up, left the church and struggled alone
with how to be spiritual without family or church
community. This pained her deeply. In the end, she felt cut
off from her son, her church and her God. That is, until she
found a "welcoming" congregation–a place where she was
encouraged to read the Scriptures for herself, allowed to
prayerfully seek God's answers for her life through Bible
study and living in community with others, and offered safe
space to journey together with her son to seek God's truth
and accept God's grace. Her joy at having found such a
place was overwhelming. It brought her and her son closer
to God, closer to each other, and closer to her church
community.

The "*welcoming church movement*" (also called the "welcoming movement") started in the late 1970s, generally in response to some very negative legislation in several denominations condemning "homosexuality" or prohibiting Gay and Lesbian pastors. Several denominations responded by establishing programs, both within and outside their denominational structures, that would allow congregations (and other church bodies) the opportunity to declare a welcome to persons of every sexual orientation. These programs are organized, funded, and run differently. Their networks of churches also range in size, each with anywhere from 20 to over 300 congregations (over 1,000 all together). The names of these programs in the various denominations are:

Affirming Congregation Programme (United Church of Canada)
More Light Presbyterians
Oasis (Episcopal)
Open and Affirming – ONA (United Church of Christ)
Open and Affirming – O&A (Christian Church, Disciples of Christ)
Reconciling in Christ (Lutheran)
Reconciling Congregation Program (United Methodist)
Supportive (Brethren/Mennonite)
Welcoming & Affirming (American Baptist)
Welcoming (Unitarian Universalist)

The intention of these programs should not be confused with those whose message of welcome is conditional–that is, reserved only for those who are closeted, repentant, celibate, or trying to change to be heterosexual. On the contrary, the *welcoming movements* proclaim a Gospel message of love and grace that is not exclusively available to heterosexual people. They seek to help shape a church that offers God's welcome, affirmation, and reconciliation to people of every age, color, gender, and ability–whether Lesbian, Gay, Bisexual or Heterosexual.

Liturgy: The Struggle and The Gift

As I compiled the submissions for this volume, a collective story emerged. A story of struggle that turns to gift as faith communities examine the issues of exclusion and grace. In the process many ideas are reconsidered, old interpretations are found wanting, and new ways of understanding are embraced. The old dualism of spirit and body–long used to name some as good and others as bad– is just one of many ideas that is explored and reevaluated.

Those who have struggled with Peter's dream about what is clean and unclean (Acts 10) hear a call to proclaim God's grace even to those who were formerly considered outcasts. Like Cornelius at the gate, they have heard the cries of those designated unclean. These communities find themselves drawing the circle of God's grace ever wider–they find their God getting bigger. Their sermons and prayers tell of a God that surprises them, does new things in their midst, and looks less like themselves than they first imagined. They find themselves more open to the movement of the Holy Spirit. Out of this experience have come not only rituals that affirm the diversity of human sexuality, but liturgies that celebrate the return from incarceration, claim a new gendered existence, or assert a fresh identity following a divorce.

Other sermons and liturgies emerge from those who have taken seriously the New Testament message against "pornia," (Greek for sexual immorality), studied scholars' insights, and grappled with the church's tradition of inhospitality to many kinds of difference. Out of this blessed struggle emerges the reality that the church does not have an impressive history of discussing or appreciating sexuality–even hetero-sexuality. Theologian and scholar James Nelson reminds us that a great deal of Christian theology "has tended to treat the human body as something other than the essential person."[1] Still, through their work, writers in this volume have found a message of God's grace to all and a spirit of hope despite much of the tradition.

And there are streams of thought arising from our earliest heritage which do point us in a more sexuality-affirming direction.
Womanist theologian, Kelly Brown Douglas, reminds us that
> the message of God's embodiment in Jesus is unambiguous: the human body is not a cauldron of evil but, rather an instrument for divine presence. It is the medium by which God is made "real" to humanity through which God interacts in human history.[2]

Douglas credits the gradual influence of Greek thought, which denigrated the body, with moving Christianity away from the Hebrew understanding of sexuality as a gift from God. In her book, *Sexuality and the Black Church,* she traces the reasons why sexuality has been a "taboo" subject for the Black church, even though African religious heritage views human sexuality as divine and, historically, those enslaved possessed a more accurate view of incarnation than their Western, free counterparts. She argues that

White culture's attacks on Black sexuality and its use of it as a tool of exploitation and oppression has effectively diminished Black valuation of sexuality. The desire for power remains a controlling force behind the continued abuse of sexuality in sexism and homophobia as well. And while we leave the analysis of the problem and its causes to the scholars, Chapter 1 offers voices seeking to heal the split between our spirits and our bodies and points to our obligation to form an embodied theology.

In *Body Theology*, James Nelson defines a viable embodied or sexual theology for our time as one that

> will understand our sexuality as intrinsic to the divine-human connection, as one of the great arenas for celebrating the Source of Life....Such theology will understand our sexuality as capable of expressing our intended destiny for freedom, creativity, vulnerability, joy and shalom. Such sexual theology will express the prophetic critique on every institutional and cultural arrangement that sexually distorts and oppresses, it will be grounded in commitments to equality, justice, and fulfillment.[3]

He goes on to argue that the ethic that might flow from such a theology will be

> strongly sex-affirming, understanding sexual pleasure as a moral good rooted in the sacred value of our sensuality and erotic power, and not needing justification by procreative possibility. It will be grounded in respect for our own and others' bodily integrity and will help us defend against the common sexual violations of that integrity. It will celebrate fidelity in our commitments without legalistic prescription as to the precise forms such fidelity must take. It will be an ethic whose principles apply equally and without double standards to persons of both genders, of all colors, ages, bodily conditions and sexual orientations.[4]

Some of the important work of living a sexual theology happens in *welcoming movement* churches. The liturgies in Chapters 5, 6, and 7 imply more than they state, but, if you look closely, you will see an underlying theology that:

- makes connections between different oppressions,
- rethinks the dualism that separates sacred and secular,
- recognizes the church's current suspicion and repression of sexuality as damaging,

- understands ourselves as deeply relational and interdependent rather than individual and independent,
- believes the trinity of God reveals God as intrinsically relational, and
- understands sexuality as integral to who we are.

This theology affirms the definition of sexuality offered by James Nelson and Kelly Brown Douglas:

> Human sexuality *is* what provides men and women with the capacity to enter into relationships with others. Sexuality is that dimension of humanity that urges relationships. Sexuality thus expresses God's intention that we find our authentic humanness in relationship.[5]

Worship Shaping Lives

The liturgy within these pages takes worship, language, and the journey as a faith community seriously. It seeks forgiveness for treating "the church as an organization in which we may or may not participate" (as the confession on page 107 states). This liturgy acknowledges that we sometimes speak and act reality into being, with feeling coming later. It encourages us to forge a unity between prayer and action. It gives expression to the belief that divine energy, joy, and abundant life are shaped in our communal spiritual practices.

Thus, it is in worship that a church makes the true journey to become welcoming. For worship is the community's vehicle for living out its identity, values and theology. These pages present challenges to modes of worship in which movement is absent; individuals gather but there is no community; where social justice is the realm of politics and not religion; and, in which the body is not present except as the ache of the tail bone against the hard pew. Instead, in Chapter 6, rituals are designed to redefine faithfulness in relationships when the relationship does not fit traditional definition, liturgies speak honestly about the messiness of change and the corporate sinfulness of the congregation, and prayers are meaningful in their complete unwillingness to look away from the realities of oppression. And you can imagine that without such liturgy—without such grappling with the parameters of renewed worship—the real work of becoming welcoming is still undone. Which is one of the reasons why this book is necessary. If a church's work of renewing, revitalizing, and recreating itself happens in its worship life, then a worship resource is needed to guide in the journey.

There is something attractive about a liturgy that does not feel the need to convince others of a particular point of view, but instead knows only that it must speak love, believing that love has the power within itself to call forth a response of the same kind. Good worship calls us to love–God, ourselves and one another. It calls us to action. It is the core energy source for the community. Thus, it is impossible for any church to change its identity in any significant way without also changing what it does in worship.

Making Connections

For many churches, their inclusiveness with regard to sexual orientation has led them to examine inclusion of others the world would also call "unclean" or unacceptable. For others, the reverse is true. Becoming "welcoming" was the result of their struggles around exclusion based on other identity categories. Many churches have a long record of fighting for civil rights and continue to fight racism, sexism, and discrimination against those with disabilities. Many are involved with issues of hunger, war, exploitation, and pollution. And an increasing number are exploring transgender awareness.

Therefore, the liturgy that develops from such churches addresses many types of exclusion. Quite often, the liturgy confronts global issues of privilege, consumerism, and our stewardship of creation. Often it speaks out against those prejudices, biases, fears and ignorance that keep us separate from one another and thus God. And it goes beyond examining our alienation from one another to speak to our relationship with the non-human world.

Thus, these pages contain a liturgical resource built on an integrated, "embodied eco-theology"– a theology that both values human sexuality and respects the environment for itself and not just for what it provides to humanity. The development and need for such a theology is offered in such books as James Nelson's *Body Theology*, Kelly Brown Douglas' *Sexuality and the Black Church* and in Sallie McFague's *Super, Natural Christians*. This last work eloquently argues that "we should love nature by relating to it in the same basic way we relate to other people; that is, with respect and care."[6]

Listening to LGBT Lives

Because *welcoming movement* churches seek to model respect and care, and because they offer a safe space, these churches have the opportunity and privilege of witnessing the lives of faithful Lesbian, Gay, Bisexual and Transgender (LGBT) persons. They have witnessed first-hand how these lives–shaped by the Holy Spirit–have built up the church. They encounter the face of Jesus Christ in the volunteer efforts of a Bisexual Sunday School teacher, the faithful service of a Transgender clergywoman, the loving raising of a child by Lesbian parents, or the attentive care for the church building and grounds by a Gay couple of twenty-two years. They have listened and discerned God in the lives of their LGBT neighbors. They have taken these lives seriously as statements of faith.

Countless current church debates over "homosexuality" would benefit from this real life experience of LGBT persons of faith. Good church people and Biblical scholars disagree about whether the Bible condemns or even addresses faithful, same-gender sexual relationships. Many mainstream denominations cannot agree on the role of Gay and Lesbian clergy or members in their churches. While some denominations state a valuing of sexuality in general and a repudiation of discrimination based on sexual orientation, there remain examples of Lesbians and Gays being forced out of their churches. Not only are ordination, covenant ceremonies, and holding church office denied to LGBT persons and their allies, stories of churches denying Gay couples holy communion and refusing to baptize the babies of same-gender couples continue to surface. Just in the past few months, two Southern Baptist churches were excluded from their national fellowship for their gay-inclusive policies. It is precisely the kind of witnessing and sharing of the lives of LGBT people that occurs in *welcoming churches* that might beneficially inform such painful situations.

Even as Luke Johnson in his book, *Scripture and Discernment*, recognizes the church's long tradition of condemning male, same-sex sexual activities, he and others commenting on his work have argued that the church must offer a place of hospitality where the gifts of LGBT persons are welcomed, a place where there is an opportunity to listen and discern from LGBT lives the new thing God may be doing in the life of the church. As with other areas of discrimination and exclusion, it took the church's interaction with

and openness to receiving the gifts of those once excluded to judge whether its continuing tradition of exclusion was appropriate. When whites excluded persons of color, it took people willing to see the suffering of slaves and the distortion of human life created by slavery to call the church to re-examine its position. It took the faithful lives of people like Richard Allen, Sojourner Truth and Martin Luther King, Jr. to offer them a new truth. When women were excluded from ordination, it took the faithful voices of Elizabeth Cady Stanton, Susanna Wesley, Antoinette Brown and many others to inspire the church to an unprecedented vision of whom God calls to ordained ministries.

The *welcoming movement* offers a place of hospitality for those in the church open to God's whisper of a new thing. It witnesses to the lives of those seeking to take seriously the incarnation, God's good creation, and sexuality and sexual orientation as part of that good creation. In so doing, it stands in the tradition of Jesus, who overturned religious and social traditions that diminished people's status as children of God. It stands with Jesus in refusing to accommodate that which excludes whole groups of people. It stands with Jesus, who saw himself as an outcast in his own land, and with a God who grants protection to the outcast. And it affirms and witnesses to the belief that God's grace is available to all.

Gathering Around the Table

It is often not that difficult for world leaders of warring countries to shake hands in front of the press, for they know that the true measure of acceptance and hospitality is sitting down to eat with one another. Eating together was an important Biblical standard of inclusiveness. Gathering around a table speaks of the willingness to share one's story, to be vulnerable, to know someone else and be known by others.

Thus, the title, *Shaping Sanctuary*. The *welcoming church movement* offers an organic shape—a bodily contour—to the institutional church, and an opportunity to turn from rigid rules of exclusion to again hear the cry of its people. *Welcoming churches* provide a sanctuary—a place set apart where the sacredness of people of every sexual orientation is recognized, where all find a place around the table of Christ. It is here where people can be vulnerable, where all can journey together to meet the Christ who goes before them. Church then is a safe, joyful space where all can shape and be shaped by an embodied theology, where sexuality is not limited to sexual acts, sexual orientation, or even our gendered-ness, but rather is a multi-faceted way of experiencing the world. Human sexuality is a vital, not optional, part of the worshiping community. It is no longer treated as a coat that can be hung on a rack at the sanctuary door, only to be retrieved when leaving sacred space.

This Resource: Using it for Worship and Study

This resource is offered as a gift to the church. It is presented as a window into the faithful journeys of LGBT persons and their allies, as a resource for justice-oriented worship, and as a tool for exploring a theology that values human sexuality and the consequences that such a theology may have for worship.

How to Use this Book

While at its most basic level, this book is a reference for those planning worship, it also provides an opportunity to examine our assumptions about sexuality and their implications for worship. Read it with an open heart and a commitment to pray, study, and work on your relationship with God and those around you, whatever their sexual orientation. I hope you will treat the contributors as resources, as additional voices, as part of the community effort to proclaim God's grace through the church's liturgy, rather than as authorities proscribing a certain point of view.

The liturgies submitted for this publication were, for the most part, written for specific occasions, within a particular context. While I have attempted to generalize these works, I hope that you will note the contextual references in the endnotes.

As this is an ecumenical publication, there are different conventions throughout the submitted liturgies. Uniformity has been created in same cases, while differences were retained when motivations of theology or convention were implied. Some are generic enough for immediate use. When context was pivotal to understanding the development and use of the piece, I included the specifics and trust that you will take the liberty to adapt the pieces as necessary. Several liturgies include specifics as an example or model to guide revisions.

There are, of course, issues of language. The *movement* in general is committed to the use of inclusive language with regard to humanity and God, and you will experience that here. The language of identification is more fluid. Whenever possible, I have used uppercase designations for Lesbian, Gay, Bisexual and Transgender to signify a claimed identity. Often, I begin with "Lesbian" rather than "Gay" in order to encourage the toppling of traditional power structures. In some congregations the acronym, LGBT is perfectly acceptable, but in others it is important to use the words. I have used Transgender as a broader designation than the past tense, Transgendered. Within the movement, the language of designating parts in litanies is in some flux. While there may be liturgical value in having high voices and low voices sound separately (as designated in this book as Female and Male), other designations of Left and Right are also used.

As a general guideline, bold text is read by the entire congregation and regular text by one voice, such as a reader, liturgist or clergyperson. Prayers of confession and affirmations of faith, while not in bold text, are generally read by the entire congregation. Note also the resources for readings. Some contributors submitted services that had contemporary readings as well as scripture readings, and while we did not have room to reprint these selections, the list is provided in hope that you will seek out these resources and excerpt them in your service. Also, the worship resource section, while not extensive, does offer some of the contributors' favorites.

Credits and Copyrights

You are welcome, and even encouraged, to use and adapt the liturgies in local worship services. Most contributors included this desire with their submissions. When using or adapting these materials, please credit the author and this publication (see the credit line on the inside title page). For those liturgies that are reprinted from other publications, please be careful to follow copyright laws and seek permission from those publishers for uses other than local worship, unless permission is specifically granted for other uses as stated in the endnotes. The references in the endnotes provide the author and publication data. The musical selections contain the copyright and type of use for which permission is granted at the bottom of each page.

Musical Notes

The music has been divided into two chapters. The first, in Chapter 9, can probably be sight-read with some ease by most congregations, but I make no guarantees. There is a song provided there that my congregation finally had a soloist sing the verses, with the congregation joining in for only the chorus. Chapter 10 contains songs that more likely to require a practice run-through before the service, or are perhaps better led by a choir. A few are from relatively inexperienced and innovative musicians, and while the notes may not always follow traditional hymn expectations, they are fine once you learn them. So don't give up!

My hope is that you will be inspired to write liturgy and music and to develop rituals that speak to your own particular community.

General liturgical writing guidelines

Here are several suggested steps to writing your own liturgy:

1. **Read scripture**. Start with the scripture for the occasion. Use a process of lectio divina (divine reading) or similar method to meditate and pray on the scripture lesson.

2. **Consider the context**. For what community is the liturgy being prepared? What are the collective needs of the group? What is the context of their ministry? What are the challenges and joys that surround the occasion? To what do the scriptures call this community?

3. **Identify a theme**. Consider the service theme or sermon topic.

4. **Revisit the scripture**. Study the scripture again for any visual concepts or word images that surface.

5. **Format.** Use the format convention for the liturgy-form being written. What follows are some examples of prayer formats. General prayers usually include adoration, confession, thanks, and supplication. Confessional prayers usually refer to both personal and corporate sinfulness and should conclude with an assurance of pardon. For some, nothing other than, "You are forgiven" will suffice. Prayers of the people usually include church concerns, local issues, and global concernswith a repeated response line (either sung or read).

see page 238

For examples of many types of prayers, read the Psalms (see also Walter Brueggeman's *Praying the Psalms*). Some Psalms are exclusively one type or another–praise, lament, thanksgiving, etc. However, you may choose to combine elements within one prayer. Choose a favorite Psalm and use its beginning line to get started and then finish with your own words. Or reinterpret a Psalm for the occasion (see page 246).

Collects, which are brief, formal prayers generally used as gatherings or before scripture readings, have five parts: 1) the God name, 2) the characteristic or attribute of God related to the name, 3) the petition related to the characteristic of God (what we are asking God to do), 4) the intended result of the petition (that which would make us more like God), 5) final doxology or affirmation.

> God, like a bakerwoman,
> you bring the leaven which causes our hopes to rise.
> With your strong and gentle hands, shape our lives.
> Warm us with your love.
> Take our common lives and
> touch them with your grace,
> that we may nourish hope among humanity.
> We pray trusting in your name, through Jesus our Christ.
> Amen.[7]

6. **Edit**. If it is a long prayer, consider cutting it by a quarter. The most common mistake in writing liturgy is wordiness. Cut words, not ideas. Simplify sentence structure where necessary. Focus on visual images, tactile themes, words that honor our embodied existence. If it will be read by the congregation, include formatting or commas to signal pauses.

7. **Cut again**. Remove long lists of items whenever possible; delete overly fussy modifiers.

8. **Be bold!** Do not be afraid to experiment, go against the rules occasionally, or try something new. It is a creative process, so you may need to close the laptop and take out the crayon.

The Study Guide

The study guide is offered as a tool to explore the essays, sermons and liturgies. It includes exercises for writing your own liturgy, and optional sessions for creating a community banner and conducting an art and spirituality class. While the study guide may be helpful to individuals, its real benefit exists for small groups. The guide is simple-to-follow and flexible; the role of facilitator rotates for each session, so no one person has to lead the course.

A Final Word

This collection is an initial offering of worship resources by the *welcoming church movement*. It offers much of the diversity and meaning of the movement, but it is not without flaws. Much imaginative work still remains if the church is to express a truly integrated, embodied eco-theology. We need to develop more body-centered rituals. In *Body Theology*, James Nelson asks if it is too much to expect the church to offer rites of passage for a female's first menstruation, a boy's coming of age, or even menopause. And for all this talk about bodies, there is precious little offered around food, which any good Methodist can tell you, is central to a religious community. We need more prayers and hymns that give voice to such occasions. Of course, some of these liturgies are offered in other works, such as Rosemary Ruether's *Women-Church*. Please see the list of worship resources for other volumes offering creative liturgies.

I am excited that the core shapers and contributors of this volume represent a broad diversity: African-American, Asian, Latino and White, persons with disabilities, parents of LGBT persons, Lesbian women, Gay men, heterosexuals, a couple of bisexuals, and at least one person identifying as Transgendered. Just about every region is represented. By design, this book serves a North American market; an international flavor is, therefore, less evident. While English is the primary language, other languages are used to remind worshipers that the Word is not the exclusive territory of any one culture. There are musical selections in several languages and translated songs from a variety of cultures.

The book includes works from seminary students, retired persons, a man living with AIDS, and a man married for sixty-three years. Many are out, some are closeted (see page 387 for the story of a closeted female, African-American, church musician). Some are single, and others partnered. There are dedicated church professionals, some lay and some clergy, a couple of Bishops and folks who do just about everything for a living, including a few who work inside the home. There are even a few children's songs, not to mention a body prayer that children will love. There are submissions from first-time composers, trained writers, professionals with several books to their credit, and even one song that "came to" a non-musician while driving to church. It has been a joy to work with this assortment of characters. Truly, churches that do not encourage diversity are disregarding wonderful gifts and robbing themselves of the blessings of the mix.

Shaping liturgy that is truly the work of *all* the people–an embodied people–is the task before the church. The sanctuary being shaped by the *welcoming church movement* proclaims God's radical grace and our desire and need to be in right relation with all of creation. It calls all of us to live out what it means to be the body of Christ, together. I hope that the discussion begun here will change and regenerate our churches in ways we can scarcely imagine.

Kelly Turney, editor
May, 2000

Chapter 1

Embodied Theology: Sexuality, Inclusion and Worship

We know that every effort to improve society, above all when society is so full of injustice and sin is an effort that God blesses, wants and demands. We have the security of knowing that what we plant, if nourished with Christian hope, will never fail.

Archbishop Oscar Romero

Integrating Sexuality and Spirituality
by Bob Treese

In the early years of my life, I saw little relationship between my sexuality and my relationship to God. My understanding of sexuality was limited to genital sex, and this was something not to be discussed. Enjoyed, yes! Understood, no! Sexual intercourse with my partner was "doing what came naturally" and was the supreme expression of our growing and deepening love for one another. Only at times when I experienced a feeling of guilt—for example, because lust had overpowered sensitive love—did I get a sense that sexuality and its expression might have something to do with my relationship to God.

Spirituality was a term I shied away from. It connoted something ethereal, unearthly, a goal toward which I was meant to grow, up and out of my earthiness toward some realm of *being* up there somewhere. Beginning in my childhood, I was perplexed by the emphasis my Sunday School teachers and others placed on another world up there somewhere. That emphasis seemed to mean denial of the world we live in. Yet we were taught that God loved this world so much that God came in Jesus of Nazareth to save it. I thought that "the Word became flesh" meant that the body was real and important and that Jesus was really human, *like me*. Why did the religion that was shaping me seem to dehumanize him? If Jesus was all good, and my natural bodily feelings were somehow bad, Jesus couldn't have been human like me—could he?

With all the confusion I felt toward spirituality, it is hardly surprising how unprepared I was when I was first forced to deal with an aspect of sexuality in a religious context. In 1965-66, I spent a sabbatical year in San Francisco on the staff of Glide Urban Center. As part of my responsibilities, I was assigned to work with the Council on Religion and the Homosexual and to serve as consultant on its Theology Committee. I went into that setting with an unexamined, typical, and naive attitude toward sexual orientation—mine was right; any other was wrong.

As I worked with that committee, however, I discovered some important things about myself. In the first place, contrary to my expectations, at our initial meeting I could not distinguish homosexual persons from heterosexuals on that committee of about a dozen men and women. I also discovered that I was scared: what would I do if one of those men tried to seduce me? (My fear was inappropriate; seductive behavior never occurred.) And, on reflection, I came to realize that I could take no credit for my sexual orientation. I had not the slightest idea how I came to be heterosexual.

As we worked together over that year, struggling with the nature and meanings of personhood of sexuality, and of the church's rejection of persons with same-sex orientation, we developed a warm, intimate relationship with strong mutual respect. Sexuality, I came to realize, is something more than, and more mysterious than, genital sex. Sexuality is present as a dynamic force in all human experiences and relationships.

That year of working with the Council on Religion and the Homosexual and the Theology Committee was a kind of new-birth experience for me, one could say a "spirituality birthing." For the first time in my life, I came to know at some depth Christians who were Gay and Lesbian. Some of these lay persons were active in congregations (though they remained closeted); others were very hurt and angry at the institution that had rejected them. All of them longed to give open expression to their faith; to be accepted as they were. And most felt accepted by God, though rejected by Christians.

As I ruminated on my responses to fear of seduction—which disappeared after our first meeting—I experienced a spiritual breakthrough. Not only did I realize that I had responded homophobically because of fear of my own impulses; I also think I began to understand how a woman must feel in the midst of a group of macho men. I felt like a sex object—objectified, robbed of my personhood—not because any of the Gay men had treated me that way but because I had imagined they would. This realization brought up the reality and brutality of sexism. I have struggled, since, with my own unconscious sexism.

I also became aware of an issue more subtle than blatant sexism. I found that I was ashamed of my own feelings of tenderness, of compassion, of the unexpected teardrop. I saw the sexism in feeling that a man should be above such "womanlike" qualities. I was forced to embrace those parts of me, finally realizing that so-called "feminine qualities" are integral parts of my being and that learned "male" attitudes are false and destructive of relationships.

Since my days at Glide, I have continued to grow in my under-standing of the intricate relationships between sexuality and spirituality. Sexism, I now know, is in reality unhealed sexual dualism, supported by our male-dominated society. Such an awakening caused me to affirm that, truly woman and man were, and are, both created in the image of the Creator (Genesis 1:27). For centuries many of the Church Fathers posited as unchallenge-able truth that women were inferior to men. St. Augustine's comment that "Man but not woman is made in the image and likeness of God"[1] is but one example. Not until the eye-opening feminist liberation movement did the male-dominated church begin to understand the profound significance that such evil teachings had had in distorting the Gospel. By contrast, Meister Eckhart, the Dominican theologian who was condemned as a heretic by Pope John XXII and who developed the theory of "creation-centered" (as opposed to sin-redemption) spirituality, said "that the reason Eve was said to be created from Adam's side was to demonstrate the absolute equality of woman to man."[2]

Gradually, I have become aware that spirituality for me is not other-worldly or ethereal; God is immanent in creation. God is not limited in the least by the affirmation that the Divine is present and active in creation. God permeates being, is present in and to me and all human beings. The incarnation of God in Jesus of Nazareth affirms all creation, including human beings. It says that flesh is important, that flesh became the medium of divine communica-tion. God's compassionate judgement was communicated in the earthly life of Jesus. The Reign of God, which was more central in Jesus' message, is here and now among us and in us.

Relationship to God is awesome. Rather than the "up-there-ness" I had been struggling with, I now see spirituality as all-embracing, a kind of web of relationships that includes communion, celebra-tion, earthiness, creativity, and hunger for ever more profound relationship to God. And an integral part of this web is sexuality, the psychological and physiological power by which we can be in community and can love. Sexuality, I now know, is essential in relationships; without it we can neither love others nor love God.

Spirituality and Sexuality: Both or Neither
by Youtha Hardman-Cromwell

How is it that sexuality has come to be viewed by some Christians as antithetical to spirituality? Spirituality is "the ways and patterns by which persons relate to that which is ultimately real and worthful to them."[1] Sexuality is our self-understanding and way of being in the world.[2] What, then, is the basis for Christian spirituality being body-denying? God, Jesus, Holy Spirit are all experienced and responded to through body, community, history. All of these are relationships, which are expressed through and, hence, inseparable from body experience.

Sexuality denotes the entire range of feelings and behaviors which we, as embodied persons in the world, have and use to express relationships between ourselves and others through looks, touch, words, and actions. Worship, or any other human activity, is, therefore, both an expression of our sexuality AND our spirituality.

How has the human being come to be viewed as dichotomized—a good spirit housed in an evil body? In this view, Christian spiritual-ity is expressed as "control, discipline, and repression of the body."[3] Such a view is clearly not supported by the creation stories. The Scriptures speak positively about human beings in creation:

> So God created humankind in God's image, in the image of God, God created them; male and female God created them. God blessed them and God said to them, "Be fruitful and multiply... And it was so. God saw everything that God made, and indeed, it was very good....
> (Genesis 1:27–31, NRSV adapted)

It is the total created being that is blessed, called good and instructed to use its body creatively and reproductively.

The source of such dichotomized thinking is related to an incorrect understanding about how God values the genders. It is not just the male who is called good and blessed, but both male and female. The Genesis creation story does not support the concept, which developed later in human thought, that the feminine is the personification of evil and the masculine of good. In this dichotomized theology, the feminine was associated with fertility, reproduction and the earth—with the material. Therefore, women represented inherent evil and that feminine evil, through sexual encounters, contaminated the male good. The male was associated with spirit and heaven. The masculine became the image of God, the one with a spiritual nature. But this view is not Biblical. It is not supported by Scripture and does not have its roots in Jewish theology.

Have you read Song of Solomon lately? Some question the inclusion of this writing in the canon. It is exceedingly sensual and celebrates the body, sexual attraction and desire as well as the power of the body in human relationships:

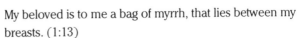

> My beloved is to me a bag of myrrh, that lies between my breasts. (1:13)
>
> How sweet is your love, my sister, my bride! How much better is your love than wine, and the fragrance of your oils than any spice! Your lips distill nectar, my bride, honey and milk are under your tongue; the scent of your garments is like the scent of Lebanon. (4:10,11)
>
> I come to my garden, my sister, my bride; I gather my myrrh with my spice, I eat my honeycomb with my

honey, I drink my wine with my milk. Eat, friends, drink, and be drunk with love. (5:1)

You are stately as a palm tree, and your breasts are like its clusters. I say I will climb the palm tree and lay hold of its branches. Oh, may your breasts be like the clusters of the vine, and the scent of your breath like apples, and your kisses like the best wine that goes down smoothly gliding over lips and teeth. I am my beloved's and his desire is for me.... Let us go out early to the vineyards.... There I will give you my love. (7:7-12)

O that his left hand were under my head and that his right hand embraced me! (8:3)

This is clearly a celebration of body-ness that stands boldly in the canon and is not refuted by other Biblical writing. Whatever theological interpretation one gives to this component of Scripture, it celebrates and affirms the human body as good. These Song scriptures may be interpreted as a celebration of human sexuality, a celebration of the relationship between God and Israel or Christ and the Church. Whichever or all, it is expressed in a very sensual metaphor. In the face of this Scripture, how can God's valuing of our sexuality be denied?

The truth is that our sexuality is intended by God to be neither incidental nor detrimental to our spirituality, but rather a fully integrated and basic dimension of that spirituality.[4] Sexuality is much more than genital sex. It is all that our bodies are and the ways in which we use them to be in the world, to be related to God, and to be in communication with other humans. This follows from the simple truth that God chose to embody us rather than leave us as disembodied spirits, a choice that God was free to make. It is also evident in the truth of Jesus' incarnation—his taking on bodily form to live and love and dwell among us. Our dualistic concepts of what it is to be human often cloud our understanding of who Jesus was, as a human being. We have difficulty affirming his humanity fully because it seems to conflict with our affirmation of his spiritual nature. To use the term "Jesus' sexuality" seems blasphemous to some Christians. But not to acknowledge Jesus' sexuality is to deny his real incarnation into human form.

It is not beyond, or in spite of, but in our fleshly state that we are loved by God and sought out for relationship, for fellowship. "Thy kingdom come on earth as it is in heaven." Right relationship with God is an earthly, and, hence, a body-state. It is in our embodiedness that we both experience and respond to the sacred.

To maintain the dichotomy of sexuality and spirituality is to give permission to the uncontrolled and indiscriminate use of our bodies in ways that are unrelated to who we see ourselves to be as God created and God-loved persons. It permits the justification of dichotomous living, strange as that may seem, in which secular and religious lives are not consistent and are not guided by an integrated ethic of behavior. This is the heresy.

There is an inevitable interconnection and interdependence between our bodily life and our life in the spirit that make them, not so much two sides of the same coin, as different lenses on the same phenomenon—truth as we know it. Our sexuality is our expression of our self-knowledge; our spirituality is our expression of our God-knowledge. Each is about personal relationship, which makes each implicitly layered with meaning that may not be universally shared:

> Neither sexuality nor spirituality are things out there; they are names for us catching ourselves in the complex act of being human, of transcending the way of being of an object to recognize ourselves as subjects, centers of interdependent activity.[5]

In *The Good Book*, Peter Gomes listed the fundamental questions of human existence:

> Who am I? Why am I here? What is the purpose of life? What does it mean to be good? What is evil, and how do I deal with it? How do I deal with death?[6]

These questions challenge simultaneously both our understanding of self and our understanding of God. We cannot pursue real answers to these questions except that we submit our whole selves to the inquiry and answer with our whole selves what we affirm to be true. I'm not just a body. I'm not just a spirit. Neither are you. I'm both, a complex integration of physical and spiritual. I'm human. So are you. If you are not yet convinced, try conceiving of anything that you do as apart from your unique identity as an individual in the world. Try expressing any of your Christian values without using your body. Our humanity is expressed in both our sexuality and our spirituality. It must be both or neither. It is a fact of our creation. And it is good.

Toward an Integrated Spirituality: Language, Images and Worship
by Carolyn Henninger Oehler

When one hears the term *spirituality*, concerns about language and imagery may not immediately come to mind. Rather, the mention of spirituality may inspire thoughts of relationship to some ethereal force or presence, some sacred being. Yet a careful consideration of just why certain ideas arise regarding the spiritual reveals that a close interconnectedness links language and imagery with spirituality.

However any of us views spirituality in relationship to our own lives, spirituality clearly is shaped and experienced through the language and images of faith. As James Nelson explains, spirituality

> includes disciplines and practices, but also myths, symbols, and rituals, informal as well as formal. It includes the affective as well as the cognitive. Significantly, spirituality includes the ways in which our relatedness to the ultimate affects our understandings and feelings of relatedness to everyone and everything else.[1]

Myths, symbols, rituals, relatedness—all these are shaped and transmitted by language. This fact demonstrates the importance that language and imagery have in influencing our perception and experience of the spiritual. The more inclusive the words and images that are used in worship, prayer, art, and literature, the more comprehensive a spirituality is possible. The use of a male-centered, patriarchal language and imagery generates a male-centered spirituality. Nelson again:

> Because our imagery and language have been so onesidedly masculine, a masculinist-shaped spirituality has resulted. Hence we have experienced God dominantly as noun, as transcendence, as order, as structure, as law, as rationality. A more androgynous theological imagery and language will help us to experience God also as verb, as immanence, as creativity, as vulnerability, as flow, and as absolute relatedness to creation.[2]

To use inclusive language and imagery in worship, in prayer, in dialogue is to open oneself and the community of which one is a part to spiritual growth and development beyond the confines of traditional restrictions. Their use also opens us to the possibility of a justice-based spirituality.

This justice-based spirituality was dreamed of by the prophets, who envisioned justice rolling down like water. This spirituality was sung of by Mary, who experienced God acting to feed the hungry, bring the powerful low, and offer liberation to those who live under oppression. This spirituality was claimed by Jesus Christ, who envisioned his ministry as good news to the poor, release to the captives, and recovery of sight to the blind.

From Dominance/Subordinance to Equality and Co-Creation

Moving to this justice-based, inclusive spirituality means leaving behind language and imagery that foster dominance/subordinance metaphors for reality and embracing those that "affirm reciprocity in action."[3] We need language and imagery that help us to claim the role of co-creator in our relationship to God and to other persons.

We have ample evidence of the inadequacy of and damage done by male-dominated language and understandings. In the traditional hierarchy of dominance, God is viewed as Lord, King, all-powerful, transcendent, demanding human submission, and fostering a sense of human powerlessness. Coming next in the hierarchy, males assume the role of dominance over those beneath them.

In this hierarchy, so-called generic language is common, with the male noun or pronoun used to represent all persons. The users of this language may not intend to be exclusive, but the effect nevertheless is to deny women's separate identity and power, both linguistically and in relationships. Dominating white male imagery and language serve to enforce subordinance of other groups as well—by race, by class, by sexual orientation.

This dominance/subordinance understanding of God and of human relationships can be replaced by images and metaphors that teach us relationships of mutuality. Beverly Harrison, for example, writes of "One present who sustains us, gently but firmly grounding the fragile possibilities of our action, one whose power of co-relation enhances and enriches our acts aimed at human fulfillment, mutuality, and justice."[4]

Traditional faith language and imagery often are heterosexist, as well as sexist. The Church as the Bride of Christ, for example, presents difficulties for those seeking inclusive imagery. The use of heterosexist words and images shapes a spirituality that is the same, allowing for sexual beliefs and practices that distort or deny the goodness of human sexuality. As Nelson writes: "[T]he re-theologizing of our language and imagery in sexually inclusive ways is a fundamental challenge of our day. At stake is a wholistic spirituality, for masculinist-shaped spirituality will only perpetuate alienation."[5]

From Dualism to an Integrated Spirituality

If we are to develop a justice-based, inclusive spirituality, we must use language and imagery that move away from dualism toward an integrated language and spirituality. Dualistic thinking supposed a division of reality into two separate and opposite categories. Some dualisms are:

God/creation	spirit/body
good/evil	spiritual/sexual
male/female	mind/emotion
white/black	rationality/intuition
heaven/earth	transcendence/immanence

These dualisms not only set up each category as opposites, they also describe God (and maleness) in the first category as good and the created world (and femaleness) in the second category as evil or "other." Using this kind of language and imagery to construct and describe reality can lead to a spirituality that supports oppression and injustice, since it denies that the creation, the body, and those equated with them must be treated with respect.

This dichotomized spirituality separates God from God's creation and suggests that some persons are more spiritual than other persons. When homosexuality is defined primarily or exclusively as sexual behavior, then this dichotomized spirituality can consider Gay and Lesbian persons as "other" and as candidates for exclusion and oppression. When people of color fall on the "other" side of the dualism, then their oppression and exploitation can be justified. Dualistic language and imagery works against a justice-based spirituality.

Dualisms like the spirit/body one have created an uneasiness in the church about the bodily implications of its worship. Leaving behind these dualisms can open us to the sacramentality that is hidden in human sexuality.[6] The links between sexuality and spirituality are profound. Rather than seeing them as opposites, inclusive language and imagery can help us to experience them as part of one whole.

From Death to Life-Giving Spirituality

Creation-centered theology and spirituality offer a third possibility that the use of inclusive language and imagery helps to make possible. One suggested metaphor to connect creation and the creator is the image of Sophia, or Holy Wisdom. Susan Cady, Marian Ronan, and Hal Taussig explain: "Sophia provides exactly the image needed to make us aware of our own collective power, not as God's puppets, but as co-creators—or potential destroyers— of this planet. Sophia's continuing creativity, too, helps to keep before us the renewal of the earth, in birth, death, and resurrection."[7]

The introduction of Sophia as a metaphor for creativity signals the importance of a neglected aspect of God, sometimes called feminine, and the possible recovery of a biblical tradition that can contribute to a more inclusive spirituality.

The links between spirituality and creativity are strong. And a creative spirituality must move away from exclusive, patriarchal imagery. Matthew Fox says:

> I think that for a theology to celebrate creativity, it must have a sense of the Motherhood of God. An exclusively paternalistic theology—which is what the West has had for three centuries, speaking and imaging God only as male— doesn't celebrate birthing, doesn't see birthing as the powerful, exciting, surprising, ecstatic, and spiritual event that it is, personally and culturally.[8]

A spirituality that is life-giving will be shaped by language and imagery that are inclusive, rather than exclusive. Instead of alienation from our bodies and our life processes, we can claim an interrelatedness and connectedness to creation and to those created to be in community with us.

Instead of being frozen in images that reinforce our powerlessness, we can become co-creators with God. Instead of accepting a spirituality that is misogynist and homophobic, we can be mothers and midwives in the shaping of a spirituality that celebrates rather than denies the world.

A justice-based spirituality needs language and imagery that are creative, egalitarian, integrated, inclusive. Virginia Ramey Mollenkott predicts that "the inclusive naming of God will train us to include all aspects of ourselves and the whole human race, and all of creation in the category of what is holy. And that in turn will help to break our bondage to a spirit-body dualism and to hierarchical structures."[9]

That spirituality will be good news to the poor and to the oppressed and to all who seek wholeness and healing. It is also our hope of creating a truly inclusive community.

Chapter 2

Proclaiming An Inclusive Community

Now is the door swinging open
to see the dance of sunlight,
hint of moonbeam.
Now do the pews bloom,
that were dry-old wood,
cut from forests long ago.
Now does a fresh wind
ruffle the memorial Bible
like a gust of Pentecost.
Now is the writing on the walls
not hymn numbers,
but God's laughter.
Now is the new covenant
not stone but heart,
not stone but heart.

Maren C. Tirabassi

Welcome One Another
by Ann B. Day

Scripture:

Isaiah 56: 3-8,
Romans 15:7-13,
Matthew 25: 31-46

Almost nineteen years ago to this day, I arrived in Holden to be the shiny new Associate Pastor at First Congregational Church. It was a long drive from Nashville, Tennessee to central Massachusetts. It was made even longer by the fact that, geography not being my forte, I imagined Massachusetts to be in the area actually occupied by Pennsylvania. When I got to Pennsylvania and Massachusetts wasn't there, it became apparent that it was even further north than I'd thought!

I did find it, however, and not long after my arrival, it was suggested to me that I should pay a call on one of the most esteemed elders of the congregation and the town, for that matter, Miss Jennie Hendricks. Miss Hendricks lived, appropriately, right on Main Street in the house where her family had lived since 1885. The last of the five Hendricks children, she was in the late years of a life that included a Master's Degree from Columbia University, a teaching career at Central Connecticut State College, education work in Chile, and a great deal of civic activity.

Fortunately, as I walked up the narrow path to her front steps, to pay my first pastoral call, I was oblivious to all her credentials. I was nervous enough just knowing that she was a long-lived and well-loved member of the community. I wanted very much to make a good impression.

After a quick tour of her house, we sat and talked in the front parlor: I, the 25-year-old pastor (the ink not yet dry on my divinity school degree) and she, the 92-year-old parishioner. I tried to say insightful things; she did say insightful things. It was, as the saying goes, "the beginning of a beautiful friendship."

It wasn't long before I was visiting Jennie in the local nursing home. There we would talk about her days at Columbia and adventures in New York City in the 1920's, about the wonders of wild mushrooms and whales, about her Unitarian leanings, and about the mystery of death.

I told her about my life, too, but I was careful what I told her. Most of the personal information, I edited out. When I fell in love, for example, I really wanted Jennie to know, but because I was in love with a woman, I didn't tell her. I didn't know how she would feel about me as a person or a pastor if she knew. I had no way of knowing if she could relate to my concerns about rejection or understand my feeling like an outsider in most Christian churches. I think now that she might well have understood because she'd had a similar experience.

Jennie's experience of rejection wasn't related to sexual orientation but to ethnicity. She was *Swedish*, and, as she tells it, around the turn of the century in Holden, being Swedish wasn't exactly the ticket to popularity. In her memoirs, Jennie writes of her family moving from Worcester to Holden in the late 1800s. "Into this environment," she says,

> came a family of Swedes, and the natives made quick work of showing them that they were not wanted. The Congregational Church, as was true in all early communities, was the center of all town activities. My parents had been active in Swedish church groups in Worcester. Since there was no Lutheran Church in Holden, they started going to the Congregational Church because it was nearby. Mother was very religious and

would have found much comfort in a "House of God." But this was not to be.

They soon began to notice that as soon as the seven of us entered the sanctuary, certain members of the choir looked askance at each other and then giggled behind their hands....At first mother and dad thought, 'Well, let's sit in the back pew and perhaps we won't be noticed.' But this rudeness continued until my people stopped going to church.[1]

Many of "*my* people" (those of us who are Gay, or Lesbian, or Bisexual) have stopped going to church too...and for the same painfully simple reason...we do not feel welcomed or wanted in most Christian churches. Now why, you might ask, do we have that impression? There are dozens of reasons but perhaps the most important is personal experience. Many of us have known indifference or hostility inside buildings which say on the outside "All Are Welcome." Too many of us understand the testimony of United Church of Christ member, Elaine Munro, when she says:

I left the church at age ten because I knew *Christians* thought homosexuals were sinners. It's been 23 years that I've been without a church family, until I joined First Congregational Church in Berkeley California.

First Congregational in Berkeley has declared itself an "Open and Affirming" (or ONA) church in the United Church of Christ. I know that many of you in this congregation are aware of what that means. But for those who may not be familiar with the language, let me define it. An "Open and Affirming" church is one which publicly declares that people of all sexual orientations are welcome in its full life and ministry. For the past ten years, I have coordinated the ONA Program—which helps United Church of Christ churches engage in education as they prayerfully consider making such statements of welcome.

I have been part of several "Open and Affirming" conversations in this church over the years; they have been some of the most lively and engaging ones that I've attended. And I know that you continue to be in a process of spiritual discernment about this. This work is two-fold. First, you must decide whether your understanding of God's love and justice as known in Jesus calls you to be a spiritual home for persons of all sexual orientations. You seem to me to be answering that in the affirmative, though more challenging discussions about all it means may still lie ahead for you. Second, if you *are* called to be such a church, you must decide whether you will claim this identity publicly; letting your light of inclusiveness shine far and wide. This is a crucial consideration. Gay, Lesbian, or Bisexual people assume the acceptance of churches at our own risk. If we guess wrong—we risk rejection, harassment, and even violence from others who bear the name "Christian." In the shadow of this uneasiness, only a declared welcome casts light.

When Cindy asked if I would come here this morning and preach specifically about Open and Affirming, I told her that I don't usually do that; I usually preach the lectionary texts—the list of Biblical readings given for each Sunday in the church year. I wish, however, to amend that. Having given it more thought, I realize that in preaching the lectionary texts, I repeatedly preach about "Open and Affirming" because so much of the Bible is about open and affirming issues. From Genesis to Revelation, we find stories and theological reflection about faithful people's struggles over who's "in;" who's "out;" who's acceptable; who's unacceptable; who's welcome; who's not.

Today's reading from Hebrew Scripture reflects one of the periods during which the Israelites wrestled with which people should be admitted to their community. At the time, they had recently returned to Jerusalem after fifty years of exile in Babylon. They set about rebuilding their place of worship, the Temple, which had been burned during the destruction of the city those many years before. As they re-established themselves in their homeland, intense debate occurred over what hallmarks would identify them as the people of God.

Some urged that, in the restored Temple, long-held restrictions continue to apply specifically to two groups: foreigners (those born outside of Israel) and eunuchs (men whose reproductive organs had been damaged or removed). There may be numerous reasons why such persons would be excluded from the community. Eunuchs could have been refused participation because part of Israel's tradition prohibited any male who could not procreate from being part of the community.[2] In addition, both foreigners and eunuchs may have worshiped gods other than Yahweh, the God of Israel, thus participating in idolatry.

The words read from the book of Isaiah this morning take a differ-ent approach. Believing that God is at work to shape "the new heavens and the new earth" (Isaiah 66:22a), the prophet reminds the people that the ultimate criterion for inclusion among God's people is faithfulness. Foreigners and eunuchs who love and serve God are welcome, declares Isaiah, for thus says the Lord:

...all who keep the Sabbath, and do not profane it,
and hold fast my covenant—
    these will I bring to my holy mountain,
and make them joyful in my house of prayer...
    for my house shall
be called a house of prayer for all peoples.

(Isaiah 56:6-7)

Time goes by. Some six hundred years later, in the church at Rome, the faces had changed but the discussion was the same; people of faith continued to be at odds over who belonged and who didn't! As you know, the earliest Christians, the disciples of Jesus, were Jews. St. Paul and some others, however, were con-vinced that God's salvation was also meant for Gentiles (those "foreigners" Isaiah spoke about.) There was big trouble in the church at Rome because members of Jewish background appar-ently felt that their place in God's plan was diminished by the pres-ence of Gentile members. Perhaps at an annual meeting one of Jewish-Christians might have said, "Wait a minute, I thought *we* were the chosen people. What about God's promises to us in the days of Abraham and Sarah? What about the dietary laws and cir-cumcision as a sign of our faithfulness? Is all that forgotten?"

Paul responds that there is room for everyone, Jew and Gentile, in God's realm. Christians of Jewish heritage should rest assured that, in Jesus, God's promises have been confirmed, not canceled. But God's love for humanity and all creation knows no limits. Gentiles, too, are recipients of God's grace and, thus, part of the faith com-munity. And so Paul exhorts mutual hospitality, *"Welcome one an-other, therefore, just as Christ has welcomed you, for the glory of God."* Paul says, in effect, let the church be that wondrous place that reflects the wideness of God's mercy and love for all of us. A community where no one is an outcast, a foreigner, a stranger.

Time goes by—some 1900 years to be inexact—and it's 1997. The scene shifts from that local church in Rome to this local church in Worcester. Once again the faces have changed, but the discussion is the same: who belongs in the community of faith? What are the criteria for inclusion and participation in the body of Christ?

As our generation's debate about inclusion of persons of all sexual orientations continues to rage in many denominations, it is easy to think that the Church must have something better to do with its time. When we wonder, "why all this fuss?" we might remember this morning's gospel reading about the last judgement. St. Matthew suggests, I think, that human beings have pressing needs, life or death needs, that we must help meet. Some are obvious to us— food, drink, clothing. But included with these is another which we may think of as optional, while St. Matthew seems to think it essential—a welcome. People *need* to be welcomed, invited, received, gathered, embraced. "Lord...when was it we saw you a stranger and welcomed you?" Learning (and for most of us it is a process of learning) to gladly open our doors and hearts to those who may *seem* strangers to us—because of their culture or their sexuality or any other factor—learning to understand and honor and love each other is how we experience Christ's radiant presence among us, is it not? On this World Communion Sunday, when not everyone feels welcome at the table or in the church, I hope that we shall break bread and drink the cup together, knowing that it is in our power, because of Christ's power, to change that. In your love for Cindy and Elaine* and theirs for you, in your outreach to other churches around ONA issues, in your conversations with each other and your prayers for each other, you have already done some powerful things to make change; and even as I rejoice in them, I hope, with God's leading, there will be more to come.

Let me close where I began, with my friend Jennie Hendricks. In 1886, she was apparently unwanted in the church. By the time of her death in 1986, just short of 100 years, she was one of its treasured members. Her Swedishness didn't change. But hearts and minds did. My partner and I have a granddaughter, Nicole, who's not quite three. I hope that in ten years or twenty years, when she asks me, "Grandma Annie, is it true that some churches won't welcome you and Grandma Donna because you love each other?" that I will be able to say, "It *was* true, Nicole, years ago, but hearts and minds change. Now, in the churches, we welcome one another, as Christ has welcomed us."

*At the time of this sermon, Cindy was the pastor of this church and Elaine, her partner.

No Longer at Ease
by Sidney G. Hall, III

Scripture:

Isaiah 62:1-7, 10-12

Kathleen Norris, in her best-selling book, *Dakota*, talks about her infatuation with the Benedictines, the gifted-ness they have brought to her life, and how she finds rest, peace, and a place apart in their monasteries. However, anyone that's ever been to a Benedictine community knows that they're not exactly places apart; they're places for engagement. A monastic community founded on the Rule of Benedict is one where every stranger at the gate is welcomed as Christ. They are places to learn about hospitality as a spiritual discipline. They are communities designed to enlarge each person's inner geography—the place of soul—so that one's outer geography also expands. Yet Kathleen also reminds us that even the Benedictines grow weary from time-to-time in their spiritual quest toward hospitality. An old story told among the Benedictines describes a seasoned abbot who, after welcoming thousands of motley strangers over the years, looked down the lane one day and saw yet another person wandering up to gate. Forgetting how tired he was, the abbot blurted out to the stranger: "Jesus Christ. Is that you again?"

We who are gathered here celebrating God's presence and prophetic voice at work in the Reconciling Congregation Program have an awesome, and sometimes wearisome job: We are here to affirm what the Benedictine monk knew before he even asked it. The answer to that question is always, "Yes." Jesus Christ, is that you again? Yes.

Every time we look into the face of a fellow human being, regardless of who that person is—regardless of how different that person is from us—we dare to see the face of Christ, always. And at the core of our spiritual journey we know that such an affirmation goes far beyond inclusiveness or even diversity. Simply stated, we are about the call to see Christ, everywhere. We also know the joy of looking across God's welcoming table and seeing the diversity of God's family, but this kin-dom vision comes with a cost. There is so much pain that has been shared. We hear the stories and we meet the people behind the stories, prophets like Jimmy Creech and Greg Dell who have both been tried for conducting a same-sex covenant service. And we know the people who sit in silent pain in the pews Sunday after Sunday who have not yet heard about the welcoming church movement. Many of these are people who wonder if they are absolutely alone in this world and have not found a way to see themselves as God's included. They have not been fortunate enough to encounter others who see the face of Christ in their face. So we come rejoicing and resting. We come reconciling. We come hoping against hope, even as we do not as yet see. We come as a people of God renewing and recommitting ourselves to go back out—to be the people of the voice, to be the people who dare to see Christ wherever we are, even with, *especially with*, those who disagree with us. It's not always easy to see the face of Christ in others. Sometimes the prejudice and fear of others even prevents us from seeing God's face in our own.

When I was in about 5th grade I terribly hurt the feelings of a friend of mine as we were riding the bus home from school. Tammy and I were old friends, even by the 5th grade, having played together since we were tiny tots. Our backyards were adjoined. She had a disability and, though Tammy tried to hide it to avoid ridicule, she was always unsuccessful. When she was born the doctors discovered that she had a congenital heart defect that would require immediate attention. Due to a brief lapse of oxygen during her ensuing open-heart surgery, she was left with some brain damage. The damage was like a persistent and annoying trickster for Tammy. She was intelligent enough to know that she was slower than most other children, a slowness that manifested itself mostly in uncouth mannerisms and the inability to discern the rhythms of etiquette so effortlessly followed by other children. Even though I was tempted to participate in the cruel antics of my friends, I knew that when they were tripping her or pulling up her dress or laughing or making jokes, I wouldn't participate. I wouldn't because she was my friend, too. But I did join in.

One spring day on the bus home from school, someone did something to her, a spit wad, a derogatory slur—I don't remember—but I laughed. I laughed because I was nervous, because I wanted to fit in, because the people that were making fun of her were my friends and I wanted to be accepted by them. Like Peter with the female accuser, I dared not look in the direction of the crucified. I did not want to see the way she must have looked at me, but the crowing cock resonated in my conscience. A few minutes later Tammy got off the bus. By the time the bus had made three more brief stops, it rounded the corner to drop me at my drive. My driveway was transfigured by the presence of my mother standing at the edge of the road with her arms crossed. Oh no. I was going to die. Do you know this stance? The kind God seemed to create just for mothers in these circumstances. It was the kind of stance that said, "This is going to hurt me more than it hurts you, but if I can make it hurt you more than it hurts me, I'm sure going to try." Now I wasn't looking at my mothers' eyes either. She said, "Look at me young man." When you hear, "young man" you may as well forget about anything you planned on doing the next few hours. "You know why I'm standing here?" she glared, and I said "No." "No" was my last ditch effort to survive her interrogation. And she says, "Well I just got a call from Tammy's mother and apparently you were making fun of her on the bus today. "I wasn't making fun of her. All I did was laugh," I quickly shot back. "You laughed at her? That's not making fun of her?" I knew what was coming next. It was my mother's way. It is the way of most mothers. She said, "Well, I want you to march right over there, young man, and I want you to apologize to her and I want you to apologize to her mother." I remember saying, "And her mother? Great!" And as I walked across the field toward Tammy's house, my mother, her eyes still burning holes in the back of head, said, "Faster. You can walk faster than that." You know that slow lead-like walk when you just can't move, like when you're being chased in a dream? Well, same thing, but this was reality. When I got to Tammy's door and apologized, she was quick at forgiving. Her mother was a different story. Pointing and scolding me, she said with tears running down her cheek, "You really hurt her feelings. I thought you were Tammy's friend." Jesus, oh Jesus, is that you again?

I didn't think for years about the experience with Tammy. Then, one day, while struggling with and praying about what it would mean to lead a United Methodist congregation toward declaring itself as a Reconciling Congregation—a congregation that welcomes and affirms all people, including Gay, Lesbian, Bisexual, and Transgender people—the memory of how I had treated Tammy surfaced to remind me of what this reconciling business is all about. I felt the Holy Spirit nudging me into the baptism of conviction, into the wilderness of coming to grips with how driven I am to please people even at the cost of my convictions, even at the cost of compromising how I understand the Gospel.

I'm convinced that there's a story like this within each of us; a story of when we really got it all wrong; when we became so afraid that we were paralyzed. There's also a story of when we were put on the outside and we didn't know if there was any way that we could be embraced and accepted for who we are—for who God made us. These are the stories that make up our lives and that re-stimulate the pain and create the possibility of hope.

The scripture passage for today is a passage of pain and hope. It reveals a sense of an in-between-ness, an already-not-yet-ness, among the people of Zion. Some of Israel's exiled have returned to Jerusalem and have begun to settle in a bit. But something is amiss. Not all is well behind the gates of the walled city. Enter the prophet, stage center. Isaiah reminds his congregation that there are still some folks not yet home. You get the feeling that they've had a retreat from reality. Rejoicing in the liberation from Babylon, now safe behind the walls of Jerusalem, and singing once again the songs of Zion, all seem reasonable responses for this broken people, but not if they forget about the other exiles not yet re-turned. The work of God's people is not yet complete. Then along comes Isaiah, disturber of the peace, noisemaker, and conscience-raiser. He reared his head in the midst of the community and called his people to see things the way they really are. He said, "Take no rest and don't give God any rest either, until everyone is home." Continuing, Isaiah reminds his people of the responsibili-ties attached to worshiping a radically inclusive God. If they are to be called a people sought out—the beloved of God—reconciled, redeemed, liberated, and made whole—they must wake up from their comfortable sleep and clear the way for more to come. Com-mentators say that this is one of those passages that seem to ex-pand while you read it. At first, you think Isaiah is referring to those Israelites still in exile; then you realize that it's not just this one group, but also the whole universe he visualizes in Zion's fold. It is something akin to Jesus' kin-dom talk. As if this weren't enough, Isaiah takes his listeners one leap further—he tells them *how* to do this. "Go—go through the gates. Go out beyond the walls, into the places that are uncomfortable, where the wild things lurk and growl in the night, and remove the rubble, the boulders that block the way for God's people to come home."

This sounds like the beginning of Mark's gospel with a wild man screaming to the people to make a smooth or straight way (we might say "gayly forward") in the desert for God's anointed to come and declare a new kin-dom. We're called to go out from our comfort zones, our idolatrous reverence to the myth of biblical inerrancy or tradition, our societal prejudices—our rubble—and clear the path for *all* of God's people to come home. Notice here that it's God who brings the people home, not us. Our job is to get our stuff out of the way to make it happen. Now, I don't know about you, but I've got some big boulders still lying around; some fear and some prejudice. I mean—it's all there. But I'm working on it and I see others here working on it, too. We're trying to remove those boulders, to get out there beyond our comfort zones, convicted to take seriously this WWJD (What Would Jesus Do?) thing. And you know what? It takes a while. Others, even others we love and respect, may not be where we are on this matter. There'll always be people still standing there—up on the gates of power—looking down and saying, "What are those goofy, reconciling people doing?"

Systems change slowly and, in that regard, churches and denominations are no different from other institutions. The people who have gained the most from the system are those most resistant to its changes. To relinquish control, to open the church to the possibility of the Holy Spirit, is to also admit that the church is still evolving, still in the process of discerning God's will, and, as Paul said, still in the process of "being saved." What the church has not yet grasped is that the exclusion of Lesbian, Gay, Bisexual, and Transgender Christians from full participation in the church is to diminish the Body of Christ. Like Isaiah's not quite completely post-exilic community of old, today's church is not the whole people of God until all may sit at Christ's banquet table. Bob Dylan could have been talking about the ecclesiastical and judicial resistance to the work of the Spirit when he wrote:

> All along the watchtower, princes kept the view
> While all the women came and went, barefoot servants, too.
> Outside in the distance a wildcat did growl,
> Two riders were approaching, the wind began to howl.
> —*All Along the Watchtower* (1968)

There is a wildness howling in the hearts of many people concerned with inclusivity across the boundaries of our American churches. The old ways of welcoming some while excluding others will no longer sustain our spiritual communities. This is a wildness that cannot be contained by ecclesial rulings or by clinging to the securities of anachronistic prescriptions. It is the wildness of the Holy Spirit alive in our churches through movements of welcoming. Its time is approaching. It is approaching. Can you hear its howl?

I know that each of us gathered today hears this message with mixed feelings. Maybe we've been able to be *out* here, with each other, in ways that we aren't safe at home. And we know that we're going to have to step back into those environs where we reside, where "princes keep the view." We don't always know how we're going to make it work. We're not sure where this journey takes us, from this point onward. But we know that we've got to go though the gates. Like Eliot's magi encountering the transforming presence of Christ's manger, "We returned to our places, these Kingdoms, But no longer at ease here, in the old dispensation."[1] And when we do, we'll learn what the Psalmist knew so well: That God hems us in before and behind (Ps. 139); and we are held. We are held in those arms of love even in the midst of our unease at seeing the world in its pain and its hope.

Jesus was a shaker, and I don't mean the furniture-making kind. He turned our world downside up, bringing a message of comfort for the disturbed, and disturbing the comfortable. Jesus set for us a banquet and the invitation read: "As you have done it to one of the least of these, you have done it unto me" (Matt. 25). We are challenged and renewed by this one, Jesus. We've been strangely warmed by this assurance. Now, by the power of the Spirit, we dare to be the people of Jesus. We dare to become the embodiment—the body—of Christ. Painfully, as we seek to embody Christ in our lives we also experience his vulnerability; and all too often, we relive his brokenness at the hands of others. I am reminded of a story told about Archbishop Oscar Romero, the slain archbishop of El Salvador, who upon looking out at the poor in his congregation who had been marginalized by military, political, and ecclesiastical oppression, gave them a word of hope. He didn't use finely-crafted theological terms like, "you are the ground of all being" or psychobabble like, "I'm okay, you're okay." With eyes of compassion and courage, Romero said, "You are Jesus. You are Jesus. You are the embodiment of God, the hands and feet of God. You are the voice that God needs now. You are Jesus." Can you believe that? Do you know that it's true? Do you realize that it is you the monk sees coming down the road? And he asks, "Jesus Christ! Is that you again?"

We've got a big task ahead of us as we approach General Conference in May. But I know that we're going to go through the gates and that whatever happens there, whatever happens, we will have been the people of God. And no one can tell us any different. And you know when we're moving slow—the voice of God is liable to sound something like: "Faster. You can walk faster than that." And when we're so weary that we can't move anymore, those same arms that prod us on will be the arms that hold us at the end of the lane and say, "Jesus Christ—it's you again." Amen.

You Do Not Know
by J. Mary Luti

Scripture:

Mark 13: 24-37

Jesus makes three simple points in this gospel lesson: First, we don't have all the time in the world. There will be an end to history, a time when time is up, and Christ reappears to gather and govern faithful people. After that, in a new world, life will flourish as it was meant to. History is not all there is. God is all there is, from the word "go" to the last hurrah. We don't have a lot of time to discover and live the difference it might make to us and others that occurs when God is the "all" of our lives. Time runs out.

Second, nobody knows when time is up and new life begins. Jesus tells his disciples that although the astute may see signs that the end is near, no one can predict the exact moment of the new world's arrival. Not even Jesus is privy to the divinely-scheduled transition from time to eternity. Only God knows. God will do it. So we have to trust God.

Third, we are to be watchful. Christ will preside over a new age someday, but what about in the meanwhile? We're to stay alert. Why? Not because we fear Jesus and judgment, but because he is wonderful, because we are confident in him. Wasn't his life one long wide-awake lookout for us? Wasn't his mission to peer into the night and spot us, the missing, and take us home? Jesus was defined by what he watched for; he took on the shape of what he loved, including the shape of our death. "Now you stay awake," he says. "Define your lives by whom you watch for. Be shaped by what you notice and by the missing things you risk your lives to find."

I was asked to preach today in view of your discussion about the Open and Affirming (ONA) process. I'm supposed to say a word of wisdom about it any time now. I'm also supposed to preach the gospel, and today the traditions that govern the first Sunday of Advent hand me this text about the end of the world; a text, alas, that has nothing to do with ONA—unless you believe that voting to become ONA will be the end of the world, or that it will be the end of the world if you don't. This passage is, obviously, not about ONA. It's about the faith of the disciples and the mission of the church.

Now, I believe that the only reason a congregation should consider the ONA process is to be more faithful to God and better fulfill its mission. Otherwise, ONA is merely a political exercise. Are you engaged in the process to become more faithful to God and better fulfill your mission? If so, this gospel may turn out to shed light on how that could happen after all. Let's look at those three points.

Start with the last: Jesus says that until he comes, the job of disciples is to be on the lookout for him. Are you? If you say "yes;" even if you say, "We'd like to be," certain things follow. For instance, since Christ is as likely to show up in the cradle of a child as in the robes of a judge, you have to watch for children. Since he is as likely to come as a prisoner or a stranger as he is a friend, you can't look only for friends; you have to look for convicts and strangers. Since he is as likely to come surreptitiously as with trumpets and heavenly hosts, you have to watch for quiet things and be ready for him to show up looking, well, just like me. Like a Lesbian. Thus, everyone who enters your field of vision requires a long look, a knowing glance.

If this church wants to be Christ's shape in the world, you'll also need to persevere. You can't sign on to watch just for a night or two, or only for the three laziest hours in the middle of the day when even God is napping and unlikely to start an apocalypse. Watchfulness is a way of life. If you persevere in it, you will take on the shape of what you peer into the darkness to see, of who you stretch into the unknown to welcome, of the missing things you take great risks to find. These are shapes of immense attractiveness. People of every kind recognize them. It won't be long before people come to you as they came to Jesus. He gave them belonging, healing, a changed life. Will you? You will, if you are awake and watching.

Becoming an ONA church could be one way of embodying a watchful mission. It could say to the world in no uncertain terms, "We're on the alert in here. If you want to know us, if you want to join us, you have to understand that watching is what we do. Lookouts—it's who we are. When we spot our Christ—and we know him, no matter what weird get-up he gets himself into—we watchers risk everything to go and meet him."

Second point: This gospel also says that the church's faith is in a God who plays some things close to the vest, a God who doesn't put every card on the table at once. The church's mission is to love this God who is freely doing whatever. The church has no inside information on God's plans. And we can't always tell when something has ended and something else has begun. The only thing we know for sure is that God is going to make something new happen. When? How? Not a clue. We can only trust.

Do you? If you say, "yes;" even if you say "We want to," certain things follow. For instance, eventually it has to be OK with you that God fiddles with things, never leaves well enough alone. Little by little, it has to be OK with you that you can't make God do what you want, or give God a deadline to meet your needs. It has to be OK with you that some doubts and anxieties hang in the air, unaddressed. It has to be OK that much of the time the only way you know whether you've done the right thing is by hindsight, and the rest of the time you're flying blind. And it has to be OK that some things you cherish go by the boards. Someday soon it has to be OK that this congregation is no one's private territory, no one's perfectly safe haven from the world, but belongs to God, whose purposes will always be good, but may not strike you that way as they unfold.

Not knowing what God is up to and being OK with that—now there's a witness the world needs! Why? Well, for one thing, because it's about freedom. Think of it this way: it's a verifiable fact of history that whenever the church thinks it has a bead on what God is up to, it starts making rules out of what it thinks God is thinking. Before long, they take on an air of eternal authority, a life of their own. Then the rules begin to rule out all sorts of agile, frisky things—like imagination and desire, daring and risk. They even rule out God. You don't need God, when you have God figured out. Rules are better than God; anybody knows that.

But by fiercely resisting all pretensions to know everything God is up to, by trusting God to have our best interests at heart, a church can itself be trusted to act in the best interests of the world. By refusing to domesticate God, we might finally succeed in un-domesticating ourselves—and others. When God is free to be God, and when people are free to be people, life gets strange, but it also gets real.

Becoming an ONA congregation could be one way of embodying a witness of trust; one way of announcing to the world that in here no one knows anything for certain; that in here no one wastes time constructing chicken-wire pens with sturdy latches to house domesticated idols and very tame creatures; that in here there is breathing room for groping towards real life together, since real life is God's only concern; that in here we've thrown caution to the wind in the hope of an unimagined liberation from death-dealing constraints; that in here, come what may, we are rock-steady reliant on a trustworthy God.

But time to live like this is running out. The first point of the story nips at our heels. We don't have all the time in the world to watch for and welcome whichever Christ happens to come down the pike today. We don't have leisure to decide to trust God. And we do not have all the time in the world to decide about ONA. ONA could be that chance of a lifetime to raise a defiant fist against settling for less; a chance of a lifetime—not only to redress a social inequity or support a nice liberal cause—but to stand with God against a lie, the lie about who has human worth and in what *amount*, the lie that has beguiled the church for centuries. Duped and deceived, the church has subsequently conspired in degrading many of the lambs Christ shepherded in life. And since Christ is best known in the ones we fear most—he said so himself—we have to face the fact that the church has also, with full authority and power, for a long, long time, blithely been invoking the anger of God on Jesus Christ himself.

ONA could be the chance of a lifetime to shout from the housetops, as Jesus commanded, the truth he bled for on the cross—that God hates nothing God has made. ONA could be the chance of a lifetime to redefine the church, to revitalize its faith and mission, to sharpen its witness. But the time to take a chance on the God of the Good and Crucified Shepherd is growing short.

Will you get ONA in under the wire? Scripture says that God's new age, when new life will be abundantly available to all, is close at hand. It's just possible that ONA could hasten its advent. ONA could make more life available now to many—and thereby also to us all. But there isn't much time. There never is when human dignity and the authenticity of Christian community are at stake.

So, as you decide, here is my prayer for you: if it turns out to be Christ who comes to the conscience of this church in the hard question about ONA, may you quickly know him in this odd disguise. May you fly to him as fast as the wings of faith can carry you.

Time is almost up. You don't know when, exactly. So be on the lookout!

It's a Question of Size
by Peter H. Meek

Scripture:

Galatians 3:23-39

John 13:34-35

I want to talk with you this morning about the issues which are being raised for Hancock Church by the work of our *Open Hearts, Open Minds* discussion group. I want to do so not only because their work is entering more and more into the life of our church as a whole, but because this is the first Sunday of Lent—an appropriate time to be investing ourselves in matters of importance to our Christian faith. I undertake very deliberately to do this with you this morning in two ways. First, as Hancock's Senior Minister, as one whom you have called to leadership and whom you have richly and wonderfully sustained as I have tried to be a leader among you. In that role, I am convinced that faithfulness to what you ask of me requires me to spend time with you here and now with these matters. Second, as the pastor to everyone who is here this morning, as one charged not simply with leadership but with love, I want to do all I can to see that all of us are both calm and open as we proceed.

Let me say at the outset that I have no intention of arguing anyone either into or out of your feelings. No one should ever try to do that to another. This is conversation, not contention; and whether or not you agree with what I say is not as important as that you know what I believe. The issue is quite simply put: what place, if any, do Gay and Lesbian people have in the Christian family; and how ought the Christian Church acknowledge the existence of a variety of sexual orientations both in the Church and in the society?

To begin with, isn't this all quite simple? Does not Holy Scripture speak clearly and vigorously in opposition to homosexuality? Is not homosexual activity condemned? Are not homosexual persons condemned? The issue has been dealt with, authoritatively.

But let us not confuse the simple with the simplistic. In the first place, homosexuality is barely mentioned in the Bible; and it is a subject entirely absent from the words and the concerns of Jesus. But more than that, those passages in both the Old and the New Testaments which do refer to homosexuality are open to careful and responsible interpretations which do not admit condemnation of anyone. It lies outside the scope of this sermon to go into this important matter in detail; I will repeat here what I have said elsewhere: to say that the Bible condemns what we think of today as "homosexuality" is neither an accurate nor a complete reading of Holy Scripture. Moreover, any reading of the Bible which turns Holy Writ into an instrument of rejection or makes Scripture into ammunition is not only wrong, but about the worst blasphemy I can imagine.

On another note, it has been my experience of this church and this people across two decades of ministry among you that Hancock is a church brimming with good will, open hands and generous hearts. We work hard at reaching out to newcomers, and we are sincere in our welcome to anyone and everyone who has ever walked across the threshold of this church. The only requirement for membership in Hancock Church is that people present themselves to the congregation, to affirm the church's covenant, and to affirm the most basic statement of historic Christian belief. We are a church of wonderful openness: that's not me bragging, it's simply something that is true about us. Isn't that enough, more than enough for us to address homosexuality as it relates to our church and to our Christian faith? One of the things about which I hope to be clear this morning is that it is *not* enough. The world, in its confusion and its complexities and, yes, its sin, needs more from us. And we need more from ourselves and from one another. It is a matter of seeking out what is just, what is faithful, what brings us nearer to the kingdom of God.

Good will and good intentions, even when they are steeped in sincere Christian belief, are not sufficient in this particular moment in history adequately to address the question of the place of Gays and Lesbians in the Church. It is not kindness that is required of us; it is boldness.

Who are these people of whom we speak? Are *they* out there, waiting for some word of encouragement from us to storm through our front door? On the contrary: them is us. To speak of homosexual persons, we must begin by speaking of members of Hancock Church, many of whose sexual orientations we know nothing about. We are speaking of children who have been raised and nurtured here. We are speaking of family members: siblings, in-laws, cousins, spouses. And we are speaking of a percentage of the general population which has remained constant generation after generation. It is simply beyond belief that any such people are less deserving of our love, less acceptable to God, or automatically excluded from the joyful flow of creation.

Most of us, I suspect, agree with that; so what more needs to be said?

There is something important that lies outside the experience of those of us in the majority. And we're not talking about racial and ethnic and educational and economic majorities, but particularly about the sexual majority. And that something that lies outside the experience of the majority is *fear*. Fear for one's physical safety. Fear that friendships and affections, even the love of parents for their children, might prove conditional on not being Gay or Lesbian. Fear that a job or a promotion depends on the prejudices of others. Fear that trying to form a family or maintain a faithful relationship might be opposed, resented, misunderstood. Fear, in short, of never being at ease in one's life—at ease in the way most of us simply take for granted. The church of Jesus Christ, of all places, needs to be a place of complete safety, especially for those who do not feel safe elsewhere in their lives. That churches are safe places needs to be clear, public knowledge. Anything less is not keeping faith with the Gospel, for the Gospel is God's word, through Jesus Christ, of love, of reconciliation, of healing for brokenness and the overcoming of all that divides us one from another.

And that is why it is not enough for this church to understand itself to be open and welcoming. We need to be sure that our welcome is known. We need not only to know among ourselves that we are open and welcoming. We need to say clearly that we are.

This is particularly important because the Christian Church as a whole has had a poor record of openness and welcome. Insofar as the church rejects Gay and Lesbian people and believes that God expects the church to be rejecting, the church is simply wrong and sooner or later that wrongness will be mended. Meanwhile, for us to be clearly and publicly a safe and an open and a welcoming place for all who seek us out, particularly right now Gays and Lesbians, means being something quite extraordinary: it means that we are *pioneers in righteousness.*

Pioneers in righteousness. A difficult task. First, because it would seem that we are then in danger of being self-righteous. And second, because the implication is that we, both as a congregation and as individual church members, have all the complicated questions of human sexuality completely figured out. Then, third, aren't we then saying that we are of one mind, in every detail, about the proper way to be an open congregation? Absolutely not. Hancock Church could not fall into the trap of institutional self-righteousness without becoming a church which none of us would recognize, nor would wish to. That simply is not going to happen. Moreover, the variety of thought and opinion among us is something to which we have pointed with pleasure over the years as a sign of Hancock's vitality and as an important reason for people to join us. Unanimity has never been a precondition of our doing important things together as a church. This is no different. What matters now is what has always mattered: we are a people of God on a journey together, learning and growing as we go, having the courage to believe that God may change our minds about things along the way. As we make it clear both to each other and to the wider community that we are a Christian Church whose welcome is without limit or condition, we are affirming that we are nothing more or less than who we in fact already are.

Being a church open to Gay and Lesbian people is not something to do because it's a nice thing for good people to undertake. Nor is it something to do so that we can be on the proper side in America's and the church's ongoing struggles with social politics. This has nothing to do with social politics: it is a matter of being faithful to the Gospel of Jesus Christ. This isn't politics; it's religion! What makes us Christians, all of us, irrespective of our own sexuality or anything else about us is, first of all, our baptism. We're Christians because we've been baptized, and the church has never, for any reason, divided baptized persons into first- and second-class Christians. Second, we're Christians because we have agreed together to follow Jesus. And that commits us to have a special care, as Jesus did, for the rejected, the despised, the fearful, the misunderstood. If churches are outposts of the kingdom of God, then churches have a special calling to offer, as does the kingdom itself, a safe haven, a loving home, to those who need it the most.

Now, does all of this mean that at some time we will stand up to be counted in, or stand up to be counted out? Do we vote on this? I don't believe that's an option for serious Christians. What would we be counted into or out of? This church? The whole Christian community? Doing and being what is right is not a matter of having enough votes, of counting up sides. Friends, we are a family of the people of God. We're here not just because we decided one day to join; we're here because God has called us. Whether or not we use the same words to talk about openness and faithfulness and justice, we go on living and growing together. We're stuck with each other, and that is both the most powerful and the most delightful thing that we can say about one another and about Hancock Church. As imperfect as we are, we're Christians. And Christians take risks; that's part of the job. The risks now before us are the risks of faith and of love; and such risks are in the end the only risks that matter. It is our task to come to terms with God's call to openness and to affirmation, to adventure and to faithfulness, to be articulate, and then to keep on being Hancock Church together. This is not an event, but an ongoing part of our journey.

Pioneers in righteousness. No one ever has a higher or a more noble calling set before them by a loving God. That such a call is now before us is cause for high thanksgiving, no matter how many questions, doubts, or uncertainties we may have. We are not called as a church to stand still and blow our own horn; nor are we called to stand still and duck, and hope whatever is going on will miss us. We are called to continue our journey while mutually loving and caring for one another, doing our best to discern what God's will is for us, trying to answer that popular question: What would Jesus do?

It's a question in the end of how big a God we believe in, of how capacious a faith we have given our allegiance to. It's a matter of the size of our religion. We can't have it both ways: either there is room in the love of God and in the church of Jesus Christ for everyone, or else everything is conditional. If there is one lesson from Christian history it is this: whenever, even in good conscience, conditions are placed on God's love or on the church's welcome it always turns out that the conditions are of human manufacture and represent human limitation and human sin. Why repeat the errors of the past? Let us, pioneers together, be on our journey, loving our way into God's future.

I have a vision I want to share. A vision of Hancock Church. Some day soon, someone will be talking with any one of us, and the conversation will turn to Hancock Church—as it often seems to when people know that we belong to this congregation. Then someone will say, "Hancock's a large church, isn't it?" And we will say, "Yes, it certainly is."

A church whose heart and whose spirit and whose courage are large enough for us to bear witness to the limitless love of God. Amen.

The Stranger in Our Midst
by Bishop Paul Wennes Egertson

In Kevin Costner's movie, Wyatt Earp is portrayed as a man intensely loyal to family, but hostile and distrusting of everybody else. To help the viewer understand this, scenes from his childhood are shown in which his father repeatedly teaches the children: Nothing counts so much as blood. All the rest are strangers. Most of us seem to know that without having been taught it. There are few things we naturally fear more than the *unfamiliar*. It is a fear so universal we have a name for it: *Xenophobia*—the fear of the foreign. It comes from the same Greek word as our English word *strange*. It refers to everything outside the circles within which we are *familiar*.

Scripture:
Matthew 25:31-46

The Strangers in Our Midst

Think of the way we view *strangers in our midst*. Are we not defensive about them and do we not work to protect ourselves from them? The warnings we give one another range all the way from Stella Bensen's advice, *Call no man foe, but never love a stranger;* through our parents' persistent counsel, *never speak to strangers;* to the urging of our police to *report the presence of strangers*. It may be a linguistic coincidence that *stranger* rhymes with *danger*, but our natural fear of the foreign and our social conditioning against those who are not familiar tie them tightly together.

With such warnings in our ears, our primary line of defense is *exclusion*. Keeping ourselves separate makes us feel more secure. So we remove ourselves as far as possible from those who are different in ways either great or small. The poor are separated from those with enough; the sick from the healthy; the old from the young; ethnic minorities from the ethnic majority; prisoners from the free; and the weak from the strong. Whatever the nature of their difference, the point is the same: *anyone not like me is bad or wrong or unworthy and therefore must be excluded from my life and my society.*

But, some would say, surely that description is no longer true in our society. We live in a time that affirms diversity, that values human differences, that celebrates multicultural experiences. *Inclusion* rather than *exclusion* is the buzzword today, at least among those who are politically and religiously enlightened. While remnants of the exclusive spirit may still be found here and there in the world, we are for the most part beyond it. Things are getting better all the time. In 1999, for example, the State of Alabama repealed its Constitutional prohibition against interracial marriage. Since South Carolina removed its similar ban earlier that year, there is now no state in these United States that legally forbids people of different races to love one another. There are no strangers among us anymore.

Is that so? Or, is there still one class of people who continues to experience *exclusion* right here in the midst of our vaunted *inclusiveness?* Robert Dawidoff, Professor of History at Claremont Graduate University, thinks there is. He calls this group "the Last Outcasts." The *Washington Post* thinks so, too. A 1999 *Post* headline identified one area where Americans still draw a line on acceptability. Based on a national survey conducted jointly by the *Post*, the Henry J. Kaiser Family Foundation and Harvard University, the article asserts that Americans have radically adjusted their moral sensibility in the last 30 years, reserving judgment on people and lifestyles they once readily condemned. A majority now finds divorce, sex before marriage, interracial relationships and single motherhood acceptable. But one group whose behavior remains firmly outside the bounds of acceptability for a majority of Americans is homosexuals.

In a recent opinion sampling, Alan Wolfe of Boston University found that middle class Americans no longer believe that Jews, Muslims or atheists are inherently less worthy than Christians. But he notes one exception to what he calls "America's persistent and ubiquitous nonjudgmentalism." He says, "most Americans I spoke to were not prepared to accept homosexuality."

Do we need studies and surveys to tell us that? Any homosexual person you meet, who has not been totally hidden in the closet, can tell you experiences of exclusion that heterosexual people find hard to believe. Here is the way that experience is described by an anonymous high school student in Massachusetts, as reported in the Winter 1999 issue of *Open Hands*.

> Nobody tells Latino kids in the high school that nobody cares if they're Hispanic so long as they keep it to themselves. Jewish kids aren't told that they're sinners and they could change into Christians if they wanted to. People don't tell Black kids they should put up with racism because they've come so far from when they were slaves. They don't have to defend why there is a Black history month, or why people want Black studies included in the curriculum. People don't say, "That's so Korean!" when they mean something is stupid or weird. People don't tell disabled kids that the community isn't ready to defend their equal rights and inclusion yet. You never hear anyone argue that breast cancer is God's way of killing off women, or that it's a good thing. If a teacher hears anyone use a slang insult for a Chinese kid, they jump on it. When foreign exchange students ask teachers about dating in school, they aren't sent to see a guidance counselor.

> But every day in the high school, I hear its okay if I'm gay so long as I stay in the closet, and that I'm an abomination against God, that I can change if I want to, and that people like me shouldn't be taught about in school. I'm told that I should be satisfied because our school is far better than it used to be, and that I shouldn't push for my equal rights and inclusion because the community isn't ready yet. I hear, "That's so Gay!," all the time, and I hear that AIDS is my punishment for being who I am, and I hear the world *faggot* all the time. It's hard not to walk around angry all the time.

If Americans are serious about building an inclusive society (and the last time I looked that was the American Dream), we are going to need a lot of people to lead the rest across this last frontier of fear in response to people who are different. If Christians are serious about building an *inclusive church* (and putting those two words side by side is redundant in the Bible I read), we have a special challenge to face. For the fact to be confessed is that Christians have been largely responsible for the inability of people in this country to accept these *last outcasts*. As the *Post*/Kaiser/Harvard survey showed, "most Americans who find homosexuality unacceptable say they object on religious grounds."

Do we need surveys to tell us that? Nancy Hanson is a Midwestern Norwegian who was transplanted to Hawaii for several years and then enrolled in Pacific Lutheran Theological Seminary in Berkeley to prepare for a second career as an ordained minister. She once sent me a copy of her book, *From Pain to Joy — Inspiring Words for Hope and Healing*, and told me this story. She spent her first Easter Sunday as a newcomer to the Bay Area in the Castro District of San Francisco, the heart of the Gay/Lesbian community there. She gave a free copy of her book to anyone willing to receive it. While there, she saw a t-shirt displaying the slogan: *Jesus hates me, this I know, for the Christians tell me so.*

Dealing with these *strangers in our midst* in this condemning and excluding way feels so normal to many Christians that it does not seem at all strange for them to do so. So, it would be strange for someone to appear among us who held a totally different attitude.

The Stranger in Our Midst

When Jesus appears among us in the gospels, he seems familiar enough. We've known his name since childhood and expect to encounter him in the Scriptures. But that very familiarity may keep us from realizing how truly strange he is. As soon as he starts talking in Matthew 25, his words sound strange to our generation. He speaks of the ultimate judgment of God. That's strange enough, because we think of Jesus as the one who reveals a God of mercy and love. None of that hell-fire talk from him! But here he speaks as though humans are somehow accountable to God for what they do and that their destiny somehow hangs on it.

What could be stranger than that? To think that we are accountable for our decisions and actions at all is an increasingly strange idea in our time. Students don't feel accountable to teachers, nor citizens to government, nor employees to employers. So why would anyone think they are accountable to God? Or, could it be that our failure to recognize a divine accountability is the source of our failure to feel responsible to others?

But this Stranger in our midst faces us with the claim that God, however loving, is going to make a judgment about us. That is a reversal of our current mind-set. It is like the story of the man who knew nothing about art taking a tour of the French Museum of Art. After looking around for awhile, he said to the curator, "I don't think much of your pictures." To which the curator replied, "Sir, it is not the pictures that are on trial here."

If the mere *idea* of judgment is strange to us, the *objects* of judgment are stranger still. We would expect strangers to be judged. If people are poor, there's a reason. If people are sick, there's a reason. If people are homosexual, there's a reason. Those are forms of judgment that come upon sinners. That's a familiar idea to the righteous. But here, Jesus is not talking to sinners. He's talking to his disciples. He's talking to us. That is strange, because we thought we were the ones to *do* the judging, not the ones to *be* judged.

Yet, the strange thing about Jesus is that whenever he has the chance to condemn a sinner, like the woman taken in adultery, he does not do it. And whenever he has the chance to reward the righteous for their hard-earned worth, he doesn't do that either. For example, a publican and a Pharisee go up to the Temple to pray. The publican confesses his many sins before God and is justified, while the Pharisee prances his impressive achievements before God and is condemned.

If the *objects* of judgment are strange, the *basis* for judgment is even stranger. If there were a final court before which all will stand, we would expect a verdict based on how well we have avoided doing bad things. We know what bad things are, the things that hurt people. In our view, we will stand up under divine judgment if we live up to the ethic of our day: *I can do anything that feels good, so long as I don't hurt anyone else by doing so.*

But the Stranger in our midst turns that dogma inside out. Divine judgment is not based on the avoidance of hurt to others; it is based on our involvement in helping others.

> I was hungry and you fed me. I was thirsty and you gave me to drink. I was naked and you clothed me. I was sick and you visited me. I was a stranger and you welcomed me. I was in prison and you visited me.

We don't need Jesus to tell us not to hurt each other. That we could figure out for ourselves. But God judges by an ethic higher than we humans would set for ourselves. Jesus introduces into the equation of accountability this second mile of responsibility for the health and welfare of others.

The idea is not new with Jesus. It appears in Moses, who taught Israel not to harvest their whole field, but to leave some grain standing for the strangers and sojourners passing through their land. The principle goes back to when Cain killed Abel and God asked Cain, "Where is your brother?" Cain replied with the question so typical of our day: "Am I my brother's keeper?" To which God's answer is *Duh!*

What's more, it is not just your brother you are to love as yourself, but also your neighbor. And worse yet, your neighbor includes not only those inside your circle, but those outside of it, too: the stranger, the foreigner, even your enemy. Or, so said Jesus. But then, what did he know? Just whom does he think he is to place such unnatural demands upon us? He is the *Stranger in our midst* indeed, calling us to responsibility for *the strangers in our midst.*

And he is more. Perhaps the strangest thing we notice about Jesus is the correspondence between what he said and what he did. He not only *taught* us to include those we would naturally exclude, but he actually *did it* himself. Look at the places where you find Jesus in the New Testament. He's in the Temple only twice: once when he was twelve and once when he drove out those who were desecrating it. The Temple was not his favorite place. You find him occasionally in conversation with Scribes, Pharisees, Sadducees and other leaders in the religious community, with their relentless concern for rigid righteousness. More often than not, those conversations were encounters of conflict over their narrowness or Jesus' graciousness.

You know where Jesus could usually be found: among *the strangers* most religious people considered unfit and deserving of exclusion from their company. He was constantly among those classes of people he taught us to care about most: the tax collectors, like Matthew and Zacchaeus; the sinners, like two thieves on the cross; the women, like Martha and Mary; the children, like those he took up into his arms and blessed, over the protest of his disciples; the Gentiles, like the Syrophoenician woman who was willing to eat the crumbs that fell from Israel's table; the poor, like the widow who gave her last mite; and the lame, the halt, the blind and *the lepers*, like the ten he healed and received thanks from only one.

What's a nice Jewish boy like Jesus doing hanging around with people like these? He is *the Stranger in our midst* because he is in solidarity with *the strangers in our midst.*

A delightful Roman Catholic Nun named Sister Jose once addressed our Lutheran Pastoral Conference in Southern California. To establish rapport with us, she explained how her family had become Roman Catholic. Her father had not been raised in the church, but was converted to Christ as an adult by reading the Bible. When he went in search of other Christians, he was bewildered by the array of churches from which he had to choose. How could he know which was the right one? It seemed obvious that Jesus would be present in the true church. So he searched the New Testament to discern where Jesus was most likely to be found. Since Jesus was always with outcasts and sinners, he concluded that the church with the most sinners would be the truest one. So that's why he joined the Catholic Church.

The Stranger in the Strangers

It is strange enough to be told that service to strangers is the basis for divine judgment. But there are stranger ideas still. We think God will judge us by what we do for God more than what we do for people. Won't we be judged by how much we love God; how much we pray to God; how much we give to God; how much we serve God? Well, in a way, yes. But the strange thing is that the way we love God is quite different from what we normally suppose. Specifically religious activities have their place and value. But the trouble with using them as a means of evaluation is that we are liable to turn those very religious activities into a justification for avoiding *the strangers in our midst.*

Jesus' story of the Good Samaritan shows this. The people who walked by the man who fell among the thieves were the priests and Levites, those primarily responsible for religious services from which they dare not be detained by people in need. When people came to worship with their generous offerings for God, Jesus asked if they had a conflict going on with their neighbor. If so, he told them to lay their checks down at the door, go be reconciled with their neighbor and then come back to offer their gift to God. Jesus will have no truck with this idea that serving God is more important than serving people. Instead, Jesus insists on the strange idea that serving people is the only way you can serve God.

Who was that man who fell among the thieves on the road? Who was that hungry woman to whom you refused a meal? Who was that prisoner you had no time to visit? Who was that stranger from whom you turned your eyes away as you passed? Who was that transgendered person you would not welcome into your congregation? The strange truth is, in every case that was Jesus! He is *the Stranger in the strangers.* So he says, "in withholding your help from the least of these strangers you withhold it from me." And the opposite is also true. "In giving your help to one of these strangers, you give it to me." He is the one we avoided and the one we helped. And, the strangest thought of all, to stand before Christ at the last judgment will mean standing before the very strangers we either excluded or included.

What are we then to do? Our first impulse may be to rush out and start accepting Gay/Lesbian people in order to build a resumé of service to strangers that will assure us a place among the sheep instead of the goats. But that will not work. For the final strangeness in this story is that neither those who helped nor those who failed to help were in any way aware of what they had done. To help others in order to gain a reward will not work, because the goodness that distinguishes sheep from goats is an intrinsic difference in the nature of their being. Sheep act like sheep because they are sheep. Goats, who try to act like sheep, hoping to be counted as sheep, are still goats and will find their destiny with the goats. People do helpful things because they are helpful people.

What we need is not a new set of actions, but a new nature. What we need is not a change in behavior, but a change in being. To naturally serve *the Stranger in our midst,* who is resident in *the strangers in our midst,* happens only as we come to know ourselves more honestly and Christ more personally. Thomas Wolfe, in *Look Homeward, Angel,* asks the question we all must ask if we are to begin knowing ourselves.

> Which of us has known his brother?
> Which of us has looked in his father's heart?
> Which of us has not remained forever prison-pent?
> Which of us is not forever a stranger and alone?

It is only as we come to recognize ourselves as strangers, who need the welcome of divine grace, that Christ will be allowed to take up residence within us and transform us into his own likeness. That is exactly what Christ comes among us to do. But the strange thing is, he may come in the guise of the very stranger you would exclude.

Reflecting on her experience with the homosexual community in the Castro that Easter Sunday, Nancy Hanson tells of the condemnation she herself experienced at the hands of a well meaning friend. Because she was going through a divorce, her friend told her that she was deceived by Satan, going against God's Word and being very selfish. That judgment had given her a taste of the dregs Gay and Lesbian people have to swallow at the hands of Christians wielding their Bibles like machetes.

But strangely, after spending a day among the Gay community, she said, "A spirit of love from the good souls I met kept me going all day." Then she made a strange comparison between her Bible-believing friend and the strangers in San Francisco. Regarding her friend she wrote, "In less than one hour, I felt hurt and invalidated by her words. After eleven hours with the folks on Castro Street, I felt energized, happy, loved, accepted and surely tolerated. "Jesus loves me, this I know, for the people on Castro Street showed me so." Jesus is *the Stranger in the strangers.*

A Sample Stranger

Let me tell you of one strange man in whom Christ was so present. Joel Workin was one of three Lutheran seminarians who publicly identified themselves as Gay in 1986 and thus were ultimately refused ordination by our denomination. Joel was a farm kid from North Dakota and a good preacher already in seminary. If our church had been up to the challenge of ordaining him, he would have become a great one. Years later I was his pastor when his beloved partner and then he himself died of AIDS. When I was preparing Joel's funeral sermon, I wondered how he would have dealt with that occasion.

I got some idea of what he would have done from the Scripture he selected for reading at his funeral. It was the story of that odd couple, Peter and Cornelius, whose unlikely encounter with each other forms the heart and axis of the book of Acts. The gospel according to Acts focuses less on *what* the gospel is than on *whom* the gospel is for. The brief version of its message is this: *The gospel is for ALL people, specifically including those classes of people our own religious tradition has taught us to exclude.*

Luke, the writer of Acts, makes his main point in a story so crucial that he tells it twice, so those who miss it the first time might catch it the second. Peter is meditating on the rooftop of a house in Joppa, on the Mediterranean coast. Suddenly a sheet drops down from heaven containing all kinds of animals, including those Jews are forbidden to eat by the 11th chapter of Leviticus. A voice tells Peter to reach in, take any one of these animals and have it for lunch. Peter just knows this is a temptation to be unfaithful to God, so he draws on a lifetime of religious discipline and resists, saying, "I have never eaten anything unclean." To which the voice responded, "Don't you call unclean what I call clean."

Now Peter may have been a good fisherman but he was a slow learner on this matter. So are the readers of Acts, even to this day. That's why the vision and its lesson are repeated three times for Peter and for us. Its called learning by rote. The drill involves several repetitions of: "Don't you call unclean what I call clean; don't you call unclean what I call clean; don't you call unclean what I call clean!" Get it? Got it! Good!

But Peter only got the literal half of it: in Christ, there are no longer prohibitions about what animals you can and can't eat. Then the doorbell rings and Peter finds some Roman soldiers standing at the door. They want him to come and share the gospel with their captain. These are not Jews, but unclean Gentiles. Jews neither enter the houses of Gentiles nor eat with them. Suddenly an explosion goes off in Peter's brain and he gets the whole point big-time! God isn't changing my mind only about what *animals* I can and can't eat; God is changing my mind about what *people* I can and can't eat with! Get it? Got it. Good!

While Peter may be a slow learner, he is not stupid. He is about to violate traditional ecclesiastical practices, so he takes six witnesses along with him. When he gets to the house of Cornelius, he acts in contradiction to his own religious conditioning, enters the house of this Gentile and begins sharing the gospel of Jesus. He has no more than started when the wind and the flame from his own Pentecostal experience is repeated. God baptizes Cornelius with the Holy Spirit. What can this mean? Only the unthinkable thought that "God shows no partiality between peoples." All are accepted into the church, even those our own religion has taught us to reject.

What has happened? *Exclusion* has just been transformed into *inclusion*. The question for Peter is now clear: "If God has baptized

Gentiles with the Holy Spirit, what is there to prohibit us from baptizing them with water and thereby admitting them into the church?" Answer: "Nothing!" Get it? Got it! Good! So, Cornelius and his whole household are baptized and the rest, as they say, is history. Or is it?

Is the acceptance of everyone into the full fellowship and service of the church a done deal? Or, are there still classes of people our religious training teaches us to exclude, unless they become different from who they are? That was the second question Peter and those first Christians had to face. After gulping hard, the church could swallow the baptism of Gentiles so long as they became Jews as well as Christians. In other words, you couldn't be Christian and remain Gentile. You were welcome to be Christian, but if you were Gentile you had to change. Or at least try! It was that second question they fought out at the first Council of the Church in Jerusalem. The decision was that you *could* be both Christian and Gentile at the same time. Get it? Got it! Good!

I've taken time to spell this out because this message was at the center of the legacy that Joel left us. I know that for three reasons. First, as already indicated, I know it from the text he chose for us to read. But second, I know it from an incident that happened during the night before he died. His hospice nurse, Carmen, sat up with him during the night while he slept. That night, he suddenly spoke aloud, saying, "We are all God's children, aren't we?" Then after a period of silence, Joel said, "Can I hear a 'Yes' or 'Amen' to that?" It was vintage Joel, in both content and form. That was his message to us.

I also know this for a third reason. Joel carried the burden of this news in his heart because he knew so many needed to hear it. Gay and Lesbian people like himself, who feel excluded by the church because of its own religious traditions, need to know that another part of that tradition includes the recognition that God's voice is sometimes heard in contradiction to the church's voice. The church also needs to hear this, so that it might respond to what it regularly asks God to do for the church: "where it is in error, correct it."

Joel's concern for this message was clear in a devotional he wrote in 1988 on the *Parable of the Prodigal Child.* When the church relates that story to the Gay/Lesbian population, it usually understands it to mean that homosexuals are those who have left their heterosexual homes for a life in the far country of deviance. The church, like the waiting father, is eager for them to come home and will welcome them if they come to their senses and return to heterosexuality. Or at least try. Joel read the story in a quite different way. For him, the church has left its gospel home of *inclusiveness* and wandered into the far country of *exclusiveness*. But that does not mean we should give up on this church. He sees Gay/Lesbian Christians as the loving ones, waiting to welcome a wandering church home when it comes to its senses. He wrote to encourage us to do so, by saying: "How shall waiting Lesbians and Gays view their relationship with the church? There has been a break, a resounding 'no' from much of the prodigal church to any form of partnership or familial bond. But is it 'No. period' or 'No-dash?' 'No. period' means that the relationship is over. It is dead, period. Go back inside the house and stop worrying about the ungrateful kid. 'No—dash,' on the other hand, means the relationship is incomplete. There is more to be said after the dash, no matter how long the intervening silence. 'No—dash' means believing, hoping and trusting that the prodigal will come home. It means waiting for the church to 'come to its senses.'"

That was a courageous thing for a young man to say who, at the hands of the church, had just been denied ordination into the ministry to which he was called by God and for which he had academically prepared himself. But even though the church hadn't *got it* yet, he still encouraged us to wait in love. I quote: "Love puts a dash behind every 'No. period' and waits. For Gay Christians, God's love is the power of punctuation, the power to turn 'No. period' into 'No- dash' and to wait expectantly for words of reconciliation. The parable says 'Hope, believe, wait, love. There is more to be said. This show is not over yet. Just you wait.'"

We can hear in these words the sense of mission Joel lived out in his life and continues to share with us today, even after his death. The God of grace we know in the gospel had captured his heart and his mind in a way even personal hurt, inflicted by his own church, could not take away. It flowed out of the vision he had of a God who includes all as children in the household of faith.

In his Certification for Ordination Exam, Joel wrote this: "The kingdom is the destiny of the whole cosmos, the big party God is planning and to which everyone is invited. It is the fulfillment of all those great scripture passages: the lion lying down with the lamb; death being swallowed up; the lame leaping; no more war anymore. Even if it kills God (and it did, the cross), even if it kill us (and it does, baptism), somehow God is going to get everybody to that big banquet feast (resurrection, the kingdom, new life). I want to continue to be a messenger and means of God's invitation, to share the good news of God's 'Yes,' to live a courageous and comforting life of faith, to incarnate Christ and the kingdom, for my neighbor, to die and rise daily. This is my 'mission.'"

Some years before his death, Joel quoted those words in a letter to a friend. Two weeks before his death, the friend quoted them back to Joel in a good-bye letter, saying "I thank you for these inspiring words. May you find satisfaction now in having accomplished that mission in a significant way.... May your leave-taking now itself be a part of the mission." In this message Joel left us, his leave-taking was a part of his mission. In this strange Gay man dying from AIDS, we encountered the *Stranger in our midst.* Through him Jesus speaks to us again: "Hope, believe, wait, love. There is more to be said. This show is not over yet. Just you wait."

Prayer

Almighty and everlasting God, you hate nothing that you have made and forgive the sins of all those who are penitent. Create and make in the Church a new and contrite heart, that in lamenting its discrimination against Gay, Lesbian, Bisexual and Transgender members and clergy, it may receive from the God of all mercy, perfect forgiveness and peace; through Jesus Christ. Amen.

Discipleship After Sundown
by Trey Hall

Scripture:
Mark 1.29-39,
see also
I Corinthians 9.16-23

As soon as they left the synagogue, they entered the house of Simon and Andrew, with James and John. Now Simon's mother-in-law was in bed with a fever, and they told him about her at once. He came and took her and lifted her up. Then the fever left her, and she began to serve them. That evening at sundown, they brought to him all who were sick or possessed with demons. And the whole city was gathered around the door. And he cured many who were sick with various diseases, and cast out many demons; and he would not permit the demons to speak, because they knew him. In the morning, while it was still very dark, he got up and went out to a deserted place, and there he prayed. And

Simon and his companions hunted for him. When they found him,
they said to him, "Everyone is searching for you." He answered,
"Let us go on to the neighboring towns, so that I may proclaim
the message there also, for that is what I came out to do." And he
went throughout Galilee, proclaiming the message in their syna-
gogues and casting out demons. (Mark 1.29-39)

L et me begin with a small confession: I generally like to be in control. I'm sure that there's no one else like me in the world or in this church, so I'll try to explain what I mean. I don't think I try to control in any autocratic fashion, but I do prefer to know where things are, who's in charge of what, what exactly I'm responsible for. I like for the projects of my life to be organized and planned out, completed before they're due. I like to have time to do a rough draft, go back over it, hone in on the weaknesses, and polish here and there to a fine-looking end-result. My control issues have occasionally made it frustrating for me to work in group settings, because I want things to go my way, the way I had dreamed about them and had aligned them with my vision. Our culture really supports this psychological disposition. Worth in our society is measured in terms of productivity: of hours booked, cases closed, heads counted, manuscripts written, home runs hit. The imperatives are staying power, rigorous endurance, faithfully finishing the task at hand—perfectly or somewhere close to perfection. The result should be marketable and make the producer look good. So, having been raised in this culture, it's a bit hard for me to hear the Gospel today, and maybe it is for you, as well. Because in Mark's story, and in fact, in his whole account of the gospel, the image of Jesus' ministry is the opposite of our condition of attachment to our products and to recognition and approval from other people. And likewise, the ministry that Jesus invites us to is the precise antidote for our culture of desire for control.

The content of Jesus' work as described in the Markan text seems fairly clear: healing, casting out demons, and proclaiming the message that the time is fulfilled, the kingdom of God has come near, to repent and believe. Though the message may be apparent, what is curious is that Jesus appears somewhat conflicted about how the message will spread. In this passage and the passage directly before, he commands the exorcized demons to keep silent, not to mention his name. Despite Jesus' mysterious demand, however, the news of his exorcism in the synagogue must have spread quickly, for at sundown, hidden by the night, the disciples go about delivering those in need to the house of Simon and Andrew, where Jesus is staying. Soon, the whole city, the text tells us, is outside of the door, offering their wounds and addictions. As we would expect, Jesus heals numerous people, and casts out many demons. But the story doesn't say that Jesus healed all of those suffering or that he freed everyone from the prison of their possession. The whole city is there, but the whole city is not healed.

Moreover, the next morning, Jesus doesn't get up early to finish the healing—as we might do to meet a deadline at school or work— he gets up while the night still hides the earth, to retreat, to withdraw to a place of desertion, a place where no one is crowded to touch him, to see him, to be healed. And he prays. He's obviously chosen a place difficult to find, because the disciples have to hunt for him, to bring him the news that "everyone is searching for you." And when we think that he will get up, dust off his feet, and return to Capernaum and the project of healing immediately at hand, he doesn't. We must move on, he says—move on to the other towns. And so they move on.

In a confounding way in Mark's account, Jesus always seems to be doing what our world might call a partial job. He doesn't seem to give 100%, doesn't follow through—in short, he shirks his responsibility. He heals many, to be sure, and disposes of some demons who know his name, but more often than not, he is moving off— dancing through Sabbath fields when he shouldn't be; climbing mountains; crossing the sea. He even tells the disciples to have a boat ready in case the crowds press him too much! He enters here and exits there. One minute he is with the people, and the next, he is seeking a place away from them.

So, my modern pretensions ask the obvious questions: Why doesn't he finish the job? Is he not really committed to the message he proclaims? Why the concealment, ambiguity, elusiveness? Why does he seem to evade us and constantly remove himself? Is Jesus the quintessential introvert? We can't know for certain, but we can certainly draw from his actions some ways of being *church* for those who name themselves to be disciples of this same Jesus.

The story provides a model for ministry for a church and social culture obsessed with holding power over others and clamoring for attention and acclaim at the same time. Jesus' attempts to conceal his full identity, in his healing the masses after sundown, in retreating from the crowds, in leaving when things are just getting started, when people are just beginning to see his face in their memories. All of these actions show us a certain way of discipleship and reveal God in the process. This is a concealed God—one who seeks a paradoxical glory, a beauty often undisclosed, vulnerable, and mysterious. This God's intention is divulged not by loud assailing proclamations, but by subtle, surprising whispers. This image of God is much more elusive—to the point of absence, especially if we are accustomed to thinking of God as the brass section of an Aaron Copland symphony. Listen closely: this is the God of the ethereal descant, barely heard, but resonating with love and empathy. This is God revealed in Christ not as the Supreme Superego but the Suffering Servant of all people. What would our discipleship convey if it were molded in this image of God? It might be an affront to many contemporary attempts to draw the masses by a zealous preacher's magnetic personality for the purpose of an influx in numbers, or shallow, poorly-supported conversions. Imagine a ministry after sundown, a ministry in the rich blackness of night, a deliberately and delightfully hidden way of mercy.

This interpretation of the passage also reveals God's concern for our development as children of God. The God revealed in Christ desires our well-being, and yearns for our participation in the process. We hear in the text that Simon's mother-in-law is healed by Jesus, but afterwards, she doesn't just sit there in a saccharine ecstasy, or lie knocked out, immobile, like something we might see on a televangelistic revival. Jesus touches her, her fever is dissipated, and she begins to serve. The healing is for relationship, for service, for proclamation and discipleship. Maybe Jesus retreats because he wants to avoid being worshiped, because he doesn't want us to confuse the weight of his message of healing with an obsession with him as cult figure. Jesus longs for our relationship, not our obsession or idolizing. The Desert mothers and fathers of early Christianity and John Wesley gently remind us that relationship requires two parties. Relationship is not an utterly Sovereign God speaking what will happen, imposing upon automatons whatever God might wish. Relationship is most certainly not having it done fully for us, without our cooperation. Nor is it doing it all for ourselves, for our friends, family, or congregations. Relationship means space for communication between God and us, space for expression, for breath and love and silence and disagreement. We are healed for the purpose of relationship, for real partnership with the One who has called us into discipleship. If Jesus didn't heal everyone in every town, or cast out every last demon, perhaps those healed were meant to share the healing. In synergy—in relationship with Christ—healing is for healing others. Jesus' leaving is not a break in the relationship, but a genuine commitment to it.

Christ's perpetual journeying also broadens our expectations of where we might encounter this revealed God. And this might be difficult for the church to hear because the church has some control issues as well. The church also likes to name everything and everyone, as the demons wanted to, and by naming, attempt to control things—like who's in and who's out, who's first class and who's last class. Sometimes, sadly, even our calling the name of Christ is an attempt to coerce and dominate others, if not an attempt to govern Christ himself. If we take this story to heart, we are astonished that Christ's identity cannot be contained; it transcends and embraces every human category. To paraphrase Paul's indictment of the Corinthians' elitist epistemology: if we think we know, then we do not know (I Corinthians 8).

Later in Paul's letter, in the Corinthians 9 passage, Paul seems to be much more emphatic and less ambiguous about what is required for the Christian life— "Woe to me if I do not proclaim the gospel!" he says. Paul is all things for all people depending on whom he is trying to win, so as to save as many as possible. He can become a Jew, one under the law, or a weak one, depending on his audience. Here Paul appears at best contextual and savvy, and at worst, manipulative and slippery, in his attempts to win people for Christ. But perhaps the Jesus of the Markan text would interpret him another way.

Last summer, while on a graduate seminar in the Middle East, I spent a day in Hebron, West Bank, a city embroiled in near constant strife between the Palestinian Muslims, who have been living and farming there for centuries, and Israeli settlers, who in past decades have set up camp, demanding strict boundaries between Israeli and Palestinian sections. The struggle continues, as Palestinian farmers and shepherds living near the Israeli settlements continue to be evicted and prevented from working their land by the Israeli military. Their houses are being demolished over and over again, often immediately after the family has tried to rebuild.

To witness this destruction, to stand in the rubble of a family's home is a reality-shattering and almost hope-shattering experience. While in Hebron, we met with a Christian Peacemaker Team, six young adults that reside with the people and try to live in their experience every day. Christian Peacemaker Teams, a project of the Mennonites, Brethren, and Friends traditions, "accompany individuals and communities who are threatened, report on human rights abuses, and plan and carry out creative, nonviolent, public responses to injustice."[1] The community that is threatened in Hebron is the Palestinian Muslim community. So the Christian team lives among them, in a small four-room apartment above the street, and heeds the call, in daily events, to sit with the vulnerable and poor, to speak up for dignity and human rights. In a violent community, they risk their lives for the sake of others. In a statement, this peace-keeping team said:

> We have heard both Israelis and Palestinians in Hebron express opinions that some violent disaster is inevitable in the near future. We reject the notion that such violence is indeed inevitable. If it happens, it will be the result of policies that promote contempt for human rights and human dignity. We continue to operate under the assumption that God's redemptive power is at work here. We reject the use of force to save our lives should we be caught in the middle of a conflict situation or taken hostage. In the event that we die as a result of some violent action, we reject the use of violence to punish the people who killed us. Should our deaths come as a result of attacks by soldiers or settlers in Hebron, we ask that our deaths be regarded as no more tragic than the murders of dozens of Palestinians who have died here in the last decade. We ask that all legal nonviolent means be taken to ensure that these deaths do not continue. We ask that the government of Israel follow the principle of logical consequences. People with guns who kill other people should be removed from society for that society's protection. Whether those people are soldiers, rabbis or students should make no difference. At present, we feel safer walking through Palestinian neighborhoods than we do when we walk past the Israeli settlements in Hebron. However, should our lives be threatened by Palestinians, we ask that they be treated by the authorities in the same way as those authorities would treat Israelis intent on harming us. If more Palestinian blood is shed by Israelis on our account, then our deaths will indeed be in vain. We also ask that the people who care about us look into the root

causes of violence found amongst oppressed peoples struggling for liberation.[2]

I asked one of the peacemakers about their ideas regarding converting Muslims to Christianity. "That's not our goal; that's not why we're here," he responded simply, and began talking about something else. Some dismissed this method as "irresponsible," as a lost chance to spread the good news of the Gospel. Yet I believe that it is indisputable that the Gospel blessings are shared in the actions of these women and men who are committed to peacemaking. These volunteers understand what it means, as Paul writes, to become weak that they might win the weak for Christ. In the spirit of Paul's words, and in the fullness and depth of their Christianity, they become Palestinian Muslims. For the oppressed Muslims of Hebron are won for Christ when their homes are saved, when the dignity of their lives is preserved, when their livelihood is honored. This is not service without changed lives—this is the good news, for all people.

The peacemaker volunteers understand—and may we also—that Jesus' identity cannot be contained: It shatters our obsessions to name and control, to claim "the Truth" to the exclusion of others' understandings of it. In a liberative sense, the proclamation of the Gospel and our notions of evangelism, are recreated. Small events are transformed into meaningful encounters. Invitations, not even in words, call us to participate in this elusive and mysterious Christ. This Christ, the One who enters here and exits there, who will not be tied down or restrained, no matter how many people are searching, no matter the size of the crowd, or the imposing might of the Israeli or US governments, or the power of Southern Baptist Convention, the United Methodist General Conference, the Presbyterian General Assembly, or any other ecclesial body. No. Jesus will not be molded into any parochial revelation, will not be solely linked with one way of being in the world, will not be constrained by the expectations of any one group, will not be strictly associated with any one uniform set of theological principles.

Jesus breaks out of the conditions we set for him, so that in relationship, we may break out of the conditions and expectations that we have set for ourselves and for others. And that is good news, indeed. Thanks be to God.

Chapter 3

Ritualizing Our Lives

The greatest gift which we are asked to accept is the gift of living our lives reverently. We are assured that Jesus came not that we may have more "prayers," or more reading of the scriptures, or more pious devotions, or more of anything, but only "that [we] may live life and have it more abundantly."

Joseph F. Schmidt

Ritual Awakening
by Kelly Turney

It was the strange odor of hot glue that let us know as we walked into the room that this would be no ordinary class. And indeed, it wasn't because the afternoon was spent exploring our spirituality through a ritual involving arts & crafts. As the teacher lit a candle and banished the voices of those who would say, "You're not good enough," or "You can't do that," a safe space was created for our "sacred play." Before us was the unglazed, but fired pots considered "failed" by the artist who made them. We made them into receiving bowls—three-dimensional, autobiographical journal pages. We began with *lectio divina* (a type of spiritual listening with the heart) as we felt our bowls with eyes closed and allowed the reading, music and silence to speak to us.

Then after a much-too-brief hour of contemplative silence and "playing" with glue, tissue, fabric, paint, flowers, tree branches, wire and all sorts of sparkling objects, we gathered the bowls together and began to tell our stories of the process of making the object our own. Stories flowed, about pieces that turned out very different than they were intended and yet became so much more meaningful in the detour. Bittersweet stories were told of coming to God and leaving the church, of discovering divinity within oneself, about symbols and colors that spoke volumes to its maker.

Rituals focusing on artistic expression can often be experienced as freeing and revelatory. At a national conference last year, one participant in my workplace-spirituality class objected to being asked to draw a ship representing her leadership and workplace relationships. A chief financial officer at her university—where she was highly-competent, number-oriented, and driven—she, like many of us, had trouble seeing the tangible benefit of such a playful activity. Only begrudgingly did she enter into the process of centering, meditation, poetry, and, finally, working with paper, scissors, and construction paper. When the group was finished and she listened to others explore the meaning of their creations, she began to understand that her military vessel had more significance than she had meant to impart. She began by saying, "I know it looks like a battleship but it's not really. It's not that I work under a military model of fighting others" and then she paused and re-thought and began again. "This is a battleship because I feel like I'm constantly battling against an army of people expecting me to fail, wanting me to blunder, but also expecting me to take no prisoners."

There are many kinds of rituals, religious and secular, that are helping people discover their spiritual core. People are realizing that far from being useless ceremonies created by ancient peoples to make our worship services run longer, rituals are an integral part of life through which we carry on, celebrate, and commemorate.

> Rituals, like myths, address the urge to comprehend human existence; the search for a marked pathway as one moves from one stage of life to the next; the need to establish secure and fulfilling relationships within the human community; and the longing to know one's part in the vast wonder and mystery of the cosmos.[1]

And rituals connect us, remind us that we are part of God and part of each other. As Kathleen Norris writes in *The Cloister Walk*, "Rituals bind a community together and also bind individuals to a community." At their best, rituals reinforce the reality that all life is interconnected.

Ritual for me is a heart-song—something that sustains me on my soul's journey. Heart-songs can be as simple and as complex as learning to meditate, visiting sacred places, listening to the hidden track 12 on the Indigo Girls' "Come On Now Social" CD, or making poetry central to your life.

When we allow ritual to engage and change us, it can disengage our frantic activity and help us take the time to breathe, and to drink deeply of the living well that springs forth within us. We realize that life is not so much trying to reach a destination as making the journey our home.

Somehow the journey is more meaningful when we see the sacred in the details; ritual can sanctify the mundane events of the world. It can infuse meaning, passion and purpose into our daily routine. One ritual that can be done in the office is based on the Buddhist monks' daily practice of getting their food in a bowl each carries to the village. Select a bowl, one that is meaningful to you. Every morning trace the rim of your bowl as you breathe in the abundance of life. Pray that you will have access to that which you need that day. Promise yourself to be present, to give what you can, to be fully available to the lessons life brings. At the end of the day, trace the edge again, being grateful. Leave in your bowl any issues or assignments that will have to be taken up again tomorrow. Kathleen Norris says it nicely, "Let the day suffice, with all its joys and failing, its little triumphs and defeats."

So treat yourself to a ritual, such as the spirituality through art workshop described in Chapter 4, or the water renewal rite described in Chapter 6, or create one that speaks specifically to your own circumstances. That is exactly what the following three authors did.

Mary Callaway Logan's first child, Hillary, was leaving home for college and the extended family needed to mark the passage. So she and her second daughter, Hannah, created a leaving home ritual. It was so meaningful that they adapted it to celebrate Hannah's leaving for college a few years later. Leslie Penrose tells the story of Daniel, an autistic child in her congregation, and of her congregation's struggle to embrace Daniel and his mother. And Lesley Brogan provides some insight into the thought process and planning of a healing ritual for a group of people from very different circumstances.

A Ritual of Letting Go, Grieving and Healing
by Lesley Brogan

Although it seems hard to imagine, there *is* a deserted beach on the panhandle of Florida. There *is* a stretch of beach where the sand is white and fine. There *is* a beach where the water is emerald and the waves are rhythmic in their comings and goings. This is the place for this service.

It is early in the morning on the Saturday after Thanksgiving. The dawn is on the way. It is still dark and the air is crisp. We gather in a parking lot, not far from the dunes leading down to the beach. Not far, on the other side of the dune, we can hear the song of the ocean. We hear a crescendo and decrescendo drawing us out of our cars, closer to the water.

We gather in a quiet that is reverent. There is a sense of the sacred even in the waiting for one another, until we are all together. When the last car pulls into the lot, our group of twenty is assembled and we start toward the beach.

There had not been a specific reason for the group's composition. Individually we have experienced a great deal of pain recently. Our stories come in many voices:

Mary Jean: Miscarried for the second time this past summer after reaching her second trimester.

Gerry: Lost his partner to AIDS.

Clark: Retired six months ago from the bank where he'd worked for thirty-five years. He is looking forward to retirement, but is not sure how he can remain useful.

Linda: Told her Christian friends that she was gay, not asking for anything from them, but hoping for their support. Instead, she was shunned.

Claudia: Broke up with her boyfriend and the following week learned that he was engaged to another woman.

Elaine: Had an abortion because she felt in her heart that she had no other real options.

Gennell: Lost her only son five years ago when he shot himself.

Rick: "Came out" to his parents, after six years of wondering whether or not he could/should. His heart told him "things would never be the same." He hoped that was true, he prayed their relationship would be better.

Amy: Is going through a divorce.

Andy: Started graduate school in August, and was laid off from his job the first of this month.

Lesley: After months of struggling, realizes that in order to have any sense of integrity in doing ministry, she must seek ordination in another denomination, not because she wants to, but because she chooses to be in a relationship with another woman.

There are also some who come this morning because they knew of the service and wanted to be a part of it. Some named their places of grief aloud, some chose not to. Some came to offer support. Each one had said that they wanted and needed to share in this service. And so, this morning, we come together. We seek to name our pain. We seek a beginning place for letting go. We seek healing.

We are each given a candle and help one another in the lighting. Cupping our hands around the flame to protect it from the breeze, we use it to help us make our way down to the water. Lesley and Amy have brought their guitars, and Bruce brought his harmonica. We start together over the dunes and to the beach. Off to the right we can see a light and silently look in that direction. There is a large Native American blanket on the ground and a kerosene lamp is close by already burning. Beside the lamp, standing upright in the sand, is a hand-carved cross.

As we walk closer, we see that other blankets have been arranged around the center blanket to form a semi-circle. We all find a place and sit down facing the water. Lesley asks us to take our hands away and let the wind blow out our candles. She then invites us to wait quietly and watch as the sun rises.

When we had arrived earlier in the parking lot, the stars were shining overhead. Minutes later, we were aware that the sky was changing. Off to our left, we began to make out colors. As the moments passed, the sky became painted in deep blues and purples, then melted into pinks and soon, a light orange. We began to make out shapes in the clouds that served as a backdrop to the changing colors. All of this took place with the continued rhythm of the ocean.

The service has been created with an understanding that it is not a typical worship service. These folks are aware that, for many of them, their pain has not been named in the conventional services. In the silence there has been discomfort and distress. There has been an intentionality of setting, here at this beach. In this place, there is, perhaps, the freedom for each one to meet God differently, as well as to see themselves and one another in a new way.

Each participant receives a note card that holds the words to the two songs. They are not given a formal order of service. Instead, Lesley briefly explains how the service will proceed and that she will serve as its leader. Prior to the service, several have been asked to participate by reading or sharing music, and those persons are aware of the order.

Gathering

[Lesley] We come together this morning to see differently. We come with hopes to hear a new song or perhaps a familiar one with a new message. We come seeking God.

Opening Music

Guitars and harmonica play "There is a Balm in Gilead." As the melody and accompaniment begin to dance with one another, the participants find themselves humming—reinforcing the melody and playing with the harmonies. As the songs ends, there is a sense of joined beginning.

Call to Worship

[Claudia] Healing Spirit, we are a people who know the weight of being burdened, who know pain. In this service, this morning, may we be reminded of your presence with us and in us. May we experience your love. Your love, God, that knows our pain, and names it with us. God, you know us, you call us by name in the midst of this pain in us.

Song "How Can We Name a Love" by Brian Wren
[sung to tune "This Is my Father's World"]

Using the note cards, everyone is invited to stand and sing this familiar melody with new words.

Readings

[Lesley has brought a Bible and passes it from one reader to the next.]

Ecclesiastes 3:1-9

[Andy] For everything there is a season and a time for every matter under heaven:
A time to be born, and a time to die;
A time to plant, and a time to pluck up what is planted;
A time to kill, and a time to heal;

A time to break down and a time to build up;

A time to weep, and a time to laugh;

A time to mourn, and a time to dance;

A time to throw away stones, and a time to gather stones together;

[John] A time to embrace, and a time to refrain from embracing;

A time to seek, and a time to lose;

A time to keep, and a time to throw away;

A time to tear and a time to sew;

A time to keep silence, and a time to speak;

A time to love, and a time to hate;

A time for struggle, and a time for peace.

Psalm 139

[Gennell] O Lord, you have searched me and known me. You know when I sit down and when I rise up; You discern my thoughts from far away. You search out my path and my lying down, and are acquainted with all my ways. Even before a word is on my tongue, O Lord, you know it completely. You hem me in, behind and before, and lay your hand upon me. Such knowledge is too wonderful for me; it is so high that I cannot attain it.

[Clark] Where can I go from your spirit? Or where can I flee from your presence? If I ascend to heaven, you are there; if I make my bed in Sheol, you are there. If I take the wings of the morning and settle at the farthest limits of the sea, even there your hand shall lead me and your right hand shall hold me fast. If I say, "Surely the darkness shall not cover me, and the light around me become night." Even the darkness is not dark to you; the night is as bright as the day, for darkness is as light to you.

[Kelly] For it was you who formed my inward parts: you knit me together in my mother's womb. I praise you for I am fearfully and wonderfully made. Wonderful are your works; that I know very well. My frame was not hidden from you, when I was made in secret, intricately woven in the depths of the earth. Your eyes beheld my unformed substance. In your book were written all the days that were formed for me, when none of them as yet existed. How weighty to me are your thoughts, O God; how vast is the sum of them! I try to count them—they are more than the sand; I come to the end—I am still with you.

[Barbara] Search me, O God, and know my heart; test me and know my thoughts. See if there is any wicked was in me and lead me in the way everlasting.

Special Music "Hymn of Promise"

Matt and Maureen sing together with guitar.

[There's an unscheduled time of silence. The tide had been slowly changing, and the water was closer now than it had been at the start of the service. There was a sense for some that the water was reaching out. For some there was a sense of the power of the waves. For some there was a growing sense of peace.]

Gospel
Luke 13:10-17

[Elaine] Now (Jesus) was teaching in one of the synagogues on the Sabbath. And just then there appeared a woman with a spirit that crippled her for eighteen years. She was bent over and was quite unable to stand up straight. When Jesus saw her, he called her over and said, "Woman, you are set free from your ailment." When he laid his hands on her, immediately she stood up straight and began praising God.

[Linda] But the leader of the synagogue, indignant because Jesus had cured on the Sabbath, kept saying to the crowd, "There are six days on which work ought to be done: come on those days and be cured, and not on the Sabbath day." But the Lord answered him and said, "You hypocrites! Does each of you on the Sabbath untie your ox or your donkey from the manger, and lead it away to give it water? And ought not this woman, a daughter of Abraham whom Satan bound for eighteen long years, be set free from this bondage on the Sabbath day?" When he said this, all his opponents were put to shame: and the entire crowd was rejoicing at all the wonderful things he was doing."

Three short stories from *Mostly True: Collected Stories and Drawings* by Brian Andreas.[1]

[Rick] When I die, she said, I'm coming back as a tree with deep roots and I'll wave my leaves at the children every morning on their way to school and whisper tree songs at night in their dreams. Trees with deep roots know about the things children need.

[Connie] I once had a garden
filled with flowers
that grew only on dark thoughts
but they needed constant attention
and one day I decided
I had better things to do.

[Mary Jean] Don't you hear it?
She asked and I shook my head no
and then she started to dance and suddenly there
was music everywhere and
it went on for a very long
time and when I finally
found words all I could
say was thank you.

Meditation

[Lesley] What brings us to this place, to this time? On the surface, we would all answer differently. We would share from our own experience, tell our own stories. For some, we have nowhere else to go—within us is the sense of being at the end. For some there is a voice inside encouraging us to "at least try this..." that "in coming together, there is strength—where two or more are gathered...." For some there is the assurance of hope—of knowing that transformation *is* possible. For some of us, we just don't know anymore, and this sounded as good as anything else. What brings us here is unique, and at the same time familiar.

The writer in Ecclesiastes reminds us of the seasons. We listened to the author's expressions of life's balances. I appreciated hearing those images playing in balance again this morning. To everything there is a season and there is a time for every purpose, for every matter. In these verses is an acknowledgment of the planting and the harvest; of losing and finding; of holding on and of letting go. As we look within ourselves this morning, we are aware of the pain. This is something that is alive and well and living right inside us. We know very clearly what the writer was talking about when the words "mourning" and "struggling" were chosen. Perhaps as we think about watching the sun come up this morning, about listening to the birds calling to one another, about listening to the rhythm of the water, perhaps we can better understand the balance of this piece.

"Mourning" balances with "dancing," "struggle" balances with "peace."

How did we make it to this beach, to this sunrise this morning? Where did our energy, our courage come from? Why is it so important that we keep trying, that we keep looking for that balance? What keeps us going? What does it matter?

It matters because we are known by God. Each one of us. And more than knowing, God has searched us. That says to me that God has a definite investment. How much easier it would be to create us, and then let go. But that's not what the psalmist believes. Instead, we heard that God has searched us, and knows us completely. The Psalm says that God knows our actions, and knows our hearts. Even to the psalmist it's too wonderful for humans to begin to comprehend.

There is a line from the song that was sung earlier that both comforts and haunts me, "In our end is our beginning; in our time; infinity; in our doubt there is believing; in our life; eternity." Can we believe those words this morning? Are we able to let them inside of us and tend to us this morning?

In the lesson from Luke there is a story of Christ that isn't shared much. I guess in the overall scheme of things, it wasn't all that significant. Another healing story, showing Jesus getting into trouble with the keepers of the law. Just another healing story, or is it? For me, there are several lessons we can take away with us from this story. Our teachers are both this woman and Jesus.

What do we know about this woman? We are told that this woman appears in the synagogue. We know that she is bent over, and that she has been so for eighteen years. Eighteen summers, eighteen winters. That in itself tells us a great deal about this woman who has no name. Obviously deformed, obviously out-of-place, she goes to the synagogue where she knows many people will be. For most of us here on the beach this morning, we carry our pain inside, and still we know its weight. At times we feel bent over. It is difficult for me to imagine going into a crowded place, when I felt bent over...and yet, here she is entering the synagogue. We can only imagine how her heart and her thoughts were racing as she chose to enter. But there is strength in this woman, and Jesus senses it.

I wonder how Jesus saw her. When she looked on her, when he looked at her, looked into her eyes, what did he see? Had she, bent over and obviously in pain, approached him and made a public spectacle of herself? Or was she back in the shadows, somewhere in a corner of the synagogue out of the way? We aren't told. Either way, anyway, Jesus saw her. We are told, Jesus saw her, and called over to her, 'Woman, you are set free from your ailment.'" And then we are told that Jesus reached out to her and touched her.

What could that moment have been like for her? Eighteen years, spent month after month, day after day, hour after hour bent-over. Her gaze had been driven downward because of the twist of her back. Looking up to see another took a great deal of effort for her. Did she look up as he touched her? Or was it only when she was released that she could stand and look on him as well? Was his touch a quick brush of the hand, or did he keep his hand there for a time as he watched her? I wonder in those past eighteen years if she had felt the touch of someone else? Or was this the first time that she'd felt another's touch? I wonder what Jesus' hands were like? Big? Small? Rough? Smooth? There is so much to this story that we aren't told. So much that is left to us. But we are told that he reached out to her. We are told that he touched her. And we are told that she experienced healing in that touch.

And in the story, the touch was enough. "Immediately she stood up and began praising God." This is a story of miracles. The story is full of them. It was a miracle that this woman found the strength to make it into the synagogue and seek Jesus. It was a miracle that Jesus sensed her pain, and, after seeing it, responded to it. We hear the miracle from Jesus' proclamation, "Woman, you are set free." There is a miracle in his touch. And there is the miracle of her standing up so straight.

What has brought you here this morning? What miracle are you seeking on this beach? Knowing that to everything there is a season and a time for every purpose, is this the day for you to let go and stand up straight?

Time of Silence

Pastoral Prayer

[Lesley] If you are able this morning, may your posture for prayer reflect the story of the woman bent over. Instead of closing your eyes, I invite you to keep your eyes open and look around with your head up. I invite you to allow your hearts to see. As we move into this time of prayer, we know that often today there is violence and abuse in ways we touch one another. Many of us have been bruised from the touch of another, some of us have been the abuser. For so many, we are genuinely afraid of touch. Like the woman bent-over, some of us have lived a long time without receiving any kind of touch from someone else. Some of us have been shunned and put aside. We've been told we are unclean.

And at the same time, we have also received life and love through touch. We have been Christ for one another. We look this morning for a time of touching in love, a time of reaching out to one another as members of Christ's community.

Let us pray:

Holy and Loving God, you are our Creator. You know us, inside and out. In this knowing, may we experience a feeling of assurance, that we are not alone. May we feel your presence with us.

Holy One, you are the God of time. May we come to understand your being with us in all of our seasons. May we come to know you in our silences, as well as the times when we speak out. May we come to know you in our weeping and in our laughing, in our mourning and in our dancing, in our being born and in our dying, in our gathering together and in our letting go.

Wondrous God, you are our healer. We hear this story of the woman who was bent-over, who Jesus saw, touched and healed. This story reminds us of the power of touch. Through touch, we can affirm one another, we can offer a connection, we can experience healing. It was through Jesus' touch that he taught us so well, "I am with you, this day, you are not alone."

We pray for our brothers and sisters who are not here on this beach this morning. We pray for those who carry their pain in isolation. In your loving kindness, Merciful God, be with them and grant them presence and peace in their struggles.

We look this morning, Holy God, for your touch in our lives. We ask to be made whole. And now, as your precious sons and daughters, we offer our prayers to you:

[After a time, one-by-one, members in the group offer prayers, of tenderness and pain, of proclamation and transformation. There are prayers of lament and prayers of thanksgiving. Several people come to the center of the group and kneel on a blanket. Silently, others surround the person in the center, some lay their hands on the person and offer silent and spoken prayers on the person's behalf. After a time, Lesley concludes the prayer.]

Loving and gracious God, we have come this morning with our hearts heavy. Through your word, through your Spirit, through your touch of those around us, we have felt your loving presence. For this gift of confidence and reassurance, we are thankful. Through Christ's holy name, Amen.

Song "Be Thou My Vision"

Benediction

To see thee is to see the end and the beginning
Thou carriest us and thou goest before
Thou are the journey and the journey's end. Amen.

As the service concludes, there are tears and hugs shared. There is a sense of lingering following the service. For many, there appears to be a sense of peace for the first time in a long time. Someone blows out the lamp and picks it up, another picks up the cross. The blankets are picked up and shaken out. There's a box for the candles. And slowly, some holding hands, some with an arm over a shoulder, we head back along the beach, over the dunes and back up to the parking lot. Before hearing the car doors slam, someone says something about a good place down the road for breakfast.

Daniel's Story & A Ritual of Hope
by Leslie Penrose

His name is Daniel. He's 7 years old, blonde, and blessed with crystal clear blue eyes. As I sat this week with Barb, Daniel's mother, in her kitchen, she remembered the day she first held him in her arms—he was just 24 hours old, and having arranged to adopt him, she had been anticipating his birth for months. "I counted 10 fingers and 10 toes," Barb said, "He was a gift from God, a dream come true. I imagined his future: a champion athlete, an academic whiz, perhaps even president!" Sixteen months later Barb sat in her pediatrician's office, hearing, but barely comprehending what the doctor was saying, "Daniel is autistic."

Autism is a mental/emotional condition that occurs when something interrupts one's ability to make connections between his/her interior world and the world around him/her, and it severely challenges the ability to connect to and relate with others—even one's own family. In Daniel's case, it means that an ordinarily curious, energetic child is growing up unable to express what he's thinking or feeling, what he's curious about or frustrated with, what he's fascinated by or afraid of. Often Daniel is unable to make anyone understand him, unable to connect with anyone. He doesn't have the words, he doesn't know how. Barb's life as a single parent of an autistic child has been a roller coaster of emotions: hope, disappointment, fear, rage, passion, loneliness, worry. "I have experienced more extravagant joy and more profound sadness in 7 years of loving Daniel than I ever imagined possible," she said, "but through it all, even in the middle of crying 'Why?' and raging 'Why me?' I have trusted God to give me the strength I have needed to care for—and to fight for—my special child."

When Barb and Daniel started coming to Community of Hope two years ago, Daniel touched our hearts, raised our awareness, and left many of us feeling inadequate as to what to say or do to express our care. But, in spite of our stumbling efforts to show our concern, Daniel and Barb found a safe and nurturing home in our midst. The last six months have threatened that. Daniel's frustration has started manifesting itself in sudden outbursts of rage—he throws things, he strikes out, he connects by wounding. There is no warning and no predicting the outbursts and so, there have been fewer and fewer places where Barb has felt "safe" to take Daniel—safe from judgmental looks, hurtful stares, shaming remarks, safe from the possibility that Daniel might scratch a stranger or slap another child, safe from those who don't understand and don't care to try. It's been weeks since Barb has even felt "safe" to bring Daniel to Community of Hope for fear of what might happen and of what we might think.

I asked Barb for the gift of a chance, and so on Sunday, September 7, Barb and Daniel came back with us for worship. An anonymous donation covered the cost of a skilled care-giver for Daniel during worship. It's not a solution, but it's "a way" to begin. It's a way for Daniel to have one-on-one attention to his needs, and for Barb to have time for "Sabbath," (holy rest), for "communion" and for fellowship. It's a way for us to act as companions on their journey, and be blessed by their presence. It's a way to hope rather than curse the darkness! "I am the way," Jesus said. So, I told my congregation that when they saw Daniel, smile, talk gently to him as you would to any child, trust that any response he makes (even an outburst of rage) is an expression of his deep human desire for relationship, and, most of all, remember, even though we call him Daniel, God calls him "Beloved!"

RITUAL OF HOPE

[This ritual was written when the family decided to participate in a new experimental treatment for autistic children]

One: Barb and Daniel, you are part of our family. The joys and sorrows of your life are our joys and sorrows too. The hopes and fears you hold, we hold too. Three years ago we covenanted to be with you in the ups and downs of your journey with Daniel's autism. Since that time we have cherished the times when you could be with us, and held you in prayer when you could not.

One: We have celebrated holy moments with you—the bike ride at Little Light House's family day, and Daniel's participation in Special Olympics. We have prayed with you as Daniel prepared to enter public schools and rejoiced with you as he negotiated that transition. We have hurt and feared with you over Daniel's increasing aggression, and cried with you when the journey has meant deep pain.

One: We give thanks for the courage it has taken for you to live abundantly in the midst of "dis-ease:"
  — for your decision to love without reservation in spite of the risk of a broken heart,

— for your commitment to care steadfastly in times of struggle as well as times of joy,

— for your insistence in celebrating the "God-stuff" in every day—the smiles, the hugs, the new worlds learned, the companionship of family, the laughter of friends for your wisdom in continuing, over and over again, to trust the power of community, and

— for your faithfulness in entrusting Daniel, yourself, and your journey to God, every single day, even when God seems far away.

Your courage has en-couraged us.

All: Today we hold with you the hope of a new treatment, and the possibility it holds for Daniel. As you follow this star from Tulsa to Chicago, not knowing what gifts or disappointments lie ahead, we offer you our fiercest prayers, our wildest dreams, our deepest yearning. We also offer you our renewed commitment to be with you come what may.

[A few representatives of the community are asked to lay hands on Barb and to sit beside Daniel on the floor, as we pray together this blessing of solidarity.]

God of grace and hope, Hold Barb and Daniel in your "fierce tenderness" as they journey to Chicago.[1] Surround them with courage, and wisdom, and strength as they continue to seek all that is possible for Daniel. Be with their friends and family as they wait and empower us, O God, to be instruments of healing and wholeness and compassion and strength as together, we face both the triumphs and the trials that lie ahead. Amen.

Leaving Home:
A Ceremony for Hillary Grace Logan
by Mary Callaway Logan & Hannah Logan

[This ceremony was held outdoors with a canopy of various-colored ribbons (one for each participant) suspended from above. There is a spiral pattern in fabric on the ground leading to the center of the canopy. Nearby, there is a fountain gurgling and a candle burning. A mirror is used and its frame was decorated with words appropriate to the occasion. Participants included family, friends, mentors, and neighbors].

Music and Gathering Flute Solo *Serenade* by Woodall

Parent A: This is a ceremony of blessing and sending forth of Hillary Grace Logan. We are gathered as your dear family, extended family, friends, the spirits of those who cannot be here, and the souls of your grandfathers. Each of us represents parts of your 18 years among us.

Parent B: We acknowledge the journey you are about to make and want to send you forth with our blessings, signs of the abiding Spirit, with solemnness and joy.

Parent A: This journey outward is a journey to the center of your independent life. It is both a journey out, and a journey to the center. Nature is one teacher of the rhythm of this journey. Symbolized by the spiral, its line is never straight.

We listen to water, which always moves in a spiral, water which mediates heaven and earth in cloud form, which meanders in the river, whose flow reflects the moon. We look to fire, which burns in a spiral, which lives lovingly in the hearth, and which must be contained. We learn from the earth, that pours forth infinite variations of life as roots seek depth, and branches seek the sun. The air carries the breath of God's spirit to us, and in incense, carries prayers back to God.

One key to living into your future is to live the movement of nature—bending, flowing, meandering, mediating, giving, receiving. This movement is a dance, infinitely creative.

Mentor: The path to the center requires direction. Your soul's journey to realization of the One, its power, its nature, and its work is yours alone to take. Along the way, each person here helped prepare you for that journey. Fate, calling, the will of God brought us and you together. And so tonight we are here to celebrate the end of this stage of your preparation and the beginning of the next.

Look around at the faces who have helped you build your way into the many worlds. We are grateful to have been called to be with you. We're grateful for your being, grateful for the opportunity you have given us to commit ourselves to a work of love, and grateful and proud to stand here with you.

This week you leave for college. Hidden among the things you will haul with you are many unopened gifts. For you to look for them is useless, but given your determination and courage, at just the precise moment, under the right circumstances, they will appear at hand. Then they will be yours to use. They are our going away gifts—those of us here you can see and the many hosts, powers, teachers, and helpers who also are present who you do not yet see.

As you ask, you will receive. I have that on the very best authority. So ask, so that your journey to the center of the One will continue and that our joy in you may be complete.

Parent B [handing the mirror to Hillary]:
The path to the center requires reflection. When you look at your reflection in this mirror, seek first to see yourself through the eyes of God who loves you like a moonstruck lover, who values you as a precious jewel. When Christ gave God's love flesh and passion, we learned that God eternally seeks us—shadow, blemishes and all. The hope is that you may embrace your whole self in beauty. Look in the mirror and be all of who you are.

Parent A: The path to the center requires love transformed. There have been many visible bonds of love—the daily nurture and protection of parents, grandparents and sister; the guiding of spiritual companions, extended family of "mothers and fathers;" your friends, schools, and travels.

[Each participant picks a ribbon and Hillary stands in the middle of the canopy of ribbons.]

Mentor: You will be cutting each of these visible bonds. Each cutting is an outward sign of the transformation of love from the visible to the invisible. Where they go is into the Mystery of the Spirits holding the Unseen. As ties to the past are transformed, we will live the faith of the seed planted in fertile ground.

Hillary [reading one her favorite quotes made popular by Nelson Mandella]:
"Our deepest fear is not that we are inadequate. Our deepest fear is that we are powerful beyond measure. It is our light, not our darkness, that most frightens us. We ask ourselves, 'Who am I to be brilliant, gorgeous, talented, and fabulous?' Actually, who are we not to be? You are a child of God. Your playing small doesn't serve the world. There's nothing enlightened about shrinking so that other people won't feel insecure around you. We are born to make manifest the glory of God that is within us. It is not just in some of us, it is in everyone. And as we let our light shine, we unconsciously give other people permission to do the same. As we are liberated from our fear, our presence automatically liberates others."

You have given me this light, through your company, your guidance and nurturing, your conversation and stories, your actions and teaching. This has nurtured my own light which shines strong as I venture into these new waters of life. Thank you.

[As Hillary cuts each ribbon, participants place the ribbon piece around her shoulders and make a comment, if they like.]

Benediction *[participants join hands in prayer]*:

The Lord bless you and keep you; may the Lord make her face to shine upon you and be gracious unto you; may the Lord lift up his countenance upon you and give you peace.

Music "Sicilano" by JS Bach

Refreshments

Chapter 4

Creating Sacred Space

What matters, therefore, is not whether God can be God without our worship. What is crucial is whether humans can survive as humans without worshiping. To withhold acknowledgment, to avoid celebration, to stifle gratitude, may prove as unnatural as holding one's breath.

John E. Burkhart

Shaping Sacred Space
by Philip Cox-Johnson

Worship spaces often come together in unexpected ways but they should not be unplanned. Shaping the look, feel, and impact of a worship space requires a willingness to be creative and to be open to the Spirit. In constructing an altar table for a large interdenominational gathering in 1999, I constructed grape vine from conduit (a light-weight metal pipe) complete with leaves cut from sheet metal and wire curlicues. I used silk chiffon for the grapes to contrast with the metal. These metal structures became the base of the altar table and two tall candle holders. When I was finishing the project, I realized the table pieces needed a bit of fencing on which to weave the grape vine. I cut a seven-foot section of wire fence and attached it to create a space on which participants could have prayers written on small pieces of paper. The prayers, laid over the fencing, created a paper parament for the table instead of fabric. As I went about my work, a casual glance at the work made me realize that I'd just created the fence where Matthew Shepard had been bound and pistol-whipped to death. This table on which we would be celebrating Holy Communion was an image of suffering and sacrifice as well as a living vineyard.

Both the work of imagination and the physical experience of worship brought this image to life. When sharing this discovery at the conference a couple of weeks later, I asked the participants to add their prayers to the fence. Even though it was not a gathering for LGBT persons, many of the prayers offered were words asking for God to bring full inclusion in the church for persons of all gender orientations.

The space in which we worship has an effect on the gathered community, whether we are aware of it or not. For the space to work for the benefit of the congregation, designing sacred space needs to be an act of creation, an act of incarnation to physical form from a thought or idea. A scripture text, idea or worship focus must be planted like a seed, allowed to germinate and be nourished until it pushes through the soil of our minds to bring abstract concepts into concrete form. Creating a physical environment for worship takes many of the same disciplines as preparing a sermon or composing a choral anthem. The visual and physical space has a unique, though often unrecognized, impact on the gathered congregation.

Just as the style and flavor of a hymn or song may have more effect than its text, so too the visual and tactile space of worship settings often have greater impact than the verbal exchange of readings and sermons. When the nonverbal, physical setting and experiential aspects don't connect with the words and ideas expressed, then the potential power of the relationship between the mind, spirit, body and soul is lost.

Sometimes the place of worship and the message conflict. For example, imagine yourself seated in a huge, half-empty gothic cathedral, on a hard wooden pew, firmly bolted to a stone tile floor surrounded by large stained glass windows. Now imagine a different surrounding: a small, intimate space with upholstered chairs in a carpeted room with a fire burning in the corner and the smell of spiced punch heating over a low flame. Location and surroundings impact our experience. While it's possible to make a large sanctuary warm and inviting and a parlor feel alienating, we must be intentional about the physical aspects of worship settings to enliven the whole people that we are.

When the space has a creative and imaginative expression born out of thoughtful and evocative planning and skillful execution, not only do ideas of worship planners come to life, but there is also more opportunity for participants to make their own connections. Sacred space needs to be an open-ended portal from the Word of God to the gathered congregation. That is one of the reasons to avoid using words on banners. Written words are an extension of a verbal rather than an experientially-oriented worship setting. And many times words are one dimensional and don't allow people to make their own personal connections from the head to the heart or from the verbal to the nonverbal. A visual of a lighted candle can be far more effective than a banner that entreats "let your light shine."

What and how we smell, hear, taste, touch and see is the environment of worship. When we allow our bodies to be involved, to play in the process of reading and study, we will approach the Scripture with more integrity and clarity. We will also help engage the imaginations of those participating in worship. In other words, through our collective imagination we can allow our bodies to participate in the hearing of the Scripture itself. When our senses are involved in worship planning and leading, we connect more of our whole being with the process of listening to and proclaiming the Gospel.

If the environment for worship includes everything we experience relating to the senses, designing this sacred space must go beyond simply making a visual explanation of the Scripture verses in a particular service. A creative expression of the intended focus is needed. For example, rather than isolating a symbol or icon on a banner or parament, it's possible to bring images to life in a variety of forms. To do this, I recommend asking questions of the symbol to help wrestle with its true meaning. If the symbol is a fish we might ask; "How does it relate to the story? Is it a fish that represents oppression, or was it intended as a secret code? Is it a sign of the bounty of God's blessings and mercy? Where does this fish live? What does it eat?" "What kind of water does it swim in—is its water clean or polluted? To what kind of fish can our community best relate?" The questions could continue, but the answers to these kinds of questions, which relate to the physical realities of the scripture stories and our own world, help link together abstract, distant themes and our current realities.

Acts of worship contain story and drama. Therefore, creating worship space is both drama and life; spiritual and physical, sacred and secular. Where these concepts intersect, we experience incarnation. A large part of the drama of worship is based on this call-

and-response model of contrast. As worship planners, we can illuminate this tension.

Just as the physical space of worship has impact even if we're not consciously aware of it, so does the process of creating that space. The "creative" part of designing space for a worship setting need not be difficult or expensive. Nor need it be reserved for the "artistic" few or "creative people" in the church. We must enable, inspire and empower creative spirits within our communities, but we must also educate those available for the task, whether they've ever thought of themselves as artistic or not. Designing sacred space isn't so much an artistic, holy vocation as much as it's a systematic process.

A step-by-step process of worship space design makes engaging the imagination of the worshiping community far less daunting. After finding the most important themes for a service, consider the space to be used and begin with what you have. While there are elements of the setting that are beyond your control, being intentional with the given realities can have tremendous impact. Engaging the space makes a statement about how you view the world and your place in that world. Likewise, leaving a space unchanged is as much a theological statement as draping a rainbow flag.

If it's a large space with lots of people, think big and bold; not subtle and detailed. Within that framework there will be many opportunities for detail, but detail need not be primary. Larger spaces are both fun and exciting but most of us are faced with limited space and resources. On a Baptism-of-Jesus Sunday in my small church, we planned to renew our baptismal vows and commission our Administrative Board, Deacons, and Elders. There were a variety of ways to express these themes visually in this square room where the congregation sits in a semicircle. The modest space meant there was no need for a twenty-foot waterfall for the 30 or 40 people gathered. Something small was more appropriate, but because we sit a circle, not everyone would be able to see the same image. The space, people, and theme offer certain limitations, (or what I like to call "invitations"), for creating a visual statement. A variety of images and locations throughout the space were used. A small but substantial fountain gurgled on the floor in front of the worship table. Two blue, silk banners (from a previous occasion) hung so that one draped onto the floor (symbolizing the water theme), and the other draped over the brocade parament on the table. Using a silk, batik banner on the table created a bridge between the earthen, rustic fountain and the formal parament. Because these banners were unlined, flexible fabric without appliqués or quilting, their use was easy and limitless.

Fabrics without appliques or quilting, solid banners, and other standard pieces can be used interchangeably for a variety of settings, themes, etc. Plain fabric, like silk or lightweight cotton is particularly good for liturgical use. Lightweight fabrics are versatile and can be hung open wide as a banner, mixed with other fabrics to provide color, wrapped around found objects such as candles, bowls, vases of flowers, shells, or tucked into a clear glass vase. These techniques provide an environment for worship that enhances the scriptural message. Living as though it is perpetually Advent by watching, actively waiting, being awake, and aware through our senses makes worship preparation more exciting, fun and fulfilling.

My experience teaches me that the Holy Spirit is sneaky and cannot be relied upon to grant inspiration in obvious places. Whether it's your favorite hangout or a retail store you're visiting for the first time, an opportunity for visual inspiration awaits. Minds can become slide carousels holding images to be pulled out and used when the worship need arises. For example, I needed offering receptacles for a national conference of folks who minister with children. There was a playground theme in the worship space complete with swings, ramps, decks, etc. So when I happened into my local discount store and discovered sand buckets for a dollar, we had our offering plates. While that store isn't my favorite, I'll never forget when the Spirit tapped me on the shoulder and said, "look." When we are ready to look and willing to see through the eyes of faith, even the most ordinary plastic buckets come alive with possibilities.

As we plan and create worship for people, especially those who have been marginalized by society and the church, we must look honestly at images and metaphors that speak directly and evocatively. How can we bring worship settings to life for people who have experienced so many "no's?" "No, you're not welcome here!" "No, your relationships cannot be blessed here." It is important not to ignore the ugly in our world or in the church. We can never truly clean a house by shoving everything in a closet. It is impossible to create a space of integrity in worship without contrasting the ugliness that exists with the hope that is possible in Christ. Worship doesn't need to be pretty. Sometimes it might even be messy, but the gospel of Christ is always one of hope. When we are faced with an environment that includes harsh and ugly images, we must offer the reality of an often elusive hope. It is the recognition of this tension, this call and response that is necessary for incarnation to occur.

As persons who have had to struggle with sexuality in very particular intentional ways, the LGBT community may be even more aware of the physical nature of worship. The issues involved are two-fold. First, it is important to include experiential aspects in all worship. Second, LGBT persons interested in the visual, musical or other worship arts must be encouraged to claim a place of leadership within the worship planning teams of their communities. Gary David Comstock in *Gay Theology Without Apology* says, "In some ways, lesbians and gay men know what no others know, just as others know what we do not but need to know."

To create sacred space requires more than an order of worship and decoration. Sacred space involves a process of examining our hearts and confronting those often painful parts that we'd rather leave alone. When we lift our pain to the body of Christ, we join with Christ in the journey from death to life. It is this hope in Christ, this joy of the banquet—that some would deny to others—that we can celebrate. When creating space for the 1999 Convocation of Reconciling United Methodists, I found that more than anything I wanted to lift up this hope. I wanted to create a space that celebrated our home within the community of faith. It gave me energy to go far beyond what I'd been able to do before. It wasn't enough to just have things be adequate, they had to be great. Even though I was greatly limited by the space, it was important to invite the eye, ear, and imagination of those gathered to enter the space and be involved. As people gathered for worship, they entered under a 25' silk rainbow canopy. The sides of the room were equipped with screens swagged with silk rainbows on which folks attached bells they'd brought from home. Each day the chancel (stage) changed to meet the needs of the services. The climax was a celebration of a loved and forgiven people with a 35' silk rainbow weaving in and out of 5 large gothic window banners.

Lesbian, Gay, Bi-gender and Trans-gender folk as well as other marginalized persons know the pain of their faith and need to know that worship is a place of celebration, joy and love, as well as acceptance.

When the verbal concepts of our head and feelings of our heart connect, the Spirit is alive and at work. As worship leaders designing space, we can be a part of this holy dance. With open eyes eager to see God in the physical aspects of our lives, the Spirit springs into birth, bringing energy, life and health. When our houses of worship overflow, not only with sounds of praise, but also with visual and environmental expressions of a community gathered in love, the Holy is even more recognized and praised. When we invite the senses of our gathered journeying souls to fully experience the truth of God's love through story and ritual, we open portals of faith. Through these portals we can travel together to a greater knowledge, understanding and assurance of the gifts we have been given and can receive. God is saying "yes" to our incarnation into physical form. God is saying "yes" to who and what we have been created to be. Let us use the worship space to exclaim God's message, "Yes, it is good!"

Creating A Community Banner
by Philip Cox-Johnson

A community banner is an extraordinary way to reflect the diversity and unity of a church. A banner can be made though the combined efforts of many church members, so that the resulting piece will be a unique symbol of the spirit of an inclusive community and a community where diversity is celebrated.

*For photo see www.
rcp.org/images/
banneridea.jpg*

This banner is made using the "fiber art" (or piecework) technique and can be completed by following the instructions given below.

Materials needed

- ✓ 2 yards of rainbow-colored fabric. The fabric should have wide bands of color that run the length of the fabric rather than the width.
- ✓ 2 yards of fabric that is a solid color or a small print. Some churches may choose to select a color that reflects their particular community of faith. If a metallic or very thin fabric is selected, it will need to have a lightweight interfacing fused to the back before cut or sewn. Interfacing is available at any sewing supply store.
- ✓ Coordinating colored thread
- ✓ Rotary cutter
- ✓ Cutting mat
- ✓ Coordinating material to be used for lining the banner. The amount will vary, depending on the size of the banner.
- ✓ Thin, fusible fleece for the edge of the pieced-together fabric

Instructions

- Pre-wash, dry and iron the fabrics prior to cutting or sewing.
- The piecing technique for the banner is called *barjello*. This means the fabric will be cut into strips and pieced together into horizontal stripes. The resulting material will be sliced again into vertical stripes and pieced together again.
- Fold both fabrics into fourths, lengthwise. To do this, first lay out the fabric on a flat surface. Fold the cut edges, or salvages, together (looking at the fabric vertically/lengthwise, you fold bottom to top) and then fold the fabric lengthwise (bottom to top) once more.
- Place the two folded fabrics exactly on top of one another.
- Using a rotary cutter and cutting mat, slice the fabric across the width into strips of variable sizes, anywhere between 1.5" to 4". Slice both sets of fabric at once to save time.
- Open up the strips of material and lay out on flat surface. Arrange strips together by alternating the rainbow and solid fabrics. Also vary the widths of

the strips for interest and appeal. Use only enough of the strips of fabric that are needed to create the desired length.

- Sew the strips of fabric together with a sewing machine using the matching thread.
- Once the strips are sewn together, iron all the seam allowances flat to one side of the fabric.
- Sew the top and bottom strips together, to form a tube. Make sure to sew the strips "right" sides together.
- Press the final seam flat in the same direction as the other seams.
- Turn tube to the "right" side.
- Fold the tube into fourths the same manner as above. The strips should now be horizontal.
- Slice the pieced fabric in the same manner as above. Slice across the width into strips of variable sizes ranging from 1.5" to 4". At this point, the strips must be kept in order from left to right.
- Beginning with the first band on the left, open the band of fabric by cutting apart the seam at the top. This will make one long strip of fabric rather than a band.
- The next band should be opened so that the rainbow design will move diagonally across the banner rather than horizontally as it did when sewn together. To create this effect, the seams of the pieced fabric will be cut open a little farther down the tube each time. For example, since the first band was cut apart at the top seam the second band would be cut apart at the seam approximately 3" to 4" down from the top. The third strip of fabric will be opened at the seam 3" to 4" further down, and so on. How far down the seams are opened varies depending on the width of the stripes, size of the banner and personal preference. This will place the rainbow pattern of the fabric further down with each new stripe and create the diagonal movement.
- Keep the strips in order by laying them out on a large, flat surface.
- Sew the strips together, being careful to match the ends up equally. Although visually the strips will appear to be different lengths, each strip of material is the same length.
- Iron down the seam allowances for each strip before sewing on the next strip. This makes the material easier to work with. Be sure to iron all of the seam allowances in the same direction.
- After all the strips are together, trim the edges and fuse with a thin, fusible fleece.
- Prior to sewing on the lining, create a rod pocket (like the top of a window curtain) on the back of the lining fabric. Sew the rod pocket at the top in two sections and leave a space in the middle open in case the banner is used on a processional pole. If desired, sew a rod pocket on the bottom also.

- Sew the lining on the banner by putting the right sides of the fabrics together and sew around the edges. Leave a 6" or 8" opening to turn the banner to the right side. Be sure to double stitch and clip the corners close to the stitching.
- After turning the banner to the right side, press the entire piece. If desired, the banner may be hand or machine quilted.

There are a variety of options that can make this project unique to the church and community.

- Piece a cross into the middle of the banner (shown on picture).
- Applique an image onto the top after the piecing is finished.
- Have the community members put their signatures on the solid fabric that is used.
- Use the banner/quilt as a backdrop to add changeable images and fabrics.

Be encouraged to make this project a symbol of the community. Remember that the process of creation is far more important than the end result, and there are few better results than the act of creation in community.

Conducting a Spirituality-Art Workshop

[This workshop was created by Mary Callaway Logan based on lectio divina format. Lectio divina is a type of divine reading. It is a process of gently and slowly listening to the scriptures with readied ears, open hearts, and searching thoughts, offering a welcoming soil for seeds of images and spontaneous connections in the human soul. The workshops usually require at least 2 hours (time for explanation, ritual, meditation, creation of art pieces and reflection). A reading is distributed a week prior to the workshop for reflection.]

Materials Needed:

- ✓ simple dowel or piece of wood to tie hanging objects from (another option: use a rectangle of hardware cloth, which allows for simple weaving).
- ✓ Small objects that will make pleasing noises when struck by other others. Suggested objects include: keys, beads, bones, sticks, bamboo cut in 6 to10" lengths, broken, fired pottery shards, china pieces, foil and tin, washers, nails, clangy materials of any kind.
- ✓ String, mylar, jute, yarn, ribbon, thin wire, etc.—to tie on objects.
- ✓ Other materials to make the wind chime colorful: acrylic paints, glitter, colored strips of fabric, tissue paper (for indoor chimes), craft foil (thicker than aluminum foil).
- ✓ Scissors, wire cutters, glue guns or other adhesives may also be necessary.

Reflections on the theme

To conduct a lectio divina workshop on the Ezekiel passage using art materials, participants should prepare themselves with the passage during some quiet time, and then continue to let the passage work on them while choosing the art supplies they will use and creating their wind chime. One of the joys of the workshop can be putting your own autobiographical spin on the materials selected, i.e., "I was taking a walk while listening to Ezekiel's encounter in the wilderness and I passed a construction site that had discarded nails and washers," or "I came upon the sun-bleached bones of something in the forest and brought them for you." Asking participants of the group to bring old keys or broken china that carry memory associations can enhance the autobiographical nature of the passage.

A week ahead, mail out a thought-provoking meditation (see below) with a challenging question about personal struggles as related to the scripture lesson to be used. Knowing the workshop topic ahead of time and having time to reflect is important for some—for others not.

Meditation *(to be distributed prior to workshop)*

"One thing is for certain, grace cannot follow denial"

Several years ago this quote stopped me still. I think of it especially when reading Ezekiel, and most particularly the dry bones-coming-to-life passage (37:1-14). As you read it, notice how Ezekiel is led to walk among the bones, clearly shown the undeniable sun-bleached and crumbling "deaths" of the people of Israel. Face the facts, see the evidence, drop the illusion, this people is "no more." Only then does grace appear.

"Prophesy to the breath...say to the breath, 'thus says the Lord God: 'Come from the four winds, O breath, and breathe on these slain, that they may live.'"

Breath re-enlivens us every minute of our lives. Breath, in Ezekiel, is God's instruction to bring back to life that which is clearly dead. Because Ezekiel is instructed to call on the four directions, God places the need in terms of the whole horizon, encompassing all, wholeness. Thus, to be revitalized, human creatures need heart, soul, body, and mind "in-spired."

Identifying those things within us that seem clearly lifeless may be a challenge. Yet as I begin to know what is deadened and name that thing, see its "bone," I can begin to call upon the breath of God to re-enliven it. Think about the spiritual song "Dem Bones Gonna Rise Again." The upbeat tempo suggests all is not lost even though every piece of evidence points to it.

To prepare for the workshop, read Ezekiel. Consider what has been "slain" or made dead, or deadened in you. It may be feelings in the body, the heart, beliefs....

Also note that Ezekiel 37: 12-14 offers a formula for transformation and restoration.

> I will raise you (from dry bones to embodied people);
> I will put my Spirit in you;
> I will place you in your own land;
> Then, and only then, you will know that I have spoken it
> and done it. You will know I am God.

During an ancient time when there were many gods vying for the devotion of the people, the prophets had the job of proving their god's superiority. That is one way to read this text, as Ezekiel envisions nothing short of a miracle resurrection of an exiled people.

Consider the promise of God—"to put my Spirit in you." What might that be for you?

Then the promise comes, "I will place you in your own land." This refers to the exile of the people, to the reality that they were estranged from their sense of home. Shame, loneliness, fear, puzzlement, longing, and dimming memory were forming a pattern of death for those who lived. The promise of a return to their own land was an enormous comfort and assurance. We, too, cannot live without some vision of what home is. And when that home is temporarily out of reach, we realize how pivotal home is.

Home may be community, a vocation, a healing circle, a river or a certain landscape that offers internally reassuring aspects. Give some thought to what it means to be "brought to your own land." How do you think of that? Are there images, pictures that you might bring? Or written descriptions? Is there mystery or uncertainty about "your own land?"

It is clear from Ezekiel that it is not enough to be restored, resurrected, en-spirited. You must be brought to a place that is somehow congruent with who you are. You must journey to your own land.

Conducting the Workshop

The day of the workshop, provide Bibles or the Ezekiel passages clearly printed, and the materials in box lids on a long table(s) covered with paper. Because wind chimes usually hang freely for the breeze to catch, for this workshop, tie heavy, long strings from the ceiling for each person to use as a workstation. This enables participants to design a balance when making their wind chime.

1. After personal preparation and preparing the space, explain to the participants the logistics of the workshop. Provide an overview of the flow of the workshop, explain the materials they have for their use, how to use any unusual supplies and allow brief introductions. (10 minutes)

2. Next, use a candle for this brief but important ritual to "banish the self-critical voices" or the "third-grade art teacher's deflating words" such as, "I'm sorry, honey, but you'll never be an artist." Explain that the lighting of this special candle signifies the welcome presence of the spirit that is more powerful than the harsh words of the past, be they words of judgment or of expectation. As the guardian spirit of the sacred space is being created, remind participants that God seeks to speak to us in visual symbols in this present moment. (3 minutes)

3. Put on soft, meditative music to prepare members for prayer with visual expression. Then, read the following introductory piece, followed by reading the passage of scripture two times, slowly (in the lectio divina tradition). When the flow is established by slow and deliberate quiet spaces between each of these readings, you can direct group members to go to the supply table and select the materials they want to use. Ask participants to maintain a relatively quiet disposition throughout the workshop. (10-15 minutes).

Introduction to the Scripture

Listen to the Ezekiel story of dry bones brought to new life by the breath/wind of God. In the passage there is both a command to Ezekiel to prophesy and the invitation to the winds of the four directions.

About human breath, we turn to Theodore Schwenck, in the book *Sensitive Chaos*. He comments on the miracle of the human larynx as it forms the movement of air. It is in the vocal cords that the soul life of a person "flows into the formation of the stream of speech, the soul's means of expression. The as yet unformed stream of air issues forth from the region of the will; at the vocal cords it receives the impulses which come from the conscious soul life of the human being, striving to communicate with the outer world...the soul uses the elasticity of the vocal cords like an instrument on which to play"

We are enabled to express human meteorology in everything from a deep moan to an aria, from a growl of rage, to the sustained tones of choral music. In ways similar to insects and birds, airborne seeds and clouds, the larynx is an organ that is literally structured by the nature of air.

When Ezekiel is asked to "prophesy to the breath," God adds divine desire to human desire. Human longing through breath and speech is met by God's desire to "make new," through the four winds—through divine-human collaboration. Letty Russell says we are co-creators with God. We present ourselves and our soul's wind, speech; we offer to co-mingle with God's desire to revive all life. Indeed, we are renewed every minute by God's breath in us.[1]

4. The creating time can vary from 45 minutes to two hours. Keep the silences, keep the soothing music, and toward your appointed ending, play music with a little faster beat and give people briefings about the time remaining.

5. To break the long silence, say "our time to step back from our work and reflect is here." Debriefing can begin as others silently walk around looking at others' pieces. Remind people that the creative act is precious, sometimes tender. Sometimes we are baffled at what we have made, other times we have had a clear epiphany. Remind participants that the candle that banishes critical voices still burns. Invite participants to continue to be "in dialogue" with their piece and the creative process throughout the next couple of weeks/months. Allow others to respond to each others' creations if permission is given to do so. Value everything that may come from this sharing time—from playfulness, creative musings and deeply personal comments. Part of the beauty is that God gives every creative impulse a different turn. One of the by-products of this experience is the restful focusing that shuts out the demands of daily lists and chores. People may be a little disoriented as they work and relax into this kind of holy play.

6. End with a prayer of thanksgiving or the following litany, which uses four voices.

From Ezekiel 37:1-14

Reader 1: Like a good Hebrew wordsmith, Ezekiel tells of God's spirit and breath.

Reader 2: "Ru'ach" is breath and also spirit,

Reader 3: Breath from the four directions,

Reader 4: Breath for the exiles who say "Our hope is lost; we are clean cut off,"

Reader 2: Breath that causes flesh to come alive on those thought to be completely lost.

Reader 1: Declares Ezekiel: "Thus says the Lord God: Come from the four winds, O Breath,

All: And breathe on these slain, that they may live."

Reader 1: And God's breath becomes the four strong winds,

Reader 2: And with God Ezekiel breathes,

Reader 3: And as the wind of God breathes,

All: Together they "con-spire," they breathe together, God and prophet,

Reader 2: to raise the exiles from the graves,

Reader 3: to bring new life,

Reader 4: to cause those "clean cut off" to rise again.

All: We of _____ [name of group], prophets in training, alike, con-spire,

Reader 1: Inspired by God's spirit,

Reader 2: breathe with God,

Reader 3: declare breath to re-enliven,

Reader 4: the marginalized, the closeted,

All: All who are exiles in our culture.

Reader 1: To cause the Spirit of God to blow,

Reader 2: the winds of strength,

Reader 3: upon those "clean cut off,"

Reader 4: the exiles of the land,

All: Those made to dwell on the edges of all institutions,

Reader 1: Except the church.

All: Except the church.

Reader 1: And so our ministry is one of con-spiring,

Reader 2: A conspiracy of healing.

Reader 3: We declare God's strong winds of hope,

Reader 4: To join our Spirit, this day,

**All: To breathe new life upon those dry bones,
And so to raise them from their graves,
And to be inspired by God,
And to walk the path of healing,
As the church in the world.**

Chapter 5

Body Parts: Elements of Worship

Be careful of simple words said often.

"Amen" makes demands

like an unrelenting schoolmaster:

fierce attention to all that is said;

no apathy, no preoccupation,

no prejudice permitted.

"Amen":   We are present. We are open.

We hearken. We understand.

Here we are; we are listening to your word.

"Amen" makes demands

like a signature on a dotted line:

sober bond to all that goes before;

no hesitation, no half-heartedness,

no mental reservation allowed.

"Amen":   We support. We approve.

We are of one mind. We promise.

May this come to pass. So be it.

Be careful when you say "Amen."

Barbara Schmich

Affirmations of Faith

*W*e are unique human beings linked with all creation
and gathered from diverse places
to share a ministry faithfully,
to raise questions hopefully,
to work for justice lovingly,

In whom and in what do we believe?

> We believe in God,
> eternal yet ever-moving one,
> who creates and is creating,
> who keeps covenant with humankind,
> who sets before us the ways of life and of death.

> We believe in Jesus, the servant-advocate,
> who lived the way of dying/rising,
> who embodied justice and reconciliation,
> who, with authority, calls us to share
> this way and this embodying.

> We believe in the Holy Spirit, sustaining presence
> and transforming power,
> who dwells among us in clarity and in mystery,
> who inspires us individually and corporately,
> who challenges, prods, emboldens.

> We believe in the church, community of faith and caring,
> covenant and promise,
> which nurtures our pilgrimage and
> through which we are called to be witnesses to
> God's truth, love, and justice.

> We believe our believing affects
> our daily walking and talking,
> our doubting and struggling,
> our decisions and choice-making,
> our responses to persons and systems.

We intend in this community in these days
to raise questions hopefully,
to work for justice lovingly,
to share a ministry faithfully,
and, by God's grace, passionately!

_____ *Barbara Troxell*

*W*e believe in a sacred power within and around us—a divine spirit that we call by many names and experience in many ways—that empowers and heals—that calls us forth.

We believe in our creativity.

Making and transforming beauty out of words and notes, images and colors, lines and pictures—and silence.

We believe in doing justice.

Justice that compels and empowers us to risk whatever we must risk to create a climate in which all people can be who they are.

We believe in our dreams.

We experience the world as it is—in both its ugliness and beauty—and we see what it can become.

We believe in making peace.

A peace that is based on openness, honesty and compassion.

We believe in hope.

We expect changes to continue to occur in our world. We rely on our courage to continue to bring about these changes.

We believe in love.

A passionate love within and around us that laughs and cries, challenges and comforts, a healing love that perseveres.

We believe in potential.

We know who we are—painful as that can be at times—yet we continue to call each other to become more of who we are.

We believe in celebrating.

We remember and we commemorate. We create rituals. We play and dance and sing and love well.

We believe in our diversity.

We affirm our many shapes and sizes, colors and traditions emotions and thoughts, differences and similarities.

We believe in life.

Life that wells up within and flows out of us like a streaming fountain.

We believe that we are good and holy—a sacred part of all creation.

Susan Karamer

O believe it is a matter of faith to stand up for those who cannot stand up for themselves.

I believe it is a matter of faith to recognize equally and love all members of God's human family. There are no exceptions to God's love.

I believe God's creation is good, beautiful and sacred; therefore to condemn any portion of God's creation is to condemn a portion of God. This is sin.

I believe Jesus Christ came to us to free all people from sin and to make disciples—people willing to live Christ's discipline of love and justice for all.

I believe the Holy Spirit is that power within us that gives us courage and stamina to face the truth and to live it, even to die for it, as Jesus died.

I believe in the resurrection, the victory over death, and the truth that is life for all in Jesus' name.

Glory is to God, the One in Three: Creator, Savior, and Holy Power of love. Amen.

adapted from Ruth Duck and Maren Tirabassi

O believe God's love will find a way to heal our wounded world,
and I believe somehow that hatred and poverty will end.
For I believe in the persistent love of God.

I believe that God is loving and healing through our tears
and I believe God can make us whole again.
For I believe in the great healing love of God.

I believe that God has made me who I am.
And I believe that God rejoices when we are able to live honest lives.
For I believe in the creative love of God.

I believe it's not too late for us to learn to live to love.
And I believe God's love can teach us to forgive and start anew.
For I believe in the forgiving love of God.

Tim McGinley

*A*s children of God, we celebrate the beauty and individual worth of all creation. We believe in God:

> who created each of us, who breathed into us our uniqueness, who delights in who we are, and what we can still become.

We believe in the love of God:

> who laughs with us in our joy, who cries with us in our pain, who wants all creation to seek peace, reconciliation, and love for each other.

We believe in the justice of God as revealed in scripture, and through the lives of prophets of yesterday and today.

God alone created us. We are not alone; God loves us. Nothing will separate us from the love of God. Amen.

Reconciling
Congregation Program _____

*W*e embrace the notion that all people are embodied, sexual creatures. And in this embodiment, we rejoice.

We proclaim our faith that there is a divine welcoming for all people into spiritual community. And we profess our belief in the role the Gay, Lesbian, Bisexual, and Transgendered community plays in the divine community.

We proclaim our faith that there is a divine calling for all of us to be in spiritual community. And we profess our belief that all of us— Gay, Lesbian, Bisexual, Transgender, and heterosexual—are called to help create that community.

As a people of faith, hope, and love, we rejoice in the spiritual community gathered here today. And we pray we may continue to gather and profess our belief in the radical inclusiveness of divine love.

GABLE _____

Benedictions/Closings

O *Thou Creative Source,*

    without which our lives could never have begun,

    Who art the Friendly Providence

    in whom our lives never end,

    Be now the Energizing Presence in our lives

    For all this interval between the

    miracle of our origin and the

    mystery of our destiny

    that we may claim

    Your light to guide us,

    Your strength to uphold us,

    and Your Love to unite us.

    To each other here and now—

    but much more even than that—

    Your love to unite us to all whom we love

    wherever they may be,

    this day and through eternity. Amen.

_____ Melvin Wheatley

One: We will not live an unlived life;   *Pentecost*

All: We will not live in fear of falling or catching fire.

One: We choose to risk our significance;

All: To live so that which comes to us as seed goes to the
next as blossom,
and that which comes to us as blossom, goes on as fruit.

_____ Spirit of the Lakes UCC

One:	Come on, it's time for the dance!
Men:	Time to choose our song,
Women:	Time to choose partners,
Men:	Time to learn the steps
Women:	and take the lead!
All:	Our God wants to dance!
One:	Some of us have had a rough year
Men:	We've lost the beat
Women:	we've been pushed aside
Men:	the music has been drowned out
Women:	by shouting and fear and anger.
All:	Our God wants to dance and no wallflowers are allowed.
One:	The dance is beginning
Men:	let those who are able
Women:	make music for those who cannot;
Men:	let those who can
Women:	hope for those who cannot
Men:	let music fill the air
Women:	bringing joy and hope to all who hear.
All:	Our God wants to dance, so let the music begin!

Jan Lugibihl

One:	Come on, it's time for the dance!
Left:	God created humankind in God's image.
Right:	In the image of God, God created us.
Left:	God blessed us.
Right:	God sees everything that has been made
Left:	and, indeed, it is very good.
Right:	And do we see anyone, anywhere who is not made in the image of God?
Left:	Do not judge so that you may not be judged.
Right:	In everything, do to others as you would have them do to you.
Left:	Invite them to the table
Right:	Invite them into the household of God
All:	Invite them to the dance.

Jan Lugibihl

One:	Come on, it's time for the dance to move out of this hall!
Women:	These walls are too narrow.
Men:	Our hearts are too full!
Women:	Let's take to the streets
Men:	leading the dance, claiming the power
Women:	spreading the news far and wide that our God is a God of love
Men:	and the last shall be first.
One:	God has opened the doors and flung out a billion stars to light our way.
All:	Our time has come! Hand in hand with God, leading the way. It's time to dance!

Jan Lugibihl

*O*n Christ we experience our wholeness,
we are a new creation.

   As you have received God's grace,
   go now and dare to reach out to others,

      to help others reconcile and make new.

         And the presence of God, who is our Creator,
         Redeemer and Sustainer, will go with you.

Kelly Turney

*L*et us covenant together that no one will be left beneath the table lapping up crumbs. The church remains dim-sighted and malnourished until all are truly we welcome to partake of your abundance.

*Based on
Matthew 15:21-28*

Now, companioned by the Spirit, go forth and be the evidence of the all inclusive hospitality of our welcoming God! **Amen**.

*Reconciling
Congregation Program*

Calls to Worship/Greetings/Invocations

$\mathcal{B}$lessing God,
Whose caring hands cupped beneath the elements of the universe
    and—like a potter—fashioned the very vessels of our being
Reach out your hand in blessing on us this morning.

As you drew the lines of our palms
and shaped the idiosyncracies of our fingers
    Teach us to reach out our hands to others in love
    Help us not to raise the threatening fist
      but to warmly grasp the possibilities of new-found
      reconciliations.

Soften our touch, O God:
    for your creation suffers from warring and pollution
    and your people reach out for help and solace
Encourage and strengthen us with your wisdom
    Until we become like You
      fashioners of justice and love
    Hands open for peace and benediction
    Gathering blessing and flourishing life for all.   Amen.

Bobbi Patterson

Voice I : We are part of the Church universal—faithful people of
      every color, gender, class, sexual orientation,
      age and ability, gathered to love and serve God.

Voice II: We are an Open and Affirming church.*
      Together, let us worship God,
      rejoicing in the good news which we celebrate this day!

All: There is a place in God's heart,
      there is a place at Christ's table,
      there is a place here and in every welcoming church
      for all people—Lesbian, Gay, Bisexual, and straight!

Voice I: Christ who gathers us,
      bids us follow in the ways of love and justice.

All: May our hearts be open to Christ's leading in our worship
      and our living, this day and always.

*use the appropriate
denominational
designation*

Ann B. Day

One: Gather us in, O God, we who are a grand spectrum of your children.

All: **Prisms that catch your light with furtive wanting and give it back in a variety of blended hues.**

One: Gather us in, O God, as dancing colors of a rainbow in the sky,

All: **For our very being is the fulfillment of your promise.**

Foundry UMC,
Washington DC

Voice I: We are the body of Christ!

Voice II: The hand clapping, toe tapping, heart pumping, mouth tasting, arms embracing,

Voice III:Justice seeking, hymn singing, love making, bread breaking, risk taking

All: Body of Christ!

Voice I: Baptized by one Spirit, we are members of one body.

All: Many and varied in gender, color, sexuality, age, class, and ability,
we are members of Christ's beautiful body.

Voice II: None of us can say to another, "I have no need of you."

All: For only together can we find wholeness.

Voice III:None of us can say to another, "I will not care for you."

All: For we are connected like muscle and bone.
If one suffers; we all suffer. If one rejoices, we all rejoice!

Voice I: Thanks be to God who in Christ has made us one.

All: Let us worship God!

Based on
I Corinthians 12:14-31

Ann B. Day

One: Come from wandering, Come into worship!
Come with your longings,
your questions and fears!
In the wilderness, remember: God is here!

All: **God is here!**

Dumbarton UMC

Based on Psalm 19

One Voice: The heavens are telling the glory of God!

All: Day to day and night to night,
unending is their silent speech of beauty and wonder.

One Voice: How shall we join their joyful witness?

All: With words that proclaim God's inclusive love,
with works that bring forth God's powerful justice,
with worship that rejoices in God's wondrous
presence, now and always.   Amen!

Ann B. Day _____

One: Just a taste of something wonderful.

All: Only a glimpse of something magnificent.

One: Just a glimmer of something holy in something so ordinary.

**All: Yet, enough to know we are in the presence of
God.**

One: Enough to cause us to stop and stare in awe,

All: Enough to stir our hearts in wonder,

One: Enough to set our feet to dancing

Reconciling   **All: And to prompt our voices to protest and praise.**
Congregation Program _____

Pentecost

One: God, you call us through your Spirit that we may gather in
celebration of the new community.

**All: Open our hearts that we may feel acceptance and
respect for our differences.**

One: We are all different and yet we share a yearning that
touches us and compels us to join together in unity with one
another.

**All: Open our minds that we may learn from one
another, and use our knowledge to bridge gaps
and build a community of faith for all.**

One: Give us strength that we may risk ourselves in the face of
discrimination and oppression.

**All: Open our spirits that we may share the message
of your Spirit.**

Spirit of the Lakes UCC _____

One: Blow through me, breath of God;
All: Bring rain to nourish growth in me;
One: Blow through me, breath of God;
All: I'll be the reed that makes your melody;
One: Blow through me, breath of God!
All: Sing your cosmic song through me!

_____ *Dumbarton UMC*

One: Holy One, open us to the movement of your Spirit:
All: Free our dreams; open our eyes, ears,
minds and hearts to the glory of life.

One: Holy One, open us to the movement of your Spirt:
All: Help us to grow! Open our senses!

One: Holy One, open us to the movement of your Spirit:
All: Open our hearts in a rebirth of wonder;
Open our defenses and delight us in our diversities!

One: Holy One, open us to the movement of your Spirit:
   Open our futures and deepen our faith,
   and make us a family in your Spirit.
All: We gather expecting the winds of love to blow through us,
the fire of passion to burn in us!

_____ *Dumbarton UMC*

Leader: Creating God, blessed are you and blessed is this time and place. Thank you for these people gathered here.

People: We are Here! Inside the Doors! We have not retreated!
We are standing in praise!

Leader: Reconciling Redeemer, you are the mender of our souls and the healer of our broken bodies.

People: Bind us together in ways that strengthen and sustain, nurture and
nourish, heal and help ourselves and the church of Christ.

Leader: Holy Fire, ignite a new spark in the heart of each one gathered here.

People: Light our way. Warm our bodies. Inspire our tongues to speak a
new word, to shout another praise and to sing an amazing song that
will bring to us life and to you glory!

Reconciling
_____ *Congregation Program*

One: We are summoned here by our holy God, who calls us each by name and gathers us together in the unity of the Spirit.

All: From the many challenges and closets and joys of our lives, we are called into God's presence.

One: Young and old and middle-aged, individuals and families, people of color and white,

All: Lesbian, Gay, Bisexual, Transgender and non-gay, we hear our names being called to join in worship.

One: This house of worship is a place to pursue God's vision for all people:

All: liberation and unity, justice and faith, expressed through different gifts. Let us worship together!

Spirit of the Lakes UCC

Leader: Praise God!

People: Praise God for all creation:

Leader: For people with all kinds of gifts and graces,

People: For disabilities and abilities with which to share our world,

Leader: For lives that struggle toward wholeness.

People: For the hope that we are given as the human family.

Leader: For hopes and dreams and the vision to bring God's vision to a reality.

People: Where all people are seen as children of God.

Leader: Praise God for all of God's children.

People: Let all God's people sing praises.

All: Praise God! Amen!

Adapted from Disability Awareness materials

One: Come! Let us gather in the presence of God.

All: In God's presence we find the community we seek.

One: Come then as a new community, a family of God's people and sing the praises of God's holy name.

All: Our voices shout out our praise to God, and our thankfulness of being once again surrounded by our chosen family.

One: The table is set, the family is gathered. Come! Let us worship God!

All: Amen! Let us worship God!

UCC LGBT National Gathering

One: We come together to this space

Left: bringing our lives

Right: each experience we have had

Left: every person met along the way

Right: each relationship formed

Left: all our loving

Right: all our struggles

Left: our failures

Right: and our dreams

Left: each story we have heard

Right: or told

Left: or been part of.

All: We come together to this space.

One: We come together to this safe space

Left: from our communities:

Right: those under siege

Left: those recovering their joy and wonder

Right: moving ahead

Left: being church

Right: rejoicing in the life and gifts and passion

Left: of all who stand beside us.

Right: Bringing each song we have heard

Left: or sung

Right: or danced to,

All: we come together to this safe space.

One: We come together to this graced, safe space

Left: to this house of welcome

Right: created for God's friends,

Left: remembering the promise that

Right: where two or three are gathered

Left: God is here among us.

Right: We bring all the songs of our lives

Left: gathered from every place we have sung

Right: and danced

Left: and loved

Right: ready to make new music

Left: move to new rhythms

Right: lead out in love and hope.

All: We come together to this graced, safe space.

Jan Lugibihl

One: We come here waiting with anticipation.

Men: Jesus is coming—Wait!

Women: He's been here—He's gone!

Men: He is here—He's coming still!

Women: Advent, Christmas

Men: Good Friday, Easter

Women: endlessly, daily happening.

One: The future stretches before us and we wait with anticipation, here in the presence of God Incarnate

Men: knowing that we may be totally surprised into a life we've never dreamed of.

Women: Sometimes the wait itself pierces us to our core

Men: turns us upside down

Women: shakes our heart loose.

One: And what does all this waiting and anticipation have in common? Perhaps all waiting is incarnation. Perhaps in becoming human God entered our waiting and showed us that the kingdom comes

Men: in the way we wait

Women: in the light we bring while we wait

Men: in those we choose to wait with

Women: in the work we do during the wait

Men: in what we choose to wait for.

Women: In the waiting is the kingdom come

Men: In the waiting is the Word made flesh

Women: In the waiting is God-with-us

All: Alleluia!

Jan Lugibihl _____

One: We come to this place in response to a call,

Left: to search for truth together,

Right: widening our hearts to invite in

Left: those we meet in our everyday lives

Right: and those we try to hide from.

One: We come to this place in response to a call

Left: to share our stories and our songs, and to dance.

Right: For a song sung together takes on new life and energy

Left: a story shared is a story made vibrant

Right: and a dance done together defeats the powers of evil around us.

One: We come to this place in response to a call

Left: because we know that what is important is not transforming the bureaucracy

Right: or fretting about what others may think of our anger or proving our point.

Left: What is most important is honoring the light of our sameness

Right: and clearing the floor so justice and peace can join hands and dance.

One: We come to this place in response to a call

Right: and the wind of the Spirit upsets us and sets us down in a new place

Left: where we are free to claim faith and hope

Right: to dream dreams and see visions

Left: to claim the gift of holy boldness

All: and to dance in the darkness alive with a billion bright stars.

_____ *Jan Lugibihl*

*P*eople of God, this day is ours!

¡Pueblo de Dios, este es nuestro día!

> **A day to acknowledge our hunger; hunger for love,**
> **hunger for respect, hunger for justice.**

People of God, this day is ours!

¡Pueblo de Dios, este es nuestro día!

> **A day to proclaim that all of God's creation—**
> **Gay, Straight, Bisexual, Trangender—**
> **must be affirmed and made to feel welcome in our communities.**

How deep is your hunger? How long can you wait

in order to be fed the bread which will sustain you?

> **Our hunger is deep! ¡Nuestra hambre es profunda!**
> **Yet even as we gather for worship,**
> **we begin to feed one another with the bread of life,**
> **a bread that will not run out even in times of scarcity.**
> **Let us seize the day and make it count.**
> **Let us seize the day and**
> **proclaim the good work that is taking place here and now.**

Reconciling
Congregation Program

[This call begins with the choir stationed at the back of the sanctuary; each choir member has a candle. The refrain "Thy word is a lamp unto my feet" and the words to, "They'll Know We are Christians" are printed in the bulletin. After the choir members' candles are lit, they may leave their candles on the altar as they proceed to the choir loft. To begin, a lone voice sings a capella from the back of the darkened sanctuary:]

"We will walk with each other, we will walk hand in hand
We will walk with each other, we will walk hand in hand
And together we'll spread the news that God is in our land..."

[The choir begins to walk forward from the back, led by a lantern or candle.]

Narrator: When the people of Israel fled from Egypt, they came to the edge of the wilderness. The Lord went in front of them in a pillar of cloud by day, to lead them along the way, and in a pillar of fire by night, to give them light, so that they might travel by day and by night.

[The choir sings]   "Thy word is a lamp unto my feet and a light unto my path."

Narrator: David spoke to the Lord the words of this song on the day when the Lord delivered him from the hand of all his enemies. "Indeed, you are my lamp, O Lord, the Lord lightens my path."

[The refrain is repeated each time between readings; the congregation joins in and the choir continues to move forward among the people, and as each reading is heard, other candles are lit among the choir.]

Narrator: Isaiah, the prophet, spoke the word of God to the people of Israel, saying, "Arise, shine; for your light has come, and the glory of the Lord has risen upon you."

Refrain

Narrator: "You are the light of the world," said Jesus. "A city built on a hill cannot be hid. No one after lighting a lamp puts it under the bushel basket, but on the lampstand, and it gives light to all in the house. In the same way, let your light shine before others."

Refrain

Narrator: "I am the light of the world. Whoever follows me will never walk without light but will have the light of life."

Refrain   [the Paschal candle is lit]

Narrator: We light the Christ candle today to remind us that we are the Body of Christ, empowered by the Holy Spirit to be the light of Christ in the world. As it is told in the scriptures, let us again proclaim that...

People: "God is light and in God there is no deception at all.
         If we walk in the light as God is in the light,
         we have fellowship with one another."

All sing: We are one in the Spirit, we are one in the Lord,
          We are one in the Spirit, we are one in the Lord,
          And we pray that our unity will one day be restored,
          and they'll know we are Christians by our love, by our love,
          Yes, they'll know we are Christians by our love.

_____ *Marcia McFee*

Collects

God, like a midwife—
skilled and wise and strong—
you are always bringing us to birth.
You nourish and sustain us
in the labor of becoming.
It gives us joy to give you
thanks and praise.

_____*Dumbarton UMC*

Jesus at the well,
        whose knowledge of our lives surprises us,
        we pray for comfort and healing.
        We bring you our dehydrated emotions and brittle bodies,
        we put ourselves on the edge and wait to be lowered
        into your living waters.

_____ *Unknown*

One God in three
whose Trinitarian nature reveals you to be deeply relational,
deliver us from our false independence.
Connect us with the whole of creation.
Draw us closer to you through our relationships with one another
so that we know the suffering of others as our own.
We pray knowing you as mother, lover and friend.

_____ *Kelly Turney*

Confessions & Assurances of Pardon

Based on Psalm 62

One voice: We are a pilgrim people, accompanied by our God,
who journeys beside us, accepting who we are;
yet goes before us, beckoning us toward who we might
become.

All: But as we move through our days,
other gods call to us, questions confound us,
direction blurs, indifference lulls; we lose our way.

One voice: So we enter into silence, to discern again the nearness
of God, who is our hope and guide.

(Moments for silent prayer)

One voice: Sisters and brothers, we can trust God at all times,
for the Holy One is our refuge and our salvation!
So with confidence, let us pour out a shared confession
of our hearts.

All: We confess to you, steadfast God, that we wander from
the path of love upon which we are meant to walk.
Fears divide us, prejudice hardens us,
violence destroys us.

One voice: But God eternally beckons.

All: We turn our hearts again to you,
God of grace and mercy.
Forgive us love that is self-satisfied,
and teach us love that is self and other affirming.
Forgive us faith that makes us rush to judgement,
and give us faith that fills us with compassion.
Forgive us peace we have made with our divisions,
and unite us in peace that passes understanding.
We pray, with thanksgiving, in the name of Christ.
AMEN

One voice: By God's mercy, our feet are set again upon the path of
faithfulness;
our hearts are set again upon the coming of God's
realm.

All: Thanks be to God, our hope and our guide forever!

Ann B. Day

O gracious and loving God,
who calls us to be your people in this age,
forgive us when we keep Christ in the past,
and the Gospel as letters on a page,
and the church as an organization
in which we may or may not participate.
  Forgive us when fellowship and mission
  is meant for and delivered to
  those we already know and love
  and we become a social club instead of your church.
    Forgive us and have mercy upon us, O God.
    Let your risen Christ reside here with us,
    and the Gospel be the power of our life,
    and the church be a people and place
    of showing your love wherever we may be.
      In Jesus' name we pray. Amen.

Church of the Redeemer

*L*et us confess together that we have not always lived as those
forgiven, set free and united in Christ.

**O God, our reconciler, we come before you as a people
of folly, who have sought the wisdom of the world. We
have built arms and prepared for war, thinking that will
bring us peace and security. Yet we find ourselves an
anxious people, isolated from one another and from you.
We have sought to make ourselves great by pointing out
the evil in others. Yet we confess that we, too, are
stained with evil. Help us, O God, to know not the folly
of the world by the wisdom of Christ, who is our hope.
Amen.**

God is even now giving us the gift of repentance. God is at work in
the world. It is not we who hope, but God who hopes in us.

Central UMC

*G*od, though we want to live as your children.
Sometimes we get confused.
Sometimes we place a high value
on things that can only turn to dust.

Thank you for loving us as we discern
the things that will endure.
Lead us to the eternal tents
where we will live in friendship with you.

Dumbarton UMC

od,

> You are the God of Huldah,
>
> of Miriam and Deborah.
>
> > You are speaking still
> >
> > through prophets in our midst.
> >
> > > You whisper an idea in our ear:
> > >
> > > we say, "What's she up to?"
> > >
> > > You rise in joy or outrage offering a vision:
> > >
> > > we say, "Whoa, she is out of control!"
> >
> > We should cover our mouths with our hands,
> >
> > amazed that You still love us.
>
> You are our God. Forgive us.

Dumbarton UMC _____

*T*hese stories have been told to us:
> **You are not fit for this.**
>
> **You cannot have the love you seek.**
>
> **You cannot come in.**

But in You, I-AM,
> **we are fit, and love, and welcome.**
>
> **Forgive our forgetting.**
>
> **Remind us we are yours.**

Dumbarton UMC _____

Leader: In the very act of praising God, we become most aware of our separations, from one another and from God. Even together, we stand alone, and alone, together we search our hearts. Let us pray.

All: Our Mother Father God,
We are accepting people, but many of our churches still bear "do not enter" signs, and we have not challenged them as we might.

We hear many congregations claiming to be open, but there are people who are still kept from their tables, and our protests, if any, have been too soft.

Forgive us God, and make us the strong, inclusive people we are called to be.

In a world that divides itself by culture, class, color and appearance, we strive to be the voice of tolerance.

Yet we sometimes tolerate the intolerance of others out of our own insecurity of fearing what we do not understand.

We allow the insulation of our privilege to protect us because we do not know how to reach the disenfranchised people of our world.

We are uneasy dealing with those who enter our well-vacuumed worlds bearing the stench of hard life.

We do not know how to get them to our tables, and we fear what might happen if we did.

We also withdraw from those who reject our acceptance of others.

How hard it is to love those who hate, and how hard to include them at our tables as well.

Forgive us God, and make us the strong, inclusive people we are called to be. Amen.

One: We belong to a God of love and compassion. We believe that God can make all things new. So I say to you, in the name of Jesus the Christ, who empowers us all, we are forgiven.

All: Thanks be to God for forgiveness.
Thanks be to God for love, and for calling us forth, ever strong, every open to new life.

Reconciling
Congregation Program

O God, deliver us.

From the anger we turn inward, or misdirect toward those we love,

deliver us.

From wanting our opponents' downfall rather than their liberation,

deliver us.

From fear, anxiety, stress, or loneliness that makes us seek a quick fix of religious or political absolutes, of drugs or alcohol, of compulsive sexual expressions or messianic lover,

O God, deliver us.

From believing what "they" say about us, devaluing ourselves or others like us,

deliver us.

For isolation from sisters and brothers, and ghettoization of our existence,

deliver us.

From lack of trust and faith in ourselves as individuals and ourselves as community,

O God, deliver us.

For denial of our integrity as spiritual-sexual creations,

deliver us.

From rejection of others because of their body-state, whether gender, race, age, sexual orientation, appearance, or disability,

O God, deliver us. Free us to live your commonwealth, O God. Clarify our vision, purify our motives, renew our hope. In the name of you who creates us, of the Christ who calls us, and of the Spirit who empowers us, Amen.

Chris R. Glaser _____

*W*eaver God, you have woven your creation together using your relationship with us and ours with each other to give rich, intricate and diverse patterns to all of life.

Forgive us when our choices tear the fabric of our lives;

forgive us when we want only to connect with those who are like us.

Challenge us to accept our differences as divine gifts,

for all are created in your image.

Help us to weave our lives together as we connect through these special gifts from you. Amen.

Unknown _____

A Prayer for Straight Men Who Are in the Closet

*G*od of creation, you made all people sexual.

We straight men confess we spend a lot of time in the closet, anxious about our sexual nature.

We are often afraid and pre-occupied with potency—how we compare with others, our "performance," and closet these fears with macho, inflated and sexist behaviors.

Teach us through our gay brothers that our sexual nature is a gift for community, not competition, to be honored in ourselves and in others.

We need the company, trust, and affection of other men, but closet these needs in stereotypical banter, jokes, and calculating behavior to avoid being thought gay.

Teach us through the example of our gay brothers that in risk and honesty with other men, we will find the company of your Spirit, and a deeper, truer understanding of what it means to be male.

We long for acceptance of who we are and what we are, but too often we closet that longing in either fear or rejection of gays and others.

Teach us through your son Jesus and through your gay servants that we cannot find acceptance of ourselves through rejection of those you have made in your image.

Through Jesus who did not hide but shared his life with all, help us straight men to leave our closets. Amen.

George M. Wilson

*A*lmighty and Everlasting God, it is so easy to focus on ourselves and forget the feelings and lives of others. We point the blame instead of accepting responsibility for our lives. We lift up perfect bodies and continue to build new churches that exclude people. We keep those who are different from us at a distance. We deny that we all have both abilities and disabilities. We close our eyes and ears, only to be isolated ourselves.

Forgive us most merciful God. Give us eyes to see the people that are gifts to our lives. Give us ears to hear the voices of hope and joy that come from the diversity of the human family. Open our hearts so that we can overcome our fears to love all persons. We pray through Jesus Christ our Lord. Amen.

Disability Awareness materials

I saw him on the edge of the dance floor.

His eyes, his head, danced to the music.

But, paralyzed from the neck down,

his body did not.

Yet a dancer can recognize a dancer,

and I found him sensual and sexy.

Forgive me, God, for not asking him to dance.

Stairs separated us, but that wasn't my reason.

He was with a friend, but that wasn't my reason.

My reason was:

I didn't want to seem patronizing,

asking him to dance.

Now I realize it was just as patronizing

not to ask.

God, forgive me:

I didn't know what to do.

Chris R. Glaser

Forgive us, God, that we have done so little with the gift of life. Made for the mighty deep, we have frittered away our energy splashing in the shallows near the shore. Endowed with minds capable of vast imaginings, we have become dull and predictable. Capable of love, we find ourselves with few acquaintances and still fewer friends. Blest with soul enough to commune with you, we have been content to lavish our affections on the passing fancies of the world. Increase our gratitude for life itself and help us henceforth to live it more nearly to the full. Through Jesus Christ our Lord. Amen.

Riverside Church, NY

Creating and Sustaining God, your great commandment in Christ is that we love one another as Christ has loved us. We confess that we fail to embrace your liberating love. We divide where you would unite. We exclude where you would embrace. We choke the breath from your Word when its truth does not accommodate our fears. Forgive our hardness of heart. Mend our broken human family. Breathe into us the living Word of all-inclusive love. We ask in the name of your Child, our Brother, Jesus, the Healer of our souls. Amen.

Park Avenue UMC

God's grace is abundant.

God's love is never ending.

Friends, the gospel affirms,

In Jesus Christ we are forgiven.

May the peace of Christ be with you.

And also with you.

Unknown

God desires friendship with all creation.

Know that you are blessed and forgiven.

Share signs of this knowledge with each other.

Dumbarton UMC

Friends, everything you are and will become has been love from the beginning.

Rejoice, and share your joy with each other.

Dumbarton UMC

Litanies

A Litany of Trust in God

Based on
Psalm 62:5-12

One voice: In the many silences of the heart, O God,
when feeling is beyond saying,
your faithful people everywhere wait upon your Spirit.
In the silence of joy—when a baby is born,
when a sunset blazes, when a loved one is restored to
health, when peace replaces strife

All: In our joy, we wait upon you, O God.
We give you thanks and praise.

One voice: In the silence of sorrow—when love is lost, when pain
is too constant a companion, when time brings change
that is hard to bear, when death seems victorious

All: In our sorrow, we wait upon you, O God.
You alone are our rock and our refuge.

One voice: In the silence of anger—
when justice is postponed until tomorrow,
when violence shatters body and soul,
when prejudice sets neighbor against neighbor,
when no one will listen

All: In our anger, we wait upon you, O God.
Teach us the ways of justice and mercy.

One voice: Let us put our trust where it belongs,
not in our positions or power or wealth,
for such things are lighter than breath.

All: In our joy, our sorrow, our anger, we trust in God's
unfailing love and guidance.
We rely upon the blessing of being a community of
faith, a Church universal.
Sisters and brothers of many colors, ages, sexual
orientations, and abilities,
we are one in Christ! Together, let us wait upon the
God of our salvation!

Ann B. Day _____

Leaving Home/Coming Home/Creating Family

L: We are God's people!

P: God's good people—Lesbian, Gay, Bisexual, Transgender and those who stand in solidarity with us.

L: We are God's people!

P: God's beautiful people—brown as the earth; pale as moonlight; black as the night; red as the sunset; golden as sunlight—We are God's living rainbow.

L: We are God's people!

P: Dancing God's seasons—
children who skip to a wordless tune;
young people who move to new rhythms each day;
adults who march and wheel to the steady beat of a distinctly different drummer;
and those elders who've danced all the other dances and now step securely in well-chosen waltz-time.

L: We are God's people!

P: A family like no other—and all like family to each other.
We leave home to come home to create family.

L: We are God's people and yet we found "home" to be a place of Exodus—a wilderness place where we cannot rest.

P: Because "home" was anger, abandonment, abuse, and denial;
"home" was closeted, painful, and oppressive;
"home" was unhealthy, uncomfortable, unloving, and unkind;
"home" was rejection, guild, damage, and brokenness.

L: And this wilderness home, this place of anguish, is a place that we should only pass through on the road to the new "home"—the "home" just barely visible and still being imagined by spirited souls full of possibility.

P: We taste the new home at table fellowship with our spiritual sisters and brothers, who in our religious communities become the family we cry with, call out to, laugh with, hug, hold and celebrate with on our special days.

L: We need that new home with friends who know our stories, parents who move beyond rejection, partners who share our dreams.

P: We hear that new home in the laughter of children: our daughters and sons, nieces and nephews, sisters and brothers, cousins and grandchildren.

L We feel that new home in the quiet presence we bring to those suffering with AIDS, their partners, families, and friends—sharing what we have: our time, our talent, our prayers.

P: We vision our new home in the breaking down of the old and the building up of the new—our new home is furnished with our stories, role models and martyrs, heroines and heroes, parades and protests, rituals and affirmations, blessings and family reunions.

L: We are your people, O God!

P: We are your people, O God! And when we come home to you, you know us as your people. Amen and amen!

Open Hands

Act of Community

All: We are many, but we are one as well.
We come from scattered places and diverse life experiences,
but today in this place we share a common vision as people who seek new life,
who seek God's guidance for ourselves, our congregations, and the larger church.
In this we are a united community, gathered at one great table to:
    celebrate our joys, share our grief,
    release our anger, examine our frustrations,
    affirm our strengths,
    and to acknowledge our common destiny.

Leader: The joy of being together leads us to praise God for life and for our lives together. Let us praise God!

*Reconciling
Congregation Program*

Litany of Change

One: How quickly we humans condemn, how easily hurtful words are spoken, acts of hate and injury accomplished.

All: **If I am different, there is no welcome; if you don't belong, there is no love.**

One: The disciple Peter refused to accept that which he thought unclean, to receive those who were impure.

Acts 10: 9-15   All: **God taught him that nothing God has made is unclean and must not be called profane.**

One: Sometimes the good news of God's love is thought to be only for some people and not for others.

Matthew 15: 21- 28   All: **Even Jesus had his eyes opened to the depth of God's inclusive love.**

One: Those who are called by the name Christian are called to be changed by God's love,

All: **so that none may be excluded, and all may be welcomed in.**

*Reconciling
Congregation Program*

Litany of Welcome

One:	Our God is an extravagant God!
Women:	A world is created out of nothing
Men:	A world is filled with light and sound and aroma and taste and texture
Women:	A world is created by a God with
Men:	a great sense of compassion
Women:	a great sense of humor and imagination
Men:	a great capacity for unrestrained, excessive love.
All:	Our God is a God of promises extravagantly made and extravagantly kept.
One:	Our God is an extravagant God!
Women:	People raised from the dead
Men:	Babies saved by midwives
Women:	The sick, the blind, the deaf, the brokenhearted healed and made whole
Men:	A poor widow's oil never runs out
Women:	Five thousand people fed by five loaves and two fishes
Men:	A stone rolled away from the tomb.
All:	Our God is a God of extravagant love.
One:	Our God is an extravagant God!
Women:	If someone sins against you
Men:	forgive not seven times
Women:	not seven times seven
Men:	but seventy times seven
Women:	forgive so many times that you just might lose count
Men:	and have to start all over again
Women:	and again.
All:	Our God is a God of extravagant forgiveness.
One:	Our God is an extravagant God!
Women:	We are no longer strangers and aliens
Men:	but members of the household of God.
Women:	We gather together in our frailty and our giftedness
Men:	and God joins us and sends out the invitation.
Women:	All who say yes
Men:	are invited to the Kingdom dance.
All:	Our God is a God of extravagant inclusion.
One:	Our God is an extravagant God!
Women:	We love each other
Men:	hurt each other
Women:	forgive each other
Men:	continue to love.
Women:	The signs of extravagance are everywhere
Men:	as close as the person next to you
Women:	as close as your own beating heart.
All:	Let us rejoice with thanksgiving in the extravagance of our God!

Jan Lugibihl

One voice: Help us open our hearts wide, Loving God.

Many: As we open our hearts, we move beyond our areas of comfort and ease.
          We learn that each of us here is worthy and precious.
          We learn that you urge us to love one another boldly.

One voice: Help us open our minds wide, Loving God.

Many: As we open our minds, we confess those areas where we need more wisdom.
          We yearn for more light for the matters we don't understand.
          We come to your house today, Loving God, to learn and to understand.

One voice: Help us open our church doors wide, Loving God.

Many: As we open our church doors, God, we learn the rich value of welcome.
          Whether gay or straight, black or white, male or female, grown or young,
          we know that you have welcomed us in, with open arms. The least we can do,
          Loving God, is learn to offer that same welcome—one to another.

One: The least we can do—and the best we can do—is to come into God's presence with openness this day.

Many: Help us open our hearts, our minds and our doors, God.
          You are teaching us to be still, and to pay heed to your wisdom.
          Guide as we listen to one another. Teach us to care for these members of our family.

One: There is wideness in God's mercy.
          May we open our hearts with care today, may we open our minds to hear God's word.
          May we open the doors of God's church, with a true and loving sense of welcome.

Many: There is wideness in God's mercy. Amen.

Claudia Brogan

A Litany for Bridging Troubled Waters

[Written as the ending of a day-long discussion of differing views of inclusion of Gays and Lesbians in the church]

One: O hear us Great Spirit of the Universe! As the twilight deepens and eventide surrounds us, we gather in praise of your gifts and your benevolence. We bow in humility, yet our hearts and minds are uplifted and we come into your presence, exalted by your love!

All: We approach you, O Creator-God, in quest of a oneness midst our diversity. We are at this time aware that you have a plan for our lives and a will for our efforts to respect and to understand each other—yet we so often fail to grasp the concepts and the examples you have set before us.

One: It is good, O Divine Mind, that we have convened this very day, coming together to learn of your wisdom through the leadership of your servants and the patience, the tolerance and the constructive counseling of the entire fellowship of these, who today have sought to be of a like mind.

All: Loving Parent of the World, we praise you for instilling within our hearts a spirit that became evident and grew this blessed day, as we struggled to identify, to admit and to overcome our own prejudices. We need—and we want to eliminate—the false knowledge, the insinuations, the propaganda we accept and often help spread. Teach us, Lord, to be always constructive in thought, as well as word and deed.

One: And, as this day wanes, and we go to our separate homes, hoping for a kinder, brighter tomorrow in our community and your world, may we long remember the blessings of our diversity. Help us to recall the smiles and the positive encouragement on the faces of these who shared our rich experiences today.

All: Loving God, be thou our guide, our mentor! Help us to be honest in facing whatever pitfalls of diversity we may encounter. Let the lessons of today be our undergirding, as we strive toward a clearer horizon. Teach us, Gracious God, to be free of prejudice and hindering phobias! May our discussions and the openness we enjoyed lead us on to new and wiser action, as we seek and work together for new alliances. These things we pray, in the name of our eternal God and our shared humanity. Amen.

Harry Akers

Litany of Affirmation

One: It is not we who have chosen God, but God who has chosen us. And we are affirmed as we hear the voice of God say:

All: I will make of the outcasts a strong nation (Micah 4:7).

One: Many of us—Gay, Lesbian, Bisexual, and Transgender—have experienced exclusion, rejection, alienation, and hopelessness, but we have heard the voice of God say:

All: I will make of the outcasts a strong nation.

One. Many of us—differently-abled, hearing-impaired, and hetero-sexual with so-called different or unacceptable relationships or families—have experienced the inaccessibility and inhospitality of many churches, synagogues, and temples, but we have heard the voice of God say:

All: I will make of the outcasts a strong nation.

One: Many of us have felt silenced, unheard, dismissed because of our language, culture, race, or gender, but in our own languages and in the midst of our life experiences we have heard the voice of God say:

All: I will make of the outcasts a strong nation.

One: Many of us have been treated as outcasts as we have lived with and through sexual, physical, and emotional abuse, HIV, breast cancer, and other life-threatening illnesses, but we have heard the voice of God say:

All: I will make of the outcasts a strong nation.

One: It is not we who have chosen God, but God who has chosen us, and we are affirmed as we hear the voice of God say:

All: I will make of the outcasts a strong nation.

Colleen Darraugh _____

A Litany of Justice

Scripture urges us to love mercy, do justice, and walk humbly with our God. What would our world look like if we all truly worked for justice? Oh, how we long for that new day!

I saw a new heaven and a new earth, for the former things had passed away.

> The issues are complex, but God we ask for justice, peace and understanding in our world. God, we pray for an end to the fighting in the world. Oh, how we long for that new day!

I saw a new heaven and a new earth, for the former things had passed away.

> There are many in our world who thirst today. In many places in our world, there is not enough water, and in other places the water is polluted and unsafe to drink, including places under siege of flooding waters. God, may there be healing, safe waters for all. Oh, how we long for that new day!

I saw a new heaven and a new earth, for the former things had passed away.

> Racial strife is still present in our world. For the peoples we pray. For all those who are discriminated against because of color of their skin, we pray. For all people to see and acknowledge race, color, and culture and to acknowledge that all are created in the image of God, we pray. What a day it will be when people can truly respect each other, and can live and work together in peace! Oh, how we long for that new day!

I saw a new heaven and a new earth, for the former things had passed away.

> We give thanks for those places in the world that have made progress in granting full human and civil rights to Gay, Lesbian, Bisexual, and Transgender people. Oh, how we long for that new day! We pray for our brothers and sisters in this country and in others who live with a constant threat against their lives because of who they are and whom they love. We pray for their safety, for their courage, and for their dreams of justice to become real. Oh, how we long for that new day!

I saw a new heaven and a new earth, for the former things had passed away.

> For the refugees and homeless of our world, we pray. For the malnourished and starving of the world; for the global economics that means a sharing of the world's resources, we pray. Oh, how we long for that new day!

I saw a new heaven and a new earth, for the former things had passed away.

> For the planet, the environment, and justice for all God's creation, we pray. Oh, how we long for that new day!

I saw a new heaven and a new earth, for the former things had passed away.

> God has promised us a new day of justice for all, a day of Jubilee. But it takes all of us working with God—loving mercy, doing justice, and living humbly with our God. Together let us commit to working for that new day when all shall say:

I saw a new heaven and a new earth, for the former things had passed away.

Je vis un ciel nouveau et une terre nouvelle, car les premiers ont disparu. *(French)*
Ich sah ienen neuen Himmel und eine neue Erde; denn das Erste war vergangen. *(German)*
Ví un cielo nuevo y un tierra nueva; porque las primeras cosas ya pasaron. *(Spanish)*

Colleen Darraugh (adapted) _____

A Litany of Unity

[Intersperse the verses of the hymn, "We Utter Our Cry" (United Methodist Hymnal #439) with the spoken words by the congregation. If multimedia capabilities are present, project pictures that correspond to the verses of the hymn with the words superimposed.]

[Instrumental introduction to the hymn begins and fades out]

People: With one voice, we utter our cry to you. We unite with all those who engage in prayer and mission with those who suffer. (Verse 1 of hymn)

People: We unite with all those who confront violence and work for peace in our neighborhoods and our world (Verse 2)

People: We unite with all those who tend the earth and hold dear all living things.
(Verse 3)

People: We unite with all those who support and engage in the process of peace.
(Verse 4)

People: We unite with all those whose action testifies to God's victory over evil and who struggle for justice. (Verse 5)

People: Spirit of promise, spirit of unity, renew in all of us the passionate desire for the coming of your kin-dom. (Verse 6)

Marcia McFee _____

Liturgical Movement

Circle of Love Body Prayer

[To create this body prayer, Marcia McFee adapted Miriam Terese Winter's confessional prayer and facilitated the following choreography with the participants' help. Groups can use these guidelines but are encouraged to design their own specific movements. The process of deciding on movements—three dimensional symbols—allows the group to explore the theology and symbolism of justice within the piece to be enacted. A child or young teenager can powerfully and slowly read the prayer. Invite the congregation to pray "open-eyed" so they do not miss the movement!]

Prayer text:

> We confess that the circle of love is repeatedly broken
> because of our sin of exclusion.
> We create separate circles: the inner circle and the outer circle,
>
> We confess that the circle of love is broken
> whenever we cannot see eye to eye,
> whenever we cannot link hand to hand,
> whenever we cannot live heart to heart and affirm our differences.
>
> We confess that the circle of love is broken
> whenever there is alienation, whenever there is misunderstanding,
> whenever there is insensitivity or a hardening of the heart.
>
> We confess that the circle of love is broken
> the circle of power and the circle of despair,
> the circle of privilege and the circle of deprivation.
>
> Through God's grace we are forgiven,
> by the mercy of our Creator,
> through the love of the Christ,
> and in the power of the Spirit.
>
> Let us rejoice and be glad!
> Glory to God! Amen.

Movement instructions:

Prior to reading the prayer, 6 or more (an even number is helpful) performers walk onto the stage and form a circle facing each other (if possible, the group encircles the communion table). Once all performers join hands, the reading of the prayer begins.

We confess that the circle of love is repeatedly broken.

BROKEN–beginning with arms bent and at waist level, abruptly and forcefully straighten arms in a downward motion on each side of the body toward the hips (as if pushing air behind you). Spread fingers apart. Hands should sweep from waist level, travel toward hips and extend behind hips with the palms facing away from the body. The gesture should symbolize broken connection.

because of our sin of exclusion.

We create separate circles: the inner circle and the outer circle,

INNER AND OUTER CIRCLE–3 people step out to make an outer circle with 3 people step closer to make a circle. The participants "explode" from the connected circle so that the isolation of individuals is expressed.

We confess that the circle of love is broken

BROKEN–repeat movement described above.

whenever we cannot see eye to eye,
whenever we cannot link hand to hand,
whenever we cannot live heart to heart and affirm our differences.

EYE TO EYE–the inner circle moves clockwise in the circle while the outer circle moves counterclockwise. All performers circle menacingly, looking away from the others and keeping hands dramatically apart from one another, using exaggerated movements.

We confess that the circle of love is broken

BROKEN–repeat movement described above.

whenever there is alienation, whenever there is misunderstanding,
whenever there is insensitivity or a hardening of the heart.

MISUNDERSTANDING–three people peel away from the circle. Each person takes three to four steps away from the group in different directions and finishes with his/her back to the center of the stage.

HARDENING OF HEART–remaining three people peel way as described above. Each person in the second group moves within one to two steps of the other performers. This prepares for the next movement, which is performed in pairs.

We confess that the circle of love is broken

BROKEN–repeat movement described above.

the circle of power and the circle of despair,
the circle of privilege and the circle of deprivation.

DESPAIR AND DEPRIVATION–One participant in each pair places a hand on the other person's head and pushes him/her down as that participant lowers to his/her knees. Pretend to use force to push the other performer to the floor.

Through God's grace we are forgiven,

FORGIVEN–performers return to the circle, facing the inside of the circle. Each performer creates X design with the one who stands on the opposite side of the circle, joining their arms crossed at the wrist. They grasp the hands of their partner. The grasped hands and arms should be layered/entwined among the other performers. This is a gesture of forgiveness and unity with each other.

by the mercy of our Creator,

MERCY–performers lift their intertwined hands in unison and re-lease the hands of their partner. Performers reach toward the ceiling or each other with arms extended straight at an angle toward the center of the circle. This symbolizes that forgiveness is made possible through our relationship with God. To symbolize God, you need not always reach "up" toward a transcendent God but can also reach toward each other.

through the love of the Christ,

THROUGH–participants quickly pull arms down and back toward body in sweeping motion, bending at the elbow until elbow extends behind their backs. Then performers thrust hands back up toward center of the circle, over their heads. Hands end up in same place as above-arms extended straight at an angle toward the center of the circle. This is a quick and sweeping movement.

and in the power of the Spirit.

POWER–performers turn to face out from the circle and reach forward with their arms. Performers should appear to be reaching for something in front of them. Performers in front reach out at waist level. Performers on either side reach out at shoulder level. Performers in the back of the circle reach out over their heads. Performers may look toward the heavens or the congregation.

Let us rejoice and be glad!
Glory to God! Amen.

Hold "POWER" pose.

[As an alternative, the closing lines can be choreographed to allow those seated in the congregation to participate by moving their arms. In this case, the movements are taught to the congregation and practiced at the beginning of the service. Performers cue the congregation to participate with them in the final movements.]

Marcia McFee,
Miriam Therese Winter
and Jaye Turney

Building a House *Choreographed to the song "All Are Welcome," (see p. 276)*

Needed:

✓ 10 participants

✓ 5 silk (or other similar fabric) banners of various solid, bright colors. Each banner should be 25' x 3'.

Participants form pairs and each pair is responsible for handling one of the banners. Each pair starts in an available aisle.

Each pair has one person at the front of the aisle (P1) and one at the back (P2). They stretch the banner between them. As the performance begins, participants raise the banner to waist level and gently ripple the banners between them.

When the music begins, the pair from the center aisle walks to the stage and creates a doorway frame with the banner. To create a doorway: find the center of the banner. Each participant holds the banner approximately 1.5' from the center. The participants stand several feet apart from each other in a line parallel to the edge of the stage. This creates a length in the fabric that the participants pull taut holding their arms over their heads. The banner stretches 3' across at the top, and the remaining fabric drapes down beside the participants. This is the "door" the other pairs walk through as they move to form the house. Practice this activity prior to the service, so the participants know approximately where to hold the material.

Once the door is created, the pair from the farthest left aisle walks toward the stage, moving the banner up and down, rippling the banner as they walk. As the lead person (P1) reaches the "doorway" the person following (P2) grabs the approximate center of the banner they are carrying. The pair continues through the doorway with the banner. NOTE: it is im-portant that the tallest participant be the leader (P1) of this pair. The tallest participant serves as the center of the house and serves much like a "Maypole" as he/she holds the center of each banner high overhead.

The center participant (C) will be the center pole and as each pair walks onto the stage, the P2 of each pair hands the center of his/her banner to the central person. "C" holds all the banners in one hand over his/her head. The remaining participants hold the end of their banners at waist level and should be far enough away from "C" so the banners take the shape of an A-frame house. One of the participants needs to hold two banner ends, since the person serving as the "C" cannot hold the end of the banner he/she carried to the stage. As each pair enters the doorway, the next pair starts walking toward the stage, so there is no delay in movement. The next pair to move forward is the pair on the far right. Then the pairs alternate until all are on the stage.

The final arrangement has two participants at the front holding the banner that forms the doorway. There is one participant in the middle of the stage holding the centers of four banners over his/her head. The remaining seven participants hold their banner ends away from the center, creating an A-frame house. Hold this position until the end of the song.

After the song is complete, "C" releases each banner one at a time and the participants holding that banner exit through the door, stretching the banner lengthwise and rippling it as they exit the sanctuary. After all pairs have exited the house, the pair holding the doorway drops their arms and carries their banner down the center aisle.

_____ Marcia McFee and Jaye Turney

Prayer of Confession and Signs of Assurance

[This body prayer uses an alternative "prayer posture" that embodies the images portrayed by inviting people to hold their head in their hands and use touch in a careful way to bless one another. Print only the final response in the bulletin.]

Introduction

The forehead is a place of connection. It is a place of caring. We go there to check for a fever, to soothe worry lines, to comfort. We cradle our head in our hands when we fell stressed, we massage our temples when we feel pain. And it is where many ministers place their wet hand and baptize an infant in the love and power of the divine Three in One. It is a place of connection.

And so, I invite you to place your head in your hands as a posture for our prayer of confession this morning. Let us pray.

Oh, God, we forget. How quickly we forget the touch of our baptism, the connection to our call.

A wet hand to our forehead, cleansing, anointing us, connecting us as members of the body of Christ. We are so often hesitant to respond.

We forget.

We forget the touch of a cool hand to our hot foreheads. We are reluctant to reach out to touch the blazing fever which rages among your people. We are afraid and so we retreat, prescribing instead of soothing, looking and not touching...unconnected.

We forget.

We forget what it is like to reflect truthfully about ourselves. We are unwilling to sit with ourselves, holding our head in our hands, hesitant to claim your possibilities for us, reluctant to name our sin.

Be with us as a parent who sits with a child. Patiently, painfully, wrapping us in your love and care—even when we refuse to be touched. Send us your merciful healing. We ask for your grace and peace and that by it, we might have the courage to stay connected. Amen.

Signs of Assurance

The good news, friends, is that the grace and peace of Jesus Christ is with us. I invite you to turn to your neighbor or neighbors and exchange names. And, as a sign of assurance and with their permission, place your hand on their forehead or shoulder or simply hand to hand—connected in some way—and speak these words of blessing and assurance to one another...

You are a child of God! Blessed are you!

[Since this prayer images God as parent, you may wish to use a parent and child in a rocking chair as a visual symbol, and the pianist can play "Jesus Loves Me" during the prayer. If used as a Christmas Eve meditation, use "Away in a Manger."]

Marcia McFee _____

The Prayer of Jesus (with movements)

[Experiencing this familiar piece of liturgy with movements can renew its beautiful meaning and bring into embodied focus the magnitude of the prayer's instructions to be WITH and FOR each other. It can be taught to the children during a time when they come forward; the children repeat the actions as they "teach" the adults. This encourages the participation of those who are hesitant about trying something new (children and adults alike!)

See lesson 3 of the study guide to explore the meaning of these movements.

Movements set to a familiar prayer such as this can give us some fresh "food for thought." They become three-dimensional, spatial theological statements (a reason to give great care to "interpretive movement").]

Start by inviting everyone to find a partner and stand facing them.

Tell them that if there is no one free around them, to join in with another pair to make a threesome. The prayer works fine with three. Teach the movements first, without telling anyone what words will be used to accompany them. Then, add the words and continue to give verbal cues for the movement.

Repeat, adding the adults, so that everyone can experience it in a prayerful and joyful manner.

The movements that accompany the words are as follows. The movements described occur simultaneously with the words which precede them on the page.

"Our Father" [or other name for God]
start with the arms bent in front of you, palms facing up

"who Art in Heaven"
place the hands on the chest over the heart

"hallowed be thy name"
extend the arms in an upward diagonal direction, meeting your partner's hands high—like London Bridge

"Thy kingdom come"
look up to one set of hands and reach up further, separating them

"Thy will be done"
bring those hands and arms down to your sides

"on earth"
look up to the other set of hands and reach up further, separating them

"as it is in heaven."
bring those hands and arms down to your sides

"Give us this day our daily bread"
cup your two hands together in front of you as if receiving something

"and forgive us our trespasses"
make a fist with each hand and press your knuckles against your partner's knuckles

"as we forgive those who trespass against us."
unclench your fists and link fingers, holding hands with your partner in front of you

"And lead us not into temptation"
continue to hold hands, turn them upside-down to reveal wrists

"but deliver us from evil."
let go of hands in a releasing, freeing quality, arms end at your sides

"For thine is the kingdom"
shake right hands as in a hand shake and don't let go

"and the power"
shake left hands as in a hand shake—now you have both hands clasped

"and the glory forever"
give your clasped hands a rousing shake on "glory" (this gets smiles!)

"Amen."
let go of hands

_____ *Marcia McFee*

Offertories/Prayers of Dedication

Call to Offering

*W*e have good news to share with all who feel forsaken and desolate. We have gifts to share with those whose resources are depleted. In those times and places where we cannot give ourselves, we offer our treasure, that others may carry forward and extend our ministry. Let us give in gratitude to God and in response to our neighbors' need.

Holy Covenant UMC

Prayers of Dedication

*A*ccept our gifts, O God, because we need to give. Use our gifts to the greatest good they can accomplish here in our midst and far beyond our individual reach. We present them in thanksgiving for all you have given us and in gratitude for the privilege of sharing in your work. Amen.

Holy Covenant UMC

*T*hank you, Creator of the universe, for the people gathered around us today.

Thank you for the things of the earth that give us means of life, plants, animals and birds that we use for food and medicine.

Thank you for the natural world, in which we find the means to be clothed and housed.

Thank you, O God, for these gifts of nature that make life abundant.

Help us see our place among these gifts. May we not squander them or consider them the means for selfish gains.

May we respect the life of all you have made. May our spirits be strengthened by using only what we need, and may we use our strength and our gifts to help those who need us.

United Church of Rogers Park

*B*lessed are you, God of all creation. Through your goodness we have this offering to bring, the result of our human efforts. May you bless its use for the mission of your church.

Blessed be God forever.

Park Avenue UCC

*G*od, you have been our shelter from one generation to another
overarching sky
shading tree
deepest waters
pulsing veins.
You have spread your vine widely
bringing us a bounteous fruitfulness
of care and nurture, fulfillment and peace.
Grow in us
that we may root ourselves in your visions
of justice and mercy.
Open our arms that we might lift another's burdens
speak through our mouths that we might comfort the afflicted
urge our feet that we might march in solidarity with the wounded.
Teach us to be the household of God,
a people spreading out the everlasting branches of love.

_____ *Bobbi Patterson*

*S*ustainer God, I am tired of this fight. I am tired of demanding a place at Your table, a voice in the pulpit, a seat in the pew. I wonder if there are any more words to say what has been said by so many, for so long. I wonder if there are any more ways of showing how destructive it is and what it means to be included out. I wonder if it is in me to continue. It matters and so, with your help, I will carry on. Guide my words and actions and may they honor you. I ask for strength in the struggle and your presence with me on this journey.
AMEN.

_____ *Lesley Brogan*

*H*oly God,
In your creation you declared all,
each and everyone
each and everything
to be good.
May I listen well
and attend to what
you declare
to be good
this day, at this time.
In this world of so many
names, faces, places, spaces,
may I remember that
there is room enough
there is love enough
for all, each and everyone
each and everything.
AMEN.

_____ *Lesley Brogan*

*L*iving memory. We cry out.

We are weary, Sore Sinew
Weary of painful struggle for some daybreak
for the simple light of a new day
when the too-long delayed justice may be ours.

We are angry, Great Passion
About racism and cruelty
unrelieved rage for long-time
rancor, which receives inadequate
resolve although much effort.

We are ready, Living Memory. Enable us
to hear what we need to hear. To dialogue
constructively. To do what we need to do.
To shatter the silences that bind us
and to act for change that shakes our
foundations for justice's cause
and for good.

Bobbi Patterson

*W*ondrous God, lover of lion and lizard, cedar and cactus, raindrop and river, we praise you for the splendor of the world! We thank you, that woven throughout the tapestry of earth are the varied threads of human diversity. Created in your image, we are of many colors and cultures, ages and classes, gender and sexual identities. Different and alike, we are your beloved people. Free us, we pray, from fears of difference that divide and wound us. Move us to dismantle our attitudes and systems of prejudice. Renew our commitment to make this a household of faith for all people—gay, bisexual, lesbian, and straight—that all who worship and minister here may know the grace and challenge of faith. In our life together, grant us minds and hearts eager to learn, reluctant to judge, and responsive to the leading of your loving Spirit. We ask in Christ's name, Amen.

Ann B. Day

Choir Prayer

*G*racious God,

Whose breath is song in the colors of creation

Whose themes of promise play hopeful rhythms

      beating the journey of our lives

Be present now and bless us who share in this common life

      as we gather our instruments, notes

      and pulse for the beginning of life.

Teach us to hear and sing new songs

      A song of praise and promise,

         of insight and hope.

Mindful of skills shaped by memory's often difficult way

Shape us with the strands of your covenant

      that ancient melody whose lines of justice and mercy

      thread imaginative patterns of harmony and dissonance

         through our common life and in the world.

Engage us in the rigors of learning

      that our efforts may weave their part

      in the larger tunes of human and natural life

Bless our sound

      binding it in your abiding love.

Commend to us the truths of fellowship and service

No longer offering our gifts as outsiders, isolated troubadours,

      but claiming our dependence on one another

         and the riches of the planet's imagination. Amen.

_____ *Bobbi Patterson*

Transfiguration

Luke 9:28-36

*R*adiant God, source of light,
as you surrounded Jesus with your glory,
so you come to us in a penetrating brightness.

You catch us off guard and expose our weakness.

We choose the limelight while you call us to explore the shadows
and brighten the darkness.

We seek the spectacular while you bind up the broken in
countless acts of mercy.

We seek to stay on the mountain or in a comfortable pew while
you walk to the valleys of need.

Radiant God,
fill us with light and courage to carry good news into all the
corners of the world and to bring back the joy of your presence.

Amen.

*Reconciling
Congregation Program*

Matthew 15:21-28

*O God, you are Hospitality. You are Welcome. You
are the Invitation, the Table, the Feast. By your spirit
may we learn to receive and offer grace, to share from
the sustenance of our lives and not simply its crumbs.
Embolden us as we serve as the voice of those who
continue to ask the church for justice and bread. In
Christ we pray, amen.*

*Reconciling
Congregation Program*

During A Time Of Discernment Regarding Making A Public Witness On Behalf Of Lesbian, Gay, Bisexual & Transgender Persons

racious God,

We give thanks for your presence in all of life and for your presence with us now as we seek to discern your will and your wisdom for this community. Remind us, Divine Spirit, that you seek to fill us with your life-giving power. Encourage us, Eternal Wisdom, to loosen our grip on our individual assumptions so that we might hear your voice speaking through our community. Disturb us, Holy Advocate, that we might be unsettled from our complacency in order to become agents of your grace to a world in need. As we gather as your people, called forth to proclaim your Word and to transform hearts turned cold, give us a clearer sense of what we are to say and do. Lead us back to our ancestors of the faith who sought your guidance when fear, confusion, and despair seemed to rule the day.

Fill us with the spirit of Moses, Aaron, and Miriam as they led the Hebrew people from slavery to freedom;

Fill us with the spirit of Queen Esther as she defied conventional wisdom to save her people from sure destruction;

Fill us with the spirit of the disciples, bereft from the departure of their friend and savior Jesus, yet able to organize a new community founded on compassion, courage, and shared resources;

Fill us with the spirit of Stephen, Lydia, Paul, Timothy, Dorcas, and other early Christians who risked living a minority faith in an empire of oppression and enforced conformity.

O God, hear the prayers of this community as we seek to make a public witness on behalf of our Lesbian, Gay, Bisexual, and Transgender sisters and brothers.

Help us to honor the voices of those who have personally known exclusion, heartache, fear, uncertainty, and even violence. Broaden our awareness of the movement of your Holy Spirit in our world, so that we might know once again that your ways are not always our ways. Call us to more fully respect the blessed worth of all your beloved children. Guide us to new ways of being church for a new age.

In passionate, eager, and joyful expectation we pray. Amen.

Allen V. Harris

New Moon

Creator God, you separated light from dark.

You placed suns and planets and moons on swirling paths with sacred destinations. You also set our lives in motion with sacred purpose as part of your creation. You have called us—and all you have made—good.

In this time when the moon is new, we look to the night and we are at peace. We are comfortably vulnerable in the darkness. We are safe because we know you created us and envelop us with your deep love.

Help us to know the goodness of the dark. As we cannot rely on our sight at times, let us be keenly aware of your gift of other senses: touch, smell, taste, hearing, intuition. As you know us and touch us, help us to honestly know and touch ourselves.

As we look at ourselves and all that is familiar to us, now colorless in the dark, help us have courage to look at the shades of gray and carefully discern truth from tradition.

Help us silently listen to our heart which sets the pace for the next cycle in our journey to you. Let us be open to the voice of our Guide, your Spirit, as we recommit ourselves and our lives to you. Guide us as we take inventory of our energy and sacred desires which come from you. Help us reinitiate plans and ideas that slipped away from us and initiate new ventures inspired in times of quiet prayer.

As the moon makes its journey toward hanging full in the sky, grant that our growth toward fullness in you be a relentless pursuit of all that is good and simple and just.

In the name of God who Creates, Redeems and Sustains us. Amen.

Jim and
Timothy Kocher-Hillmer

Family Prayer During Coming Out Process

*W*e cry today, God
 and feel very real pain
 but we ask you to forgive our selfishness as we dwell only on our grief.
We cry for our dreams that we now see as lost,
 and lose sight of the miracle of life in our midst.
We cry out of fear for what our love one may now face in an intolerant world,
 and forget that you are God and care more deeply than we ever can.
We cry for the hurt that we have ignorantly caused,
And neglect to work for justice here and now.
We perpetuate our sadness,
 and forget all our reasons to celebrate.
Oh God, have mercy.
Oh God, hear our hurts.
In your power and love, God, please make us whole.
Amen.

_____ *Jennifer Pope*

A Father's Prayer of Thanks

O God, thank you for the example of love and the gifts of grace
 which Gay men and Lesbians continue to bring to the
 community of faith.

They know your acceptance even though they have been denied
acceptance from family, friends, and community; they have that
sense of wholeness which can come only from putting one's being
in your hands; they cope with misunderstanding, fear, and hatred
because they know that you love them; they joyfully realize their
sexuality is a gift from you, and part of your creation; they experience humility learned from adversity, know compassion rising out
of suffering, give unconditional love through your example; they
understand the value of each day's life even though they face
death from persecution and disease; and they rejoice in the conviction of the reality of life beyond death because of Jesus Christ.
Thank your, God, for our daughters and sons!

_____ *Merrill M. Follansbee*

A Parent's Prayer

O God, what can break this dark mood of sadness and despair? Silence enfolds me.

Dear God, thoughts, like colors, run wild until the silence brings order from chaos.

Spirit of God, break through the darkness, the brooding, unwelcome thoughts. Despair must not win!

Ever-present God, kindle love and hope; open hearts and minds of all. Let justice enter in. Amen.

Muriel S. Follansbee _____

*G*od of all colors:
the one who made me want
to speak and to write
with quiet, eloquent significance,
was black.
Yet, though principal of my high school,
his family was not allowed
to buy a home in our neighborhood.

God, forgive us.
God, deliver us.
For we have accepted the gifts of many
while rejecting their body-selves
because of color, gender, age,
disability, sexual orientation, appearance.

Help us to realize
if the gifts are beautiful, so are they.
Help us to celebrate others' value
by their fruits
not the shape of the trees.

Chris R. Glaser _____

Prayer for an Inclusive Church

*G*od, who revealed to Peter
both the circumcised and un-circumcised
are welcome into your kingdom;
God, who promised your spirit
will be an advisor to the faithful,
and a comforter to the hurting;
We pray your spirit will lead the church
toward insights on how all your people
can experience the welcome
that Peter, in your name,
offered to the un-circumcised Gentiles,
especially those whom the church rejects
due to race, sex, and sexual orientation.

Then Peter said, "Can anyone withhold the water for baptizing these people who have received the Holy Spirit just as we have?" Acts 10:47

God, whose grace knows no boundaries,
teach us to avoid erecting barriers
to human experiences
that cannot be found in your kingdom.

Euguene G. Turner

*S*pirit of Truth, you often seem elusive to us:
to speak truth
 can result in being shunned
 by parent, siblings, or children;
to be honest
 can jeopardize our pastorate or job.
Why does embracing you run the risk
of discrimination and pain?
Spirit of Truth,
fill my heart, my breath, my soul.
Encompass me
with your ever-changing form.

As long as my breath is in me and the spirit of God is in my nostrils, I hold fast my righteousness, and will not let it go. Job 27:2,6a

Ease the bitterness
of my constant struggle.
Strengthen me against those
who would use you to hurt me.
Let me never doubt
 my own integrity,
 my own freedom to disclose,
 the authenticity of my faith.
Guide my vision
to your ultimate manifestation. Amen.

Mark Bowman

Chapter 6

Molding Occasional Services and Ritual Designs

*The rugged American individualist—
impatient, as always, with the
inconvenient social structure of
Christian belief and praxis—
prefers the friendly, pliable agendas of
personal prayer to the intractable—
often harsh and dreadful—demands of
an ancient historical and public cultus.
For the liturgy of the Christian
assembly stubbornly resists the
manipulations of both politics
and civil religion.*

Nathan Mitchell

AIDS Liturgies

World AIDS Day Liturgies

One: How have you come to this time and place?

All: We've come this far by faith!

One: How has your heart weathered the many losses of friends and lovers?

All: We've come this far by faith!

One: How has your mind grappled with the constant specter of death?

All: We've come this far by faith!

One: How has your soul maintained wholeness?

All: We've come this far by faith!

One: It's not because of government support;

All:	We've come this far by faith!
One:	It's not because of the research and medical communities;
All:	We've come this far by faith!
One:	It's not because of health insurance companies;
All:	We've come this far by faith!
One:	It's because of the grace of God.
All:	We've come this far by faith!
One:	It's because of the presence of Christ.
All:	We've come this far by faith!
One:	It's because of the sustaining power of the Holy Spirit.
All:	We've come this far by faith!
One:	We've come this far because the love of God is made visible through the care of lovers, friends, family, and caregivers.
All:	We've come this far by faith!
One:	We've come this far because the love of God empowers us to love, to hold, to be a healing presence.
All:	We've come this far by faith!
One:	We've come this far because nothing, nothing at all can separate us from this love.
All:	We've come this far by faith!
One:	We've come this far by faith, and we will go even farther, knowing that in every step we take,
All:	God hasn't failed us yet!
One:	In every burden we carry,
All:	God hasn't failed us yet!
One:	In every setback we face,
All:	God hasn't failed us yet!
One:	Our God is a constant presence on which we can lean.
All:	God hasn't failed us yet!
One:	We can trust in God's presence.
All:	God hasn't failed us yet!
One:	Alleluia! Amen!
All:	Amen and amen!

_____ *Karen P. Oliveto*

One:	At the dawn of creation, God's light burst into the world.
All:	Don't let the light go out!
One:	God's light sustains all living things.
All:	Don't let the light go out!
One:	All that is good, all that is right, all that is just, dwells in the light.
All:	Don't let the light go out!
One:	The light of God's love resides in each one of us.
All:	Don't let the light go out!
One:	In the eyes of our lovers, in the lives of our friends, in the acts of compassion by strangers, we have encountered the light.
All:	Don't let the light go out!
One:	That light sustains us, throughout all the changes of life.
All:	Don't let the light go out!
One:	Even in the midst of illness and disease, the light shines in our lives.
All:	Don't let the light go out!
One:	Nothing can separate us from the light of God's love.
All:	Don't let the light go out!
One:	Our sexuality cannot separate us from the light of God's love.
All:	Don't let the light go out!
One:	Our antibody status cannot separate us from the light of God's love.
All:	Don't let the light go out!
One:	Sickness cannot separate us from the light of God's love.
All:	Don't let the light go out!
One:	Death cannot separate us from the light of God's love.
All:	Don't let the light go out!
One:	Tonight, we hold the light of God's love in our hands and in our hearts.
All:	Don't let the light go out!
One:	Tonight, we hold the light of those we have loved who have died.
All:	Don't let the light go out!

One: Tonight, we embrace the light.

All: Don't let the light go out!

One: Tonight, let us open our lives to the healing presence of the light.

All: Don't let the light go out!

One: Tonight, let it fill our lives.

All: Don't let the light go out!

One: Don't let the light go out!

All: Don't let the light go out! Don't let the light go out!

_____ *Karen P. Oliveto*

World AIDS Day Service

Hymn "O Christ, the Healer, We Have Come" Fred Pratt Green
Tune KENTRIDGE

A Litany of Gathering

We gather this evening to remember.
We come to affirm our faith and our hope.
We come longing for the caring One who calls us from
darkness into the light of love.
We gather this evening to be drawn together.
Embraced by nurturing arms of all who sojourn along this path
we call life.
We gather this evening in sadness and frustration.
Remembering friends and loved ones who have died of AIDS
and acknowledging the indifference of many religious
communities, our society, and the continuing slowness of
our human response to the changing nature of the
epidemic.
We gather this evening in compassionate support.
Embracing well those who are living with HIV, AIDS, and the
worried.
We gather this evening seeking to live our lives in prayer that
we all might be moved from suffering to healing, from
fear to confidence, and from silence to celebration.

Prayer of Unburdening & Confession

Powerful, merciful God, some of us confess that we have not kept our promises to be more open, better educated, and more willing to give of ourselves to those with HIV infection or AIDS. Some of us have not completely changed our judging attitudes or our risky behavior. Some of us continue to be frozen with fear that AIDS will touch us or those we most dearly love. We are all angry that medical research still has not discovered a cure, now almost two decades into the epidemic. And we are angry that too many have died. Hear and honor our strong feelings, O God, and accept our deep regrets. Heal us from all that is broken and hurting within us that we may be renewed and empowered to be your agents of healing and change. Give us confidence that with the strength of your marvelous grace at work within us, we can make a life-bearing difference in the midst of so much death. Amen.

Assurance of Pardon & Passing of the Peace
(Adapted from the Jewish tradition)

Magnified and sanctified be God's great name in the world which has been created according to the divine will, and let us say: Amen. May God grant us abundant peace and life to us and to all of creation and let us say: Amen. May God, who ordains harmony in the universe, grant peace to us and to all of creation and let us say: Amen.

May the peace of Christ be with you.
And also with you.
(Please exchange greetings of peace.)

The First Lessons

(Background: The Book of Lamentations responds to a people devastated by crisis. Historically, that crisis was the conquest by the Babylonians of the holy city of Jerusalem. But the church has often turned to this beautiful and poetic text to express its grief in times of crisis during Holy Week, in the time of war, or as we do this evening, in the face of widespread and devastating disease. In acknowledgment of the world-wide nature of the AIDS epidemic, these selections will be read in several languages. You are invited to follow the text, if you wish, by using the pew Bibles.)

The passages will be read as follows:

Lam 1:1-6 in Hebrew

Lam 1:11-17 in English

Lam 2:10-13 in English

Lam 2:18-22 in English

Lam 3:1-15 in French

Lam 3:16-33 in English

Lam 3:48-63 in Spanish

Lam 4:1-5 in English

Lam 4:14-15; 17-20 in German

Lam 5:1-5; 9-16 in Spanish

Lam 5:17-22 in English

The Second Reading
Poem, "The Unveiling (Making A Memorial Panel),"
by Dean Kostos

Psalm 121

The Gospel: John 11:1-44

Sermon

The Feast of the Eucharist

All who respond to the love taught by Christ are invited to share in Communion.

Remembrance

As the names of those to be remembered are being read, the congregation is invited to come forward to light candles from the flame of the paschal candle and place them in the stands around the communion table. We will light candles until all the names have been read.

The Prayers of the People

Healing, loving, compassionate God:
Tonight we come before you with heavy and aching hearts
heavy because of a devastating disease that has run rampant
over our world, aching because so many have fallen victim to
this monstrous menace.

We pray, this evening, for all those whose lives have been invaded and shortened by HIV, who have suffered swollen glands and panicked over colds and rashes and pneumonia. We lift up those who have felt the sting of being ostracized, shut out, closed off, and where prejudice has divided one from another.

We give thanks for those tireless workers who give of their time and energy to bring hope in the midst of despair, for gentle and faithful care-givers, for researchers, doctors and nurses seeking to find a sure cure, a vaccine to end this dark night of the soul, for those determined ones raising funds to support every effort to see this crisis to an end.

O, Love that will not let us go, help us cling to one another when sorrow and suffering surrounds us and almost overcomes us, when hearts are breaking and pain persists and lives are torn asunder.

How we need you in these days, dear God, and in these moments to shore up our saddened spirits and mend our broken hearts. Give the church courage to reach out—to reach out— and touch each suffering son or daughter, or parent, or partner or lover, or colleague, so that each can feel a warm and tender inclusion in the family of God.

Forgive us if we have alienated anyone so stricken with AIDS, keep us mindful that Jesus loves everyone—everyone who labors and is heavy laden.

And, now, we seek your blessing, holy and caring God, thanking you for celebrating with us in times of joy and upholding us in times of sorrow. Hold us tightly so that nothing—nothing can separate us from the love of God. And it is through Christ, our healing and hopeful Savior, that we offer this prayer. Amen.

An Invitation to Give and Receive

Blessed are you, God of all creation. Through your goodness we have this offering to bring, the result of our human efforts. May you bless its use for the mission of your church.

Blessed be God forever.

Hymn   "Draw Us in the Spirit's Tether" by Percy Dearmer, alt., *New Century Hymnal*

The Great Thanksgiving

Blessed are you, God of all creation. Through your goodness
we have this bread to offer, which earth has given and
human hands have made. It will become for us the bread
of life. Blessed be God forever.

Blessed are you, God of all creation. Through your goodness
we have this wine to offer, fruit of the vine and work of
human hands. It will become our spiritual drink.
Blessed be God forever.

Lift up your hearts.
We lift them up to God.

Let us give thanks to God.
It is right to give God thanks and praise.

The Preface

"... we raise our voices in thankful praise."

**Holy, holy, holy Lord, God of hosts. Heaven and
earth are full of your glory. Hosanna in the highest.
Blessed is the One who comes in the name of the
Lord. Hosanna in the highest.**

Consecration and Christ's Prayer

Words of Institution for the Bread and Cup

Prayer after Communion

The feast has ended. With thanksgiving, depart in peace.
May God be with you.
And also with you.

Let us pray.

We thank you, God, for renewing our spirits, for helping our
souls to speak in any season, for showing us how to love
without reason, simply because we can. We thank you, God,
for remembering us in candlelight, for remembering us in
daylight, for making us shine, remarkably, in any light.

We thank you, God, for this glowing amber, our footprints
made of fire, dancing the possibility of forever. Amen.

Hymn   "We Shall Overcome" Afro-American spiritual

Blessing & Benediction

*Park Avenue
Christian Church*

Prayer for All Living with AIDS

*J*esus went throughout Galilee,
teaching in their synagogues
and proclaiming the good news of the kingdom
and curing every disease and every sickness among the people.

Matthew 4:23

O Dios nuestro sostén,
estamos llenos de agravio y confusión,
temerosos en nuestro dolor y soledad.
Tu eres quien puede levantarnos
y darnos la fortaleza y esperanza que necesitamos.

Amado Dios, escucha nuestra oración. [1]

We come to you that we may be healed.
We are hurt and suffer from this disease called AIDS.

Loving God, hear our prayer.

Consuela a los que están temerosos, anciosos, y perplejos.
Ilumina a los que juzgan en ignorancia.

Amado Dios, escucha nuestra oración. [2]

We pray, too, oh God,
for the brokenness in our relationships
and our world.
We ask you to heal these wounds,
especially the ones which thrust us apart.

Loving God, hear our prayer.

Presentamos nuestros hermanos y hermanas
que están muriendo.
Quita toda lágrima de sus ojos.
Fortaléceles en su lucha por integridad y libertad;
que ellos puedan encontrar paz en tu presencia.

Amado Dios, escucha nuestra oración. [3]

Create in us a holy place
where we can care for ourselves
when we feel hopeless,
when we feel we can no longer bear

the suffering from this terrible disease.
Enable us to nurture and care for each other,
for we know that we are both healers
and in need of healing.

O Dios abre nuestros ojos para ver
y nuestros oídos para oír,
que podamos entender
y que entendiendo
podamos clamar
por misericordia y justicia
para aquellos que sufren.
Permítenos traer luz en las tinieblas de nuestra sociedad,
que seamos dirgidos por tu Espíritu en nuestro esfuerzo
hasta alcanzar la cura de esta plaga.
Todo esto oramos en la confiranza de que tu te complaces
en oír nuestro clamor porque tu eres nuestra vida,
nuestra esperanza, y nuestra paz. Amén. [4]

_____ *[A translation of the Spanish by Jim Anderson]*

1. O God our Support,
   we are full of aggravation and confusion,
   frightened in our pain and loneliness.
   You are the One who lifts us up
   and gives us the strength and hope that we require.
   Beloved God, hear our prayer.

2. Comfort those who are frightened, anxious, and perplexed.
   Enlighten those who judge in ignorance.
   Beloved God, hear our prayer.

3. We present our brothers and sisters who are dying.
   Wipe every tear from their eyes.
   Strengthen them in their battle for integrity and liberty,
   that they may find peace in your presence.
   Beloved God, hear our prayer.

4. O God open our eyes to see
   and our ears to hear,
   that we may understand and that, with understanding, we may cry out
   for compassion and justice
   for those who suffer.
   Permit us to carry light in the darkness of our society,
   that we may be guided by your Spirit in our effort
   to attain a cure for this plague.
   All this we pray in the confidence that you welcome
   our cry, for you are our life, our hope, and our peace. Amen.

_____ *More Light Update*

1 Thessalonians
4:13-18

Funeral Liturgy for AIDS

L: For those who are dying,

C: Almighty God, receive our prayers.

L: For those who are sick and frightened of what might be, for those who are dying alone, for those who are trying to comfort loved ones, for those who are trying to find a cure,

C: Christ, receive our prayers.

L: Dear Creator, it is hard not to curse you for allowing AIDS to be, hard not to hate those who say it is your punishment for Gay men, hard not to shut the door on those who clumsily try to help, and hard not to despise those who will go on living.

C: Holy Spirit, melt our hearts and soften our smiles that we may remain open to all the possibilities of this moment.

L: As the light fades from the eyes of our partners, as the death of another friend barges unwanted into our already restructured and diminished lives, as our own colds and sores do not heal, and as our despair deepens,

C: help us remember, dear Partner, that you are here with us, and will care for us no matter what hell we find ourselves pulled into.

L: As friends and relatives try to understand and support, yet sometimes feel left on the side, pushed away or closed out when they want to be so close,

C: Give them, dear Friend, eyes of understanding and hearts of compassion.

L: For those who do not understand and do not want to,

C: Remind us, dear Parent, that we are all your children, and that you love us all very much and want all of us to grow into fullness.

L: For those who have died, for those who are dying, for those who are afraid they are getting sick, and for those who have lost or are losing loved ones,

C: Help us see, gentle Spirit, your presence in the caring hands of others, and know that you, too, grieve over the tragedy of AIDS, ARC, and HIV.

L: Where there is so much gloom,

C: Where there is so much distress,

L: Where there is so much despair,

All: Enter now, God, with your enduring hope.

L: Let us offer the names of those we are concerned about:

C: (either silently or aloud, name those persons for whom we should pray).

L: Dear Creator of Life, we often don't know where to begin when there is a tragic loss. Today we have so many feelings piling up on each other that it takes all our strength just to keep them under control. We do not understand the reason for this death. We do not accept the injustice of it. We are angry that you would allow anyone to die in this way, especially the death of our dear friend. We feel forgotten and betrayed. Even our faith in you seems to be hanging by a trembling thread. Yet, we do not ask you to make everything better. We do not ask you to restore our faith right away. But we do ask that if you will not take away the pain, you will at least come close and comfort us. Calm our angers and heal our wounds. In due time, help us see again the goodness of life. Assure us in the corners of our doubts that we do not die here with our friend. In remembrance of another life that was taken early, we offer our prayers.

Be assured, dear ones, that God hears the prayers of those who grieve, feels the anguish of those who are in pain, and will send a balm that heals.

C: Amen.

Mark Liebenow

Remember,
an AIDS prayer at a Memorial Service for Martin

*R*emember that tears are cleansing as well as painful.
Remember that telling the stories
not only reiterates, but also renews hope.
Remember that holding one another
is how we re-weave the world.
With the sacred joy that was and is Martin's
in the dancing heart of God.

Bobbi Patterson

Blessings

Blessing the Home

A group of friends gathers in the entry of the home with a Blessing Candle—any candle that has been chosen with the "home-makers" in mind. We often use a rainbow candle with the names of the "home-makers" or the word "home" carved into it. The candle then remains as a reminder of the blessings that have been offered.

*G*od of Hospitality and Hope,
Be present with us, gathered together in this place to claim this house as a home. May it be for _____ and _____ *[names of homemakers]*, both a place of shelter and respite, and a place of challenge and growth. As the days and nights lived in this home turn into weeks and months and years, may they be increasingly filled with the awareness of your presence and the blessings of your companionship. Amen.

Lighting the Candle of Blessing

The gathered community then move from room to room carrying the lighted candle and blessing each room. If there is a musical refrain that the group can sing together, it creates a nice way to aid the transition from room to room.

LIVING ROOM

May the couple who dwell here live and love and dream and hope and laugh and cry and play and pray, knowing you are in their midst. And through your love and grace, may their lives and their love grow stronger, may their kinships and their friendships deepen, and may strangers always be welcomed as angels.

Bless, O God, all those who will enter this home in the days to come.

PIANO ROOM

May the music that is made in this place be an instrument of peace and healing both as it is played and as it is heard, and through it may player and hearer glimpse you.

Bless, O God, all those who will share music here in the days to come.

GUEST BEDROOMS

In these rooms, O God, may guests rest in Your care. May they know comfort in times of joy or distress, and may gentle, healing dreams fill the journey of each night.

Bless, O God, all those who will rest here in the days to come.

OFFICE/EXERCISE ROOM

May the work done here be life-giving and creative, both for the body and for the world. May it be done in solidarity with your dream of shalom, and may it bear fruits of compassion and justice.

Bless, O God, all those who will work here in the days to come.

PRIMARY BEDROOM

In this room, O God, may _____ and _____, rest in your care and in one another's love. May the love that is nurtured here be filled both with passion and with compassion, and may the blessing they find in one another's love strengthen them to reach out in love and service to your world.

Bless, O God, those who will share rest and love here in the days to come.

PATIO AND POOL

May those who come to this place of respite and these waters of life find their bodies refreshed, their spirits renewed and their lives baptized anew by shared recreation.

Bless, O God, all those who will play here in the days to come.

SUN ROOM

Here, O God, may _____ and _____ create bonds of love and memories of joy as they rest and play with one another, with family, with friends. In this room, may needs and fears be expressed in safety, and may laughter flow freely.

Bless, O God, all who will gather here in the days to come.

Hanging the Celtic Knot

[or some other symbol of friendship and trust]

KITCHEN AND DINING ROOM

In this room, O God, food will be prepared, bread will be broken, special times will be celebrated, and life-journeys will be shared. May the sharing both of the food and of the community be a blessing, and through both may bodies be nurtured and spirits strengthened.

Bless, O God, all who will feast here today and in the days to come. Amen!

Feasting on Bread and Wine and Friendship

Part of the planning of this ritual is deciding with the couple or person where their cross or other symbol of friendship will hang. Words may accompany the hanging, such as, "This will hang just above the doorbell to symbolize welcome." or "This cross will hang above the door to bless each coming and going." This is done before the last room (the kitchen) is blessed, so that the feasting and fellowship can immediately follow blessing the kitchen as a continuation of the ritual. The blessing time thus reminds those gathered that blessing continues each time people gather to feast together.

_____ *Leslie Penrose*

Animal Blessing Service
in Honor of St. Francis of Assisi

*[This service was held in a park with participants seated on blankets
and a hay bale as an altar. Human companions were encouraged to
bring their animal companions for blessings whenever feasible or to
bring the collars or photos of those unable to attend. A guitar and re-
corder were used for musical accompaniment. On the bulletin cover was
a quote from Father Zossima in Fyodor Dostoyesvsky's* The Brothers
Karamazov: *Love the animals, love the plants, love everything. If you
love everything, you will perceive the divine mystery in things. Once you
perceive it, you will begin to comprehend it better every day. And you
will come at last to love the whole world with an all-embracing love.]*

Hymn   "All Things Bright and Beautiful," words by Cecil Frances
Alexander, music 17th century English melody

Scripture Lesson Genesis 1

Lesson from our Spiritual Ancestor

Apprehend God in all things,
for God is in all things,
Every single creature is full of God
and is a book about God.
Every creature is a word of God.
If I spent enough time with the tiniest creature—
even a caterpillar—
I would never have to prepare a sermon.
So full of God is every creature.
—Meister Eckhart

A Prayer for the Animals

One: So many authors have written about the importance of recognizing that we are all a part of the natural world—that we
are a community—that all of us exist together. Alice Walker
says, "As we treat animals, so we treat people and vice
versa." She reminds us that profound connections exist between oppressing other people and oppressing nature.

So as we pray this day, let us remember this relationship of
mutual influence. Let us seek to respect nature and acknowledge animals—both non-human and human—for who
they are. For quite often our global concern and care for the
earth arises from our local encounters. Big caring and small
caring are related. To care for the whole, for a sustainable

planet, is also to care for its parts—for the local, particular bit of the planet in our own neighborhoods, in our own houses. If we learn to care for our local communities, might then the whole planet have a better chance? This, then, is what we are about today—experiencing, sensing, taking responsibility for the inter-relatedness that St. Francis recognized in the world.

So in the spirit of the connectedness of all life, let us pray together:

All: Receive our humble prayer, O God, for our friends the animals, especially for the non-human animals who are suffering, for any that are hunted, or lost, or deserted, or frightened, or hungry; for all that are put to death that we might wear their coats.

We entreat for them all your mercy and pity, and for those who deal with them, we ask a heart of compassion, gentle hands and kindly words.

Make us to be true friends to animals, to respect their existence in the world, and so to share the blessings of the merciful.

We are thankful for those companions who were loved but are no longer with us and whom we name in our hearts.

O God, bless, keep and protect each of our animal companions, make us to care for their needs that they may live according to your plan and be a source of love and joy to those with whom they dwell, through Jesus Christ our Savior, Amen.

Prayer of Blessing

[Participants are invited to bring their animal companions forward for a prayer of blessing. The pastor prays for each animal and human companion saying: Bless, O God, this creature _____ (name of animal) and fill our hearts with thanksgiving for its being.]

Hymn   "The Friendly Beasts," Medieval French melody, harmony by Carlton R. Young

Dismissal with Blessing

May God, who created the animals of this earth, continue to protect and sustain us all, now and for ever. Amen.

Blessing our Graduates and their Journeys

*G*od of Grace and Glory,
Ancient of Days, Bearer of the New Day,
and Source of all Life and Being,
Be present with us, gathered together in this place to affirm the life-journey of those in our community who are graduating from high school. The ritual of graduation recognizes, in our society, the achievement of having completed 12 years of school; however, in the lives and families of those who are graduating, it symbolizes much more. Graduation is a symbol of the transition from child-hood into adulthood; it is a time both of closure and of new begin-nings, a time of letting go and of reaching forth.

Graduation brings with it opportunities for starting fresh, for begin-ning again, for claiming a whole new journey. Therefore, _____ *[names of those graduating]*, as we celebrate together your gradu-ation, we celebrate also the journey we have had with you, how-ever long or brief that journey has been for each of us. As you have lived and loved in our midst, we, as your community of faith, have struggled to model the ways of life; we have sought to do justice, to love kindness, and to walk with God. We have not been perfect, and we have failed in many ways.

Today, we affirm together your own journey in the faith from this day forward. We affirm that in your own faith-seeking, you will re-ject some of what we have given you and accept other things—that is as it should be. Our prayer is that with God's help you will "choose life" for yourself and for your neighbors.

[a bowl of water is brought forward]

As you begin the journey that lies for you beyond graduation, we invite you to leave behind you, old fears, old grudges or guilts, old ways of relating that weigh you down and get in the way of new life! Whisper them softly into your cupped hands...and with this water, the same water with which you were baptized, we ask the God of new life and new beginnings to wash them away.

[As graduates dip their hands into the water, the minister or the community says:]

We send you forth, blessed by the water, to claim the promise of new of life and to re-claim the original blessing of harmony and peace among all people and all of creation.

And further, as you begin the journey that lies for you beyond graduation, if there are things from your journey that you wish to claim for what lies ahead—you are invited to speak them aloud for all creation to hear and to know....

[Graduates are invited to share gifts and graces they hope will strengthen their future.]

With this salt—the ancient symbol of preservation and strength and blessing—we ask the God of all times and places to strengthen you in the things you have named and in all the ways of justice and peace.

[Each graduate places salt on his/her own tongue.]

We send you forth, blessed by the salt, to claim the ways of Truth and justice—love in all you become and all you do. May God grant you courage and hope for the journey.

[Each graduate is given a cup with his/her name on it, and water is poured into each cup.]

And now you are invited to carry your Cup of Blessing among this community, gathered in the name and the spirit of God, to receive their blessings.

[Graduate pass their cups around congregation and those present are invited to speak their blessings into the cup. After the cups are passed, the graduates are invited to drink from them.]

Drink in all that has been offered you, in the name of the Creator, the Christ and the Spirit of Life.

May your eyes see the ways of life; may your mouth speak the ways of truth, and may your life reflect the ways of love. Amen.

_____ *Leslie Penrose*

Blessing/Commissioning of Mission Team

Reading: John 1:35-39

Reader 1: Weaver God, time and again you have called your people to leave their homelands and seek your dwelling place in foreign lands.

Reader 2: "Come and see" you have invited your people;

Reader 3: "Come and see my face in the face of a stranger."

Reader 1: And along the way, you have woven the lives of your people together,

Reader 2: Strangers and neighbors, kindred and foe.

Reader 3: Bound together by your grace into one family.

Community: **We gather now to seek your blessing for these companions to whom you now offer the invitation to seek your face and your life in the faces and the lives of the people of _____** *[name country to which team is traveling]*. **Through our prayers, our giving, and our support, we go with them. And with them we pray that through the reconciling power of your spirit, their presence, their work, their learning and growing might participate in the mending of your tattered world and the reconciliation of your kin-dom.**

Team: We journey together as a people shaped by your love, freed by your forgiveness, and called by your vision of shalom. We pray that through the power of your spirit, as we work hand-in-hand with our brother and sisters—both on this team, and in _____ *[name of country]*—that we might be humble enough to know we go seeking you; and open enough to discover anew the unity that is ours in you:
> —sisters and brothers of a common family,
> —created and loved by the same God,
> —sharing a single home on this, our earth.

In gratitude and hope we pray. Amen.

Community Blessing

[The entire congregation is invited to lay hands on the team members and bless them either with silent prayers or with spontaneous sentence prayers.]

Leader: Come, Spirit of the Living One, pour out your spirit on these our brothers and sisters. We pray that by this commissioning, their hands and hearts might be strengthened to be compassionate to human need, tender in their care for one another, and faithful to your hope of a world made one by love.

Song   "It Takes A Whole Village" on *Pieces of our Lives* by Jim and Jean Strathdee

Leslie Penrose _____

Blessing on Becoming a PhD Recipient

_____, *[name of PhD recipient]* you have worked for and received one of the highest honors of academia—your PhD. As your community of faith and struggle, we know some of the work that has preceded this moment, and we value the gifts and skills that it recognizes and affirms. It is with great joy that tonight we celebrate with you both the accomplishment and the potential that this degree represents.

Are there thoughts or feelings you would like to share with us about meeting this goal in your life?

> *[Response from PhD recipient.]*

One: As we celebrate with you the honor this degree represents, we also celebrate with you the authority that your voice will derive from it. We are grateful that you work and teach in a place where you can influence the future of the church and the Christian community. We are hopeful that because of your voice and others, the future of the church holds the promise of more justice and more compassion, and we are proud that for the present time, you have chosen to live out your faith and share your journey as a disciple, in our midst.

We take our role as your community of faith seriously and, therefore, as we celebrate with you, we also call you to remember that authority carries with it responsibility, and the authority to speak and teach within the tradition of Jesus carries with it the responsibility to risk:
speaking the truth, working for justice
and living with integrity and compassion.

_____, as your community of faith and hope, we offer you our prayers of support and encouragement and joy. And we would like now to symbolize that support and joy by the laying on of hands.

Community Laying on of Hands and Blessing

God of Wonder and Presence, bless Dr. _____ *[full name]* in this time of celebration and accomplishment. Grace her/him with the courage to continue to seek integrity and justice in her/his living and her/his teaching. May s/he know both the comfort and the challenge of faithful companionship along the way. Amen.

_____ Leslie Penrose

Blessing on Defending A PhD

_____ *[name]*, you go forth tomorrow to defend your dissertation. It has been a long and difficult journey to this moment. Much of your life energy has been poured into this project. We invite you now, in the presence of those who love and value you to speak your hopes and your fears.

[PhD candidate speaks.]

And now we gift you with this symbol of our solidarity—a candle of hope. May it be a reminder to you that you are a part of us, that, PhD or not, you are a gift to us and that our prayers go with you.

[The candle is lighted and the community prays together.]

_____, may you claim with joy the journey that
has brought you to this day.
May you speak with a voice of confidence and truth,
And may you know every moment that you are a
child of God and our companion.

Leslie Penrose

For Blessing the Journeys of those Leaving the Church

*T*he community of faith is a covenant family on a journey of hopes—a family created by grace, bound together by hope, and nurtured by the blessing of companionship—a family of companions who for awhile find both their way and their home together. Like every community of faith, ours has formed and is reformed over time, as companions are born and as they die, as strangers join our journey and become friends, and friends leave our midst to make a new home in a new place.

> All: _____ and _____, *[names of those leaving]* for a holy time you have lived and loved with this community as companions on our journey. We have shared good times and bad, joys and sorrows, successes and failures. We have grieved the loss of friends together and celebrated the joy of life and the gift of diversity. You have been a blessing to us and among us.

[Members of the community then speak some of the significant contributions the person/ family has made and some of the special moments/events/activities they have shared.]

> All: For a while, _____ and _____, you have found your way and your home in our midst. Your stories are in our hearts. Now you are moving to a new home. We feel deep sorrow in your leaving, and yet we are grateful to have shared this part of our journey of faith and hope with you. Thank you, for who you have been in our midst and what you have done "on the way" with us.

As symbols of our continuing companionship we have a gift for you. This rainbow candle is a reminder that wherever you go, you will find God in the struggle for justice and abundant life for all people; and hope in the companionship of those who have committed their lives to that struggle.

[The whole community is then invited to lay hands on those leaving as this sending forth is prayed together.]

> **Companion God,**
> **We give you thanks for the life, the witness, the friendship, of these our companions, _____ and _____. Accompany them in their continuing journey and bless them each day with enough hope to dream, enough courage to risk, enough passion to insist on justice, and enough laughter and bread to remember you with their lives. Amen.**

Leslie Penrose

Companioning

Ritual of Betrothal

*B*rothers and Sisters, we who are called "Christian" believe and experience loving relationships to be one way in which God is made manifest in our midst. As part of a community of faith which spans the continents and the centuries, we are heirs to a number of ways of interpreting, socializing, legalizing, and ritualizing the relationships that are important to us. We are living now in a time and culture that is struggling with changing understandings of the nature of holistic, life-giving, loving relationships. In our daily living, we no longer hold firmly to the limit of two simple options—celebrate singleness or monogamous marriage for life—and yet, in our religious life we do not yet acknowledge any alternatives. The result is increased compartmentalization of our life and our religion, often leading to secrecy and shame, and avoidance of a deeply necessary dialogue.

As we gather today, many of us are still unclear about issues of partnering, marriage, and covenant relationships; many of us still struggle with clarity about boundaries for sexual expression. What is promiscuity, what is not? What does commitment require, what does it allow? What honors and nurtures human dignity and life-giving relationship, and what does not?

And so, we come to this celebration of "betrothal"—a celebration of commitment to one another that is faithful, serious, and public, but not necessarily for life—from the very midst of the struggle—without knowing what the journey will be or where the questioning will lead, but knowing that honesty, solidarity, and open communication must be the foundation for our continuing search for answers. We come giving thanks for the gift of love in our lives and entrusting our questioning and our struggling—to God and one another.

I present to you _____ and _____. This couple comes celebrating the loving relationship they have found with one another and committed to nurturing it and one another. _____ & _____ are not yet ready to commit the rest of their lives to one another in marriage or holy union, but they have decided to take the step of sharing one home as they continue to grow with one another toward right-relationship. They seek our blessing and our support.

_____ & _____, as you prepare to betroth yourselves to one another and then grow your relationship among us, what do you need and expect from your community of faith and hope?

   [Response from Couple]

And now, _____ & _____, as companions on your journey, we ask you:

Have you made the decision to live together with mutual respect and concern for one another's well-being?

   We have.

Will you seek the wisdom and support of companions and mentors in times of struggle and growth?

   We will.

Will you be faithful to one another as you grow this relationship?

   We will.

Prayer of Blessing:

Faithful Companion of us all,
Pour out your fierce and tender love upon those who have come to name and to celebrate their growing relationship in our midst. Bless these two in their loving, that it may be a source of strength and creativity and hope. May this community be a source of wisdom and support for them. May they find in us a safe place to question, to learn, to fail, to grow; and together may all of us continue to seek ways to live and love that honor you and one another.

_____ *Leslie Penrose*

Words for the Ending of a Relationship

*T*he arrows have fallen beyond you,
   and it is time to depart.

We gather up a richness of ordinary days,
   sharp edges of some angry memories,
   the echo of laughter, the shadow of tears.

We will always be in one another's prayers,
   but the stones of blessing and distrust
      are piled between our lives.

   May God watch between us, for
we choose to be absent from one another.

Go well, grateful for the love we've known.

_____ *Maren C. Tirabassi*

Death & Dying

A Worship Service for Gathering Around One Who Is Dying

[This is a gathering of loved ones that provides intentionally giving thanks and letting go. This service is fluid and is open for all to participate. Participation is done through the spoken messages to the one who is dying, the sharing of stories, the offering of prayers, and the singing of songs. Participants are encouraged to bring photos, mementos or other visual reminders to surround the group. Quiet spaces between words are part of this time. One person is chosen to guide the others.

Music for this service is about weaving. Any songs or hymns can be used. They can be sung by one or by everyone. If one song is to be used throughout, it is best to have a familiar tune. Some suggestions for songs include: "It's in Everyone of Us," "How Can I Keep from Singing," "I Want Jesus to Go with Me," "O Come, O Come Emmanuel."]

Opening Prayer

Holy and knowing God, we gather with our friend and ask that you be with us. In this tender time may we remember how well we are known to you. May we be reminded that you loved us first and love us still. Comfort us in this time together. May we feel your presence now and in the time to come. In your name we pray. AMEN.

see p. 306 **Song**   "Lullabye" by Cris Williamson
[Sung between messages]

Stories / Messages

Prayer

One: We offer our painful and fearful places to you, O God,

Many: The path of love is sure, unhurried and filled with mystery.

One: Help us to have a heart that is open to your loving ways,

Many: The path of love is sure, unhurried and filled with mystery.

One: Reshape our hearts and steady our spirits,

Many: The path of love is sure, unhurried and filled with mystery.

One: May we always know your companioning presence,

Many: The path of love is sure, unhurried and filled with mystery.

Stories / Messages

Song   "Lullabye" *[Sung between messages]*

Stories / Messages

Prayer of Petition

Each person is invited to share a petition for the one of this service or for him/herself. Following each petition all join together and say,

> In your loving-kindness, O God, receive our prayer.

Stories / Messages

Prayer

> Great God of all mystery,
> if in the presence of death our thoughts are startled,
> and our words flutter about like frightened birds,
> bring us stillness.
> Give us grace to wait on you silently and with patience.
> You are nearer to us than we know,
> closer than we can imagine.
> Before we felt pain,
> you suffered it;
> Before the burden came upon us,
> your strength lifted it;
> Before the sorrow darkened our hearts,
> you were grieved.
> As you walk in the valley of every shadow,
> be our good shepherd
> And sustain us while we walk with you.
> Receive O God, our prayer, AMEN.

Stories / Messages

Song   "Lullabye" *[Sung between messages]*

Closing Prayer

> Loving and Merciful God, we are thankful for this time that you
> have shared with us. We are grateful for the love that is shared in
> this circle. Bless and comfort our dear friend in the time to come.
> May your light continue to guide us and lead us to you. In your
> name we pray. AMEN.

Benediction (traditional Celtic prayer)

> Calm us, O Lord, as you stilled the storm.
> Still us, O Lord, and keep us from harm.
> Let all tumult cease.
> Enfold us, O Lord, in your peace. AMEN

Lesley Brogan

Funeral Procession Litany

*To be read at a
slow, walking pace
as the ministers and
choir slowly process
in. After each line,
there is a slight
pause. Soft music in
the background may
be helpful.*

L: Yes, yes, God is good.
C: Yes, yes, life is good.
L: We have come as family,
C: as close friends and community,
L: for this life was one of us
C: and touched deep inside of us.
L: Come, hear, life is good.
C: Come, hear, God is good.

L: Yes, yes, God is good.
C: Yes, yes, life is good.
L: We have come to celebrate
C: all that life commemorates,
L: and to share with those we love
C: all our grief and pain thereof.
L: Come, near, life is good.
C: Come, near, God is good.

L: Yes, yes, God is good.
C: Yes, yes, life is good.
L: Come and see that death is here,
C: come with faith and with your fears,
L: come to talk and share your love,
C: singing hymns of hope above.
L: Come, hear, life is good.
C: Come, hear, God is good.

L: Yes, yes, God is good.
C: Yes, yes, life is good.
L: We hold high the faith we trust
C: for the love that circles us,
L: and to pause with reverence
C: sharing words of confidence.
L: Come, near, life is good.
C: Come, near, God is good.

L: Oh, yes, God is good.
C: Oh, yes, life is good.
L: With the hope that lives in us,
C: and the dreams that empower us,
L: we will witness to our faith,
C: that this life won't dissipate,
L: Come, hear, God is good.
C: Come, near, life is good.

Mark Liebenow

Litany for a Service of Worship after Violence

One: We gather to remember that we are all created.

All: We acknowledge our need for divine help.

One: Blessed are the poor in spirit,

All: For theirs is the realm of heaven.

One: Today we feel our many losses to indifference and violence.

All: Today we mourn what hatred has done.

One: Blessed are those who mourn,

All: For they shall be comforted.

One: In our pain we know that hate must end.

All: Together we find strength to resist hatred by our caring.

One: Blessed are the gentle,

All: For they shall inherit the earth.

One: Our hearts protest injustice and are unable to remain silent.

All: Together we search for true peace in word and deed.

One: Blessed are those who hunger and thirst for righteousness,

All: For they shall be satisfied.

One: We pray for those who hate and do violence,

All: Because we know our own temptations and failures.

One: Blessed are the merciful,

All: For they shall obtain mercy.

One: We pray for love, for compassion and healing.

All: We empty ourselves of hatred to make room for genuine love.

One: Blessed are the pure in heart,

All: For they shall see God.

One: We appeal to everyone to stop the hate.

All: We will start with our own actions, reactions and inactions.

One: Blessed are the peacemakers,

All: For they shall be called children of God.

One: Every human life is precious to God and the human community.

All: Each human path of faith is a sacred journey within life.

One: Blessed are those who have been persecuted for the sake of righteousness.

All: For theirs is the realm of heaven.

One: Some will call us names and tell lies about us.

All: Many will do so in the name of religion.

One: Blessed are you when people cast insults at you and say all kinds of evil against you falsely on account of me.

All: Rejoice and be glad, because your reward is great in heaven, for so they persecuted the prophets before you.

Originally designed and used for Memorial Services for Matthew Shepard and Billy Jack Gaither

based on Matthew 5:3-12

_____ *Helene H. Loper*

For the death of a church

[This liturgy was adapted from the death and resurrection service in the United Methodist Book of Worship for the closing of a reconciling congregation. Adjust the scripture and other references to be appropriate for the denomination. The service follows the regular death service with the following adapted liturgies.]

Call to Worship

Friends, we have gathered here to praise God and to witness to our faith as we celebrate the life of _____ *[name of church]*.

We come together in grief—acknowledging the loss of our church, yet joyful for its ministry and its enduring spirit in each of us.

Let us name those members who are separated from us by death—but not by love *(congregation may say aloud or silently the names of these persons)*. May God grant us grace in this moment, that in pain we may find comfort, in sorrow, hope, in death, resurrection.

Let us celebrate and say goodbye to the ministry that has inhabited this place thus far. Let us praise God. Amen.

Confession

Holy God, before you our hearts are open, and from you no secrets are hidden. You are ever more ready to hear than we are to pray. You know our needs before we ask. We bring to you now our sorrow for our sins.

Gracious God, forgive us when we have forgotten that our life is from you and unto you. This building, this community of faith, is not of our own making but of yours. Forgive our inability to celebrate completely the many years of ministry of your servants in this place. For in the midst of our celebration, there is also pain. Comfort us in our grief and deliver us from the fear of change. Lift us from our sins, our distractions, and our disappointments. Free us from the desire to remake a new church in our image. Help us to freely return this church to you, trusting in your goodness unto the end. Speak to us, loving God, of the cycles of life and death. Enable us to die as those who go forth to joyfully live, so that living or dying, our life may be in you and that nothing in life or death will be able to separate us from your great love in Christ Jesus. Amen.

Consecration to Ministry of Reconciliation *[form a circle]*

"Therefore, if they are in Christ, they are a new creation; the old has passed away, behold, the new has come. All this is from God, who through Christ reconciled us to himself and gave us the ministry of reconciliation." II Cor. 5:17-18

In _____ *[date of welcoming decision]*, as a community of faith, you made a decision to welcome all people fully into the life of this church and have celebrated your designation as a reconciling congregation throughout the years. You promised then to _____ *[list welcoming vision statement]*. As you leave this place, to wherever God leads you, carry with you this commitment to witness to the Gospel message of reconciliation.

We honor the bold decision of this congregation to become reconciling by committing ourselves to be a reconciling presence in the world and the churches we serve. Amen.

Commendation

God of us all, your love never ends.

When all else fails, you still are God.

We pray to you for one another in our need, and for all, anywhere, who rejoice and mourn with us this day.

Keep true in us the love with which we hold one another.

In all our ways we trust you.
O God, all that you have given us is yours.

As first you gave this church to us, now we give it back to you.

Receive it and your servants as we seek new ministries in your service. Amen and Amen.

Kelly Turney

Prayer for One Who Has Died

[Before beginning this rite, gather a candle and symbols that represent the life of this friend. Place the candle and symbols on a table or altar. Use this prayer as a guided meditation or as a corporate prayer. During the times marked "silence," you may write your reflections or share them with a friend. You may also want to use a bowl of water and some seeds as part of the prayer. Make this prayer your own.]

*S*pirit of Life, we gather to remember the life of _____. You are the Creator of life, the Comforter in death. Be present with us in our remembering, our celebrating, our letting go.

Light the candle.

We remember the life of our friend, _____. We remember times of laughter...time of sharing...times of frustration...times of crying...times of growing...times of loving... (silence)

We remember times of pain, of anger, of regret, of guilt. (silence)

We feel God's Spirit washing over us like healing waters. Let the waters wash away that which must be released. Enable us to let go of the crusty, stale, prickly memories that block us from life. Let go as the waters wash them away. (silence)

We celebrate the gifts that _____ has given to us and to the world. We celebrate the seeds that _____ has planted, seeds that are growing and will bear fruit. Remember the gifts that _____ has given to friends, to the church, to family, to the world. *(silence)*

Sustainer of Life, we are thankful for the water, thankful for the seeds, thankful for the life of _____. Teach us to live again and to bless life through our own living. Send us out as faithful, life-giving, celebrating people. Shalom. Amen.

_____ *Beth Richardson*

A Service of Re-membering, Healing, and Wholeness
For Victims & Survivors of Abuse

[The service is used to promote a structure for healing from personal violence; to connect/re-connect to the sacred and allow the sacred to provide comfort; and to validate the anger, pain and confusion of survivors (and the loved ones of non-survivors). The clergyperson or lay leader is encouraged to seek out personal testimony from survivors and allow these voices to be the nexus around which the rest of the service revolves. The planners encouraged further dialogue after the service by listing in the bulletin counseling resources including the phone numbers for the local rape crisis center, and the men's anti-violence group. The following quote appeared on the bulletin cover:

*M*y heart is moved by all I cannot save:
    so much has been destroyed.
        I have to cast my lot with those
            who, age after age, perversely,
                with no extraordinary power,
                    reconstitute the world.
                          —*Adrienne Rich*

Musical Invocation "23rd Psalm" by Bobby McFerrin

Welcome

Reading Psalm 55:4-8, adapted from Marie Fortune

Witnessing

We are here because violence exists in our homes, our communities, our country.

We are here because we, or those we love, have been violated.

We are here to mourn, to cry out our fury.

We are here to share our grief at the harm done to children and women, and our anger at those who perpetrate that harm.

We are here in victory, in celebration of our survival.

We are here in solemnity, in honor of our mothers and grandmothers and sisters and friends who did not survive.

We are here in solidarity, as we commit ourselves to the elimination of rape, child abuse, and woman battering.

We are here in fearlessness, to speak the truth, to begin the healing.

We are here together—with each other, and with God.

[Remarks from survivors]

see p. 278

Lamenting Song "By the Waters of Babylon"

Litany of Naming

Sisters & brothers, we acknowledge that violence exists in our families and in our land. We commit ourselves to exposing that violence and to freeing those who suffer such violence from its crippling effects. Out of our commitment, let us pray responsively:

For children who suffer pain, degradation, and rejection from those responsible for their care,

Grant them safety and protection, Sacred Comforter.

For parents who suffer the anguish of their failures as parents,

Grant them insight and healing, Sacred Comforter.

For those who are abused and battered by those who profess to love them,

Grant them strength and courage, Sacred Comforter.

For those who batter those they profess to love,

Grant them the repentance that can change their lives, Sacred Comforter.

For women and men who have been wounded by sexual violence,

Grant them healing and empowerment, Sacred Comforter.

Let us now name before God and this community gathered those whom we know and love who seek healing and reconciliation:

[response after each name] **We stand beside you.**

Oh God, in you all struggle is reborn to strength, all pain is remolded to promise, all wounds are re-created to wholeness. Keep us in your love with compassion for each other. Amen.

Cleansing and Forgiving

For those who have experienced sexual or domestic violence, the issue of letting go of anger and moving on is of critical importance. It bespeaks being able to forgive, which is a necessary precursor to healing. Many survivors of sexual or domestic violence find that the issue of forgiveness is often raised by other people first: "It's over. There's nothing you can do about it anymore. Why don't you just forgive and forget?"

I say to you now: our task is not to forgive and forget, but rather, to forgive and remember. Let us join in the healing experience of forgiveness.

First, may we forgive ourselves: for the times we stood by, or looked the other way; for the times we allowed fear or embarrassment to keep us from reaching out to a child or woman in peril, or from speaking out against injustice. We ask God's help in forgiving ourselves.

Next, may we forgive the abusers: for their violence, their insensitivity and rejection, their selfishness, their theft of the innocence to which children are entitled, and the ability to trust which women deserve. We ask God's help in forgiving the abusers.

Then, may we forgive God: for allowing pain and abuse into our lives and lives of those we love; for allowing our prayers for deliverance to go unheeded. We ask God's help in forgiving God.

When we forgive, we free ourselves from the shackles of anger and vengefulness. Forgiveness does not mean that the wrongs done to us are no longer wrongs. Forgiveness does allow us to emerge, although changed forever by what we have experienced and witnessed, as whole and integral persons.

Thus, may we forgive and remember—remember our worth and dignity; remember those who have helped and listened to us in our despair; and remember the solace and comfort of God's constant presence in our lives, from which we may ever draw strength, courage, and healing.

Let us read now responsively.

Touch with your healing power the minds and hearts of all who suffer from sickness, injury, or disability, and make them flourish again.

Receive our prayer, O God of life.

Touch with your healing power the minds and hearts of all who live in confusion or doubt, and fill them with your light.

Receive our prayer, O God of life.

Touch with your healing power the minds and hearts of all who are burdened by anguish, despair, or isolation, and set them free in love.

Receive our prayer, O God of life.

Break the bonds of those who are imprisoned by fear, compulsion, secrecy, and silence.

Come with your healing power, O God.

Fill with peace those who grieve over separation and loss.

Come with your healing power, O God.

Teach us self-and other-forgiveness, that our anger, grief, humiliation, degradation, and anguished guilt may become a re-membering of empowerment and love.

Come with your healing power, O God.

Affirming

God of Grace, you nurture us with a love deeper than any we know, and from your river flows healing and salvation always.

We praise and thank you, O God.

God of love, you enter into our lives, our pain, and our brokenness, and you stretch out your healing hands to us wherever we are.

We praise and thank you, O God.

God of strength, you fill us with your presence and send us forth with love and healing to all whom we meet.

We praise and thank you, O God.

Blessing

Benediction "The Hero in You" by Mariah Carey

Silence *(Feel free to leave as you are ready)*

Mary Krueger & Bobbi Patterson _____

Ritual of Healing Touch

One: We are here because our sister/brother, _____, is preparing again for the regime of chemotherapy and stem cell transplant. Her/his body is being threatened by a cancer.

All: _____ *[name]*, we come to this ritual of healing tonight as your family. You are part of our life and we cherish you. We rejoice in your laughter, we celebrate your determination, and we marvel at your courage.

One: As your companions, we are also willing to hear your fears, and to be with you in your pain, and to honor your right to make your own decisions about your treatment and your health care.

All: We are committed to walking with you as you struggle against this disease.

(Two matching candles are lighted. One will remain in our sanctuary and be lighted each day as part of a prayer vigil. The other will go with _____ to remind her/him s/he is being held in prayer.)

One: Tonight, _____, we give thanks for your presence in our midst, and we pray with our whole hearts for the success of your treatment. Some of us will travel with you to the hospital; some will care for your home, your pets, your business. Some of us will encourage you with cards and letters and calls; some of us will hold you in prayer each and every day.

All: All of us will hope with God for your healing.

[The community is invited forward to lay hands on the person desiring healing and pray together the following prayer of support and hope.]

May the life-giving spirit of God which first breathed life into you, now surround you, uphold you, and flow through you. May God's tender compassion heal your wounded body and renew your weary spirit. May Her "fierce tenderness" surround with the assurance of support and care and His gentle peace be a safe retreat for your fear. May our courage encourage you in times of fear or loneliness, and our strength be a resource when the way is long and hard. May the light of Christ be faithfully present with you and give you hope as your body struggles toward healing. Amen.

The phrase, fierce tenderness, is from Mary Hunt's *Fierce Tenderness: A Feminist Theology of Friendship.*

_____ *Leslie Penrose*

Celebrating Recovery

One: _____ and _____, we are your family. The joys and sorrows of your life are our joys and sorrows too. We grieve with you when failure and loss and pain are part of your journey, and we celebrate with you when success and renewal and joy are part of your life.

All: Today we celebrate with you! We celebrate and give thanks to God for the gift, and the hard work, of sobriety!

One: _____ *[name of recovering person]*, we celebrate the courage it has taken for you to get sober: to ask for help when you have needed it, to seek out and complete treatment, to faithfully attend meetings even when you don't want to, to continue, over and over again, to claim the power of truth and honesty as healing and life-giving, and to entrust yourself and your journey to God, even when God seems far away.

One: We give thanks for the support of your family, given and chosen, and your employer in the midst of your decision not to let alcohol steal any more of your life. And we celebrate the new life you are discovering as a result of your sobriety.

One: _____ *[partner's name]*, we also celebrate with you, your commitment to recovery from your own kind of dependency and your decision to participate in Al-Anon.

One: _____ and _____, we recognize that recovery is an on-going process—a journey one cannot do alone—a journey in which we all participate and for which we all need one another. We also acknowledge that we all share a need for God's grace and empowerment in our lives.

All: Today we celebrate with you the gift, and the hard work, of sobriety! And we pledge to you, as companions in the journey toward wholeness, our solidarity in the struggle to stay sober.

Community Blessing of Solidarity
[symbolic gesture of surrounding the couple and praying for them]

God of Grace and Glory, Bearer of the New Day, and Source of all Life and Being, embrace _____ in your liberating power as s/he continues to fight for a life free of alcohol. Give her/him courage, and wisdom, and strength. Hold _____ also as s/he strives to love and support _____ in life-giving ways. Surround them with the power of this gathered community and walk with them through both the trials and the triumphs of each day.

Help us, O God, as a community of faith and struggle, of forgiveness and hope, to live in ways that model life and wholeness. Empower us as we journey with _____ and _____ and one another, to seek justice, to offer respect and compassion, and to trust your promise of shalom. Amen.

Leslie Penrose _____

[The following four services were developed around the broad theme of Proclaiming Jubilee; each has a separate focus within that theme: renew, release, reconcile and rejoice.]

Renewal Service

[Worship service with water renewal ritual designed more broadly than a baptism renewal. Materials needed include: water pitcher; water; 4-5 small bowls (large enough to fit fingers in); marbles or other glass beads available at craft store (enough for each person in the congregation to take one). Depending on the size of the congregation, plan for 4-5 water-bearer stations.

Prior to the service, fill the pitcher with water and ensure there will be enough water to fill all bowls 2/3 full. Divide the glass beads & place in bowls. Arrange bowls & water pitcher on the communion table. Give water bearers suggestions on what to say to the congregation as each person dips her/his hand in the bowl and takes a glass bead. Suggestions include "Go with God," "God bless you," "Peace be with you," "Amen."

During the ritual, water is poured from the pitcher into each bowl and each water bearer is given a bowl and moves to a designated station. The congregation is invited to come to one of the water stations to dip their fingers and take a glass bead. After all participants have had a chance to visit a water station, the water bearers place the bowls on the table and return to their seats.]

Gathering Hymn "Bring Many Names" Brian Wren *see p. 277*

[A Shofar is blown (or, as an alternative, bells around the room are rung at random) to introduce the scripture reading]

Hebrew Scripture Leviticus 25:9-10

One: We have come proclaiming Jubilee!

All: We have gathered to renew, release, reconcile, and rejoice.

One: Renewing of mind, body, and spirit,
        Releasing the captive within us,
        Reconciling the alienated,
        Rejoicing in God's great mercy.

All: The day of atonement has come.
        The trumpet has sounded.
        Let the Jubilee begin!

Response "Halle-Halle-Halleluja!" *see p. 298*

Centering Prayer

Great and mighty God, as the clarion blast fades,
we gather as one mind and body to listen to your word.
Open our hearts to understanding.

Hebrew Scripture Isaiah 43:19-21

Behold, I am doing a new thing; now it springs forth, do you
not perceive it?
I will make a way in the wilderness and rivers in the desert.
The wild beasts will honor me, the jackals and the ostriches;
for I give water in the wilderness, rivers in the desert,
to give drink to my chosen people,
the people whom I formed for myself that they might declare
my praise.

Psalter Psalm 104 with sung response

Sermon

Hymn of Commitment "Go Down Moses" Afro-American
spiritual, adapt and arr. by William Farley Smith
(verses sung by cantor, congregation sings bolded refrain)

When Israel was in Egypt's land, **let my people go**;
   oppressed so hard they could not stand,

let my people go. Go down, Moses, way down in Egypt's land;

tell old Pharaoh to **let my people go!**

Your foes shall not before you stand, **let my people go**;
   and you'll possess fair Canaan's land,

let my people go. Go down, Moses, way down in Egypt's land;

tell old Pharaoh to **let my people go!**

We need not always weep and mourn, **let my people go**;
   and wear those slavery chains forlorn, **let my people go.**
   Go down, Moses, way down in Egypt's land;

tell old Pharaoh to **let my people go!**

O let us all from bondage flee, **let my people go;**
   and let us all in Christ be free,

let my people go. Go down, Moses, way down in Egypt's land;

tell old Pharaoh to **let my people go!**

Blessing of the Water

[During the reading of the blessing, several participants offer movement as a way of symbolizing the water. One participant is needed for each aisle and uses a banner to mimic water waves.

Holding onto the end of the rods, participants move the banners over their heads and around their bodies to create shapes such as figure eights, circles, zigzags and spiral designs. Participants walk slowly up and down the aisles to keep the banners flowing, beginning on the cue "In the beginning..." and ending on "Amen."]

Materials needed for each participant:

8' long by 1' wide silk banner in various shades of blue

1/2" diameter by 1' dowel rod

Each banner should be securely fastened to one end of a dowel rod.

*G*racious God, we thank you that in every age you have
made water a sign of your presence.
In the beginning, your Spirit brooded over the waters and they
became the source of all creation.
You led your people Israel through the waters of the Red Sea
to their new land of freedom and hope.
In the waters of the Jordan, your Son was baptized by John
and anointed with your Spirit for his ministry of
reconciliation...
May this same Spirit bless the water we use tonight, that it may
be a fountain of deliverance and new creation.

This is the water that comes to us as rain in drought...
This is the water that slakes our staggering thirst.

This is the water through which we experience the healing
and wholeness of your Spirit as hope in oppression
promising us that a time will come when all is good.

May this water remind us in your name
to banish discrimination...
to wash its wounds away...
to break the bread of freedom...
and to declare a holy day.

*C*ome, Spirit, come and be a new reality.
Renew us as we acknowledge that you are the victory, you are
the grace,
And you are the reason this gathering is a holy place.

*C*ome, Spirit,
renew the hearts of all gathered for prayer and praise,
renew the structures that order our lives,

renew the lifestyles that structure our days,
renew the earth with countless initiatives for justice and
    peace,
liberation and life now and every day.
Let the people say: **AMEN!**

Invitation to the water

Come now to one of the stations near you to touch the water
and be renewed.

Words of Meditation

Water flows from high in the mountains.
Water runs deep in the earth.
Water comes to us from God
    and sustains all life.
Water flows over these hands,
    may I use them skillfully to....

Response Refrain from "Water of Life" by Jaime Cortez, Bob
Hurd

Anthem "As Water To the Thirsty" by Timothy Dudley-Smith and
Brian Coleman

Prayer of Thanksgiving

One: Let us rejoice in the faithfulness of our covenant God.

All: **We give thanks for all that God has already given
us. As members of the body of Christ and in this
gathering of Jubilee, help us to claim your promise
as our own, that we might faithfully participate in
the ministries of the church by our prayers, our
presence, our gifts, and our service, that in everything God may be glorified through Jesus Christ.
Thanks be to God, AMEN.**

Hymn "Blessed Assurance" Words by Fanny J. Crosby; music by
Phoebe P. Knapp
   (Add this new refrain after third verse)

This is our story, this is our song, praising our Savior all the
day long, this is our story, this is our song, praising our Savior
all the day long.

Release

Call to Worship

Leader   In the beginning was God, and God begat the rhythm of creation, and the rhythm begat everything else, and the dance began. *[slow, rhythmic drum beat begins]*

People   **As the rhythm sounds, creation happens.**

Leader   We are a people bound together through sacred sound.

People   **As rhythm sounds, communion happens.**

Leader   Our faith leads us to a world reverberating like a thousand different thunders.

People   **As rhythm sounds, work and play become one.**

Leader   We are part of a rhythmic universe as we listen to one another.

People   **As rhythm sounds, opposition ceases.**

Leader   We are all companions of life's rhythms in our stillness and motion; in the sound and silence, our souls are uplifted.

People   **As rhythm sounds, we are standing on sacred ground.**

[Continue the drum beat and transition into the opening song]

Hymn "All Creatures Raise your Bells and Ring!" *adapted from* "*All Creatures of our God and King*"

Substitute the words "All creatures raise your bells and ring!" in the opening line. Sing last verse slowly.

Litany of Lamentation

[Based on Lamentation 5 and excerpts from personal stories. The scripture verses are read by reader 1. Various readers, seated throughout the congregation, stand and read their lines.]

Reader 1   Remember, O LORD, what has befallen us; look, and see our disgrace! Our inheritance has been turned over to strangers, our homes to aliens. We have become orphans, fatherless; our mothers are like widows.

Reader 2   When I told my family the truth about myself, they decided I no longer belonged to them. They return my cards and letters unopened. In their world, I do not exist.

Reader 1   We must pay for the water we drink; the wood we get must be bought. With a yoke on our necks we are hard driven; we are weary, we are given no rest.

Reader 3   I've been elected to General Conference as a delegate again. I remember the pain of last time. Can I bear it once more? Can I continue to hold the door open for those who despise me?

Reader 1   We have made a pact with Egypt and Assyria, to get enough bread.

Reader 4   I'm the pastor of a reconciling congregation. I worry that I might not be appointable to another congregation.

Reader 1   Our ancestors sinned; they are no more, and we bear their iniquities.

Reader 5   "...we do not condone the practice of homosexuality and consider this practice incompatible with Christian teaching.... Since the practice of homosexuality is incompatible with Christian teaching, self-avowed practicing homosexuals are not to be accepted as candidates, ordained as ministers, or appointed to serve The United Methodist Church" (quoted from the United Methodist *Book of Discipline*).

Reader 1   Slaves rule over us; there is no one to deliver us from their hand. We get our bread at the peril of our lives, because of the sword in the wilderness.

Reader 6   I'm scared coming home late at night because of the rainbow sticker on my car. I've been run off the road before.

Reader 7   My partner and I met at work. After our relationship became public, we were told that we would need to find other employment.

Reader 1   Our skin is burned from the heat of famine.

Reader 8   My partner and I were active members of our congregation. But after the Judicial Council's ruling that ministers could be tried for conducting holy unions, we felt we could no longer remain loyal to a denomination that refuses to affirm the sacredness of our committed relationship.

Reader 1   Women are raped in Zion, virgins in the towns of Judah.

Reader 9   For thirteen years, I tried to live in a heterosexual marriage, denying my passions and the truth about who I am. Finally, I could no longer deny the wholeness God wants for me.

Reader 1   Princes are hung up by their hands; no respect is shown to the elders.

Reader 10   I graduated with honors and awards from seminary, but my conference will not ordain me because of whom I love.

Reader 1   Young men are compelled to grind, and boys stagger under loads of wood. The old men have left the city gate, the young men their music.

Reader 11   I was afraid to admit my love for the arts, to show my feelings—living up to the stereotype proscribed by my father kept me in a confusing place, a lonely closet.

Reader 1   The joy of our hearts has ceased; our dancing has been turned to mourning.

Reader 12   As a fourth generation Methodist minister, I have been proud to claim my heritage. But now as this church struggles, I feel my own passion for ministry waning under the weight of threatened division.

Reader 1   The crown has fallen from our head; woe to us, for we have sinned!

Reader 13	I'm scared to take a stand for what I know to be God's justice. What if someone questions MY sexuality? What if someone asks me if I'M gay?
Reader 1	Because of this, our hearts are sick; because of these things, our eyes have grown dim,
Reader 14	As a teenager, growing into a realization of my own sexuality, I felt so bad about myself that I just wanted it all to end. I didn't want to live.
Reader 1	Because of Mount Zion, which lies desolate; jackals prowl over it.
Reader 15	Until the church proclaims the holiness of all of God's people, including Gay, Lesbian, Bisexual and Transgender persons, society will condemn us and those who stand with us and degrade us to a "less than human" status.
Reader 1	But you, O LORD, reign forever; your throne endures to all generations.
ALL	**Convict and transform us, O God, with your reign of love. Restore the church and release us from bondage. Give us the courage to proclaim and celebrate Jubilee. Amen.**

Sung Response "Inspired by Love and Anger"   *see p. 350*

Prayers of the People & Congregational Response
(use an appropriate musical antiphon)

Out of the depths I cry to thee; Lord, hear me, I implore thee!

Scripture Luke 4:15-21

Proclamation

An Improvisation on "Re-"
[Dancer requests from congregation three or four words that begin with "re" that typified the struggle in the church and then creates a dance movement symbolizing those words; the last word improvised is used to transition the congregation into the singing of the final song "Freedom."]

Song "Freedom" (South African)   *see p. 296*

Closing Song of Release "When Israel Camped in Sinai" Text: Laurence G. Bernier, Music: George J. Webb.

Benediction

Reconcile

Gathering Music

Song of Confession "Help Us Accept Each Other" Words by Fred Kaan, Music by John Ness Beck.

see p. 123 for movement instructions

Body Prayer of Confession —*Circle of Love*

Signs of Peace and Response "Ubi Caritas"

A Contemporary Story, *The Three Little Wolves & the Big Bad Pig* by Eugene Trivizas

Anthem "We are the Body of Christ" by Jaime Cortez and Bob Hurd

Ancient Sayings 1 Cor 3:18-23, II Cor 5:13-20

Proclamation

Prayers for the Church

*G*racious God, we pray for Your holy church...
We come knowing that the night is very dark but we remember that...
"Only when it's dark enough, can you see the stars."*

from Dr. Martin Luther King Jr.'s speech "I See the Promised Land," April 3, 1968

*W*ondrous God, we come to you with open arms and outstretched hands, we come with open eyes, not deceiving ourselves.

*W*e know, "it's alright to talk about 'long white robes over yonder,' in all of its symbolism."*
But ultimately people who are Gay, Lesbian, Bisexual or Transgendered need to know that you, oh God, can cover them in love right now.
It's alright to talk about "pearly gates," but help us open our doors to those who feel shut out and lonely.
It's alright to talk about "mansions in glory," but youth who have been kicked out by their parents and families need a roof over their heads.

It's alright to talk about "streets of gold," but young men and
women like Matthew Shepard and Billy Jack Gaither need
a safe place to walk without fear.

Eternal God, we come knowing that all things belong to you,
life, death, the present and future.

Forgive the church, O Merciful God, for trusting in the wisdom
of this age. Help us to come as fools who are willing to
trust in Your Wisdom.

Oh God, who reconciled the world through Christ Jesus, open
the minds and hearts of an unwilling church to see a new
creation.

Help your church to answer the dilemmas of today with "a
kind of dangerous unselfishness."*

Help your church "to rise up with a greater readiness, and
stand with a greater determination."*

Urge us on to be ambassadors for Christ and claim the message of reconciliation.

Closing Song "All Are Welcome" Text and Music by Marty
Haugen see p. 276

*[Liturgical movement can be used during this song to "build the house"
where all are welcome. See page 126 for a description of the movement.]*

Benediction

Rejoice

[For this service: 6x8 foot free-standing panels may be used with a variety of small bells tied to them. Ensure that there are enough bells for every participant to have one. Participants will remove a bell of their choosing and "ring" the Jubilee as the benediction].

Call to Worship

One: May justice roll down like waters renewing our desert experiences,

Many: **And may the rhythm of love release us from our fear.**

One: Rejoice, and know that the land belongs to God, we belong to God—all is restored, all are reconciled.

Many: **Let the spirit of Jubilee ring throughout our lives. Amen**.

[Have pre-arranged individuals shake the panels of bells so that they ring out.]

see p. 324

Bell Choir Anthem "The Year of Jubilee is Here" adapted and bell arrangement by Carl Wiltse.

Hymn "Jesus Christ, Hope of the World" music by Joao Carlos Gottinari, text by Edmundo Reinhardt, translation by Pablo Sosa

see p. 349

Offering of Ourselves & Sung Response (refrain from "Jesus Christ, Hope of the World")

We often think that giving an offering to God means giving money, but our commitment to give involves so much more than our financial contributions.

It is about our time, talents, gifts and our service. It is also about our willingness to be vulnerable—to open ourselves up to the very hard work of reconciliation. We offer our willingness to continue in the face of setbacks, failures and limited success.

Our theme of Jubilee reminds us that no human authority—be it bishops or the judicial council—can ultimately control the UMC and force it in directions determined by their own limitations. At the heart of the gospel is the message of God's love, which values all persons equally. Practices and structures that deny this stand in violation of the divine will and must be overturned.

We, therefore, must be engaged in the work of reform. We must challenge the church's oppression no matter the intensity of the opposition. The Reconciling Congregation Program is charged with holding before the church the truth of the gospel, proclaiming the year of Jubilee—the time of deliverance and freedom.

To begin the challenging journey, we'll have several groups bring their reports—their "offering"—to say just a sentence or two about what they're planning in the year to come. Then, later on in the service, we'll give you an opportunity to complete a card offering your own commitment to this work.

Let the youth, LGBT group and persons of color come forward and make their offering, and we will respond with the refrain from "Jesus Christ, Hope of the World." Then, the parents, students/ seminarians and clergy groups will come forward, and we will again respond with the refrain from "Jesus Christ, Hope of the World."

Invitation to the Table

Reader 1: Why do we keep coming back to this table which some would argue offers a meaningless, ancient ritual which no one fully understands and makes the service too long? And we ask the same question of the church. Why do we keep coming back to this church which specifically excludes Gays, Lesbians, Bisexuals, and Transgender persons?

Reader 2: I come, and I suspect it is the same for many of you, because it is here, at the table and in the community of believers, where we experience God's acceptance, grace, forgiveness and hope. And we come because it is often at the altar when we are surprised by God's presence.

Reader 1: Far from being a useless ritual created by ancient peoples to make our worship time longer, this is a time and place when we are reminded that there is no separation between our time and God's time—all time is holy.

Reader 2: So we take time to come to the table, to breathe in the faith of each other, to experience that trust has tasted good.

Reader 1: We keep coming back, because here we are offered a
new beginning—
a chance to feast on the bread of life
and to be the bread that feeds a tired and weary world.
And we drink deeply of the living cup—
to quench our thirst for the desert times to which we
are called.

Reader 2: The Eucharist is not something we do, but something
we are.
Holy Communion is the way we will be in the world.
We take the body of Christ into the world and live it—
we become the Eucharist for the world.

Reader 1: And so let us again come to the table to experience
Eucharist.

Reader 2: This is Christ's table, so all are invited to partake,
whether you're a member of this denomination or any
church. Christ invites to the table all who love him, who
earnestly repent of their sin and seek to live in peace
with one another.
Therefore, let us acknowledge now those things that
have separated us from God.

Silent Confession and Choral Response "Kyrie eleison"

Hebrew Scripture Isaiah 62:6-12

Anthem "Revival in the Land"

Proclamation

A Moment of Reflective Silence

Offertory

Doxology Words by Brian Wren

Praise God, the Giver and the Gift.
Hearts, minds and voices now uplift:
Alleluia! Alleluia!
Praise, praise the Breath of glad surprise,
freeing, uplifting, opening eyes,
Three-in-Oneness, Love communing,
Alleluia! Alleluia! Alleluia!

The Great Thanksgiving

May God be with you.

And also with you.

Lift up your hearts.

We lift them up to our God.

Let us give thanks to our God.

It is right to give our thanks and praise.

Blessed are you, O God, who created us to love one another and who called us to be a covenant community.

We come today, gathered in gratitude: grateful for this community and for your creation, all of which belong to you, grateful for the cycles of sowing and reaping, for the joy of work & play & rest, and for your Jubilee that restores the equality of all persons.

And so, we join our voices in song, as our ancestors have done before us, to praise your name and join their unending hymn: *see p. 300*

> **Le lo le lo lay lo,   Le lo le lo lay, lo,**
> **Le lo le lo lay lo lo   Lay lo lo le lo le lo lai.**
> *(Repeat)*

Leader: Holy, holy, holy, God of power and might

People: **Holy, holy, holy, God of power and might**

Leader: Heaven and earth are full of your glory

People: **Heaven and earth are full of your glory**

Leader: Hosanna in the highest.
Hosanna in the highest.

People: **Hosanna in the highest.**
Hosanna in the highest.

Leader: Blessed is the One who comes in the name of the Lord.

People: **Blessed is the One who comes in the name of the Lord.**

Leader: Hosanna in the highest.
Hosanna in the highest.

People: **Hosanna in the highest.**
Hosanna in the highest.

All: **Le lo le lo lay lo,   Le lo le lo lay lo,**
Le lo le lo lay lo lo   Lay lo lo le lo le lo lai.

> *(Repeat)*

Holy are you, God, and blessed is this gathering today, for we come around this table as a foretaste of the heavenly banquet—as a model of your realm on earth. This day we are reminded that you created and are creating a world of diversity and change—of new things. By coming to this table, we participate in your creation.

At this table, we can be present with Jesus on the night before meeting with death, when he took bread, was thankful for it, and broke it for his disciples saying, "This is my body which is given for you. Do this in remembrance of me."

And likewise after an evening of fellowship and eating together around the table, he took the cup saying, "This cup poured out for you is the new covenant in my blood. Drink of it, all of you."

And so, he initiated this holy sacrament—a way to remember your presence through Christ—a way for us to celebrate your presence among us. And in our participating, we become for others a continual remembrance of your presence among us.

And so, we participate in this holy mystery and offer to make real the memory of Christ in the world. Christ is present for us so we can be present for the world as we proclaim the mystery of faith:

**Christ has died, Christ is risen,
Christ will come again.**

Pour out your Holy Spirit on us gathered here and on these gifts of bread and the fruit of the vine.

Make them be the bread of life and the quenching cup of blessing, so that we may feast and drink deeply and be the Eucharist for the world, co-creating the realm of God until all are reconciled, and we feast at your table forever.

Through Christ, with Christ, in Christ, in the unity of the Holy Spirit in your holy church, all honor and glory is yours, Almighty God, now and forever.

And now, with the confidence of children of God, let us pray:

**Beloved, our Father and Mother, in whom is heaven,
Hallowed be your name.
Followed be your sovereign way,
Done be your will and rule,
Throughout the whole creation.
With the bread we need for today, feed us.
In times of temptation and test, strengthen us.
From trials too great to endure, spare us.**

**For your reign is the glory of the power that is love,
Now and forever. Amen.**

The minister breaks bread while saying:

> Like the grains gathered from the field, we, who are many, are
> one body.
> The cup over which we give thanks is a sharing in the new
> covenant of Christ.

Sharing the Bread & Cup

The bread and fruit of the vine are given to the people, with these words
being exchanged:

> The bread of life, for you. **Amen.**

> Drink deeply of the living cup. *Or*
> The promise of a new covenant. **Amen.**

Post-communion prayer

Loving God, we thank you that you fed us in this Sacrament. Help
us remember that the Eucharist is not a passive activity. For when
the Eucharist stays in the sanctuary, it is distorted. Rather, gather
us to be reminded and restored, so that we may scatter to be the
body of Christ for the world. Be with us as you take us places that,
on our own, we would not go. Help us make real the power of love
in the world. Amen.

Hymn "Guide Our Feet" African American Spiritual, harmony by
Wendell Whalum, words adapted

> Guide our feet while we run this race...
> Hold our hands while we run this race...
> Stand by us while we run this race...
> We're your children while we run this race...
> for we don't want to run this race in vain!

Dismissal Jeremiah 29:11

Thus says the Lord, "For surely I know the plan I have for you,
plans for your well being and not for harm, to give you a future
with hope." *(NRSV adapted)*

Musical Benediction

*(Please take a bell from the wall and add your voice to the sounding of
Jubilee. Continue to proclaim Jubilee as you go from this place and witness throughout the world!)*

*Reconciling
Congregation Program*

Justice

A Ritual of Social Exorcism

[The occasion for a social exorcism needs to be carefully chosen. Above all, there should be a shared context of ministry and social witness. This ritual unmasks the power of evil and should be treated as a very solemn, God-given and even risky undertaking. Because this is an unusual ritual, some people may need time for orientation to the ritual and its presuppositions. It needs to be emphasized that this liturgy is genuine and not a form of guerrilla theater or show. At the close of the ritual, participants are likely to feel exhausted not only because it may have taken several hours, but also because they have been struggling with very real principalities and powers. A time of relaxing and breaking bread together is appropriate.]

Invocation and Introduction *[An introduction should emphasize the ritual's serious intent and the central focus of the power of God in Jesus Christ rather than the power of evil].*

Scripture *[Mark 11:15-19, Romans 8:35-39, Colossians 1:11-17, or other pertinent passages may be used.]*

Discernment of the Spirits and Powers *[Following a period of silent prayer for discernment, the gathered community identifies the spirits not of God which hold captive the given institution; for instance, these may be the Spirits of Mammon, Domination, Fear, Greed, Arrogance, or Contempt for the Poor. There can be a sharing or general listing of the spirits which the group identifies as well as a common sensing of the key ones to name in the ritual. If the service involves a large group, this discernment could be done in advance by smaller groups.]*

Confession *[It is critical for participants to search their hearts for ways in which they collaborate with the spirits and powers named.]*

Absolution *[A clear and compelling absolution is pronounced in the name and power of Jesus Christ.]*

Holy Communion *[This emphasizes Christ triumphant over the powers of sin and death.]*

Words of Deliverance

We discern that there are influences and spirits not of God which are preying upon *[name of the institution, government, or entity]* and holding it captive to alien principalities and powers.

In the name and power of Jesus Christ, we bind these spirits and powers not of God so they can do no more evil.

Receiving God's forgiveness, and with confidence in Christ, who cast out demons and drove the agents of Mammon from the temple, we declare these spirits are exposed, discredited, and stripped of their power.

In the name and power of Jesus Christ, we declare that all ties have been severed between *[the institution]* and any previous incidents; influences; history; policy; traditions; theories; customs; authorities; financial or political groups; and government institutions or individuals who have become conduits, advisors, or channels misdirecting it, or person who are connected to it, for ungodly ends.

Let us now order the ungodly spirits to depart.

Spirit of *[insert name]*, in the name and power of Jesus Christ, we order you to depart from *[the institution]* and surrender before God.

Spirit of *[insert name]*, **in the name and power of Jesus Christ, we order you to depart from** *[the institution]* **and surrender before God.**

[Continue for each spirit, and repeat as you feel led.]

Prayer for Renewal of the Institution's Purpose

O God, we thank you for your power over spirits that defy you. We ask you now to fill *[the institution]* with a clean heart.

Where there was _____, fill it with _____.
Where there was _____, fill it with _____.

[continue with each spirit named above. Examples of couplets in the above prayer would be: Fear-Love, Patriarchy-Mutuality, Domination-Humility, Greed-Generosity, Arrogance-Humility, Contempt for the Poor-Solidarity with the Poor.]

[You may at this point also wish to pray for the renewal of the baptismal vows of any known Christian leaders of the given institution. It might include the actual names of the participants and of the decision makers of the institution. The prayer could take the following form:]

God, we pray that Christian decision makers, and we ourselves, may be strengthened in our resolve to renounce the spiritual forces of wickedness, to reject the evil powers of this world, and to repent of our sin. Enable us to accept the freedom and power you give us to resist evil, injustice, and oppression in whatever forms they represent themselves and to be faithful to the in-breaking of your reign.

Prayer of Thanksgiving and for the Continuing Witness for Justice

[This prayer could embrace both the particular context for this service as well as situations in which others are working for justice.]

Exhortation *[Ephesians 6:10-18 is especially appropriate here. "Finally, be strong in Christ and in strength of Christ's power. Put on then the whole armor of God..." At the end of the reading, participants could accept this empowerment and protection by repeating a Litany of Confirmation based upon the passage.]*

I take upon myself the whole armor and protection of God. I fasten the belt of truth around my waist. I put on the breastplate of righteousness.
On my feet I place that which makes me ready to proclaim the gospel of peace.
I take up the shield of faith to quench all the flaming arrows of the evil one.
I put on the helmet of salvation and the sword of the spirit, which is the word of God.
I will pray in the spirit at all times, keep alert, and persevere in supplication for all the saints.

Benediction (from Ephesians 3: 20-21)

Now to the One who by the power at work within us is able to accomplish abundantly far more than we can ask or imagine, to God be glory in the church and in Christ Jesus to all generations, forever and ever. Amen.

George McClain

A Litany of Repentance, Healing, and Commitment

[*This litany was offered by a coalition including Affirmation, In All Things Charity, Methodist Federation for Social Action, and Reconciling Congregation Program in response to the trial of a United Methodist clergyman, who, on November 17, 1999, was found by a Church Trial court in Nebraska, guilty of "disobedience to the Order and Discipline of the United Methodist Church." They rendered that verdict because the Reverend Jimmy Creech had conducted a service of Holy Union for two men. As penalty, the trial court removed Jimmy's clergy credentials.*

The coalition stated that "in taking this action the United Methodist Church again inflicts injury on its own body. It not only dismisses a gifted, courageous, and faithful pastor; it also continues the spiritual violence of the church against lesbian, gay, bisexual and transgendered persons. All of the body of Christ is wounded by such an injury. God grieves the church's sin and brokenness."]

Leader/**People**

We come this day as a broken and wounded people.

In our pain we turn to God for healing and forgiveness.

One more expression of the church's violation of God's children is upon our hearts.

What we have done and what we failed to do enabled this injury. We have tolerated that which is intolerable: the rejection by our church of God's gift of love and dignity for part of our family.

We repent.

In the midst of our hurt, our anger, our guilt, we pray for God's forgiveness, for God's healing, for God's strength.

We offer prayers for ourselves, for one another, for our brother Jimmy Creech, his wife Chris and their family, and for our church. *(Pray in silence)*

Our prayers are not complete with silent or spoken thoughts and cries. If the desperately needed healing is to continue, our prayers must also take the form of commitment and action.

God's grace reaches out to us, to our world and to our church. But we must respond with our hearts and our lives.

Let those who are willing and able come forward to offer themselves for the work of justice, healing, and faithfulness to which God calls us in this critical time. *(You are invited to come forward to receive the blessing of this gathering for your commitment. If you are not able to come forward but wish to make this commitment, please indicate your participation in a visible way possible for you.)* Let those now gathered receive and extend this commitment and blessing.

We will not rest until this injury and sin is gone from our midst. From the cauldron of our tears, anger, hope, and faith, our commitment is born. Only by God's presence and power will that commitment be realized. Only by our action and support for one another will we be agents for that presence and power. We offer ourselves to be God's people for this time. May the Spirit be with us as we challenge the violence, the hatred, the ignorance and the injury within us and around us.

So be it.

Amen.

UM Coalition

Light One Candle for Solidarity

[In response to an investigative hearing of a charge against 67 United Methodist pastors who conducted a ceremony of blessing for a California lesbian couple, churches from across the country created ritual blessings of solidarity candles that were then shipped to California to be lighted at the hearing.]

Reader 1   As members of the community of faith, we stand with those accused of violating church law for blessing the committed love of a couple.

Reader 2   God, said, "Let there be light."

People   **We light one candle that it may be a symbol to us and to sisters and brothers far away of the warmth of our community in Jesus Christ. May the heat of this candle give warmth and compassion to the testimonies as they are given and heard.**

Reader 1   We light one candle in solidarity with those who will witness on behalf of an inclusive church.

Reader 2	Jesus said, "You are the light of the world...let your light shine before others."
People	**May the light give wisdom and courage to those being questioned. May the light of God's love and justice shine in the hearts and minds of all persons.**
Reader 1	We light one candle in solidarity with those who are Lesbian, Gay, Bisexual, and Transgender—out, closeted, lay, clergy, alone, in community—our sisters, our brothers, our friends, ourselves.
Reader 2	John said, "God is the light and in God is not darkness at all. Whoever says, 'I am in the light' while hating a brother or sister is still in the darkness."
People	**May the energy generated by this candle empower us to remain faithful in our ministries of grace and acceptance.**
Reader 1	We light one candle to send our spirit of community, offering a message of hope, a prayer for justice, and a shout of gratitude to those who have stood courageously for the inclusion of all people. May they be guided by the light of Christ to lead the whole church into the light of God's love.
Reader 2	For the message you have heard from the scriptures is that "we should love one another."
All	**May the flame of this candle continue to burn beyond this day until the time arrives when all people shall be able to freely honor, celebrate and share the covenants they make with each other, with their families, and with God.**
Reader 1	And all God's people said,
All	**Amen. And amen.**

[The candle is lit.]

Euclid, University, and Wheadon UMCs

A Ritual of Solidarity

*[This litany was used at the Biennial Meeting of American Baptist
Churches, USA, to dedicate candles brought by welcoming churches.
After the meeting, candles and copies of the litanies were returned to dis-
fellowshipped churches and other churches under fire with the following
note: This candle and litany are shared with you as a Welcoming and
Affirming expression of solidarity from other American Baptist persons
and communities. Receive and use them however they may benefit and
encourage your ministry.]*

Leader   From the very beginning, the Divine Word of meaning,
love, and divine creativity has been generating a new
day.

People   **The Word was with God, and indeed the Word
was God.**

Leader   All things came into being through this Word of divine
insight and graceful creation,

People   **And through the love of Christ we have met
this Word face to face.**

Leader   In this Word was life, and this life was the light of all
humanity.

People   **Nevertheless, throughout the ages, women and
men have sought the comfort of denial.**

Leader   The impulse is to hide.

People   **They have chosen a reality which is made of
fig leaves.**

Leader   In the garden, they asked "Why would God create us to
look like *this*?"

People   **And even in our churches today, some ask
"Why would God create anyone to *be* like
that?"**

Leader   So men and women continue to recreate God in the
image of their own denial and fear.

People   **But the light shines in the darkness, and the
darkness has not overcome it.**

Leader   Yet, some prefer to "turn out" out the light;

People   **Others who claim to be "of the light" just turn
their backs;**

Leader	And still others seek the shadows of caution for the sake of "unity;"
People	**Meanwhile, there is this candle.**
Leader	This candle comes to us from friends who stand with us in solidarity.
People	**This candle is a tangible prayer and declaration—an affirmation that the light still shines in the darkness.**
Leader	*(Singing)* Blest be the tie that binds our hearts in Christian love;
People	*(Singing)* **The fellowship of kindred minds is like to that above.**
Leader	O God, our choice is not to be rebels in search of a name.
People	**Our prayer is for an authentic place to stand and lives that ring true from the very depths of our souls.**
Leader	We thank you for others who walk this path with us;
People	**Accept us all as instruments of your peace.**
Leader	Grant us the serenity, the courage and the wisdom to let our lives be like this candle—
People	**Burning brightly in testimony to the light that shines in the darkness—and that the darkness has not, cannot, and will not ever put it out.**
Leader	The Lord is risen—
People	**Christ is risen indeed!**
Leader	And so are we!
All	*(Singing)*
	This little light of mine, I'm going to let it shine.
	This little light of mine, I'm going to let it shine.
	This little light of mine, I'm going to let it shine.
	Everywhere I go!

Terryl & Marvin Marsh

Transition

This ritual was created for a clergy woman leaving the UM ministry in order to take a job where she could live fully and openly as a Lesbian.

Sending Out to New Ministry

_____ [name], this is a powerful time of transition and change in your life. As companions with you in faith and struggle, we know some of the work that has preceded this moment, and we value the gifts and skills that it recognizes and affirms. It is with great joy that tonight we celebrate with you both the accomplishments and the potential that this calling to a new ministry represents. We also know that this, like any transition, brings both anticipation and grief.

You are leaving a place and a form of ministry that you have been part of for many years, and you leave behind a part of who you have been. You leave:

— a network of co-workers, friends, and companions in ministry:
— a group of students who have in many ways become your family,
— a familiarity with how things are done and with what is expected,
— an official appointment with insurance and retirement benefits and certain guarantees.

There will be grief, and perhaps even moments of regret. And soon, you begin anew—a new job, a new ministry in a new place with new people and new procedures.

This new job will have its challenges, its frustrations, its disappointments, just as the old one did, but it also holds the potential for greater use of your creativity and energy. It offers the possibility of new learnings, and the opportunity to develop new skills. And perhaps, most importantly, this move signals an intentional step in your ongoing commitment to live with integrity and to honor your call to a ministry of justice and hope.

Are there thoughts or feelings you would like to share about this time of endings and beginnings?

[Response of one leaving.]

Congregational Response

As we celebrate with you the joy and hope of this new ministry, we also celebrate with you the authority that your voice will derive from it. We are

grateful that you will be working and teaching in places where you can influence the future of the church. And as your community of faith, we call you to remember that authority carries with it responsibility, and the authority to speak and teach within the tradition of Jesus carries with it the responsibility to risk. We are hopeful that because of your voice and others, the future of the church holds the promise of more justice and more compassion for all God's people.

[A candle bearing the word "Hope" is lighted and presented to the one leaving as the community repeats the fellowship litany used to open each service.]

One: Lighting this candle is our witness that in all things, we have chosen to hope rather than curse the darkness.

All: **We live in God's world. We are called to be God's people. In life, in death, in life beyond death, we are not alone.**

Song "Go Now in Peace" by Natalie Sleeth

_____ *Leslie Penrose*

Celebrating Homecoming after Incarceration!

One: _____ *[name]*, you are part of our family. The joys and sorrows of your life are our joys and sorrows too. Three years ago, we grieved with you when you were incarcerated, and since that time we have held you in prayer...

as your child was born and cared for by others in our community,

as hopes for parole were raised and crushed time and time again,

as promises were made and broken, time served was lost,

privileges were denied, and hope grew weary.

All: **Today we celebrate and thank God for your release from incarceration and your presence among us. We share your joy, and offer our hope and our support for the gift and the hard work of this new beginning!**

One: We celebrate the courage it has taken for you to claim an honest memory...

> to use the time you were incarcerated for reflection and self-evaluation,
>
> to take seriously and complete your treatment and training programs,
>
> to reject labels that limit and dehumanize you,
>
> to continue, over and over again, to claim the power of truth and honesty as healing and life-giving, and to entrust yourself and your journey to God, even when God seems far away.

Your courage has en-couraged us.

One: We give thanks for your family's constant support over the last three years...

> their loving care of your child,
>
> the thousands of miles they drove as they visited each weekend,
>
> the hours on the telephone, the parole hearings, the sleepless nights,
>
> their refusal to let the system steal their compassion or harden their hearts,
>
> their shared tears and laughter, their witness of courage and hope in our midst.

We have seen God's faithful love through theirs.

[Response by the one returning.]

All: _____, **today we celebrate with you and with your family, the joy of your home-coming and the hope for the journey that lies ahead. We pledge our support to you, as companions in the journey toward life and wholeness.**

Community Blessing of Solidarity *[symbolic gesture of surrounding the person/family and praying for them]*

Song "This is the Day of New Beginnings" words by Brian Wren, music by Carlton R. Young

Leslie Penrose

Naming Ritual After Separation

Used by a woman to claim a new name after a divorce.

One: _____ [first name], as your community of hope and trust, we acknowledge with you this day that for too long women have been named by others—by fathers, by husbands, by masters, by cultures. We also recognize with you that names hold great power and possibility: the power and the possibility to hold and to free, to limit and to encourage, to dehumanize and to personalize. Naming ourselves is a power women have often not claimed—a power we celebrate that you are claiming this day.

_____ [first name], you have lived with the name _____ [last name] for ___ years. There are both wounds and dreams that accompany that name. We grieve with you the lost dreams and offer you our hope and presence toward the healing of the wounds.

And as you choose a new name. There are hopes and there are fears that accompany that choice. We invite you now to share with us your new name and your journey into claiming it.

[Response by the one claiming new name.]

Community Blessing

[Laying on of hands by the community]

Thanks be to you, God of our Endings and our Beginnings, for the power of this woman's name and the blessings of her life!

Community response

As a community, we now speak with joy your new name:

_____ _____!

_____ Leslie Penrose

*Designed for those
claiming new names
after covenant
ceremony.*

Naming Ritual

One: _____ *[first name]*, we have known, loved, and valued you as a participant of this community. We have celebrated the faith together, we have struggled together to resist the injustice society places upon Gay and Lesbian persons, and we have shared the honor of standing with you and your partner as you vowed your commitment of love and faithfulness to one another in a covenant service. We have been blessed by the journey and are grateful now to share in the celebration of your choice to take a new name.

_____, what name do you now let go?

[Response]

And what new name have you chosen for yourself?

[Response]

All: **For too long, Gay and Lesbian persons have been denied the legal rights and the benefits of marriage. For too long, taking the name of a life-partner in Christian marriage has also been denied same-sex couples. Today, we recognize your decision to resist that denial and to affirm your love and commitment to your partner by taking his/her name.**

From this day forward, we will know you as _____ *[full name]*. Thanks be to God for the power of your name and the blessings of your life!

Leslie Penrose

"I Am"
A Liturgy of Re-Naming for Transgender Persons

Scripture Revelation 21:1-6

One: Dearly beloved, as a people of faith, we know that God continues to shape and mold us in our growth, inviting us to claim for ourselves the people who God created us to be. Each new day is an opportunity to live more fully the promise of who we are.

Throughout history, individuals, as they have claimed their unique personhood more fully, have been given a new name, a testimony of their faithfulness.

All: **Abram was renamed Abraham.**

One: Sarai was renamed Sarah.

All: **Simon was renamed Peter.**

One: Saul was renamed Paul.

All: **We know that renaming is an important way to reflect our new nature found in Christ.**

One: Today, a child of God comes forward in an important renaming. It has not been an easy journey, yet we know that the road of faith is not an easy one. We have been asked to witness this renaming and become companions for the journey.

My friend, throughout your life you have been known as
_____ *[former name]*. The Holy Spirit, however, continued to call forth within you something more. Today, you stand before us, your life a testimony to the God who makes all things new. What name do you choose for yourself?

I am _____ *[new name]*.

One: You have known the waters of baptism, when you were claimed as God's own. Today, we again use water, as a reminder to you that God continues to claim you and sustain you. May these waters refresh and renew you in your journey of faith.

[(New name) cups hands over a basin while water is poured from a pitcher. He/She draws this water to his/her lips.]

One: _____ *[new name]*, you are God's beloved child. May you continue to be a faithful follower of Jesus, glorifying God through all that you do and all that you are.

My friends, I present to you _____ *[new name]*.

Congregational Response

_____ *[new name]*, **we rejoice with you for all that God has done for you, and for all that has yet to be revealed. As your sisters and brothers, we pledge to walk with you, as you will walk with us. Together we shall drink water from the well of life. May the life and ministry we share always reflect that love of God, which calls us all to wholeness.**

Hymn Response "Hymn of Promise" by Natalie Sleeth

_____ *Karen Oliveto*

This ritual was designed to help a community accept the healing and dating of a member whose partner had died of AIDS. The community wanted to allow the person to become someone other than "____'s companion." This ritual could be adapted for someone after a divorce.

Transition After Separation from a Partner
(from death or divorce)

Introduction: *[The reason/need for the ritual is 'confessed' in the midst of and on behalf of the community.]*

One: ____*[name]*, we have loved and celebrated who you have been in our midst as part of a couple dear to this community. *[Add words appropriate to the experiences shared with the couple such as: We have prayed and danced and laughed and cried and worked and played with you. As a couple we shared with you the birthing of this community of hope and faith; we witnessed your holy union, blessed the home you both shared, struggled with you both through your partner's illness. After his death, we grieved with you the loss of his companionship, and clung with you to the memory of his smile, his gentle spirit, his terrible jokes!]*

All: **____, believing that our histories are sacred, we invite you to speak those names and words that describe who you have been with ____ [partner's name].**

[Response]

One: ____, these names and descriptions are forever a part of who you are, but they are not the limit of who you are. Tonight, we want to acknowledge and claim with you the possibility of what is not yet.

All: **We want to affirm your returning hope and encourage your continued becoming! We invite you now to share with us your hopes and dreams for your future.**

[Response]

One: We stand with you at this point of new beginnings, linked forever by our history but not limited to it, strengthened by what has been and anticipating what is yet to be.

One: We want to journey with you into the future—to share the struggles of learning to be single again, the risks of deciding to love again.

One: As things change in your life and new relationships evolve, some of us may struggle with memories of your partner, and with expectations for and about your life.

All: **We commit to name that struggle as ours, not yours! And we covenant to walk with you in solidarity and companionship into whatever future God's grace brings forth.**

Blessing for the Journey

S: Great Spirit of the North, give me the courage I will need to...

All: **Great Spirit of the North, give us the courage we will need to support and journey with ____.**

S: Great Spirit of the East, give me the hope I will need to...

All: **Great Spirit of the East, give us the hope we will need to support and journey with ____.**

S: Great Spirit of the South, give me the strength I will need to...

All: **Great Spirit of the South, give us the strength we will need to support and journey with ____.**

S: Great Spirit of the West, give me the wisdom I will need to...

All: **Great Spirit of the West, give us the wisdom we will need to live with our lives, what we have said with our lips.**

All: **O Great Spirit, bless our brother/sister, guide his/her journey, keep us on your way!**

_____ *Leslie Penrose*

A bowl of water is passed among the congregation, and people are invited to offer their prayers of blessing into it. Then the subject of the ritual (S) is invited to wash his/her face in the waters of new birth and face each of the four directions, asking the Great Spirit for what s/he will need on the journey.

Visioning

Organizational Visioning or Retreat Service

[Several stations with prayer bundle supplies should be placed with ample access on all sides. Allow at least one station for every 20 participants. For prayer bundles, supply enough materials for each participant to make one bundle: 6-inch square pieces of cloth (in a variety of fabrics), 12-inch lengths of various colored ribbon, 4-5 various bowls with different seeds (plan for a variety of bowls: wood, clay, glass, metal, etc. to complement and accentuate the cultures represented in the seeds.) Seed suggestions include: Indian Corn or maize, wildflower seeds, sushi rice (rice is used in Buddhist prayer rituals for offering, etc.), dried beans (pintos provide pretty red & white variegated color), pumpkin seeds, mustard seeds (very Biblical), wheat or some other standard grain (representing that which would become bread for the table), sesame seeds, "Money Plant" seeds, or other seeds that have meaning for the group.]

Gathering Song "A Dazzling Bouquet" (see p. 355)

Words of Welcome

Song of Praise "God of the Sparrow, God of the Whale" words by Jaroslav J. Vajda, music by Carl F. Schalk,

Litany of Praise (based on Psalm 65)
> Praise to You, our God;
> **We come to You with praise and prayers,**
> You are the hope to the ends of the earth,
> **You are to the hope to the farthest seas,**
> You established the mountains,
> **You calm the roaring waters,**
> Those who see your signs are bound in awe,
> **You make the gateways of the morning and the evening shout for joy.**
> You enrich the earth and the seas,
> Rain showers softly fall,
> Grain in pastures grow,
> **Hills and valleys are clothed in abundance,**
> Your blessings overflow,
> **And we, your people, shout and sing together in joy.**

Sharing of the Word Matthew 13:3-10

Small Group Reflection
> Where are you in this parable?
>> What kind of seed are you? What kind of soil are you in? Are you already in a stage of growth? Do you have enough light and water? Do weeds needs to be pruned

away from you or do you need to be pruned? Do you produce food, flower or shade? If you are not a seed, what do you identify with in the parable? Are you the sower, the birds, or the soil?

Where is this organization in this parable?

What kinds of seeds need to be planted for this organization?

Where are the strategic places for this organization to plant our seed?

Song for Reflection "Sois La Semilla" words & music by Cesareo Gabarain, trans. By Raquel Gutierrez-Achon and Skinner Chaves-Melo

Ritual Action (make prayer bundles containing seeds)

Participants are invited to the tables to make their own prayer bundle.

In Native American traditional religious practice, a prayer bundle (sometimes called a "medicine" or "mystery" bundle) containes objects that connect the individual to the Great Mystery—God. These bundles sometimes contain a crystal, a stone, pollen, feather, or other objects that remind the person of a time or place where God was very powerful and present. The bundles we make today will contain one or more kinds of seeds.

The prayer bundle is for you to:
— take with you on your journey
— offer to someone with whom you want to share the strength of this event
— take home to plant
— tie to a tree or bush so that the prayers will continue to return to God

Silence for Prayer

Song of Dedication and Commitment

Sending Forth
Jesus said, "I am the vine."
And we are the branches.
Those who abide in Jesus,
Will bear much fruit, because apart from Jesus we can do nothing.
Jesus said, "If you abide in me, and my words abide in you, ask for whatever you wish and it will be done for you."
Let us abide in the love of Jesus. Amen and Amen.

Sharing Signs and Words of Peace

_____ *Chip Aldridge & Gloria Soliz*

"Called to be Moses" Devotion

Hymn "Lift Every Voice and Sing" (verses 1 and 3)

Scripture: "Let My People Go" from *God's Trombones* by James Weldon Johnson

Meditation

Moses and his helpers were sent by God six thousand years ago for the slaves in Egypt, who were caught under the heel of slavery.

Harriett Tubman, the Quakers, and others were sent by God for the persons of African and African-Caucasian descent who were held by the lash of the whip of slavery in the United States.

Ghandi was sent by God to the East Indians who were colonized and oppressed by British colonialism.

Martin Luther King, Jr. and the cadre of civil rights workers—Black and White—were sent by God for those who were cut off from full participation in the life of this country by Jim Crow laws and skin color discrimination.

Nelson Mandela, Desmond Tutu and others were sent by God for the South Africans who were disenfranchised and strangled in their own land by apartheid.

The list goes on.

God says over and over again, "Let my people go!"

God sends a "Moses" to those who suffer oppression and inhumanity from other human beings. Each Moses is unique for each unique time and place and situation. God chooses from time-to-time, someone to go, someone to stay, someone to persist and insist in ways unique to that time and place and situation.

Who has God sent to the Gay, Lesbian, Bisexual, Transgender Christians, excluded from full participation in the life of the church and full acceptance as worthy human beings in matters of our larger society?

Is it us? *(moment of silence)*

Prayer (adapted from Duke Ellington's "Have Thine Own Way")

Let us pray:

Have your own way, God, have your own way.

Wounded, unsure, and weary, help us today.

Power, all power, surely is yours.

Touch us, sustain us, Savior divine!

Use us, direct us, and make our steps sure.

God, dear God here with us now, God Almighty,
God of love,

please look down and see our people through.

For life is hard, our path unclear,
and we must lean on you. Amen.

Song "Where God Leads Us" (adapted) sing all four verses, then end with the chorus.

1. Can we hear our Savior calling,
    can we hear our Savior calling,
    can we hear our Savior calling?
    Take your cross and follow, follow me.

* General Conference (GC) and Judicial Council (JC) are decision-making bodies in the United Methodist Church. Substitute your own denomination's groups.

2. We'll go with him through the garden,
    we'll go with him through the garden,
    we'll go with him through the garden,
    we'll go with him, with him, all the way.

3. We'll go with him through the GC*,
    We'll go with him through the JC*,
    We'll go with him through the trials,
    We'll go with him, with him, come what may.

4. He will give us grace and glory,
    he will give us grace and glory,
    he will give us grace and glory,
    and go with us, with us, all the way.

Chorus:

    Where he leads us, we will follow, where he leads us,
    we will follow, where he leads us, we will follow,
    we'll go with him, with him, all the way.

Youtha
Hardman-Cromwell

A Service of Vision

Bienvenidos/Welcome

Leader: Eterno Dios, known to us in many forms and languages, we gather to listen to the whispers of your voice. Sea tu nuestra vision *(be thou our vision)*.

People: Lord, we come from many places, representing the great diversity of your table. Somos *(we are) [congregation is invited to speak all of the following words that apply to themselves as they are said in the order presented]:*
women,
men,
older ones,
younger ones,
    tired,
    impassioned,
    despairing,
    hopeful,
        Latino/a,
        African-American,
        European American,
        Asian-American,
           single,
           partnered,
           students,
           lay,
           clergy, and
_____(participants are invited to speak additional realities).

Leader: Creator God, we celebrate all of the diversity in our midst and thank you for welcoming us to the table of Christ.

All: Help us to listen more than talk. Help us to let go of our agenda in order that we might know your will.

see p. 308 **Hymn** "Singing For Our Lives" by Holly Near

An Invitation to Listen

"So that, with the eyes of your heart enlightened you may know what is the hope to which God has called you."
Ephesians 1:18

Silence

Hymn "Tu Has Venido A La Orilla" (verse 1,3 English, Verse 1,3 Spanish)

Listen and Reflect

"Where there is no vision, the people perish"
Proverbs 29:18, KJV

La Paz De Dios

Write the vision; make it plain...so that a runner may read it."
Habakkuk 2:2

Silence

Congregation is invited to reflect and write down thoughts on the following:

In listening, I understand God's vision to be _____

Offering Glimpses of the Vision

Hymn "Pues Si Vivimos" (verses 1-2 in either Spanish or English)

Blessings of One Another

Congregation is invited to share their name and reflections on their understanding of God's vision.

Congregational Response;

_____ *[name]*, may the eyes of your heart be enlightened.

"Pues Si Vivimos" (verses 3 and 4)

Acting on the Vision

Leader: "Behold," says the Lord, "I am doing a new thing."

People: Now it springs forth, do you not perceive it?

Leader: Our presence here suggests the answer.

All: So let us move boldly with open hearts to listen, discern and participate in God's new thing.

Reconciling Congregation Program

Welcoming

New Staff

One: _____, you have chosen to work in our midst as an "_____"
[name position], as one who will seek both to use your gifts
and skills to empower us to live out our commitment to ministry and mission, and to discover and deepen your own
skills for pastoral ministry. We celebrate that, for a time, you
have chosen to embody your companionship among us as
"staff" and invite you to share with us your hopes and fears.
We also invite you to share what you need from us as companions on the way.

[Response of new staff member.]

One: As a community we have heard the cry of God's people and
together we have responded "here I am."

All: Now we call you as a "leader" in our midst to empower us
to live out that commitment to discipleship,

One: to hear us into our own calls to discipleship,

All: to organize and coordinate the offering of our gifts in mission & ministry,

One: to support us as we walk with one another through pain and
joy, through failure and success, through fear and faith.

_____, as we begin this journey together, we ask you:

Will you help us to integrate our vision of God's hope for
shalom and the use of our resources? And will you facilitate
the connection of our life and work as a community with
the life of the larger world?

I will.

Will you journey with us in our living and in our dying, stand
in solidarity with us in the midst of grief and persecution;
rejoice with us amidst celebration and good news; and continue to struggle with us against sexism, racism, class-ism,
homophobia, & injustice?

I will.

Will you care for yourself even as you care for others? Will
you take time to rest, to play, to create, to dream? Will you

say "No" when "No" is life-giving, and model among us a striving for healthy boundaries? Will you say "Yes" when "Yes" is life-giving—even when it requires a risk—and model among us a commitment to God's justice and love?

I will.

Then, _____ take this "staff" as a symbol of your commission to work with us and among us in mission and ministry for the life of God's creation.

And receive this blessing of our hands as a sign of our support and a reminder of God's faithfulness and blessing.

Community Blessing

God of Presence and Promise, pour out your spirit upon _____ as s/he begins her work among us...and upon this community as we recommit ourselves to the work of compassion and justice-love in the world. Accompany us in our continuing struggle to follow in the way of Jesus' life-risking love and bless us each day with enough hope to dream, enough courage to speak the truth, enough compassion to touch, enough passion to insist on justice, and enough strength to stand for integrity. Amen.

Song "Here I Am, Lord" by Dan Schutte

_____ _Leslie Penrose_

A "staff" is individually created and given to the staff person. A member of the congregation personally chooses a "walking stick" for each person and adorns it with symbols of the work their ministry will include.

Chapter 7

The Contour of Grace: Sacraments, Covenants and Pride Liturgies

The very elements of bread and wine presume a symbiotic

relationship between humankind and nature, especially for

the sustained production of these elements....the ritual

implicitly acknowledged the need for people to cooperate

with nature and with God.

Edward Foley, Kathleen Hughes, Gilbert Ostdiek

Blessing Prayer for Infant

*G*entle God, we give you thanks for _____,
received with water, words and the whisper of God,
into the Church of Jesus Christ
and this community of faith.
We pray grace on this young life as
infancy stands up into childhood
and childhood reaches out for adolescence.

> Grant, O God, strength for the journey,
> insight appropriate for years,
> laughter in home,
> and blessing in all places.
> We acknowledge the painful truth
> that the very love in this family
> may cause people to wound
> this child with hurtful words, isolation,
> and even playground violence.
> Be present for this child as confidence before insults
> and a hug for tears.

May these parents find courage;
may godparents share wisdom;
may a friend arrive for every loneliness;
and may the community of faith
be alert always to the needs and hopes
of all God's children. Amen.

Maren C. Tirabassi

Words for Godparents' Commitment

*Y*ou who stand here as godparents are chosen by these parents because of their affection for you and confidence in your wisdom.

The important task of a parent in nurturing God's children often requires the loving support of people who stand apart enough to be objective, yet close enough to understand.

Godparents are called to give birthday presents, to attend recitals and ballgames, and to sit in fast food restaurants for hours of adolescent conversation.

There may come a day when this child asks you something because of your gender or your orientation or your faith. You are called to be honest, even when you feel awkward, and helpful, even when you are confused about the "right" answer. Most of all, you are called to pray love, grace, fun and common sense around this fragile, beautiful family.

If you are willing to do so, please respond,
"I will, with God's grace."

Maren C. Tirabassi

Sacrament of Holy Baptism for Adults

The Charge

*S*isters and brothers, baptism is a sacrament of the church. It is the sign that God's love is acting on our lives. As such, it is a reproduction or rehearsal of that which has already happened and will continue to happen. Those receiving the sacrament are marked in the act as Christian disciples and initiated into the family of Jesus Christ throughout the world.

Baptism reminds us, regardless of age, that we are always to some extent helpless, needy, dependent infants insofar as our relationship with God is concerned. Yet it is hard to let go, to be plunged under the water—especially in a culture that encourages us to believe that we are in control and that we have earned or deserve everything we have.

Baptism also brings the liberating word of grace. It is a revolutionary action that cuts to the core of any shallow, negative images of ourselves, and challenges many of our superficial values. In a world asking too little of itself, barely sticking its toes into the waters of life when what is needed is a faithful plunge, Christian baptism is a liberating, revolutionary act.

In the use of water, baptism deals with death. The ancients said that the act of a person passing under water is a rehearsal—an affirmation of death. Baptism says we all will die. But if we accept our death, we can be free as we were never free before. To be free in that way is to receive life in such a way, it is like rising up from the drowning waters or being born again. Therefore, baptism is the beginning of life in Christ and among Christ's people. It implies the dedication of a person to a life of freedom and freeing others.

The vows

_____, do you accept God's call to resist evil, injustice and oppression in whatever guise they present themselves?

I do.

Do you truly and earnestly recognize your human limits and brokenness and desire to grow in grace?

I do.

Do you accept Jesus as the symbol of unconditional grace, the source of your freedom to act—to act boldly—in this world?

I do.

Do you desire to be baptized in this faith?

Yes, by God's grace, I do.

[To the sponsors] Will you who sponsor _____ support and encourage him/her in him/her Christian life?

I will.

The Baptismal Prayer

Merciful God, we pray that as _____ confronts her/his weakness and limitations, s/he will continually be confronted by your grace. Strengthen her/him when s/he doubts; challenge her/him when s/he becomes too self-assured. Let her/him struggle for justice and meaning and love; and be filled and surrounded by your spirit. And, O God, we pray especially that you will at all times remind us that s/he is ours and we are her/his, and that all of us are yours. Amen.

The Baptizing

_____, we baptize you in the name of our God, Jesus Christ and the Holy Spirit. Amen.

May the power of the Holy Spirit work within you, that being born of water and Spirit you may ever be a faithful witness to Jesus Christ.

Through baptism, you are incorporated into Christ's new creation by the power of the Holy Spirit and share in Christ's royal priesthood. With joy and thanksgiving, we welcome you as a member of the universal body of Christ. Amen.

The Community's Response

Members of the family of God, we commend _____ to you. Do all in your power to increase her/his faith, confirm her/his hope, and perfect her/him in love.

We give thanks to the Spirit for the faith that has been worked in you. We pledge to you our care, our challenge, and our support as sisters and brothers, servants, guides and deliverers of God's grace. Together with you and with all the people of God, we seek the unity of the Spirit in the striving for and celebrating justice, meaning, and wholeness. May our common journey serve the glory of God in the coming of God's new creation.

Adapted from Broadway UMC

Eucharist

Eucharistic Prayer

*Y*ou, O God, our Maker, Sustainer and Redeemer, are to be praised. We give you thanks that you love us, mold us and invite us to be your people. Open to us your Word and move your Spirit among us that in hearing your Word and celebrating the feast of your life among us we might be enlivened and empowered to serve the oppressed and work for justice in every place. Amen.

Tú, O Dios, nuestro Creador, Sustentador y Redentor, debes ser alabado. Te damos gracias porque nos amas, nos moldeas y nos invitas a ser tu pueblo. Abre ante nosotros tu Palabra y permite que tu Espíritu se mueva en nuestro medio para que al oir tu Palabra y celebrar la fiesta de tu vida entre nosotros, podamos ser animados y fortalecidos para servir a los oprimidos y trabajar por la justicia en todo lugar. Amén.

*Reconciling
Congregation Program* _____

Calls to Communion

*F*rom lonely places deep in our hearts and from busy places just around the corner, we come to this feast of longing and fulfillment.

We come knowing that often our expectations of what we will receive outweighs our certainty of what we will give. Nonetheless, we come knowing that we will give what we can and receive abundantly the grace which knows no bounds.

We are keenly aware that at this table all barriers are mute, all distinctions are neutral, all grievances are pointless for the invitation of the host is clear: all are welcome at the banquet feast. Rich dine with poor, friends dine with enemies, men, women, youth, and children gather to remember a love born in a stable, transfigured on a mount, crucified on a hill, and resurrected in our hearts each time we set this table.

Divine presence, spirit of wisdom, holy grace: Come and dine with us today. Amen.

Allen V. Harris _____

Here at this table we once again reenact the great story of salvation.

We do not simply remember the story, but in the mystery of faith, we relive it.

We relive the faith of the matriarchs and patriarchs. With Sarah, we laugh and give birth to impossible possibilities. We walk and dance with Moses and his sister, Miriam, as they bring a great people from the bondage of slavery to a land of great promise. With the shepherd boy, David, we fight against unimaginable odds to make our dreams come true. With Queen Esther, we use our wisdom and our courage to maintain justice in the face of audacious evil.

We relive the blessed humanity of the disciples of Jesus. With Peter we are bold to claim the faith. With Martha and Mary, we long to serve and to learn of God's marvelous ways. With John we see visions of how the world could be. With Gregory of Nyssa, we are drawn from the solitude of life to service in God's name. With Francis and Claire we set our hearts on the simple things in order to clear a path for God. With Martin Luther and Pope John XXIII we hear the voice of God calling in new ways.

We relive the passion of the martyrs. With Stephen we are stoned for refusing to claim false gods as our own and handmade idols as the Living God. With Perpetua and Felicitas we hear only the voice of our savior calling us through the trials of life. With Joan of Arc we stand firm in our belief that God does, indeed, communicate with us and that we may be called to unusual and incredible means to justify righteous ends. With Martin Luther King, Jr. we risk the piercing finality of a bullet to keep alive the dream for a better world.

We relive the commitments of twentieth century prophets of peace.

With Mahatma Gandhi we garner the power of the people to overturn systems of oppression. With Dorothy Day we live in the midst of the poor in order to understand God's love more fully. With Rosa Parks, we acknowledge that sometimes we are simply tired of the prejudice and we just want to sit where we want to sit. With Harvey Milk we engage in the politics of our world so that all persons might be seen as being worthy of dignity and respect.

At this table, barriers of time and tradition peel away, and the essence of our faith becomes clearer. Christ has invited us to this table to help us recognize our common destiny as people of faith: to live in harmony with God and with one another. Let us accept the invitation, eager to receive and eager to give. We receive the gift of those throughout the ages who have lived lives of peace and of promise. We give the gifts of time, energy, and money so that their lives might not be in vain. We give, so that through the work of this great community of faith, others might be inspired by our lives.

Come to the table, for the feast has been prepared.

Allen V. Harris

*A*t table with his disciples, Jesus brought down nations, transformed social orders, and softened human hearts. In the simple act of offering another person a piece of bread and a sip from a cup, Jesus did the most powerful thing a human being could do: he gave himself in love.

We, too, gather at a table seeking to give ourselves in love, and in so doing resurrect the power of God again and again. Let us not make this an arduous task. Let us not put up barriers so that some might feel unwelcome.

Let us not forget the power of the simple. The gifts of God for the people of God. We come bringing our gifts for the work of Christ through his Body, the Church. Praise be to God.

Allen V. Harris

Easter

*G*ather now, dear friends, around the banquet table of Christ. Come from near and far, from the familiar and the unknown. We are invited to this feast by Christ, who has opened the invitation to you and to me, not because we have earned it, but simply because it is God's good pleasure to do so.

Come as you are. God does not rely on human divisions and prejudices, but welcomes all who yearn to be whole, who see in Christ Jesus the hope of the world. Open your arms to embrace the abundance which Christ's resurrection embodies. Bring gifts of thankful praise and offerings from your heart so that Christ's work in the world might be made real through the work of this congregation.

Alleluia! Christ is risen. Let us come to the table.

Allen V. Harris

*J*oined together as one people, we are gathered around this table in order to embody the hope we have for the unity of all people. This hope was given to us by God, and it is in God's name that we come back to this table each week.

Our host at this glorious banquet is Jesus Christ, who not only prayed that we might all be made whole, but who gave his life for the sake of that unity. It will not be in the proclamations of world parliaments nor in the brutality of war that our world will be saved. Rather, it will be in the simple routines of life, such as breaking bread and sharing the cup, that we will recognize our neighbor as our sister and our brother.

We are invited to this holy meal from wherever we are in life. We are not required to bring anything but ourselves. This gracious gift calls many of us to respond with acts of charity and thanksgiving. You are therefore invited to share your gifts of gratitude in the offering of prayers, talents, and financial resources for the work of this church in our community and world. Come, for all things are made ready.

Allen V. Harris

*A*t this table we are called to gather as Christ's beloved community, a people committed to nurturing the divine light in all whom we meet, friend and stranger alike. We are given strange tools for such an important task: bread to break and share, a cup from which to drink our fill.

This is the paradox of the Christian life. We are charged with the task of transforming the world. Yet we must do it one heart at a time, with each small flame as important as another. We are reassured, however, that this spirit is sustained by our coming together to share our memories of what God has done for us. This bread is broken; this cup poured out. Come, therefore, and eat and drink. Share your memories with one another. Bring your offerings, as simple or as grand as they might be, so that others, too, can keep the flame alive.

Allen V. Harris

Come to the table, for wide is God's welcome.
You are welcome here!

If you are young or old, you are welcome.
If you have black skin, white skin, yellow, brown, or red skin, you
    are welcome.
If you are married, not married, or share your life in a holy union,
    you are welcome.
If you are sick, infirm, or well, you are welcome.
If you walk, roll, crawl, or are carried to the table,
    you are welcome.
If you cannot hold the cup or eat the bread, you are welcome.
If you cannot hear me or see me, you are welcome.
If you are Gay or Lesbian, you are welcome.
If you are not Lesbian or Gay, you are welcome.
If you are man or woman, you are welcome.
If you are Bisexual or Transgender, you are welcome.
If you are happy or sad, you are welcome.
If you are rich or poor, powerful or weak, you are welcome.

You are a child of God, and you are welcome!
And so we come, all of us, together.
We come with our gifts, our pain, our hope, our fear.
We come with our traditions, which comfort and sustain us, our
    pews and our pulpits are open.
We come with our experience, that we may observe our trespasses
    and never repeat them.
We come with reason, to take all into account and discern the
    spirit of truth.
And we come, clinging to the Scriptures which command us to:
love our neighbor wholeheartedly,
remember God continually,
receive grace, seek justice, create peace, and do good works.
Amen.

Gordon W. Brown _____

Great Thanksgivings

*F*riends, let us gather from wandering,
    at the table of friendship and communion with God.
    God is with you!

And also with you!

Lift up your hearts.

We lift them up to God.

Let us give thanks to our God.

It is right to give our thanks and praise.

It is right, and a good and joyful thing,
always and everywhere to give you our thanks and praise, O God!

**When we were mad with thirst and cursed your
prophets in the wilderness, you gave us water.
When we railed against you and believed we would
starve, you gave us bread from heaven.**

Now make this bread and cup a sign for us to your continuing
presence within us and among us.

(The bread is broken)
As you feed us, make us bread for the world.

Make us bread for the world.

(The cup is offered for blessing)
As you quench our thirst, make us water for the world.

Make us water for the world.

(We are welcomed to the feast.)

_Dumbarton UMC

*T*he Lord be with you.
And also with you.

Lift up your hearts.
We lift them up to the Lord.

Let us give thanks to the Lord our God.
It is right to give our thanks and praise.

It is right, and a good and joyful thing,
always and everywhere to give thanks to you,
God Almighty, creator of heaven and earth.

You created us, unique, human creatures,
created to love and be loved,
created to seek relationship with you and each other.
We give thanks to you for your gift of our sexuality,
that which calls us into intimate relationship with each other.
We give thanks to you for your gift of those we love and who love us,
especially those in covenant relationship with us,
who embody your presence to us in many and holy ways.

And so,
with your people on earth
and all the company of heaven
we praise your name and join their unending hymn:

Holy, holy, holy Lord, God of power and might,
heaven and earth are full of your glory.
Hosanna in the highest.
Blessed is the one who comes in the name of our God.
Hosanna in the highest.

Holy are you, and blessed is your Son Jesus the Christ.

Through him, you showed us a new way to be
in relationship with you and with each other,
to care for one another and the stranger,
and to see you in different ways.
Through him, you showed us a new level of acceptance
and new ways to worship you.

By the baptism of his suffering, death, and resurrection
you gave birth to your church,
delivered us from slavery to sin and death,
and made with us a new covenant
by water and the Spirit.

Through this community which you have called together
through our concern, our passion,
and our seeking to know you,
we learn more about you, your sustaining love,
and your own passion for justice and liberation for all.

On the night in which he gave himself up for us
Jesus took bread, gave thanks to you, broke the bread,
gave it to his disciples, and said:
"Take, eat; this is my body which is given for you.
Do this in remembrance of me."

When the supper was over, he took the cup,
gave thanks to you, gave it to his disciples, and said:
"Drink from this, all of you;
this is my blood of the new covenant,
poured out for you and for many for the forgiveness of sins.
Do this, as often as you drink it, in remembrance of me."

And so,
in remembrance of these your mighty acts in Jesus Christ,
we offer ourselves in praise and thanksgiving
as a holy and living sacrifice,
in union with Christ's offering for us,
as we proclaim the mystery of faith.

Christ has died; Christ is risen; Christ will come again.

Pour out your Holy Spirit on us gathered here,
and on these gifts of bread and wine.
Make them be for us the body and blood of Christ,
that we may be for the world the body of Christ,
redeemed by his blood.

Strengthen us for our witness and our service in your name,
Increase our courage and wisdom as we live and work
for your realm.

By your Spirit make us one with Christ,
one with each other,
and one in ministry to all the world,
until Christ comes in final victory,
and we feast at the heavenly banquet.
Through your Son Jesus Christ,
with the Holy Spirit in your holy church,
all honor and glory is yours, almighty Creator,
now and for ever.

Amen.

And now, with the confidence of children of God, let us pray:
[Insert the congregation's Lord's Prayer.]

Words for serving.

The bread of Life, given for you.
The cup of Joy, given for you.

Ben Roe _____

Commissioning Spiral Around the Altar

*B*efore the service, place the communion table behind the congregation. At the beginning to Communion, move from the front of the sanctuary in a spiral around the edges of the congregation, turning the usual spacial order upside down and symbolizing the circle of God which encompasses us all and moves to the margins.

UCC Coalition _____

Post-Communion Prayer

O God, you have bound us together in common life, which we have celebrated at your holy table. Help us, in the midst of our struggles for justice and truth, to confront one another without hatred or bitterness. Empower us to stand together, to walk together, and to work together with mutual forbearance and respect. Teach us to abide in your love. Amen.

Park Avenue UCC _____

Maundy Thursday Footwashing Service

[The Rite of Footwashing dramatizes vividly the humility and servanthood of Jesus. Some scholars argue that footwashing is a sacrament that Jesus initiated. For the rite, prepare stations that include a chair, water basin with warm, soapy water, and a dry towel. This service does not include a sermon; instead there is time for reading and reflection. Time is allowed between each reading, during which participants are invited to discuss the reading with those sitting nearby. Participants are invited to use this time to meditate on the meaning of the Passion of Jesus, to deepen their understanding of Jesus' life and death for their own life, and to contemplate the mystery of the ritual Jesus initiated at the Last Supper.]

Gathering and Welcome

Collect

Loving God, who gave all things into the hands of Jesus and inspired him to wash the feet of the disciples, draw us now into the story as participants, not as mere observers. Help us to recognize one another as sisters and brothers united in the body of Christ for service in the world. As you love us into wholeness and joy, enable us to love others in ways that evoke their response to your love. **Amen.**

Prayers of Confession and Pardon

O Christ, in your presence we discover who we are.

You wash our feet, and we learn how reluctant we are to serve one another. We have not learned to love others without conditions or to serve them without pretense.

Christ's way is not yet our way; his truth is not yet our truth; his life is not yet our life. Though we lift the cup and break the bread with him tonight, tomorrow he shall die alone.

We shall forsake him, for we do not yet understand that you have written upon our hearts the truth of the cup and loaf.

And the *truth* of the cup and the loaf is that you shall be our God, and we shall be your people. And the *life* of the cup and the loaf is knowing you—

***all* of us knowing you, from the least of us to the greatest.**

Assurance of Forgiveness

God has heard our voices and listened to our supplications. We are welcomed by Jesus Christ to the table where all may eat and drink and find a welcome. Our host bows down to wash our feet and invites us to do the same for one another. Embrace this opportunity to love as we have been loved.

Foot Washing Rite

Those who wish to participate in the Rite of Footwashing may remove their footwear and place it under their seats. An appointed person will kneel before each basin and wait for a person to be seated in the chair in front on the basin. The appointed ones place that person's feet in the basin one at a time, lift and dry each foot, and rise. The person whose feet have been washed kneels and washes the feet of the next person waiting in line. Persons who have had their feet washed and have washed the feet of another may be seated and replace their footwear. The feet of the ones who began the footwashing will be washed last.

(During the rite, participants sing "They Will Know We Are Christians by Our Love;" "Jesu, Jesu;" or other appropriate, well-known tunes)

Gospel Lesson Luke 22:14-23

Reflection—What is the new covenant of which he speaks? What is this new and living way Christ opens?

Hymn "Remembering the Supper" by Lavon Bayler; sung to tune ST CHRISTOPHER

> Remembering the supper
> Christ shared with friends that night,
> When common things found holy worth,
> And shadows turned to light,
> We gather now in Jesus' name
> To find a presence here,
> That washes, feeds, and sends us forth
> As servants cleansed of fear.

We bring our hungry spirits
To find the bread of life.
We seek a cleansing, healing balm
To ease our pain and strife.
Renew our sense of covenant
As bread and wine are shared,
As towel and basin show us how
Your love is best declared.

Prepare us for our journey
through life as day by day
We learn and grow to understand
And follow Jesus' way.
Receive our thanks and praise, O God,
And by your love equip
Your children here and everywhere
For true discipleship.
Amen.

Reading Excerpts from "Crucifixion" in *Memories of God*
by Roberta Bondi

Reflection—Is it your suffering shame that consumes you with
anger, that renders you passive, that swallows you in depression, that keeps you from loving and knowing yourself to be
loved? How can we be rescued from our shame?

Reading Excerpts from *The Rainbow People of God* by
Archbishop Desmond Tutu

Reflection—In life there is both bitterness and sweetness;
struggle and hope.

Holy Communion

Post Communion

When people turn from the table where bread is broken and
candles glow, be sure you have invited them not to your
house but to their own, and offered not your wisdom but your
love. Let it be so.

Blessing and Dismissal

Stripping of the Church

Kelly Turney

We who are family praise you.

We cherish and do not relinquish

to traditional lifestyles

our particular vows,

the vow Scripture writes

for unexpected, unusual,

and unacceptable

relationships:

Wherever you go, I will go,

and where you lodge,

there will I lodge.

Your people will be my people

and your God...my God,

and not even death shall part us.

Maren C. Tirabassi

A Celebration of Same-Gender Covenant

Greeting

Brothers and sisters in Christ, may the love of God that passes all understanding be yours now and forever more. Amen.

Human companionship is essential in the Biblical view of human fulfillment. These two persons are here this day to publicly declare their covenant with each other and God. They have come into the presence of family and friends to affirm their relationship and what each brings to that relationship, making it like no other.

We gather to witness the declaration that _____ and _____ are about to make. We pledge to each of them our continued love and support.

Let us rejoice and be glad!

Music of Celebration

Statement of Covenant

_____ and _____, you are meant, as persons chosen by God, to live lives of compassion, kindness, humility and patience. Forbear each other; forgive each other. As God has forgiven you, you too are asked to forgive.

Above all, love. Love binds everything together in perfect harmony. Let the peace of Christ dwell in you. Be thankful for all that God has given you and that you give to each other. Let all you do, in word or deed, be done in the spirit of Christ, giving thanks to God, the creator of us all.

Vows

Will you now say your vows to each other?

_____, I promise to love you, to be patient with you, to be with you in joy and pain as long as we both shall live.

Covenant Service Resources

Blessing Ceremonies: Resources for Same-Gender Service of Commitment *published by the United Church of Christ Coalition, Open and Affirming Resources, P.O. Box 403, Holden, MA 01520-0403. www.coalition. simplenet.com*

Same-Gender Services of Union: A Planning Resource from the Office of Lesbian & Gay Concerns. *Unitarian Universalist Association, 25 Beacon Street, Boston, MA 02108. www.uua.org*

Valentine's Resource Book *published by Affirmation, United Methodists for Gay, Lesbian, Bisexual and Trangendered Concerns, P.O. Box 1021, Evanston, IL 60204*

Prayer

Gracious God, you are the very source of our life and our love. May your love be with _____ and _____ throughout their lives. May their love for each other enable them to serve you more fully, to love others more deeply. Guide them to serve you all the days of their lives. Through Christ our Sovereign. Amen.

Declaration

You have spoken vows to each other in the presence of these persons and God. May you have the wisdom and strength to keep these vows. May no one seek to destroy the covenant you have affirmed today in our presence. May peace come to you and to all people. Amen.

Benediction

University United
Methodist Church _____

Prayer for the Service Uniting a Man and a Woman That Affirms the Variety of Relationships

*G*od, who has formed the love
between _____ and _____,
keep it as open as it is tenacious,
as honest as it is earnest,
as dynamic as it is romantic.
Weave their fingers close with intimacy
but keep them hand in hand with family, friends,
and the strangers on their path.

And may God bless all who commit themselves
to make home with one another—
not only men and women
who love each other,
but men who love men
and women who love women.
O God, may all our relationships—
those blessed by law
and those blessed by spirit—
be heart-sealed, strong as life
and strong as death.
May many waters
neither flood our kindled passions,
nor quench the wick
that carries light
down from this day into old age.

And may we be festive as Cana,
fruitful as Eden, star-lit as Bethlehem,
and may the God who promises
to dress all Jerusalem
like a wedding in heaven,
wipe away the tears from our eyes.
Amen.

_____ *Maren C. Tirabassi*

For use in denomina-
tions which prohibit
officiating at a same-
sex covenant ceremo-
nies when a clergy
from another denomi-
nation has been asked
to officiate.

Opening Music

Request for Sanctuary

*[following three knocks on the door from the back of the sanctuary, the
Pastor of couple says]*

> We are _____ (name of denomination). Because
> our _____ (name book of rules for the denomina-
> tion) has disallowed a service of Holy Union for ____ and
> _____, we come seeking sanctuary for the purpose of cel-
> ebrating their love and commitment.

Response from Host Pastor

[from the altar, the Pastor who will officiate at the service replies]

> I bid you welcome in the name of Jesus Christ.

Procession

Presentation of Couple

[facing the host pastor, the visiting pastor presents the couple saying]

> For the past _____ years I have been privileged to counsel
> ____ and ____ as they have explored their relationship. I
> have witnessed the power of God's spirit that calls them to-
> gether and their courage in responding to that call. They rec-
> ognize that God's pure unbounded love, released and through
> their relationship, heals and strengthens them as individuals,
> unites them as One with God and celebrates their covenant
> with each other in the presence of God and their community
> of faith as an outward and visible sign of this inward and spiri-
> tual grace. As a representative member of the holy, catholic
> and apostolic church, will you officiate?

Response from Host Pastor

> Empowered by the Holy Spirit, I will.

[Visiting Pastor is seated in the congregation and the service continues]

L. Annette Jones _____

*L*oving Spirit of all that is true and of all that is calm and warm, join us here in this sacred place as we celebrate the love and life you have created in us and that you are so present in.

Lord, with your love,

receive our prayer.

Let us rejoice ourselves today, sweet God. Allow us the comfort of knowing that we are exactly the way you have created us to be, and are becoming exactly what you want. Be with us as we continue to surrender ourselves to your love and live in a world that harbors so much fear. God we invite you to be an active presence in each one of us as our commitment grows stronger towards a healthy, whole, confident way of loving you.

Lord, with your love,

receive our prayer.

Enflame our entire community, dear God, and be the force that drives us to honesty, clarity, commitment, and truth. Clear our ears so that together, we may hear your call to unite. Be with us as we strive to create a world that is safe for closet doors to open everywhere, and for the spirited and the lovely to emerge.

Lord, with your love,

receive our prayer.

In you, Lord, we entrust all our fears. Today we ask you to move bleakness to beauty and our insincerity to empower-ment. We turn our lives over to you in all ways, and are assured that in all ways your will shall prevail. Thank you for leading us to a point in our lives where we can feel safe, secure, and strong within ourselves, with those we love, and with you. We thank you for the spirit that moves within us and breathes out of us so that we may touch others deeply in our commitment to you and your profound love.

Amen.

GABLE

Prayers of the People

One: You are above us, you are beneath us. You are beside us, you are within us as you...

All: **Companion us on our journey, O God.**

One: When we are afraid to ask for help, when we are too proud to acknowledge our weakness and pain, when we feel unworthy because of what others say against us or when we do the same diminishing of our self worth,

All: **Companion us on our journey, O God.**

One: We thank you for the sanctity of our bodies, the miracle that we are. May we always look at ourselves with tenderness. May we honor the temple in which you dwell.

All: **Companion us on our journey, O God.**

One: We pray for those who lead us. Those in government and those in our community. Give them clear vision to lead us in the way of freedom, peace and love. Raise up among us your wisest and most loving children to lead us. Keep us mindful that they need our support and energy to create a world that you envision.

All: **Companion us on our journey, O God.**

One: We pray for our sisters and brothers who are living with dis-ease. We pray for those whose minds are filled with fear. Send your Spirit to fill them with healing and give us grace to carry them when they are too weak to go on alone. *(The people may add their intentions silently or aloud for those who are ill.)*

All: **Companion us on our journey, O God.**

One: We pray for those who have died and gone before us leading the way. We miss their presence next to us. We entrust them into your ever-loving care knowing we all share the journey with you. We remember especially this day: *(the people may add their intentions silently or aloud for those who have died).*

All: **Companion us on our journey, O God.**

One: We celebrate our uniqueness, our worth as daughters and sons. We are your prophets and your clowns, your dreamers, your sages and your mystics. We are fathers and mothers, brothers and sisters. We are Black and White, and all hues between. We are Lesbian and Gay, Heterosexual and Bi-sexual, Transgender, and questioning. We are celibate. We are partnered and single by choice, death or divorce. May we always know you are our companion on our journey, O God.

All: **Amen.**

Gerry Hoyt _____

Evening Prayer

Leader: God of light, you enfold us in arms of love, as a mother for her child, as a shepherd for his sheep.

Assembly: We light these candles with gratitude for your unconditional love. Open our hearts so that we may reflect your love selflessly and with concern, not just toward family and friends, but toward enemies as well.

Leader: God of light, you surround us with the glow of your infinite goodness and the warmth of your compassion.

Assembly: We light these candles in thanksgiving for your call to serve as an example to others. May we be your beacons to the world, bringing justice to the oppressed, freedom to the enslaved, light to those in darkness.

Leader: God of light, you protect us from hatred, from injustice, from those would seek to do us harm.

Assembly: We light these candles in thanksgiving for the gifts of hope and healing. Fill us with your Spirit so that all whose lives touch ours may also know the power of forgiveness and love.

All: Creator God, we gather to thank you for your countless gifts to us. We are ever grateful for your love, compassion and faithfulness. But we also thank you for our history, our sexuality, our families of choice, and our uniqueness—all truly special gifts to us and our Gay, Lesbian, Bisexual and Transgender communities of faith. We praise you and bless you, this night and every night. Amen.

*Pride Interfaith
Coalition at Harvard*

adapted from a
Native American
prayer

Prayers of the Community

Leader: Great Spirit, whose voice we hear in the winds,
and whose breath gives life to the world,
hear us, we your people made of sacred earth.

Assembly: May we reverence all good things in the natural order
of our universe by using our resources for noble
causes. In gratitude, we pray, *(community is invited to
add their prayers aloud or in silence)*

Leader: May we be conscious of beauty, our eyes beholding
the red and purple sunset, our hands respecting the
creation you have made, our ears sharpening to hear
your many voices.

Assembly: May we preserve the integrity of the arts and sciences
that nurture our body and spirit. In gratitude, we pray,

Leader: May our wisdom hold the things you teach, the lessons
you hide in every leaf and rock. May our strength not
yield to condescension, but to your greater power of
love.

Assembly: May we do the work of creating and maintaining the
spiritual and political dimensions of the Gay, Lesbian,
Bisexual and Transgender community. In gratitude, we
pray,

Leader: May we be ready to come to you without fear, so when
life fades, our spirit may come to you without shame.

Assembly: May we never forget Matthew Shepard, whose
shameful death galvanized many to reject hatred's fear
and embrace power's pride. In quiet tenderness and
reflection, we now call him and the other victims of
hate crimes to our minds and hearts, *(silence)*

Leader: We ask this in the name of the Great Spirit.

All: Amen.

Pride Interfaith
Coalition at Harvard

Litany of Joys

Leader: We recall those events and people that give us joy in our lives, that have made freedom in our lives possible, that have made beauty in our lives visible. Please remember now vocally or silently those people and joys in your life.

One: We celebrate the liberation found in coming out.
We celebrate our bodies and desires,
our sexual intimacy, pleasure and friendship.
We celebrate freedom, we celebrate Being Out—

All: **As we celebrate, we shall liberate and be liberated!**

One: We celebrate the journeys that have brought us here, our loved ones and communities. We celebrate those who have helped us to this place, their example and inspiration, and the courage of those who have gone before us—

All: **As we celebrate, we shall love and be loved!**

One: We celebrate the expressions of our voices—joining the chorus of voices universally. We celebrate those who stand against discrimination and who work for equality:
Sister Jeannine Gramick and Father Robert Nuguent,
The European Court of Human Rights,
The South African Bill of Rights,
Stonewall—

All: **As we celebrate, we shall listen and be listened to!**

One: We celebrate increased recognition of same-sex partnerships, in communities, corporations and nations:
Denmark, Sweden, Iceland, Greenland, France, and the Netherlands. We celebrate media coverage, positive television exposure, organizations that work for equal rights, celebrations of our identity like Coming Out Day and the hope they all bring—

All: **As we celebrate, we shall find courage and encourage!**

One: We celebrate the diversity of Lesbian, Gay, Bisexual and Transgender communities, the possibility of openness, honesty and integrity. We celebrate coming out, and all that it has meant, means and will mean in the lives of human beings, in their loves, and in their journeys—

All: **As we celebrate, we live and give life!**

GABLE

Leader:	For those who fear us, for those who despise us, for those who love the sinner but hate the sin,
All:	God of Compassion, hear our prayer.
Leader:	For those who know but can't come out, for those who know but won't come out, for those who keep their knowing at the edges of their consciousness,
All:	God of Integrity, hear our prayer.
Leader:	For those in the church who want to cleanse their parishes and dioceses of our presence, for those in the church who are uncomfortable and vocal, and for those who are uncomfortable and silent,
All:	God of Wisdom, hear our prayer.
Leader:	For those who practice sexual fascism whatever their own orientation,
All:	God of Mercy, hear our prayer.
Leader:	For those who quiet the slurs, for those who challenge the stereotypes, for those whose embrace excludes no one,
All:	God of Justice, hear our prayer.
Leader:	There are different gifts, but it is same God who gives them. There are many sexualities, but it is the same God who bestows them all.
All:	God of Joy, hear our prayer. Amen. Blessed be.

Gail Dekker

Based upon the ritual of baptism, this rite is designed to be a celebration of the goodness of a Gay man or Lesbian's life—a goodness given by God.

Coming Out Ritual

Gathering

Leader: Dear Friends, all life is a sacred and blessed gift. We are here today to bless the life of _____, who has invited us to join her/him in celebration of her/him-self as a Lesbian/Gay man. As we welcome this sister/brother with joy, we proclaim the sacred worth of every child of God.

Prayer for Truth

God of truth and justice, may our worship here help us to practice truth in speech and in thought before you, to ourselves, and before one another. We pray

in the name of Jesus who promised: You shall know the truth, and the truth shall set you free. Amen.

A Hymn or Song of Praise

Self-Blessing (adapted from Psalm 139)

[The one coming out recites these words]

Holy One, you examine and know me,
you know if I am standing or sitting,
you read my thoughts from far away.

Where could I go to escape your spirit?
Where could I flee from your presence?
It was you who created my inmost self,
and put me together in my mother's womb;
for all these mysteries, I thank you;
for all the wonder of myself,
for all the wonder of your works.

Community Blessing

[The celebrant and other friends and family sprinkle water on the one coming out, and address her/him with any or all the following words or other spontaneous words of blessing.]

For a woman:
Born of a woman, beloved of God, lover of woman, you are blessed. You are the light of the world.

For a man:
Born of woman, beloved of God, lover of man, you are blessed. You are the light of the world.

Words of Welcome

All: We welcome you, sister/brother and friend, into this community. With you we make a commitment to integrity. We promise to oppose injustice, and we embrace with joy the gifts that come to us from the Holy One's hand.

Hymn

Benediction

All: Go in peace.
Love God and do what you will.
Be a blessing to the world. Amen.

_____ *Rebecca Parker*

Chapter 8

Voices of Wisdom

Celebrating the liturgy should train us to recognize justice and injustice when we see it. It serves as a basis for social criticism by giving us a criterion by which to evaluate the events and structures of the world. But it is not just the world "out there" that stands under the judgement of God's justice, sacramentally realized in the liturgy. The first accused is the church itself, which, to the degree that it fails to recognize what it is about, eats and drinks condemnation to itself.

Mark Searle

Scriptural

The Beatitudes – A Litany

Based on verses from Matthew 5

One voice: Blessed are the poor in spirit, for theirs is the kingdom of heaven.

All: God our Center, we are grateful for your presence within and among us. May all that we are and do arise from our love for you.

One voice: Blessed are those who mourn, for they will be comforted.

All: God our Comfort, be with all whose hearts are filled with grief. Let Christ's peace uphold them. May we bear with them the burden of sorrow, and bring to them faith's message of hope.

One voice: Blessed are the meek, for they will inherit the earth.

All: God our Inspiration, may we have the mind of Christ as we relate to one another. Let love be our guide and reconciliation our desire. May people of every color and class, age and ability, sexual and gender orientation be truly welcome and valued among us.

One voice: Blessed are those who hunger and thirst for righteousness, for they will be filled.

All: God our Advocate, let our righteousness be born, not of arrogance, but of yearning to do your good will. May we hunger for churches where all belong, where diversity of humanity and unity in Christ create community and promote justice. May we thirst for right relationship with you and all our neighbors.

One voice: Blessed are the merciful, for they will receive mercy.

All: God our Refreshment, as your forgiveness restores us, so may we offer the blessing of restoration to those who wrong us, and accept it from those we have wronged. Help us to find our way when the paths of justice and compassion seem to diverge. Give us hearts ever open to mercy's possibilities.

One voice: Blessed are the peacemakers, for they will be called children of God.

All: God our Hope, plant deep in us the longing for a world where children do not suffer at the hands of adults, where lover's quarrels do not end in violence, where nations do not battle. May we pray peace, make peace, live peace. Amen.

Ann B. Day

Interpreting Psalms 23, 42, 43, 69

O say, 'The Lord is my shepherd"
BUT, O Lord, I DO WANT...

I want fairness,
I want justice for
those concerned about international saber-rattling
and survival of humankind;
liberals struggling to know how faith
becomes deeds of love,
women weary of being subjected to a theology that views
them as second-class creatures in God's realm,
people of color,
Cubans, Haitians, Rwandans,
Puerto Ricans in New York,
Mexicans in Texas,
Asians and Pacific Islanders in California,
the divorced who are judged "failures" and never whole,
youth experimenting with drugs and struggling to make sense
of a reality imposed by a sick society,
the alcoholic trapped in a downward spiral of chemical dependence,
prisoners "warehoused" to relieve our fear,
the homeless ignored to relieve our responsibility,
the Gay or Lesbian person: gifted, alone, terrified.

The Lord is my shepherd,
BUT, O Lord, I DO FEAR EVIL:
The evil of my enemies.
Jesus, protect me from your followers!
(Jesus stopped for blind Bartimaeus even though the church
"should stay out of those concerns.")

The Lord is my shepherd,
BUT, O Lord, I DON'T FEEL ANOINTED
and my cup seems empty!
Help me feel your "goodness and mercy"
that I may come to trust your love, feel your compassion,
and dwell in your house forever.

I thirst for the living God, yet find not food but tears.
Why does the enemy harass me?
My enemies exult in my anguish.
Defend my cause against a people treacherous and unjust.

Save me, O God...
The waters are up to my neck;
I sink in deep mire,
I find no secure foothold
My throat is parched from SPEAKING OUT;
I am afflicted and in pain.

How large a cup of tears must I drink?
O God, do you forget your servant?
Have you forgotten my name?
Will neglect and disease do me in?
How long must I remain in this pit?

Rachel's cry for her children is my cry!
I will not be comforted.
How long must I wait in this place of grief?
How long must I wait in the darkness
without a candle to light my way?

Come, Holy One, lift to my lips a cup of cool water
that I find my voice and sing your praise.
Come, O God, into my deep darkness.
Lead me from this exile,
deliver me from the evil that surrounds me
that I may praise your name and dwell
at last in your holy place.

Kay L. McFarland

Don't Fret, Don't Fret

Based on
Psalm 37:1-13

*D*on't fret, don't worry, even in the midst of scoundrels,
and don't be jealous of them or their doings or their stuff;

They are gonna dry up and blow away in the shadow of your goodness.

Be kind in your heart, do the right thing, and you will have nothing at all to worry about;

Trust God, be happy and delight in knowing God, and you will have your heart's desire.

Remember that God is not on your schedule; quietly wait, listen for God in your mind;

You will rise and shine in the presence of the wicked, and make peace and justice all around you.

Don't fret because some crook gets his way, some cheat wins the prize, or some brute succeeds;

Think about God, be calm, unafraid, and don't get mad or you'll get sucked into their ways and schemes.

In a while the crooks and the cheats and the brutes are gonna get cut off;

Even if you wanted to go out looking for them, you won't find them anywhere.

The scoundrels will plot against you and God, but don't fret, don't worry;

God chuckles at the wicked in their stumbling, and God laughs out loud at their stupidity.

For the kindhearted and right-minded will prosper forever.

Gordon W. Brown

Psalm 30

One: I will extol you, O God, for you have drawn me up, and did not let my foes rejoice over me.

Left: I cried to you for help, and you have healed me.

Right: You brought up my soul from the depths, and restored me to life.

One: Sing praises to God, faithful ones, and give thanks to God's holy name.

Left: For God's anger is but for a moment; God's favor is for a lifetime.

Right: Weeping may linger for the night, but joy comes with the morning.

One: As for me, I said in my prosperity, "I shall never be moved." By your favor, you had established me as a strong mountain; you hid your face; I was dismayed. To you, O God, I cried, and to you I made supplication: "What profit is there in my death, if I go down to the Pit? Will the dust praise you? Will it tell of your faithfulness? Hear and be gracious to me! O God, be my helper!"

Left: You have turned my mourning into dancing;

Right: You have taken off my sackcloth and clothed me with joy, so that my soul may praise you and not be silent.

All: O God, I will give thanks to you forever.

Jan Lugibihl

Psalm 150 Responsive Reading

Can also be used as a call to worship

One: Praise God!

Left: Praise God in the sanctuary;

Right: Praise God in the mighty firmament!

Left: Praise God for God's mighty deeds;

Right: Praise God according to God's surpassing greatness!

Left: Praise God with trumpet sound;

Right: Praise God with lute and harp!

Left: Praise God with tambourine and dance;

Right: Praise God with strings and pipe!

Left: Praise God with clanging cymbals;

Right: Praise God with loud clashing cymbals!

One: Let everything that breathes praise God!

All: Praise God!

Jan Lugibihl

Contemporary

Luke 8:5-8

Voices 1 and 2 read alternatively without allowing a break in the rhythms of the phrases. The result should be the sound of one voice with relaxed continuity. Bold letters indicate the two voices reading simultaneously. A chorus could also be used for the bold passages. Places marked by ~ indicate that the words are to be repeated almost simultaneously with the previous word in a staccato fashion by the other speaker.

Readers' Theater for two voices

Voice 1: Lying **sleepily** (pause) within is the **warm, mindless comfort** of the seed

Voice 2: (spoken quietly) **Resting** in a sundrenched~

Voice 1:   sundrenched

Voice 2: softening soil

Voice 1: Then God bids a new morning to greet and stir her. And says to the root,

Voice 2: "Come out!" and the seed says

Together: **"I will grow."**

Voice 1: A tiny hand **emerges.**

Voice 2: Your **root** holds all the energy~ of the **universe**

Voice 1:   energy

Voice 1: An immense **energy** as **full** as the relentless ocean's **crash** (spoken loudly)

Together: **Against the shore.**

Voice 2: (quietly) As **full** as a breast's desire to be suckled.

Voice 1: And the seed says:

Together: **"I WILL grow."**

Voice 1: The root **presses** through the dying case of the seed

Voice 2: not hesitating

Together: **NOT HESITATING**

Voice 1: **It must wound** its confinement,

Voice 2: **It must wrestle** with its friend.

Voice 1: Yet, a wound it is, as the pressing tears aside~

Voice 2:   tears aside

Voice 1: what once was dear. Yet, a wound it is, a God wound,

Voice 2: calling new life **out of the stillness,**

Together: (slowly) S E A R C H I N G **in the dark soil with a tiny spark of light.**

Mary Callaway Logan _____

A Psalm of Discipleship

Choir 1

Bless these hands that reach out
and into the lives
of so many people,
pausing to touch
with tenderness
the hardened heart
where hurt is buried far
beyond all feeling,
where love is a four-letter word
that has no meaning
beyond the now.

Choir 2

Bless these feet that run
through the day
after day
after day
without ceasing,
standing firm
upon principle,
dancing rings around
wanting to quit,
stopping to catch up
with what is important
in the long run,
then and now.

Choir 1

Bless this heart that holds within it
far more than it can carry
of grief
and the disabling
disempowering pain
of multitudes,
yet knows
that You would ask of it
no more than it can bear
and so it bows
in gratitude,
making the most of
amazing grace.

Choir 2

Bless this spirit determined to be
an extension of
Your Spirit,
with a reservoir of compassion
that is conceived
of enough
and more than enough
of serenity
and patience
for all Your cherished children,
even if every
replenishing source
by You
were running dry.

Choir 1

We are Your disciples, Shaddai,
may we live for
and love
one another.

Choir 2

Bless our hands to Your service,
out feet to Your path,
out heart to Your purpose,
our spirit
to dwell in the depths
of Your Spirit
for Your glory
now and forever.

Miriam Therese Winter

Prophetic Voices

Reader 1: We are called to the prophetic edge of witness. The prophetic voice is rarely welcome. No one wants to give it voice, no one wants to hear it.

Reader 2: Jeremiah speaks:

Reader 3: "Execute justice in the morning, and deliver from the hand of the oppressor anyone who has been robbed." No more injustice!

Reader 1: It is speech that makes a demand, a judgment and is non-negotiable.

Reader 2: Jesus speaks:

Reader 4: The captives will go free. No more bondage!

Reader 1: It is the voice that says No more! Enough!

Reader 2: Sojourner Truth speaks:

Reader 5: I toiled and slaved, and no one but Jesus heard me; and ain't I a woman? No more slavery!

Reader 2: Martin Luther King, Jr. speaks:

Reader 6: I have a dream today. No more racism!

Reader 2: Oscar Romero speaks:

Reader 7: "In the name of God, I ask you, I implore you, I demand you stop the oppression!" No more rulership of the rich over the poor.

Reader 1: It is the voice crying in the wilderness reaching out to those who would open their hearts.

Reader 2: The voices of women speak:

Reader 8: We will not stand for the violence, the economic oppression, the devaluing of ourselves anymore.

Reader 2: The voice of Gays and Lesbians, Bisexuals and Transgender speak:

Reader 9: Stop the lies. Stop the hypocrisy. We will not be silenced. Not even by force or violence. We are everywhere. No More!

Reader 1: The prophetic voice calls us to create the future now, beginning now, ever now, always now, a kairos, the moment in which we say, Enough: No More!

Readers 3-9 : Our commitment is strong. We will not be silenced. We are called to be people of witness.

Reader 2: The people of God say:

Readers 3-9: Enough! No More!

Carter Heyward (adapted) _____

Overheard from the Prophet's Heart

Voice 1:   I said

Voice 2:   I will be on my guard.
            I am afraid to speak
            and seem a fool.

Voice 1:   I said

Voice 2:   A muzzle on my mouth
            preserves me from the taunts
            of those who hate me.

Voice 1:   I was silent

Voice 2:   and my heart was hot.

Voice 1:   I was silent

Voice 2:   and my heart was not.

Voice 1:   I mused.

Voice 2:   I burned.

Voice 1:   And finally

Voice 2:   I spoke

Voice 1:   I said

Voice 2:   My days are just a breath.
            Holding my peace may never bring me any.

Voice 1:   I said

Voice 2:   I'll speak. And what I speak
            might one day come to be.

_Dumbarton UMC

Ever-Present Grace: A Psalm

I called upon the Lord in my hour of despair and God heard me.
Even though I did not fully sense the wonder of your grace.

When I uttered my first baby cry
I was known before the throne of God.
> **When I was baptized with water and a word**
> **the Holy Spirit grabbed by heart.**
When I sang my nursery songs
the Lord heard my voice.
> **When I spoke the words of confirmation**
> **God stood beside me.**
When I first knew the desire to touch another man
God's love touched my soul.
> **When I prayed to deliver me from this desire I felt was sin,**
> **the Lord answered me,**
> **And my eyes were opened by the grace of God.**
I heard your words of acceptance, not change,
"My grace is sufficient for you."
> **Because of your changeless love, oh God,**
> **Your spirit will not let me go.**

If I hide in the darkest closet of self-denial,
You are there–calling.
> **If I travel to the mountain of acceptance and openness,**
> **You are there–smiling.**
If I pass through the desert of painful rejection and words of scorn,
You are there–healing.
> **If I sing your praise to others like myself,**
> **You are there–rejoicing.**
If I weep from the loss of brothers and sisters with lives cut short,
You are there–consoling.
> **If I find the earthly love that binds my heart with another,**
> **You are there–embracing.**
Or if I go to the farthest reaches of the earth,
You are there–guiding.

> **There is no place I can go**
> **That you have not already been, oh Lord.**
For the steadfast love of God
is broader and deeper
than the places of our mind.

Robert W. Gibeling, Jr. _____

"We are the They"

Lines relevant to the context may be added in the second half of this response.

Reader 1: This is about

Reader 2: accessibility.

Reader 1: So that all may worship

Reader 2: so that all may serve.

Reader 1: Access.

Reader 2: Access.

Reader 1: For them.

Reader 2: For whom?

Reader 1: For them.

Reader 2: They.

Reader 1: They who...

Reader 2: They who what?

Reader 1: Wait, back up.

Reader 2: Access.

Reader 1: Access.

Reader 2: The act or opportunity of coming to or near; admittance.

[one person tries to walk past the other and is stopped]

Reader 1: A way of approach or entrance; passage; path.

[again, one person tries to walk past the other and is stopped]

Reader 2: The state or quality of being approachable;

Reader 1: accessible;

Reader 2: obtainable;

Reader 1: attainable...

Reader 2: The visible ways we are unable to gain access

Reader 1: But there are also the more invisible ways we are unable to access each other.

Reader 2: We

Reader 1: are the

Reader 2: "They"

[the next lines are read by individuals in the congregation]

Reader 3: we who sit in classrooms struggling to grasp, alone in our unperceived and misunderstood differing ability to learn;

Reader 4: we who wrestle with the darkness of depression, having to function daily while ever climbing out of the pit;

Reader 5: we who are frequently tired, faced with shallow resources of energy while others continue easily,

Reader 6: we whose dreams are thwarted by an oppressor's weight;

Reader 7: we whose abilities change daily with the onslaught of symptoms related to AIDS, MS, cancer and countless others;

Reader 8: we whose memories elude us, our friends becoming strangers, our families seemingly passers-by;

Reader 9: we who awake with pain and must merely manage it, praying for fleeting moments of relief;

Reader 10: we who find it uncomfortable to touch, to be touched, to risk conjuring unmentionable memories or to risk opening ourselves to another;

Reader 11: we who gaze in the mirror–not lovingly at God's expression of love–but with contempt for the wrinkles, for the imperfections.

Reader 1: We

Reader 2: are the

Reader 1: They

Reader 2: visible or invisible

Reader 1: perceived or not perceived

Reader 2: already

Reader 1: now

Reader 2: in our congregations

Reader 1: congregations that are made up of the "They"

Reader 2: For the They

Reader 1: is

Reader 2: Us.

All: **Spirit of energy and change, pour out upon all of us renewed perspectives. Help us break away from the old–accessing new realities, accessing new relationships, accessing the divine. Amen.**

Marcia McFee

Good News About Good News:
A Readers' Theatre for Four Voices

[The piece is designed for female Voices 1 and 3 and male Voices 2 and 4.]

Reader 1: The Bible is a love story that teaches people to love God, to love each other, and to love themselves. Jesus said,

Reader 2: Love God with all your heart

Reader 3: and with all your soul

Reader 4: and with all your mind.

Reader 1: Jesus wants us to love God with all of ourselves.

Reader 2: He wants us to love every part of ourselves—including our sexuality.

Reader 1: Jesus refused to accommodate traditions that excluded whole groups of people, such as the Samaritans and Gentiles. He loved the powerless:

Reader 3: women and children and beggars.

Reader 2: He valued compassion and reconciliation above the law.

Reader 4: He healed people on the Sabbath, he touched lepers, he broke bread with outcasts.

Reader 1: Jesus' life also suggests that he has a strong love and understanding for individuals who do not fit the sexual norms of their times.

Reader 3: As psychotherapist and former Jesuit, John J. McNeill, reminds us, Jesus' mother Mary was a member of the sexually disenfranchised. To all appearances, she was an unwed mother and thus liable to the severe penalties of Jewish law.

Reader 2: Jesus urged his friends to redefine the family. For Jesus, family was more than biological kin. In Luke, Jesus states,

Reader 4: My mother and my brothers are those who hear the word of God and do it.

Reader 3: In a society that valued heterosexual marriage and reproduction, Jesus and his twelve disciples remained unmarried and childless.

Reader 1: Jesus loved one of these disciples, John, above the others. John records this love at the Last Supper, when Jesus announced that one of the disciples would betray him. The gospel states,

Reader 3: The disciple Jesus loved was reclining next to Jesus. Simon Peter signed to him and said,

Reader 4: Ask who it is he means,

Reader 3: so leaning back on Jesus' breast, he said,

Reader 2: Who is it Lord?

Reader 1: According to McNeill, Peter recognized the special relationship between Jesus and John, and other gospel events corroborate it.

Reader 4: John ran ahead of Peter and was the first after the women to see the empty tomb and know that Jesus had risen.

Reader 3: At another time, while fishing with Peter after the resurrection, John was the first to recognize Jesus when he appeared on the shore.

Reader 2: John alone of all the male disciples stood under the cross and tried to comfort Jesus. And it was to John that Jesus entrusted the care of his mother.

Reader 1: The early church recognized and honored faithful same-sex love.

Reader 2: According to Yale history professor John Boswell, records of church-sanctioned same-sex unions date from the eighth to the eighteenth centuries. In 1578, thirteen same-sex couples were married at Mass at St. John Lateran in Rome with the cooperation of the local clergy,

Reader 4: taking communion together, using the same nuptial Scripture, after which they slept and ate together.

Reader 3: One thirteenth-century Order for the Solemnization of Same-Sex Union called on God to

Reader 4: vouchsafe unto these thy servants...grace to love one another and to abide un-hated and not a cause of scandal all the days of their lives, with the help of the holy mother of God and all the saints.

Reader 3: The ceremony ended with these words:

Reader 4: And they shall kiss the holy gospel and each other, and it shall be concluded.

Reader 2: This ceremony also invoked the names of Saints Serge and Bacchus, Roman soldiers of high standing who, in the early fourth century, were executed together because of their Christian faith. Many Christian philosophers and artists recognized their love for each other as a married couple. In the sixth century, Severus of Antioch explained,

Reader 4: We should not separate in speech [Serge and Bacchus] who were joined in life.

Reader 2: In a tenth-century Greek account, Saint Serge is openly described as the sweet companion and love of Saint Bacchus. There are many paintings and carvings of this couple, always portraying them joined together by their halos.

Reader 1: Joining people together in love is what the Christian church should be about, but unfortunately, many who call themselves Christians have hurt numerous Gay, Lesbian, Bisexual, and Transgender people—and their allies.

Reader 2: The tide, however, is turning back to Jesus's message of justice and inclusive love.

Reader 3: In 1968, Troy Perry founded the Metropolitan Community Church for Lesbians and Gays.

Reader 4: In 1969, the Roman Catholic organization, Dignity, was created. It was the first gay-lesbian organization within a major church.

Reader 1: Currently there are GLBT organizations within several mainline denominations:

Reader 2: United Methodist,

Reader 3: Presbyterian,

Reader 4: Lutheran,

Reader 2: American Baptist,

Reader 3: Episcopalian,

Reader 4: and the United Church of Christ.

Reader 1: The United Church of Christ has paved the way for other mainline denominations to advocate gay rights and to bring Jesus's message of inclusive love to Gay, Lesbian, Bisexual, and Transgender people.

Reader 2: In 1969, two months before the Stonewall uprising in New York—the beginning of the modern gay rights movement—the United Church of Christ Council for Christian Social Action declared opposition to all laws criminalizing private homosexual relations between adults. The Council also opposed the exclusion of homosexual citizens from the armed forces.

This final section celebrates the United Church of Christ's work and a local church's Open and Affirming Covenant. Adapt to celebrate the specific denomination's history and church's welcoming covenant.

Reader 3: In 1972, the United Church of Christ was the first mainline denomination to ordain an openly gay man.

Reader 4: In 1985, the UCC General Synod called on all UCC congregations to study homosexuality and to declare themselves Open and Affirming.

Reader 1: In 1993, UCC president Paul Sherry joined the March on Washington for Lesbian, Gay and Bisexual Equal Rights and Liberation.

Reader 2: He has denounced the military's discrimination against Gays and Lesbians.

Reader 3: He has denounced the violence that took the life of Matthew Shepard.

Reader 4: He has affirmed equal marriage rights for same-gender couples.

Reader 1: Under his leadership, the UCC published a comprehensive curriculum for AIDS awareness and prevention designed for use in Christian education.

Reader 4: In 1999, the United Church of Christ and the Unitarian Universalist Association published the first component of *Our Whole Lives: Sexuality and Our Faith*, a comprehensive educational program aimed at people of all ages. In an inclusive and developmentally appropriate manner, it includes topics that are typically excluded from both secular and faith-based sexuality education resources. It explores and affirms several issues of sexual diversity, including homosexuality, bisexuality, and gender identity.

Reader 2: Today there are some 300 Open and Affirming churches in the United Church of Christ.

Reader 1: In 1992, Faith UCC was the first mainline church in Iowa to declare itself Open and Affirming. The following statements are excerpts from its Open and Affirming Covenant:

Reader 3: We openly support the concerns of those who find themselves exiled from a spiritual community—including Lesbian, Gay, and Bisexual people. We condemn

Reader 4: racism,

Reader 1: sexism,

Reader 2: ageism,

Reader 4: heterosexism,

Reader 1: injustice,

Reader 2: discrimination,

Reader 4: violence,

Reader 1: indifference,

Reader 4: and hatred

Reader 3: as the antithesis of Christian faith.

Reader 1: God calls us to Christian faith manifested in love—love of God, of neighbor, of self. Such love honors diversity while seeking peace and wholeness within community. As the apostle Paul wrote,

Reader 2: There are many parts,

All: **yet one body.**

Reader 1: We acknowledge God's gift of sexuality with its joyous power and challenging mystery.

All: **We affirm Lesbian, Gay, and Bisexual people as persons of God who are deeply valued by their Creator.**

Elizabeth Thiel,
Jon Trouten, and
Mary Vermillion

On Remaining Silent

I continue to be amazed by the inability of the heart to fluently
And openly speak its mind;
We are too often prisoners of our own lack of capacity to articulate
What our innermost selves desperately long to
Breathe into space.
Our souls seethe with passions so profound that they cannot easily—
Perhaps never—
Be uttered by our oh-so-human tongues.
Our spirit cries from the very depths of our being,
"Help me say what I really feel!"
And yet, we remain trapped within the confines of our finite language
And our socially derived
Barriers of convention and propriety;
We cannot seem to break free of the arbitrarily imposed bonds—
Shackles that
We have purposely or perhaps even unwittingly placed
Upon ourselves—
And so we live quietly in our pain,
And our secret longings remain silent, unknown by anyone
Other than our most private selves
And the One who created us.
You are the God who comes to us
and meets us as we are.
In Your presence we discover the freedom for which our souls cry
out.
You are the God who gives us life
and who enters into that life in wondrous, amazing ways.
You are the God of music, of prayer, of preaching,
of the Gospel of Liberation.

You are the God who comes to us when we cry alone at night,

and who laughs with us in our joys.

You are the God of white, straight, rich, Euro-American people,

Some of whom have attempted to co-opt your gospel truth and

claim exclusivity for it—

But we know better.

We know that you are also the God of black and brown and red
and yellow

and Gay and Lesbian and Bisexual people,

And people who are poor,

and people who simply hurt,

All of whom you love passionately, fiercely and tenderly

With a love that refuses to ever let us go.

You are truly the God of diversity,

Who created the stars and red hair and mother's milk

and puppies and sunsets—

Yes, and Transgender people, too.

You are the God who gives us hope

and liberation from this world's oppression,

And You are the God who will always love us

With a love that is indeed everlasting and incomprehensible in its
completeness.

Yes, You are God and we are Your people.

May we bless You and each other without ceasing.

Amen, and amen.

Vanessa Sheridan

Based on
I Corinthians 13:1-13

Voice 1: What's the "good word" we have for the world?
What do we say through the worship and witness of our church?

Voice 2: We say, "We believe in God, known in Jesus Christ."
We say, "Let there be justice and peace!"

Voice 1: We say, "Come, accept the cost and joy of discipleship."
We say, "Our congregation is Open and Affirming."*

* The appropriate program title in a denomination may be substituted for "Open and Affirming."

All: It is good to voice our beliefs and commitments.
But say what we will, even in angelic tones,
if we do not love each other, our talk is cheap.
We shall sound to the world like clanging symbols.

Voice 2: We thank God for the joy of learning!
We are curious about the world within us,
the world around us and the worlds beyond us.
We wonder about the Creator of it all.
Exploring tradition, scripture and experience,
we pray and reason together.
Our faith seeks understanding.

All: It is good to grow in knowledge and wisdom.
But even if we knew everything,
even if we have mountain-moving faith,
if we do not love each other,
we have gained nothing.

Voice 2: What does love ask of us?

All: Love asks that we be patient and kind
as we build an inclusive faith community,
that we abandon arrogance,
that we risk new things,
that we not delight in the failings of others,
that we rejoice in discerning and living God's truth.

Voice 2: Love is strong!
It believes and hopes and endures.
But sometimes even love falters.
Then we may forgive and accept forgiveness,
so that love may be renewed.

Voice 1: Sustained by God's Spirit,
three things abide within and among us,
faith, hope, and love.

All: And the greatest of these is love.

Ann B. Day

Resources for Readings

Maya Angelou. *Even the Stars Look Lonesome*. Random House, New York, 1977.

Audre Lorde. *Uses of the Erotic: The Erotic as Power*.

Denise Baker. *Julian of Norwich's Showings From Vision to Book*. Princeton University Press, Princeton, NJ, 1994.

Joseph Beam. *In the Life: A Black Gay Anthology*. Alyson Publications, Boston, 1986.

Roberta Bondi, *Memories of God: Theological Reflections on a Life*. Abingdon Press, Nashville, 1995.

Judy Chicago, *The Dinner Party: A Symbol of our Heritage*. Anchor Press/Doubleday, Garden City, NY, 1979.

Rosamund Elwin, ed. *Tongues of Fire: Caribbean Lesbian Lives and Stories*. Women's Press, Toronto Ontario, Canada, 1997.

Julia Esquivel. *Threatened with Resurrection (Amenazado de Resurreccion)*. "No Tengo Miedo a la Muerte." Brethren Press, Elgin, IL, 1994.

Marcia Falk. *The Song of Songs: A New Translation*. HarperSanFrancisco, San Francisco, 1993.

Carter Heyward, *Our Passion for Justice: Images of Power, Sexuality and Liberation*. Pilgrim Press, New York, 1984.

_____. *Touching Our Strength: The Erotic as Power and the Love of God*. Harper & Row, San Francisco, 1989.

_____. *The Redemption of God: A Theology of Mutual Relation*. University Press of America, Washington, DC, 1982.

Mary E. Hunt. *Fierce Tenderness: A Feminist Theology of Friendship*. Crossroad, New York, 1991.

James Weldon Johnson. *God's Trombones: Seven Negro Sermons in Verse*. Viking, New York, 1955.

Audre Lorde. *The Collected Poems*. W.W. Norton and Company Inc, New York, 1983.

Brian McNaught. "I Like It" in *A Disturbed Peace: Selected Writing of an Irish Catholic Homosexual*. Dignity, Washington, DC, 1981.

Nelle Morton. *The Journey is Our Home*. Beacon Press, Boston, 1985.

Mary Oliver. "Wild Geese" in *Dream Work*. Atlantic Monthly Press, New York.

Jan L. Richardson. *Sacred Journeys: A Woman's Book of Daily Prayer*. Upper Room Books, Nashville, 1995.

_____. *In Wisdom's Path*. The Pilgrim Press, Cleveland, 2000.

Will Roscoe, editor. *Living the Spirit: A Gay American Indian Anthology*. St. Martin's Press, New York, 1988.

Aaron Shurin, "The Truth Comes Out" from *Gay Soul: Finding the Heart of Gay Spirit and Nature with Sixteen Writers, Healers, Teachers, and Visionaries*, edited by Mark Thompson. HarperSanFrancisco, 1994.

Howard Thurman. *Disciplines of the Spirit*. Friends United Press, Richmond, Indiana, 1995.

Desmond Tutu. *The Rainbow People of God*. Doubleday, New York, 1994.

The following are only a sampling of resources from which excerpts were taken for the worship services submitted for this publication.

Chapter 9

Musical Shapes: Congregational Singing

The Lord could do without our intercessions and our praise.
Yet it is God's mystery to demand of us,
God's co-workers, to keep on praying and never tire.

The Rule of Taizé

List of Welcoming Favorites

*T*hese following hymns were selected for their inclusive language and imagery from the commonly-used denominational hymnals. The *New Century Hymnal* is produced by Pilgrim Press primarily for the United Church of Christ but is used by several denominations due to its justice-oriented focus and inclusive language. Also, the Unitarian Universalist Hymnal, *Singing the Living Tradition* (Beacon Press, 1993), has a reputation for broadly inclusive hymns.

Hymn Name	Episcopal Hymnal 1982	New Century Hymnal	Presbyterian Hymnal	United Methodist Hymnal
All Things Bright and Beautiful	X	X	X	X
Be Now (Thou) My Vision	X	X	X	X
Bring Many Names		X		
*Blessed (Blest) Be the Tie that Binds		X	X	X
Christ Loves the Church				X
Camina, Pueblo de Dios		X	X	X
Cantemos al Creador (Senor)		X		X
Come Christians, Join to Sing			X	X
Come, My Way, My Truth, My Life	X	X		X
Cuando El Pobre			X	X
First One Ever, The	X			X
Forgive Our Sins as We Forgive	X		X	X
Gift of Love				X
God is Here			X	X
*God of Grace and God of Glory		X	X	X
God of Many Names				X
God of the Sparrow		X	X	X
Heal Me Hands of Jesus				X
Help Us Accept Each Other		X	X	X
I Come with Joy	X	X		X
I Sing a Song of the Saints of God	X	X	X	X
I Was There to Hear Your Borning Cry		X		
Jesu, Jesu	X	X	X	X
*Just As I Am**	X	X	X	X
Let Justice Flow Like Streams		X		
Let My People Seek Their Freedom				X
Like the Murmur of a Dove's Song	X	X	X	X
Lord, Whose Love Through Humble Service	X		X	X

Love Divine, All Loves Excelling	x	x	x	x
Many Gifts, One Spirit		x		x
Now the Green Blade Riseth	x	x		x
Not Here for High and Holy Things	x			
O For a World		x	x	
O God of Every Nation	x		x	x
Of All The Spirit's Gifts to Me				x
One Bread, One Body				x
Open My Eyes			x	x
*Precious Lord Take My Hand		x	x	x
Saranam, Saranam				x
Sent Forth by God's Blessing		x		x
*Shall We Gather At the River		x		x
Silence, Frenzied, Unclean Spirit		x		x
Sois la Semilla		x		x
Spirit (Spirit of Gentleness)		x	x	
There is a Wideness in God's Mercy	x		x	x
This is a Day of New Beginnings		x		x
This Is My Song		x		x
Una Espiga		x	x	x
We Shall Overcome		x		x
We Would Be Building		x		
What Wondrous Love is This	x	x	x	x
You Satisfy the Hungry Heart			x	x
(Lord God,) Your Love, O God, Has Called Us Here	x	x		x
Your Love, O God, is Broad				x

* Baptist favorites
** "Just as I Am," which is often associated with Baptist revival or evangelistic meetings, was actually written by an Episcopal woman (Charlotte Elliott) who was living with some disabilities and was challenged by her priest to consider what it was she truly offered to God. This poem, and then the hymn, came from that experience. Through the "coming out" process, this hymn has taken on new meaning for many as a way of affirming that people are invited to come to God, "just as I am."

Songbook suggestions

Everflowing Streams, edited by Ruth Duck and Micahel G. Bausch. © 1981 Pilgrim Press.

Hymns Re-Imagined by Miriam Therese Winter features familiar hymn tunes with contemporary texts that proclaim a fully inclusive and justice-based message. Medical Mission Sisters, Hartford, CT, mms@hartsem.edu.

Gather–Second edition © 1994 from GIA Publications, Inc.

Lift Every Voice and Sing by Cooperative Recreation Service including "Hello."

Sing Justice! Do Justice! is a collection of new hymn and song texts to familiar and new tunes including the five winning entries and many Honorable Mentions from the over 200 entries in the international contest co-sponsored by Alternatives and The Hymn Society in the United States and Canada. Words and music come ready for personal or group use. Published by Selah in 1998 and available from Alternatives at www.simpleliving.org.

A Singing Faith by Jane Parker Huber. © 1987 Westminster Press, is a collection of 63 hymns, most set to familiar tunes, featuring inclusive language, notes about each hymn and useful indices.

Singing in Celebration: Hymns for Special Occasions. © 1996 Westminster John Knox Press. Includes 52 hymns, familiar tunes, inclusive language, author's notes about the hymns, and index.

The Shaker Gift of Song by Ann Black Sturm

Songs of Shalom songbook, UM Board of Discipleship, 1983, including Janis Ian's "What About the Love?" Dorie Ellzey's "We Are Gathered Here Together."

Songs for a New World from the United Methodist Board of Discipleship.

Recordings Submitted

Melissa Etheridge, "Scarecrow" on *Breakdown*, 1999. The track is a moving tribute to Matthew Shepard, the young gay man murdered in Wyoming.

Indigo Girls, "Philosophy of Loss," hidden track 12, on *Come Now Social*, 1999. Speaks of church doors that are "open wide to all straight men and women but they are not open to me."

Bill Harley, "I'm Gonna Set at the Welcome Table" from the CD of the same name, Round River Records.

Bobby McFerrin, "23rd Psalm," from *Medicine Man*, EMD/Capitol Records, 1990.

Marsha Stevens, "Blessing You" on *I Still Have A Dream*, 1993. BALM Ministries, P.O. Box 1981, Costa Mesa, CA 92628, 714-641-8968. Speaks of the "holy vow" made between two people and their commitment to make a home and family together.

New Words to Familiar Tunes

The Bells of the Season

(Advent) by Karen Oliveto

Tune: TRURO, LM.
Song: "Lift Up Your Heads, Ye Mighty Gates"

What are those bells that call to us
To open up our broken hearts?
Bells that connect, bells that unite
Bells of the season, ring so bright.

What are those bells that call to us
To open hands to those in need?
The bells of justice, God's new day!
Bells of the season, help us pray.

What are those bells that call to us
To dance, to laugh, to embrace life?
The bells of joy, for God's great gift.
Bells of the season will uplift.

What are those bells that call to us
To praise the Christ whose birth we sing?
The bells of faith, our Savior's come!
Bells of the season, bring us home.

Earth Day Hymn

by Timothy Kocher-Hillmer, 1995

Tune: TERRA PATRIS.
Song "This is My Father's World"

This is our Father's world
And to our list'ning ears
All nature sings and round us rings
The music of the spheres.
So let us hear this world
And may we be aware
Of rocks and trees, of skies and seas,
This wonder that we share.

This is our Children's world!
Unthinking, we consume.
God's gifts abound yet we are found
Preparing our own tomb.
So let us fill this world
With new alternatives;
When one lives in simplicity,
Another simply lives.

It is our Mother's world
Which sings a gentle song,
"Return to me and set me free.
Together we are strong."
Now let us heal this world
By working hand in hand.
Our hands in earth will bring re-birth,
New hope for every land.

God gifts us in this world,
With creatures everywhere,
With sounds and sights,
With great delights,
For all to love and share.
So let us love this world
With all our heart and soul.
Be open, learn and in return
This earth will make us whole.

For the Goodness of our Bodies

by Ruth Duck, 1997

Tune: EL CAMINO. Song "Cuando El Pobre"

For the goodness of our bodies
    made for caring,
for the longing of two hearts
    learning to love,
for the joy that lovers find in
    one another,
for these good gifts we would thank you,
    loving God.
For these good gifts we would thank you,
    loving God.

For the vows a man and woman
    honor daily,
for the pledge two women keep
    with all their hearts,
for commitments two men keep with
    one another,
for these good gifts we would thank you,
    loving God.
For these good gifts we would thank you,
    loving God.

For the courage that burns bright in
    seeking justice,
for compassion to show love
    where there is fear,
for the rainbow, sign of promise
    for your future,
for these good gifts we would thank you,
    loving God.
For these good gifts we would thank you,
    loving God.

see endnotes for copyright statement

A Hymn of Reconciliation

by Harry A. Akers, alt., 1991

Tune: REST, 86.886.
Song: "Dear Lord and Father of Mankind"

Dear God, Parent of Humankind,
Forgive our foolish ways.
Take from our minds the fear and stress
that fester in out prejudice
and let us sing Your praise!

"Let those who are without sin
be first to cast a stone"
The Savior, in the seamless robe
seeks not a trial, nor a probe—
But pleads we all atone!

God made us Human, one and all,
yet none of us the same.
No one is perfect—still, within,
despite our dif-fer-ence and sin,
all bear God's mark and name.

Forgive us, Lord, for all the times
we point, accuse, deride.
If someone's lifestyle's not our own
why must we always be so prone
their decency to hide?

Teach us, dear God, to do your will;
We're not here to condemn.
Help us to hear what others say,
To tolerate another's way,
and be to all a friend.

Lazarus, Come Out! A Coming Out

by Peter J.B. Carman

Suggested Tunes: LANCASHIRE, LLANGLOFFAN, ANGEL'S STORY, ST. CHRISTOPHER, AURELIA; 7.6.7.6.D.

As from the tomb stepped Lazarus
and drew a ragged breath,
You opened up fear's fortress,
and drew me out from death.
O God of truth and wisdom,
of holy dignity,
I thank you for the opening
through which you set me free.

When I was hid in secrets,
I could not find the day:
Enclosed in self-deception,
my spirit slipped away.
In pain I sought to slumber,
bone weary, still, alone,
Until at last you found me,
and called me through the stone.

I pray for all God's children
whose lives stay cloaked in shame,
And pray for all whose hatred
drives them to pointless blame.
I pray for greater courage
to stand and face the crowd,
An heir to sacred promise,
who names your love aloud.

No longer shut in anger
nor sealed in desperate fear,
No longer forced in anguish
a stranger to appear,
No longer wrapped in secrets
in death's dishonest game,
I praise you, Sweet Redeemer,
and rise to bear your name.

Let There Be Light

by Harry Ackers, 1998
Tune: CONCORD, 47.76.

Let there be light,
let there be understanding,
let all the people gather.
Let them be face to face.

Let there be truth,
truth that gives birth to freedom,
breaking the bonds of hatred,
granting to all, God's grace.

Let there be love,
for every son and daughter,
created by our maker.
Help us be their shalom!

Let there be peace,
love for our sister, brother,
respect for one another.
let our church be their home.

Let there be joy,
in our concerning, caring,
help us to be more daring,
as we defend what's right.

Let there be light.
Christ's love for future ages,
gleaned not from mildewed pages.
O, God, let there be light!

Questions—Still Unresolved!

by Harry A. Ackers,1999
Tune: VICAR, 11 10.11 10.
Song: "Hope of the World."

Who will stand forth,
        against the bigot's blindness?
Who will speak out, 'gainst prejudice and fear?
God needs brave people,
        filled with love and kindness,
To spread God's great compassion,
        far and near.

Where can we find strong advocates for justice,
Who value all God's cherished humankind?
Where are the faithful, whose full promise,
        "Trust us,"
Will see that others won't be left behind?

When will we learn, O Church, in all our glory,
That every child of God—each daughter, son –
Must be accepted, if the "good news" story
Is to be finished and Christ's life work done?

How can we learn to hear what Jesus told us?
Shake off the fears and hatreds of the past!
The wrathful gods that ancient tablets sold us,
Languish in dust—Christ's love prevails at last!

Why can we not all follow Jesus' teaching,
Both Straight and Gay, in fellowship divine?
The church will die,
        if it should stop out-reaching.
But serving all, its mission is sublime!

O Spirit, Spring of Hidden Power
by Ruth Duck

Tune: JESOUS AHATONHIA.
Song: "Twas in the Moon of Wintertime"

O Spirit, spring of hidden pow'r
that hallows day and night:
You are the force that prods the flow'r
through pavement toward the light.
You are the song that brings release;
in prison cell you do not cease.
Spring of pow'r, fire of love, giver of life:
come, renewing Spirit, come.

O Spirit of the holy cry
for human dignity,
you are the pride of head held high
before all bigotry.
Your rhythm rouses weary feet
to move to freedom's steady beat.
Spring of pow'r, fire of love, giver of life:
come, renewing Spirit, come.

O Spirit of undying life,
O breath within our breath:
You are the witness to our strife
that love surpasses death.
You are the gift that we desire;
anoint our heads with tongues of fire.
Spring of pow'r, fire of love, giver of life:
come, renewing Spirit, come.

see endnotes for copyright statement

We Gather Round the Table Now
by Jane Parker Huber

Tune: AMAZING GRACE, CM.

We gather round the table now
In gratitude and awe.
Christ is the host, the nourishment,
The message without flaw.

In joy and solemn praise we come
To celebrate and sing.
Our visions and remembrances
Alike to Christ we bring.

The shadowed garden where Christ prayed
That God's own will be done
Reminds us that humanity
In Christ alone is one.

So now Christ's strength can feed us all
In common daily bread.
We drink the life poured out and find
Our souls and bodies fed.

Around this table, in this place,
Are all named by Christ's name;
An unseen cloud of witnesses
With us the gospel claim.

see endnotes for copyright statement

We Limit Not the Truth of God
by John Robinson, alt.

Tune: MATERNA, CMD. Song Suggestion: "America the Beautiful."

We limit not the truth of God to our poor reach of mind.
By notions of our day and sect, crude, partial, and confined
No, let a new and better hope within our hearts be stirred–
The Lord hath yet more light and truth to break forth from God's Word.

Who dares to bind to their dull sense the oracles of heaven,
For all the nations, tongues and climes, and all the ages given?
That universe, how much unknown! That ocean unexplored!
The Lord hath yet more light and truth to break forth from God's Word.

O Father, Son and Spirit, send us increase from above;
Enlarge, expand all Christian souls to comprehend thy love
And make us all go on to know with nobler powers conferred,
The Lord hath yet more light and truth to break forth from God's Word.

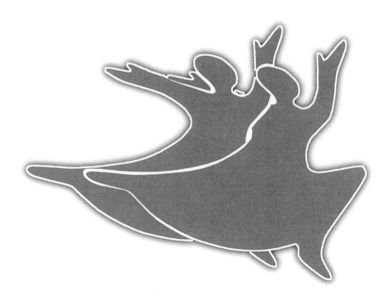

Hymn Music

*The music was kindly
submitted by a variety
of individuals and
publishers.*

All Are Welcome

Words and music by Marty Haugen
Tune: TWO OAKS

1. Let us build a house where love can dwell and
2. Let us build a house where proph - ets speak, and
3. Let us build a house where love is found in
4. Let us build a house where hands will reach be -
5. Let us build a house where all are named, their

all can safe - ly live. A place where saints and
words are strong and true. Where all God's chil - dren
wa - ter, wine and wheat; A ban - quet hall on
yond the wood and stone, To heal and strength - en,
songs and vi - sions heard And loved and treas - ured,

chil - dren tell how hearts learn to for -
dare to seek to dream God's reign a -
ho - ly ground, where peace and jus - tice
serve and teach, and live the Word they've
taught and claimed as words with - in the

give. Built of hopes and dreams and vi - sions, rock of
new. Here the cross shall stand as wit - ness and as
meet. Here the love of God, through Je - sus, is re -
known. Here the out - cast and the stran - ger bears the
Word. Built of tears and cries and laugh - ter, prayers of

faith and vault of grace, Here the love of Christ shall
sym - bol of God's grace; Here as one we claim the
vealed in time and space, As we share in Christ the
im - age of God's face, Let us bring an end to
faith and songs of grace. Let this house pro - claim from

end di - vi - sions:
faith of Je - sus;
feast that frees us;   } All are wel - come, all are wel - come,
fear and dan - ger;
floor to raft - er:

all are wel - come in this place.

Bring Many Names

Words by Brian Wren

Music by Carlton R. Young

By the Waters of Babylon

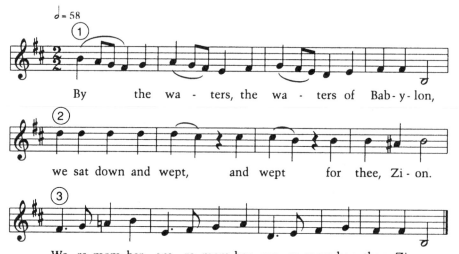

By the wa - ters, the wa - ters of Bab - y - lon,

we sat down and wept, and wept for thee, Zi - on.

We re - mem - ber, we re - mem - ber, we re - mem - ber thee, Zi - on.

Words: Psalm 137
Music: William Billings, 1746–1800

BILLINGS
Irregular

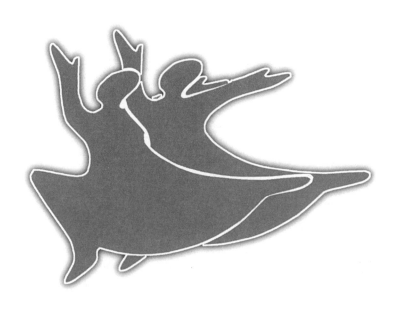

Circle of Love

Words and music by Miriam Therese Winter

♩ = 84

Throw a peb - ble in a pond, see a cir - cle.
Rain up - on a pud - dle falls in cir - cles. An
Lit - tle birds learn to fly in cir - cles.
Mar - riage vows are sealed with a cir - cle.

Dance and we'll re - spond with a cir - cle.
e - cho - ing can - yon calls in cir - cles.
Earth com - pletes the sky: a cir - cle. The
Rain - bows are re - vealed as a cir - cle.

Sing a hap - py sound, and the song comes cir - cling round, 'til
Share some hap - py news, it will cir - cle back to you, 'til
Some set out to roam, yet all come cir - cling home, for
life we live ex - tends through a widen - ing circle of friends, 'til

all are caught and held in a cir - cle of love.
all are caught and held in a cir - cle of love.
all are caught and held in a cir - cle of love.
all are caught and held in a cir - cle of love.

Refrain

Reach - ing out, reach - ing in, a cir - cle game: all will win.

Teach - ing you, teach - ing me, how to live in - clu - sive - ly.

Ev - 'ry - one knows a cir - cle grows, all a - round the globe it goes, 'til

all are caught and held in a cir - cle of love.

Come, Holy Spirit

Words and music by Jorge Lockward

Refrain: Ho - - - - ly Spi - rit! Ho - ly

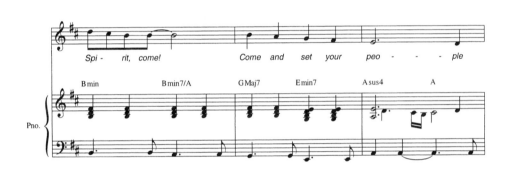

Spi - rit, come! Come and set your peo - - - ple

free

1. Come, Breath of God,
2. Come, Ho - ly Balm,
3. Come, Ho - ly Dove,

© Jorge Lockward, 2000

Congregations may reproduce without restriction for local worship use provided the copyright owner is
acknowledged. For other uses, contact the copyright owner

4.- Come, Joy Divine,
fill us with a song.
May our hearts be glad
and our faces shine.

5.- Come, Holy Fire,
burn, break, and destroy.
Challenge every life
Come, and shake our souls.

6.- Come, Holy Light,
ageless wisdom, come.
Show us how to live,
so we may be one.

7.- Come, Power Divine,
give your people strength,
as we heed your call:
Open wide the door!

Come, Holy Spirit -2-

Creation of Peace

Music by Carolyn McDade

1. We'll build a land where we bind up the bro - ken.—
2. We'll build a land where we bring— good tid-ings to
3. We'll be a land build - ing up an - cient cit - ies,—
4. Come, build a land—— where man - tles of prais-es re-

We'll build a land where the cap - tives go free, where the
all the af - flict - ed and those— who mourn. We'll then
rais - ing up dev - as - ta - tions from old, re -
sound from— spir - its once faint and once weak, where like

oil of glad - ness dis - solves all mourn-ing. Oh,—
give them gar - lands in - stead of ash - es. Oh,—
stor - ing ru - ins of gen - er - a - tions. Oh,—
oaks of right-eous-ness stand her peo - ple. Oh,—

Words adapted from an address by Barbara Zarotti at the Riverside Disarmament Conference
(based on Isaiah and Amos).

we'll build a pro - mised land that can be.
we'll build a land where peace— is born.
we'll be a land of peo - ple so bold.
come build the land; my peo - ple we seek.

Chorus: Come build a land— where sis - ters and broth-ers, an -

oint - ed by God,— then cre - ate peace— where

just - ice shall flow——— down like wat - ers, and

peace like an ev - er - flow - ing stream.

Creation of Peace -2-

Come, Spirit

Words and music by Miriam Therese Winter

Sing, my soul, a Spirit song,
Dance, my heart, at your re - birth,
When con - strained by thoughts or things,

call - ing all to sing a - long. Fill the world with
part - ner to the dance of earth. Thirst - ing spir - it,
hear the word the Spir - it brings: life is larg - er

joy - ful sounds: God is here and grace a - bounds.
drink your fill: love goes danc - ing where it will.
than it seems, hope is har - bin - ger of dreams.

Refrain

Come, Spir - it, come and be a new re - al - i - ty. ___

___ Your touch is guar - an - tee of love a - live in me.

Dance with the Spirit

Words and music by Jim Strathdee

Spirited
♩. = 126

Dance with the Spir - it ear - ly in the morn - in', __ walk with the Spir - it through-

out the long day. Work and hope for the new life a - born - in', lis-

ten to the Spir - it to show you the way.

Descant

O __ Spir-it come, come a - to- day, O __ Spir- it come, come a - my way.

Drops of Water

From the teachings
of Jesus and Ghandi

Words and music
by Jim Strathdee

Drops of Water -2-

EarthSong

Words and music by Miriam Therese Winter

Refrain 1
1. Heart - song, sing a - long,_ can't go wrong: it's earth - song. Heart - song,

1. 2. To Verse 1 / Fine 3. To Refrain 2

grow - ing strong. Come, sing a - long_ to earth - song.   earth - song.

Verse 1
Fly, soar - ing high, like a bird on the wing.

Lift up your heart, let your caged spir - it sing.
Sing Refrain 1
one time only

Refrain 2
2. Heart - beat made com - plete_ by re - peat - ing earth - beat. Heart - beat,

1. 2. To Verse 2 3. To Refrain 3

pas - sions meet_ with danc - ing feet._ Feel earth - beat.   earth - beat.

EarthSong -2-

Esther Round

Words and music by Ann Freeman Price

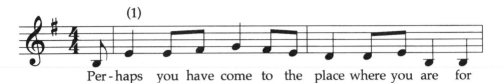

(1) Per-haps you have come to the place where you are for

just such a time as this; Per-haps you have come to the

place where you are for just such a time as this.

(2) Speak out! Don't keep si-lence! Be true to God;—

Speak out! Don't keep si-lence! Be true to God!

Esther Round was used as a theme for Methodist Federation
for Social Action (MFSA) during General Conference 2000.

Hold On

Words and music arrangement
by Ann Freeman Price

1. Pe - ter thrown in pri - son chains, Sol - diers
2. While in pri - son Pet - er stayed, Peo - ple
3. Then one night in dark - ness deep, An - gel
4. When you're tired and things are tough, God still

guard-ing him in Her-od's name, God is with you each
fer - vent-ly to God did pray. God is with you each
came and said, "Just fol-low me." God is with you each
pro - mis - es to be e - nough. God is with you each

day. Hold— on.——— Hold on.——— Hold— on.———
day. Hold— on.——— Hold on.——— Hold— on.———
day. Walk— on.——— Walk on.——— Walk— on.———
day. Hold— on.——— Hold on.——— Hold— on.———

__ God is with you each day. Hold— on.———
__ God is with you each day. Hold— on.———
__ God is with you each day. Walk— on.———
__ God is with you each day. Hold— on.———

Wide Is the Welcome. . .

Extend the Table

Words by Vickie Pruett

Music by Carl Wiltse (ASCAP)

I re-mem-ber from my child-hood Go-ing to my grand-ma's house_ And the

food would fill the ta-ble, Then all the folks would gather 'round._ There would

be so man-y mouths to feed;_ Would there be e-nough for me? But

at my grand-ma's ta - ble There was room for man - y more.

Ex - tend the ta - ble, There is plen - ty to share 'Cause

at our Lord's_ ta - ble There are man - y who care. Christ's

arms are al-ways o-pen wide To all who want to come in-side

Ex-tend the ta - ble, The Ta - ble of— the Lord. Now

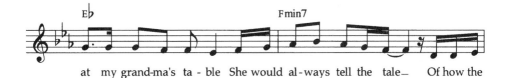

at my grand-ma's ta - ble She would al-ways tell the tale— Of how the

Lord sent in-vi-ta-tions To all the folks ev-'ry - where.— There were

man-y who sent back re-grets—'Cause they did-n't want to sit With the

poor and the lame and the out-casts At the Ta - ble of the Lord.

Extend the Table -2-

Ex - tend the ta - ble, There is plen - ty to share 'Cause

at our Lord's— ta - ble There are man - y who care. Christ's

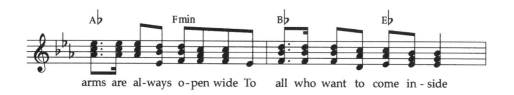

arms are al-ways o-pen wide To all who want to come in - side

Ex - tend the ta - ble, The Ta - ble of— the Lord. 'Though

Grand-ma died— years a - go, I re-mem-ber that ta-ble of love, And the

les-sons she taught me so long a - go A-bout the ta-ble of the Lord.— If

Extend the Table -3-

she were still a-live to-day— I know that she would say, "Don't

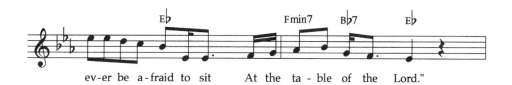

ev-er be a-fraid to sit At the ta - ble of the Lord."

Ex-tend the ta - ble, There is plen-ty to share 'Cause

at our Lord's— ta - ble There are man - y who care. Christ's

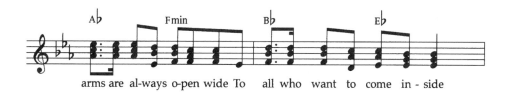

arms are al-ways o-pen wide To all who want to come in - side

Ex-tend the ta-ble, The Ta-ble of— the Lord. Ta-ble of the Lord.

Extend the Table -4-

Freedom is Coming

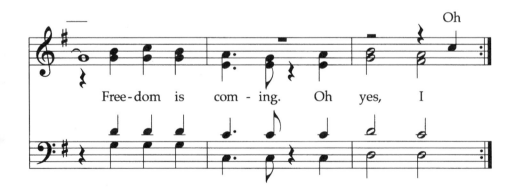

public domain

Freedom is Coming -2-

Halle, Halle, Hallelujah

Words by George Mulrain

Music: Caribbean Folk Song
arr. Carlton R. Young

Add voices in small notes on repeats.

Hal - le, hal - le, hal - le - lu - ja.
1 I AM the rock of a - ges cleft for me;

Hal - le, hal - le, hal - le - lu - ja.
I AM the let me hide myself in thee;

Hal - le, hal - le, hal -
I AM the Rock of a-

These words may be sung ad lib by a soloist, as shown in the score for stanza 1.
The group sings the Hallelujas at the end of each stanza, and may sing the entire chorus,
Halle, halle, halleluia between stanzas.

1. I AM, the Rock of Ages cleft for me; I AM, the Let me hide myself in thee;
   I AM, the Rock of Ages cleft for me; (all), Halleluja. *Halle*, etc.
2. I AM, the Nothing in my hands I bring; I AM, the Simply to thy cross I cling;
   I AM, the Nothing in my hands I bring, (all) Halleluja. *Halle*, etc.
3. I AM the Bread of Life, feed on me; I AM the One True Vine, grow in me;
   I AM the Bread of Life, feed on me; (all) Halleluja. *Halle*, etc.
4. I AM the Resurrection, live in me; I AM the Way, the Truth, follow me.
   I AM the Resurrection, live in me; Halleluja. *Halle*, etc.

Halle, Halle, Hallelujah -2-

Holy, Holy (Le lo le lo lay lo)

Words and music by William Loperena.

Pronounciation in English: le = leh, lay = lie, lo = loh.

Music © Order de Predicadores, Convento Nuestra Señora de Rosario, Bayamon, PR 99060.
Spanish/English edition © 2000 General Board of Global Ministries,
GBKMusik, 475 Riverside Dr., New York, NY 10115. All rights reserved. Used by permission.

Holy, Holy (Le lo le lo lay lo) -2-

A Home Where All Belong

Words by Ruth Duck

Music by Jim Strathdee

1. This is a song for all who live a-lone,
2. This is a song for all who car-ry on,
3. This is a song for homes of man-y kinds,
4. This is a song for all who la-bor long,

form-ing webs of friend-ship, a fam-'ly of their own.
rais-ing sons and daugh-ters, a part-ner new-ly gone.
of-fer-ing loves shel-ter with o-pen hearts and minds.
build-ing on this plan-et a home where all be-long.

Chorus: May we weave cre-a-tive pat-terns of laugh-ter, love, and

tears. May__ grace be in-ter-wo-ven__

1.-3. ____ in the fab-ric of our years.

4. fab-ric of our years.

How Can I Keep from Singing

Verses

1. My life flows on in end-less song A-
2. Through all the tu-mult and the strife, I
3. What though the tem-pest 'round me roar, I
4. When ty-rants trem-ble, sick with fear, And
5. The peace of Christ makes fresh my heart, A

bove earth's lam-en-ta-tion. I hear the real though
hear that mu-sic ring-ing; It sounds and ech-oes
hear the truth it liv-eth. What though the dark-ness
hear their death knells ring-ing; When friends re-joice both
foun-tain ev-er spring-ing. All things are mine since

far-off hymn That hails a new cre-a-tion.
in my soul; How can I keep from sing-ing?
'round me close, Songs in the night it giv-eth.
far and near, How can I keep from sing-ing?
I am his; How can I keep from sing-ing?

Refrain

No storm can shake my in-most calm, While to that rock I'm

cling-ing. Since love is Lord of heav-en and earth,

How can I keep from sing-ing?

(public domain)

Journey to Commitment

Words by Rodney R. Romney

Theme Hymn, 1974 American Baptist Convention   BLOTT EN DAG IRREG.
Oscar Ahnfelt

1. God of love and God of our sal -
2. Broad - er lands in space de - clare Your
3. Let our jour - ney be to new com -

va - tion, To a bro - ken, hun - gry world You've
glo - ry, As be - yond our earth we pierce the
mit - ment, To a deep - er life with - in Your

come, With Your gifts of whole - ness and a -
sky; Soar - ing flights be - yond our high - est
grace, Let us reach in love to one an -

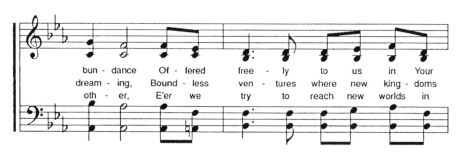

bun - dance Of - fered free - ly to us in Your
dream - ing, Bound - less ven - tures where new king - doms
oth - er, E'er we try to reach new worlds in

Son. Yet our world is still with hate di -
lie. Yet no flight can e'er out - run Your
space. Glo - ry be to God who rules the

vid - ed, Ghetto - ed lives be - tray our des - perate
pres - ence, There's no realm your truth has not been
heav - ens, Glo - ry be to Christ the ho - ly

fear. Walk a -gain our streets of lone - ly
spread, There's no king - dom but Your own e -
one. Yours the king - dom, pow - er and the

liv - ing, Show the king - dom in its beau - ty here.
ter - nal, Bring - ing life where once all life seemed dead.
glo - ry In this world and in all worlds to come.

Journey to Commitment -2-

Lullabye (Like a Ship in the Harbor)

Words and music by Cris Williamson

Lullabye (Like a Ship in the Harbor) -2-

Singing for Our Lives
(We are a Gentle, Angry People)

Words and music by Holly Near

1. We are a gen-tle, an-gry peo - ple, and we are sing - ing, sing-ing for our lives.
2. We are a jus-tice-seek-ing peo - ple, and we are sing - ing, sing-ing for our lives.
3. We are young and old to-geth - er, and we are sing - ing, sing-ing for our lives.
4. We are a land of man-y col - ors, and we are sing - ing, sing-ing for our lives.

We are a gen-tle, an-gry peo - ple, and we are
We are a jus-tice-seek-ing peo - ple, and we are
We are young and old to-geth - er, and we are
We are a land of man-y col - ors, and we are

sing - ing, sing - ing for our lives.
sing - ing, sing - ing for our lives.
sing - ing, sing - ing for our lives.
sing - ing, sing - ing for our lives.

5. We are gay and straight together,
And we are singing, singing for our lives.
We are gay and straight together,
And we are singing, singing for our lives.

6. We are a gentle, loving people,
And we are singing, singing for our lives.
We are a gentle, loving people,
And we are singing, singing for our lives.

Singing for Our Lives (We are a Gentle, Angry People) -2-

The Song of Letting Go

Words and music by Thew Elliot

Accompaniment Figure: The Song of Letting Go

Start simply. Play the accompaniment figure as many times as you like for an introduction. Begin with the first voice only, then add the second voice to it, and finally add the third voice. The first voice (main melody) may be sung by men and/or women. While the harmonies work in any voice, they are most effective if the second voice is women, and the third voice is men. Once all the voices are singing, the song can build. Other instruments or solo singers may improvise over the top of the "wash" of sound. Gradually, it should come back to a quiet state as in the beginning. The final ending is indicated by the double bar line in the vocal score.

This may be accompanied by guitar. When using guitar, it is more easily sung in A major. The guitar accompaniment is simply one measure of A, one measure of Asus4, in the rhythm indicated above.

Tempo suggestion: quarter note=80

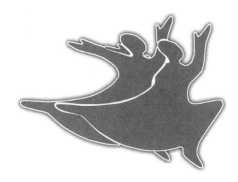

The Song of Letting Go -2-

Song of the Soul

Words and music by Cris Williamson

1&4. "Love of my life,"—— I am cry-ing;
2. What do you do—— for your liv-ing?
3. Come to your life—— like a war-rior;

I am not dy-ing: I—— am danc - ing,
Are you for - giv-ing, giv - ing shel - ter?
noth-in' will bore yer. You can be hap - py.

danc-ing a - long—— in the mad-ness; there is no
Fol-low your heart;—— love will find you; truth will un -
Let in the light;—— it will heal you; and you can

sad-ness, on - ly a song of the soul.—— And we'll
bind you. Sing out a song of the soul.——
feel you sing out a song of the soul.——

sing this song. Why don't you sing

Alternate words can be used for the beginning of verse 3:
"Come to your life like a lover; and you'll discover you can be happy."

Song of the Soul -2-

Spirit, I Have Heard You Calling

Words and music by Thew Elliot

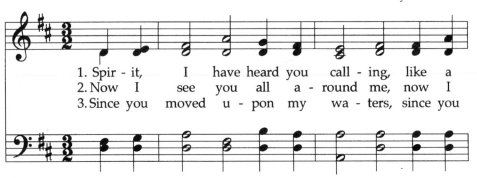

1. Spir - it, I have heard you call - ing, like a
2. Now I see you all a - round me, now I
3. Since you moved u - pon my wa - ters, since you

mem - 'ry long grown dim, cry - ing from cre - a - tion's
hear you call my name. Now I speak the words you
spoke and set me free, I have yearned for this com-

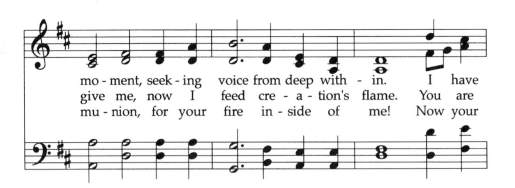

mo - ment, seek - ing voice from deep with - in. I have
give me, now I feed cre - a - tion's flame. You are
mu - nion, for your fire in - side of me! Now your

heard   you   in   my   long - ing.   I   have
speak - ing through my   long - ing.   You   are
love   de - fines my   long - ing.   Now   your

heard   you   in   my   pain.   Now   I   feel   you mov-ing
speak - ing through my   pain.   Now   I   feel   you mov-ing
love   shines through my   pain.   Now   we   dance in end-less

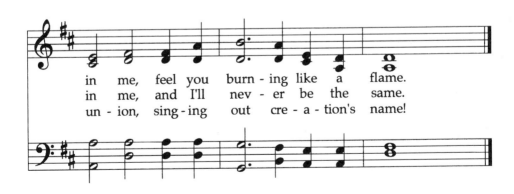

in   me,   feel   you   burn - ing like   a   flame.
in   me,   and   I'll   nev - er be   the   same.
un - ion, sing - ing out   cre - a - tion's name!

Spirit, I Have Heard You Calling -2-

Song of the Body of Christ

Hawaiian song adapted by David Haas

Walk With Me

Words and music by John S. Rice

Walk with me, I will walk with you and

Fine

Build the land that God has planned where love shines through.

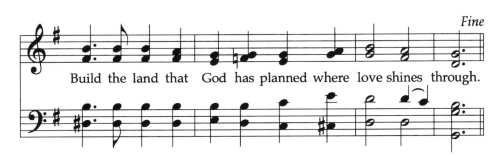

1. When Mo-ses heard the call of God, He said, "Lord don't send me."
2. Now Pe-ter was a most un-like-ly Man to lead the flock;
3. Young Ma-ry Mag-da-lene was sure her life could be much more,
4. And when you share your faith with me and work for life made new,

D.C.

But God told Mo-ses "you're the one to set my peo-ple free."
But Je-sus knew his ho-li-ness And he be-came the Rock.
And by her faith she dared to let God's love un-lock the door.
The wit-ness of your faith-ful-ness Calls me to walk with you.

What Does the Lord Require

Words and music by Jim Strathdee

Micah 6:8

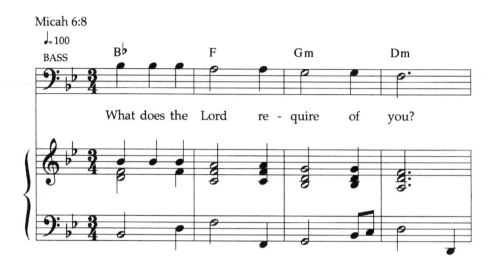

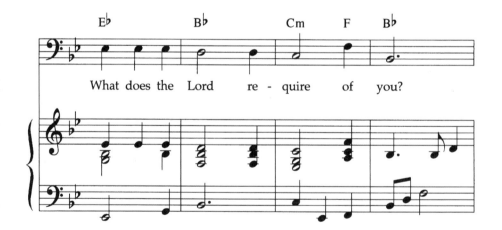

What Does the Lord Require -2-

What Does the Lord Require -3-

Weave

Words and music by Rosemary Crow

Weave, weave, weave us to-geth - er. Weave us to-geth - er in
u -ni-ty and love.___ Weave, weave, weave us to-geth - er.
Weave us to - geth - er, to - geth - er in love.___

1. We are man - y tex - tures,
2. We are dif - ferent in - stru - ments
3. A mo - ment a - go___ we

we are man - y col - ors,___ Each one dif-ferent from the
play - ing our own mel - o - dies, Each one tun - ing to a
did___ not___ know___ our u - ni - ty, on - ly di-

o - ther.___ But we are en - twined with one an-
dif - ferent key.___ But we are all play-ing in
ver - si - ty.___ Now the Christ in___ me___ greets the

oth - - - er in one great tap - es - try.
har - mo - ny, in one great sym - pho - ny.
Christ in thee in one great fam - i - ly.

Walls Mark Our Bound'ries

Words by Ruth C. Duck 1994

Music: PENROSE by Jim Strathdee, 1996

1 Walls mark our bound'-ries and keep us a - part; walls keep the world from our eyes and our heart. Ta - bles are round, mak - ing room for one more, wel - com - ing friends we had not known be - fore. So

2 Walls make us sure who is in and who's out; walls keep us safe from all ques - tion and doubt, but at a ta - ble in o - pen ex - change new ties are formed as our lives re - ar - range. So

3 Once we were strang - ers, di - vi - ded, a - lone. Hate and dis - trust built a wall stone by stone. Now at a ta - ble the bread that we share joins us to Christ in a cir - cle of care. So

Walls Mark Our Bound'ries -2-

Chapter 10

Songs Beyond the Basics

A new inspiration springs forth with every time, with every age, with every place. In the song of the church there is always one more measure, one more note, one more verse, more lyrics, and above all, more deeds to perform, deeds that build the temple of the kingdom of God.

Ricardo Ramirez

Choral Submissions

Christmas is a Covenant, choral arrangement by Judith Hanlon available from Passage Music Ministries, P.O. Box 60127, Worcester, MA 01606

The Year of Jubilee is Here, choral and bell choir arrangement by Carl Wiltse of A Minor Music Company, 932 Virginia, SE, Grand Rapids, MI 49506

Music

The music was kindly submitted by a variety of individuals and publishers.

All the Days of Your Life

Words and music by Mike Stern

Be for Us a Model

A hymn for the blessing of a committment

Words and music by Timothy Kocher-Hillmer

Bring the Feast to Every Hillside

Words: Joan Prefontaine, 1996　　　　　　　　　Music: FEAST by Jane Ramseyer Miller

1. Bring the feast to ev-ery hill-side where the hun-gry peo-ple wait.
2. Bring the feast to ev-ery hide-out where the poor and thirst-y dwell,
3. Who will love de-sert-ed spa-ces? Who will share a strang-er's cup?
4. Danc-ing at in-clu-sive tab-les gay and straight to-ge-ther sing.

Loaves and fish-es mul-ti-ply-ing: com-mon mir-a-cles cre-ate!
cries of pain and des-per-a-tion, card-board shel-ters, pri-son cells.
Who will bless those no one bless-es? Who will speak and dare stand up?
Join with us to strength-en, nur-ture, let our just-ice voic-es ring!

While some choose to keep their ta-ble where a weal-thy few can dine,
Where there is no grass to rest on, where the earth's been paved and torn,
O Cre-a-tor, Life Sus-tain-er, spark of hope in young and old,
Bread that knows no gen-dered lan-guage, grapes of sol-i-dar-i-ty;

Let us praise a wid-er ven-ture: mov-ing ban-quets, bread and wine.
let us spread com-mu-nal ta-bles 'till in-jus-tice is out-worn.
help us spread and move the ta-ble where we of-ten fear to go.
Sis-ters, bro-thers, join the Love Feast, dance to shape com-mun-i-ty!

The Call of God

Words and music by Julian Rush

1. IN CONG - RE - GA - TIONS LARGE AND SMALL, WE GA - THER WITH OUR DREAMS, SUR - ROUN - DED BY A BRO - KEN WORLD IN WHICH CON - FU - SION TEEMS. THOUGH CRIES OF HU - MAN SUF - FER - ING MIGHT LEAD US TO DES - PAIR, AS

2. THE SAINTS WHO WALKED BE - FORE US HAVE PRO - VI - DED US A GUIDE. LET NOT THEIR SELF - LESS WIT - NESS OF DE - VO - TION BE DE - NIED.

3. A DIS - TANT FU - TURE BEA - KONS WITH UN - CER - TAIN - TY. WE PRAY THE LOVE OF CHRIST WILL GUIDE US AS WE FACE THE COM - ING DAY.

The Call of God -2-

Christmas Bells

Words and music by Jeanne Knepper

Descant: Al - le - lu - ia, Jus - tice

1. An-gels sing of peace to all peo-ple. Jus-tice is born in the
2. Shep-herds heard the an - gels_ sing-ing songs to in-clude them in
3. We still come with hearts full of long-ing, hop-ing to hear words of

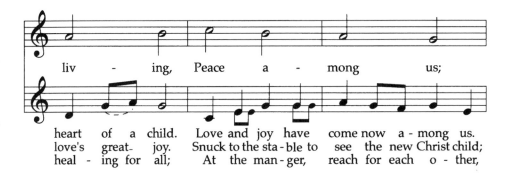

liv - ing, Peace a - mong us;

heart of a child. Love and joy have come now a - mong us.
love's great_ joy. Snuck to the sta - ble to see the new Christ child;
heal - ing for all; At the man - ger, reach for each o - ther,

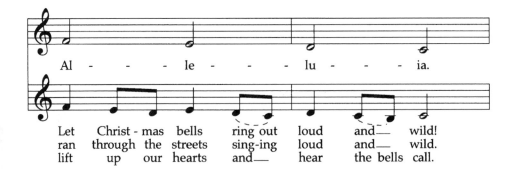

Al - - - le - - - lu - - - ia.

Let Christ - mas bells ring out loud and_ wild!
ran through the streets sing-ing loud and_ wild.
lift up our hearts and_ hear the bells call.

Al - le - lu - ia,   Jus - tice

Chorus: Peace a - mong us!   Jus - tice liv - ing!   Joy comes to us in the

liv - ing,   Peace   a - mong   us;

light of a star.   Let   us sing out   Christ - mas bless - ing;

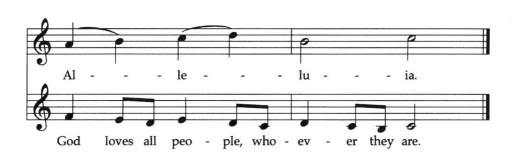

Al - - le - - lu - - ia.

God   loves all   peo - ple, who - ev - er they are.

Christmas Bells -2-

Christmas is a Covenant

Words and music by Judith Hanlon

1. Chris-tmas is a cov-e-nant, a__ prom-ise from the past. a__ hope for all to-mor-rows,__ lovethat will__ last.__ Christ-mas is a
2. Keep your ba-bies near to heart, hold tight the el-der's hand, gen-e-ra-tions of the Pro-mised One bring-ing Christ in-to the land.__ Sing car-ols to the
3. O come, come all ye faith-ful ones, a__-round the mang-er kneel. With our child-ren, friends and fam-i-ly,__ this cov-e-nant we seal.__ We'll walk as peo-ple
4. Chris-tmas is a cov-e-nant, a__ prom-ise from the past. a__ hope for all to-mor-rows,__ lovethat will__ last.__ O come,come all ye

Christmas is a Covenant -2-

Christmas is a Covenant -3-

Dona Nobis Pacem

Words and music by Jan Powers

Do - na___ No - bis___

Pa - - - - - cem.___

Show us your face,___
Child - - - ren of song___

Fill us with grace;___
Wo - - - ven and strong,___

© 1989 Jan Powers

Congregations may reproduce without restriction for local worship use provided the copyright owner is
acknowledged. For other uses, contact the copyright owner.

Make gen - tle all we do,
Shar - - ing the gos - pel call;

As we live in you;_____
Reach - ing out to all._____

Help us leave be-hind all hin - drance from the past;
Daugh-ter pro-phets of a new day com-ing soon,

Free us to love and to heal;_____
Young sons with free - dom to dream;_____

Dona Nobis Pacem -2-

Dona Nobis Pacem -3-

The Color of Grace

Words and music by Judith Hanlon

From cre - a - tion to e - ter - ni - ty on God's
Each____ day is a____ treas - ure in____
I am called to il____ - lu - mine re -

can - vas of____ life,____ we're____ the light of
God's mas - ter____ plan. We____ ren - der
demp - tion's ta - pes - try____ wo____ - ven on the

mer - cy____ brought to dark____ strife.____ The
beau - ty____ by be - ing God's____ hands.____ By
paths that____ lead to Cal - va - ry.____ With

brill - iance of our co____ - lors can____ on - ly be rea -
heal - ing and____ hold____ - ing the____ lost and the de -
Es - ther and____ A - bra - ham, Ma - ry, Dan - iel and____

The Color of Grace -2-

Come to the Table

Words and music by Julian Rush

1.THRU THE DE - SERT WE HAVE BEEN LED,
2.THOSE DE - JEC - TED, LIV - ING IN FEAR,
3.FROM THE - VAL - LEYS, THRU - OUT THE LAND,

BY GOD'S MAN - NA WE HAVE BEEN FED.
THOSE IN - FEC - TED, SUF - FER - ING HERE,
HOPE IS RIS - ING. WE UN - DER STAND

PEO - PLE OF FAITH WHO WOULD FOL - LOW THE WAY,
MAR - GIN - AL PEO - PLE WHO LIVE IN THE FRAY,
WE HAVE BEEN SENT TO ALL PEO - PLES TO SAY,

COME THIS DAY___ COME TO THE
COME THIS DAY___ COME TO THE
COME THIS DAY___ COME TO THE

Come to the Table -2-

For the Sky

Words and music by Jan Powers

1. For the sky and for the land,
2. Make this time a wel - come place,
3. Through all cyc - lic sea - son song,
4. For the tune in na - ture's call, for
5. May the cos - mic thread of peace be
6. For our la - bor yet to be:

Mys - tic u - ni - fy - ing hand, we
Full of laugh - ter, hope, and grace for
Join our voic - es, clear and strong in
All things liv - ing, great and small, we're
Wo - ven here, by all who cease their
May we birth it joy - ful - ly in

thank you, we thank you, we thank you, we thank you.
friend,___ for friend,___ and strang - er, and strang - er.
glad - ness, in glad - ness, in glad - ness, in glad - ness.
danc - ing, we're danc - ing, we're danc - ing, we're danc - ing.
hat - ing, their hat - ing, and judg - ing, and judg - ing.
praise,___ in praise___ to you,___ to you.___

May the Spir - it show - er us with love. Let it be.

For Those Tears I Died

Words and music by Marsha Stevens

way. But just like you pro-mised, You came there to—
be.   Your love loosed my chains,— and in You I'm
doors, and I thank You, and praise You from earth's hum-ble

stay.———————— I just had to pray.——
free.———————— But Je - sus, why me?——
shores.———————— Take me; I'm Yours.——

— And Je-sus said, "Come to the wa - ter, stand by My—

For Those Tears I Died -2-

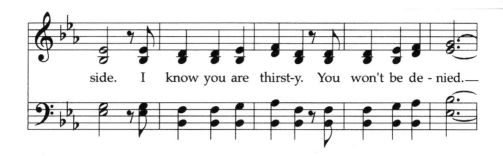

side.   I   know you are thirst-y.   You   won't be de - nied.——

—— I   felt ev - 'ry   tear - drop when in dark-ness you

cried,————   And I   strove to   re - mind

you   that for those tears I   died."————

For Those Tears I Died -3-

A Gift for the Altar

Words and music by Amanda Udis-Kessler

1. Jane has a gift for the al - tar: She brings peace she has found, peace to pass all a-round, sweet peace; God's peace for the al - tar but she comes with her lov - er to hon - or the day. The church in its fear turns the wo - men a - way, Late at night they join hands and in sad - ness they pray that the doors of the church will be o - pened AND THE ONE

2. Bob has a gift for the al - tar: He brings cour - age and trust that the world can be just good faith, God's faith for the al - tar but he's nev - er been shy a - bout who shares his life The ring on his fin - ger is not from his wife. The cold - ness they show him cuts deep as a knife and he leaves through the doors still un - o - pened BUT THE ONE

3. We have a gift for the al - tar: We bring all we can give all the days that we live These lives, our lives for the al - tar. Will the al - tar stand emp - ty? The church must de - cide. With our heads bowed in prayer and lift - ed in pride we have light for the world that can - not be de - nied Yes the doors of the church will be o - pened FOR THE ONE

A Gift for the Altar -2-

I Am that Great and Fiery Force

Words and music by Jane Ramseyer Miller

1. I am that great and fier-y force, spark-ling in ever-y thing that lives. In shin-ing of the riv-er's course, in green-ing grass that glor-y gives.

2. I shine in glitt-er on the seas, in burn-ing sun, in moon and stars. In un-seen wind in ver-dant trees I breathe with-in, both near and far.

3. And where I breathe there is no death, and mea-dows glow with beaut-ies rife. I am in all the spir-it's breath, the thund-ered word, for I am Life.

Jesus Christ, Hope of the World

Words and music by Reinhardt & Gottinari
(translated by Pablo Sosa)

1. A lit - tle be - yond this our time, the fu - ture an-nounc-es with gladness: no war, no dis - as - ter, no crime, no more des - o - la - tion, no sad - ness.

2. We want to cast out all our hate, we long for a world of pure beau-ty, in which peace will nev - er a - bate and jus - tice for all our du - ty.

3. We hope for a new world of trust: no one will be fee - ble nor strong. The sys-tems we have are un-just: they al - ways di - vi - sions pro - long.

4. The seeds of your kin - dom we bear, your fu - ture is draw-ing so near: the earth with your help we pre - pare un - til you in full - ness ap - pear.

God, break the walls, set us free! Trans-form this la-ment in-to danc-ing. Our hope and all of our long - ings, trans - form in the full-ness of life; our hope and all of our long - ings, trans - form in the full-ness of life. A - ieh, e - iah, a - ieh a-eh a - eh. A - ieh, e - ieh, a - ieh a-eh a - eh.

Inspired by Love and Anger

Words and music by Iona Community

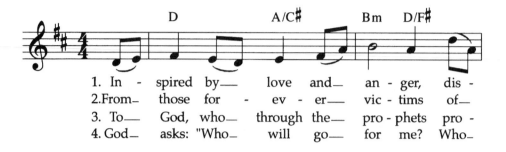

1. In - spired by— love and— an - ger, dis -
2. From— those for - ev - er— vic - tims of—
3. To— God, who— through the— pro - phets pro -
4. God— asks: "Who— will go— for me? Who—

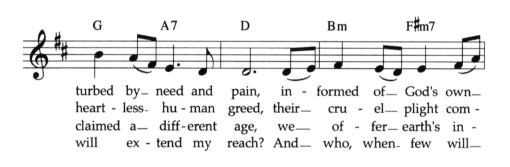

turbed by— need and pain, in - formed of— God's own—
heart - less— hu - man greed, their— cru - el— plight com -
claimed a— diff - erent age, we— of - fer— earth's in -
will ex - tend my reach? And— who, when— few will—

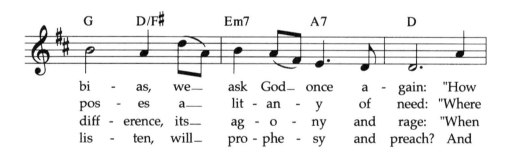

bi - as, we— ask God— once a - gain: "How
pos - es a— lit - an - y of need: "Where
diff - erence, its— ag - o - ny and rage: "When
lis - ten, will— pro - phe - sy and preach? And

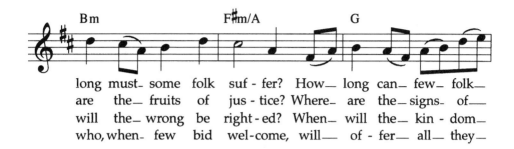

long must― some folk suf - fer? How― long can― few― folk―
are the― fruits of jus - tice? Where― are the― signs― of――
will the― wrong be right - ed? When― will the― kin - dom――
who, when― few bid wel-come, will―― of - fer― all― they―

mind? How― long dare― vain self - in - terest turn―
peace? When― is the― day when― pris - oners and――
come? When― will the― world be―― gen - erous to――
know? And― who, when― few dare― fol - low, will――

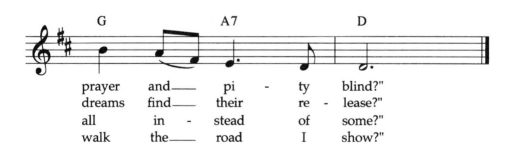

prayer and―― pi - ty blind?"
dreams find―― their re - lease?"
all in - stead of some?"
walk the―― road I show?"

Inspired by Love and Anger -2-

Jesu tawa pano

Words and music by Matsikenjiri

Other stanzas may be improvised: Savior; Master; Spirit

* sometimes sung B, sometimes sung ** D2

Justice Round

Words and music by Thew Elliott

All a - round me voic - es ring: "Jus - tice!" is the song they sing! And with - in this song I'll sing my part; I will rise and speak what's in my heart! I will rise!_____ I will rise!_____

Accompaniment Figure: Justice Round

The accompaniment and the singing should sound like bells. Pianists can achieve this effect by using the sostenuto pedal and striking the keys lightly, coming off almost immediately and letting the pedal sustain the sound (refresh the pedal whenever the sound begins to get too muddy). Singers can achieve a bell effect simply by thinking "I will make my voice sound like a bell!"

Tempo suggestion: half note=80

Leading the Dance

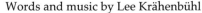

Words and music by Lee Krähenbühl

2. Dance at the table, dance at the wall.
   Dance in the place where they're never seen dancing at all.
   There's no waiting for any permission this time
   Because nobody bothered to ask
   When the clear voice of Jesus says, "Rise up and walk,"
   You don't say, "May I please?" You just lead in the dance.

REFRAIN

3. Dance in the light-stream through broken prison bars
   Dance in the darkness alive with a billion bright stars
   This is not time for fretting what others will think
   'Cause you never know when it's your turn.
   Just remember Christ's teaching: the first will be last.
   The ones who were last are now leading the dance.

REFRAIN (2x)

The ones who were last are now leading the dance.
The ones who were last are now leading the dance.

Mine is the Church (A Dazzling Bouquet)

With a Cajun swing feel, or boogie woogie

Words and music by Bret Hesla

Refrain: Mine is the church where ev-ery-bo-dy's wel-come.
1 Come here, all you six - foot glad - i - o - las.
2 We don't sim - ply tol - er - ate each oth - er.
3 Our de - mons keep try - ing to di - vide us;

I know it's true 'cause I got through the door.
Come, all you pur - ple li - lacs shin - ing bright.
We ask and tell, we don't just turn a - way.
They doc - u - ment their lies to make them true.

We are a dazz - ling bou-quet of ev-ery kind of flow - er
Come, let us all bloom to-geth - er in the gar - den:
We give at - ten - tion to ev - ery bud and blos-som.
To - day we're freed from our judg - ing and ex - clud-ing.

Sing refrain at beginning and end.
May also be sung between stanzas.

Jump in the vase, 'cause we've got space for more.
A car - ni - val of fra-grance and de-light.
Let ev - 'ry face come grace the grand bou-quet.
Just look a-round, en - joy the love - ly view.

Text and tune © 1995 Bret Hesla, admin. Augsburg Fortress; arrangement from *Global Songs II: Bread for the Journey* © 1997 Augsburg Fortress. Reprinted by permission.

On My Honor

To my dear friends, Jim Carlson and Kevin McConnell for the ocassion
of their celebration of love and their life-long commitment to covenant.

Words and music by Judith Hanlon

On My Honor -2-

Ours the Journey

Words and music by Julian B. Rush

1. In the midst of new di-men-sions, in the face of
2. Through the flood of starv-ing peo-ples, war-ring fac-tions
3. Through the years of hu-man strug-gle, walk a peo-ple
4. We are Black and we are A-sian, In-di-an, His-
5. We are man and we are wo-man, all per-sua-sions,
6. Should the threats of dark pre-dict-ions cause us to with-

chang-ing ways, Who will lead the pil-grim peo-ples
and des-pair, Who will lift the ol-ive branch-es?
long des-pised, Gays and les-bi-ans to-geth-er
pan-ic, White, We a rain-bow co-a-li-tion,
old and young, Each a gift in thy cre-a-tions,
draw in pain, May thy blaz-ing phoe-nix spir-it

wan - der - ing their sep - arate ways?
Who will light the flame of care?
fight - ing to be re - al - ized.
all of val - ue in thy sight.
each a love song to be sung.
res - ur - rect the church a - gain.

God of rain - bow, fier - y pil - lar, lead - ing where the

ea - gles soar, We, thy peo - ple, ours the jour - ney

now and ev - er, now and ev - er, now and ev - er - more.

Ours the Journey -2-

Mothering God, You Gave Me Birth

Words © Jean Wiebe Janzen, 1991,
based on the writing of Julian of Norwich

Music MOTHER ROUND
by Jane Ramseyer Miller, 1996;

```
[1]
1 Moth - er - ing   God,    you   gave   me   birth
2 Moth - er - ing   Christ,  you   took   my   form,
3 Moth - er - ing   Spir - it,     nur - t'ring  one,

[2]
in    the    bright   morn - ing   of    this   world.
off - er - ing   me    your   food   of    light,
in    arms   of    pa - tience   hold   me   close,

[3]
Cre - a - tor,   Source   of    ev - 'ry   breath,   you
grain   of    all    life,    and   fruit   of    love,   your
so    that   in    faith    I    root   and   grow   un -

[4]
are   my    rain,    my    wind,   my    sun.
ver - y    bod - y    for    my    peace.
til    I    flow'r,   un - til    I    know.
```

Reconciling People

Words by Carole Elizabeth

Music by Gerald. W. Holbrook

1. Walls of co - lor, ways of lov - ing, Mo - ney, pow'r, and war
2. Gays and les - bi - ans and straight folks Should not dis - a - gree.
3. Shall we hide in de - gra - da - tion? Shall we fear each oth - er?
4. It is truth, God's truth, that frees us; Fear that walls us in.

Keep us locked in lone - ly __ pri - sons; God calls us to more:
God who formed us, calls and __ loves us, Made us to be free:
Join hands, all God's pre - cious __ peo - ple, Sis - ter, bro - ther, lov - er:
Shout for free - dom, joy, and __ vis - ion; Come now, let's be - gin:

Re - con - cil - ing, build - ing bridg - es 'cross the gap be - tween

Vi - sions of what ought __ to __ be And what we know and see.

Seeking Healing in Our Journey

Words and music by Jane Ramseyer Miller
arr. Madelin Sue Martin

Stand Up

Words and music by Mike Stern

First they came for the com- mun- ists then they came for the Jews
Then they came for the un- ion- ists and they came for the priests
Then they came for the pac- i- fists and they came for the gays
Still they come for the out- casts for the poor (and) re- fu- gees

but I was- n't a com- mun- ist and I was- n't a Jew
but I was- n't a un- ion- ist and I was- n't a priest
but I was- n't a pac- i- fist and I was- n't gay
(and) though I am not an out- cast (and) I'm not (poor) or (a) ref- u- gee, (To Coda)

so I did- n't stand up and I did- n't ask why

by the time they came for me there was no one left to ask why

now I'm gon- na stand up and I'm gon- na ask why
yes we're gon- na stand up and we're gon- na ask why

and if some time they come for me I hope there's some- one stand- ing by my side,
and if some time they come for us there'll be lots of peop- le stand- ing side by

side, a whole lot of peo- ple stand- ing side by side.

© 1985 Mike Stern

Congregations may reproduce without restriction for local worship use provided the copyright owner is acknowledged. For other uses, contact the copyright owner.

Survivors

Words and music by Ann Freeman Price,
arr. Carolyn Gray

1. The times— have been tough. The bar - riers— have been
2. The days— have been long. The strug - gle— has been
3. We stand— in the storm. The thun - der— e - choes
4. The dreams— have been born. The vis - ion— starts to

strong.— The laws— have been rig - id, And the
hard.— Real change— has come slow - ly, And we've
round.— We stand— firm to - geth - er, And we
grow.— We all— form a cir - cle, And we

Survivors -2-

We are Not Going Away

Words and music by Lee Krähenbühl

Note from Lee Krähenbühl: This song was inspired by the following Biblical accounts (in order of appearance): Luke 11:5-8; Luke 18:1-8; Genesis 32:24-30; 2 Kings 4:8-37; Matthew 15:22-28; Luke 18:9-10; and by the final speech in Tony Kushner's play Angels in America, Part II: Perestroika.*"Kindling" performed it at the Sierra Song & Story Fest. I wanted it to have a life of its own and to grow, like any good folk song, after I had turned it loose. I've added about five or six verses (not printed here) to fit certain special occasions. I invite you to do the same, in the spirit of those who open their arms in love and goodwill to people who haven't been able to bring themselves to do the same—yet.*

See verses on next page➡

Repeat the melody in the measures beginning with the words "There once was a man" for each couplet throughout each verse. Please note that some verses have more couplets than others. Also, the number and rhythm of the words change from verse to verse. Be free in setting them to the melody. Repeat the chorus after each verse.

1. (continued) "We're all in bed for the night, old pal; we're in for the night, I say.
   It's much too late for your room and your board; no hard feelings, but please go away."
   But the man he did knock and the man he did pound 'til the rooster crowed in the day,
   And the weary friend finally opened the door and asked him in to stay.
   And Jesus said God gives more freely than this, if only we will pray.
   So sisters and brothers, believe in his words—we are not going away!

   Chorus

2. There once was a judge, so Jesus has told, who thought he could live on his own,
   But there was a widow who had a case and would not leave him alone.
   Now the judge cared not for people or God, and he wished that the widow were dead.
   But just to get the old gal off his back, he granted her wishes instead.
   And Jesus said God gives more freely than this, if only we will pray.
   So sisters and brothers, believe in his words—we are not going away!

   Chorus

3. Now Jacob wrestled an angel at dawn—that sure seems like a dumb thing to do;
   But the angel gave him a name and a blessing, 'cause Israel would not let go.
   And the prophet Elijah was much too busy to perform resurrection one day,
   But he raised the son of the Shunammite woman; she was not going away.
   And we believe God gives more freely than this, if only we will pray,
   So sisters and brothers, believe in his Word; we are not going away!

   Chorus

4. Jesus' people hated the Canaanites; they thought they were lost in sin.
   So Jesus himself was caught by surprise when a woman of Canaan came in.
   And when he compared her people to dogs, she did not flee or sway.
   And she changed the mind of the Lord and he blessed her because she would not go away.
   The old Pharisees thought when they put him to death that in the grave Jesus would stay.
   But just like our Lord, we are rising again; we are not going away!

   Chorus

5. Now Jesus said "ask" and Jesus said "seek," and Jesus said "knock on the door."
   And it will be given and we shall find and it will be opened for sure.
   Now you might shut us out and go hide in your room. "Out of sight, out of mind," you might say.
   But we believe in the promise of Jesus, and we are not going away.
   We're partnered and single, we're wealthy and poor. We're straight and we're lesbian and gay.
   We're brown and pink and all shades in between. We're young and lived many a day.
   And we're singing and praying in spirit and soul, and try to ignore us you may.
   But why not get to know us? We'll be here awhile; we are not going away!

   Chorus

We are Not Going Away -2-

What Does the Lord Require of Thee

Words and music by Mike Stern

You Gave Me Life

Words based on prayer
by Edward Hays

Music by
Timothy Kocher-Hillmer

You gave me life, you know me. Your

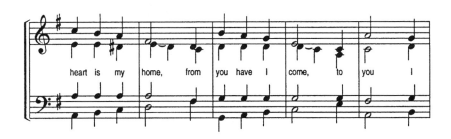

heart is my home, from you have I come, to you I

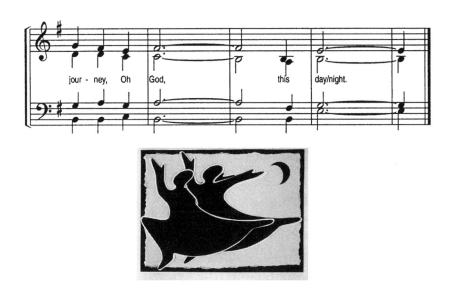

jour - ney, Oh God, this day/night.

Chapter 11

Selected Worship Resources

"Worship that liberates is powerful because it gather the tears of the past and the dreams of the future into the hearts of those desiring to live fully in the present."

Kittredge Cherry & Zalmon Sherwood

See also the Resources for Readings on page 265

Alexander, Marilyn Bennett and James Preston. *We Were Baptized Too: Claiming God's Grace for Lesbians and Gays*. Westminster John Knox Press, Louisville, 1996.

Ayers, Tess and Paul Brown. *The Essential Guide to Lesbian and Gay Weddings*. Alyson Publications, Boston, 1999.

Butler, Becky, ed. *Ceremonies of the Heart: Celebrating Lesbian Unions*. Seal Press Feminist Publishing, 1997.

Cherry, Kittredge and Zalmon Sherwood, ed. *Equal Rites: Lesbian and Gay Worship, Ceremonies and Celebrations*. Westminster John Knox Press, Louisville, 1995.

Duck, Ruth, ed. *Bread for the Journey: Resources for Worship*. United Church Press, Cleveland, 1981.

_____ and Maren C. Tirabassi, eds. *Touch Holiness: Resources for Worship*. Pilgrim Press, New York, 1989.

_____. *Finding Words for Worship: A Guide for Leaders*. Westminster John Knox Press, Louisville, Kentucky, 1995.

Eiesland, Nancy and Don Saliers. *Human Disability and the Service of God*. Abingdon Press, Nashville, 1998.

Fortune, Marie. *Violence in the Family: A Workshop Curriculum for Clergy and Other Helpers*. The Pilgrim Press, Cleveland, 1991.

Glaser, Chris. *Coming Out to God: Prayers for Lesbians and Gay Men, Their Families and Friends*. Westminster John Knox Press, Louisville, 1991.

Huck, Gabe, ed. *A Sourcebook about Liturgy*. Liturgy Training Publications, Archdiocese of Chicago, 1994.

Lewin, Ellen. *Recognizing Ourselves: Ceremonies of Lesbian & Gay Commitment.* Columbia University Press, 1998.

Liebenow, Mark. *And Everyone Shall Praise: Resources for Multicultural Worship* and *Prepare the Way.* Pilgrim Press, Cleveland, 1999.

Loder, Ted. *Guerrillas of Grace: Prayers for the Battle.* LuraMedia, San Diego, 1984.

More Light Update. Monthly newsletter of Presbyterians for Lesbian & Gay Concerns. Communications Secretary and Newsletter Editor James D. Anderson, P.O. Box 38, New Brunswick, NJ 08903-0038.

McClain, George. *Claiming All Things for God: Prayer, Discernment, and Ritual for Social Change.* Abingdon Press, Nashville, 1998.

Open Hands: Resources for Ministries Affirming the Diversity of Human Sexuality. Chris Glaser, editor. Published by the Reconciling Congregation Program, Inc. 3801 N. Keeler Avenue, Chicago, IL 60641.

Preach Out! Open and Affirming Sermons of the United Church of Christ. United Church Board for Homeland Ministries, 1999. Contact ONA Program-The Coalition at onaabday@aol.com or 508-856-9316.

Ricciuti, Gail and Rosemary Mitchell. *Birthings and Blessings II: More Liberating Worship Services for the Inclusive Church.* Crossroad, New York, 1993.

Richardson, Jan L. *Night Visions: Searching the Shadows of Advent and Christmas.* United Church Press, Cleveland, 1998.

_____. *Sacred Journeys.* Upper Room Books, Nashville, 1995.

Roberts, Elizabeth and Elias Amidon. *Earth Prayers From Around the World: 365 Prayers, Poems, and Invocations for Honoring the Earth.* HarperCollins, San Francisco, 1991.

Ruether, Rosemary Radford. *Women-Church: Theology and Practice of Feminist Liturgical Communities.* Harper & Row, Publishers, San Francisco, 1986.

Schaffran, Janet and Pat Kozak. *More than Words: Prayer and Ritual for Inclusive Communities.* Meyer-Stone Books, Oak Park, IL, 1986.

Skinner, Don. *Prayers for the Gathered Community: Resources for the Liturgical Year.* United Church Press, Cleveland, 1997.

Stuart, Elizabeth. *Daring to Speak Love's Name: A Gay and Lesbian Prayer Book.* Hamish Hamilton, London, 1992.

Tirabassi, Maren C. *An Improbable Gift of Blessing, Gifts of Many Cultures: Worship Resources for the Global Community.* United Church Press, Cleveland, 1995.

_____. *Blessing New Voices: Prayers of Young People and Worship Resources for Youth Ministry.* United Church Press, Cleveland, 2000.

Weems, Ann. *Reaching for Rainbows: Resources for Creative Worship.* The Westminster Press, Philadelphia, 1980.

Whitcomb, Holly. *Feasting with God: Adventures in Table Spirituality.* United Church Press, Cleveland, 1996.

Winter, Miriam Therese. *WomanWord.* Crossroad, New York, 1990.

Welcoming Program Denominational Websites

Baptist

Association of Welcoming and Affirming Baptists – members.aol.com/ wabaptists/index.html

> Members are churches, organizations, and individuals who are willing to go on record as welcoming and affirming all persons without regard to sexual orientation, and who have joined together to advocate for the full inclusion of Lesbian, Gay, Bisexual and Transgender persons within American Baptist communities of faith.

Rainbow Baptists – www.rainbowbaptists.org

> A joint venture of American Baptists Concerned for Sexual Minorities and Honesty (an association of local groups that provide support, education and advocacy for Gay, Lesbian, Bisexual and Transgender Baptists). Information on coming-out issues, regional and national support groups, homosexuality and the Bible, welcoming & affirming churches and resources for youth and families, and links to affirming Christian organizations in other denominations and general links of interest to LGBT people. Includes a link to American Baptists Concerned, a support, education and advocacy group for Lesbian, Gay, Bisexual and Transgender Baptists that also provides support and resources to families and friends of sexual minority Baptists, churches and clergy.

Brethren/Mennonite

Brethren/Mennonite Council for Lesbian and Gay Concerns – www.webcom.com/bmc/welcome.html

> Provides support for Mennonite and Church of the Brethren Gay, Lesbian and Bisexual people, their friends and families, by fostering dialogue between Gay and non-gay people, and providing accurate information about homosexuality from the social sciences, biblical studies, and theology.

Catholic

Dignity/USA – www.dignityusa.org/index.html

> Organized to unite Gay, Lesbian, Bisexual and Transgender Catholics, as well as families, friends and loved ones in order to develop leadership, and be an instrument through which they may be heard by and promote reform in the Church.

Disciples of Christ

Gay, Lesbian and Affirming Disciples (GLAD) Alliance –
www.gladalliance.org
> A presence working for the full dignity and integrity of Gay, Lesbian,
> Bisexual and affirming people within the Christian Church (Disciples
> of Christ).

Eastern Orthodox

AXIOS – qrd.rdrop.com:80/qrd/www/orgs/axios
> Organization of Eastern & Near Eastern Orthodox, and Byzantine &
> Eastern-rite Catholic Gay & Lesbian lay Christians.

Episcopal

Integrity – www.integrityusa.org
> Integrity's mission is to be a witness of Lesbian, Gay, Bisexual, and
> Transgender persons in the Episcopal Church and to the world.

The Oasis – members.aol.com/TheOasisNJ/
> Ministry of cultural and racial diversity in the Episcopal Diocese of
> Newark with all who experience prejudice and oppression because
> of their sexual orientation, as well as their families and friends, offer-
> ing reconciliation, education, liberation and hope to all who seek
> sanctuary, empowerment, justice and peace.

Alliance of Lesbian and Gay Anglicans – www.alga.org
> Working for the unconditional inclusion and full participation of Les-
> bian and Gay people in every facet of the Church's life throughout
> the Anglican Communion.

Lutheran

Lutherans Concerned North America – www.lcna.org
> Advocates for positive change within the Lutheran church; started
> the Reconciling in Christ program to recognize Lutheran congrega-
> tions which welcome Lesbian and Gay believers.

Metropolitan Community Church

Metropolitan Community Church – www.ufmcc.com
> An inclusive worldwide Fellowship of Christian congregations with a
> special outreach to the world's Gay, Lesbian, Bisexual and
> Transgender communities.

Presbyterian

More Light Presbyterians – www.mlp.org
> Seeking the full participation of Gay, Lesbian, Bisexual and Transgender people of faith in the life, ministry, and witness of the Presbyterian Church (USA).

Quaker

Friends for Lesbian and Gay Concerns – www.geocities.com/WestHollywood/2473/flgc.html
> An association of Lesbian, Gay, Bisexual, Trans, and non-gay Friends (Quakers) who seek spiritual community within the Religious Society of Friends. This fellowship, seeks to know God within and to express God's truth in the Quaker and Lesbian/Gay/Bisexual communities.

Q-Light – world.std.com/~rice/q-light/intro.html
> Place for discussion of topics of interest to Lesbian, Gay, Bisexual, and Transgendered (LGBT) Quakers in an atmosphere of harmony and mutual respect, and a place to seek clarity on issues relating to the place of LGBT Quakers in the Religious Society of Friends in accordance with Friends' principles of gospel order.

Unitarian Universalist

Interweave – www.qrd.org/www/orgs/uua/uu-interweave.html
> A membership organization affiliated with Unitarian Universalist Association, dedicated to the spiritual, political, and social well-being of Unitarian Universalists who are confronting oppression as Lesbians, Gay men, Bisexuals, Transgender persons, and their heterosexual allies, and facilitates the celebration of the culture and lives of its members.

United Church of Canada

acpucc@aol.com – email address for the Affirming Congregation Programme of the United Church of Canada.

United Church of Christ

Open and Affirming Program – www.coalition.simplenet.com/ona/onaindex.htm
> Calls on United Church of Christ Congregations to declare themselves "Open and Affirming" (ONA). The central affirmation of an ONA congregation is that "Gay, Lesbian, and Bisexual people" (or "people of all sexual orientations") are welcome in the full life and ministry of the church.

Lesbian and Gay issues in the UCC – www.ucc.org/headline/gayfac.htm
> Facts about Lesbian and Gay issues in the United Church of Christ.

United Methodist

Affirmation – www.umaffirm.org
> An activist caucus of Lesbian, Gay, Bisexual, and Transgendered people organized to proclaim a gospel of respect, love and justice and empower people to undertake works of inclusion and justice where they are.

Reconciling Congregation Program – www.rcp.org
> Movement of United Methodist individuals, congregations, campus ministries, other groups which publicly welcome all persons, regardless of sexual orientation.

Other Worship-Related Sources

- EarthMinistry – www.earthminstry.org – offers a variety of worship materials to draw attention to the Christian's call to care for all God's creation.

- Gospel Colors – www.gospelcolors.com – is a company that specializes in fiber art for worship settings.

- Passages Music and Ministries – original music by Judith Hanlon and the "The Color Of Grace" CD sung by Passages and friends. www.passagesmusic.com

- Jan Powers' song collection is published by Judson Press in three volumes, "Breathing New Life Into Lent," rooted in the Revised Common Lectionary themes. A Christmas musical, "A Holy Wonder," is in the works, a setting of seven poems by Gordon M. Forbes for easy-choir, flute, and solo voice.

- Scarritt-Bennett Center's Liturgical Design Institute in Nashville, Tennessee, is a source of programs, liturgical needlework, and consultation on worship visuals and arts. Contact LDI at 615-340-7543.

- Shower of Stoles – www.showerofstoles.com
  A collection of hundreds of liturgical stoles from GLBT people of faith from across North America, from Canada to Cuba, Alaska to Hawaii. They are active leaders in their faith communities—ordained ministers, elders, deacons, seminarians, church musicians, missionaries and other gifted people—who have been barred from serving their faith communities because of their sexual orientation. This collection was created as a witness to give a voice to these faithful people, many of whom have been forced to choose between serving in silence or losing their livelihood.

- Michael Stern Music – featuring poet and songwriter Michael Stern, who serves as resource leader and presenter for worship services, conference, retreats and special events for all ages. CDs available. www.home.earthlink.net/~mikesongs

Chapter 12

Study Guide

How to Use this Study Guide

This curriculum is designed to be both flexible and easy to use. It offers a six-week basic course and two optional sessions: one that involves fabric and sewing, and the other providing an arts and crafts experience.

Before you gather for the first meeting, read the study guide introductory materials and the essays to be discussed at the first meeting.

Course Goals

Your own goals and hopes will vary, but the goals that guided the writing of this course are:

- to make connections between faith, embodiment and worship,
- to build a sense of community and support within the group,
- to understand the importance of affirming the diversity of sexuality in the church,
- to encourage worship and living that more deeply reflect the gospel message of incarnation, hospitality and the interconnectness of all life.

Course Organization

Adapted from *Simpler Living, Compassionate Life: A Christian Perspective*

Facilitator: The role of facilitator is designed to rotate each week; the course does not require an experienced leader, expert, or teacher. This contributes to a shared sense of ownership, responsibility and community in the course. Whoever organizes the class will likely be the facilitator for meeting one. Some groups may find it helpful to designate the facilitator for the remaining meetings during meeting one. Others may wish to choose someone to facilitate the next meeting at the end of each meeting. The facilitator should read all the material (readings and curriculum) for "their" meeting thoroughly before the group meets to have a feel for timing, flow and content.

Setting and timing: Ideally, this course should be offered in an informal setting that contributes to a relaxed, community-building atmosphere. With the exception of the two optional "activity" sessions that require tables and craft supplies, chairs set in a circle should be sufficient.

Allow enough time (45 minutes to 1 hour) to experience the material. Decisions regarding how much time should be spent on each section should be made according to the flow of the discussion and the interest of the group.

The two optional activity sessions take more than one hour to complete. You may choose to select a time when 2 to 3 hours are available for these sessions or divide the activity over several weeks.

Group size: Ideal group size is between six to twelve participants. If your group is larger, break into smaller groups for the discussion periods.

Journal: You may wish to bring a journal or notebook to take notes, record feelings and chart how your thoughts have changed over time.

About the readings: This study guide is an attempt to help you form a learning community that hears from a variety of voices–some from within your group, some from the readings. The readings are meant to offer additional voices of persons who could not join your discussion in person, rather than authoritative sources. The goal is not that everyone will emerge from the class believing the same things, but that, in an open sharing of ideas and experience, each individual's own exploration of the issues will be enhanced and supported.

Course Ethos

This course seeks to value individual perspectives, life-experiences and wisdom. You are encouraged to interact with each other and the materials honestly and to be open about your questions, misgivings and hopes. Participants should know, however, that they need to determine their own comfort level in sharing personal information. No one is obligated to participate in ways that make them uneasy.

Cecile Andrews has a number of helpful guidelines for creating a community-oriented group:

- No leaders. Be participatory. This is a circle, not a pyramid, so no one can be a dictator. Everyone is responsible.

- Respond as equals. In this course, we act on the idea that we are all equal.

- Be authentic. We spend a lot of our lives trying to look successful. No one really gets to know us. In this group, try not to pretend. Describe what you really think or feel.

- Focus on the heart. Some conversations come just from the head. When you communicate from the heart, you bring in the whole of yourself: emotions, imagination, spiritual insight and thoughts.

- View conversation as barn-raising instead of battle. Ways to do this include:
  - Listen and focus on understanding. As others speak, try to suppress the instinct to criticize or compare;
  - No attacking, dismissing or denigrating. The facilitator should be especially committed to responding to others with support, thus modeling a caring response;
  - No persuading. It is enough to state what you think–you do not have to convince people that you are right;
  - No playing devil's advocate. Although this is a common form of communication, it violates just about all of the above guidelines.

- Question conventional wisdom and seek out alternative explanations and views.

- Discover wisdom through stories. Throughout human history, people have learned through story-telling. Everyone can tell their story and there's no right or wrong interpretation. Ultimately, stories connect people; in listening to someone else's story, we often hear strains of our own.

Meeting Format

The meeting format is fairly self-explanatory. Each meeting has all or most of the following components:

The Facilitator Overview should be read by the facilitator prior to the meeting. Specific instructions for the meeting are given in this section.

Tools Everyone Needs generally includes this book and, if you wish, a pen and journal/notebook. Other suggested supplies, such as a flip chart, are indicated in this section.

Participants should be familiar with the *Purpose and Overview* sections before the meeting starts.

The *Opening Prayer* provides a brief centering time. This time can be led by the facilitator or whoever feels comfortable doing so. Feel free to bring in prayers of your own or pray spontaneously as you are comfortable. This goes for the *Closing Prayer* as well.

Each meeting's discussion emanates from that week's readings. There are more questions offered than can probably be discussed in the given time; therefore, the facilitator should make some decisions regarding the questions to discuss.

Finally, there is a section, *Read Before Next Gathering*, that lists readings for the next meeting.

A Final Note

This is your course. Use it as a resource to engage your life with the ideas presented, not as a course to be "mastered." You may find you don't have time to answer every question, or feel drawn to discuss only a few questions or interject questions of your own. You may want to spend two weeks on certain meeting topics. Please modify as desired.

Meeting 1

Listening to Our Lives

Tools Everyone Needs

Shaping Sanctuary

pen or pencil

Optional:
journal or notebook

Purpose

To briefly introduce the course and clarify/discuss course guidelines;

To create a "safe space" and sense of community within the group by telling life-stories;

To share expectations and hopes for this course.

Read Before Next Gathering

Introduction p. vi

Integrating Spirituality and Sexuality p. 2

Spirituality and Sexuality: Both or Neither p. 5

Facilitator Overview

This meeting sets the tone for the rest of the course. As facilitator today:

— Welcome everyone and make sure everyone has access to a copy of this book;

— After the introductions, follow the flow of the readings and associated questions;

— Ensure that a safe space for discussion is created by reviewing the guidelines for discussions and agreeing upon confidentiality standards for information shared in the group;

— Lead (or ask someone to lead) the opening meditation, prayer, and songs;

— Read aloud the group reading (we suggest members take turns reading);

— Keep track of time to ensure that all have adequate time to tell their own stories;

— Determine how the group wants to choose each meeting's facilitator, and designate one for the next meeting.

Overview

This first meeting is dedicated to hearing a portion of each person's life story and a little about why they feel drawn to this course, which explores the theological implications of human sexuality, the integration of spirituality and sexuality, and examines the liturgy which seeks to include people of every sexual orientation. The entire course emphasizes and values individuals' experiences and wisdom.

Opening Prayer

Loving God–Creator, Redeemer and Sustainer–thank you for the gift of another day and for the chance to be together. We remember that you have promised your presence where "two or three are gathered." May we bring our whole selves to this endeavor. May we learn from our own lives, from each other and from your presence in our world. Amen.

Introductions

Have group members briefly introduce themselves (they will have a chance to say more soon.)

Opening Meditation *(Read aloud to the group)*

> Now is the door swinging open
> to see the dance of sunlight,
> hint of moonbeam.
> Now do the pews bloom,
> that were dry-old wood,
> cut from forests long ago.
> Now does a fresh wind
> ruffle the memorial Bible
> like a gust of Pentecost.
> Now is the writing on the walls
> not hymn numbers,
> but God's laughter.
> Now is the new covenant
> not stone but heart,
> not stone but heart.
>
> — *Maren C. Tirabassi*

"It takes a great deal of time and love for us to learn how to let go of our senses of separateness, isolation, and self-control, and risk not only reaching out to touch others but also allowing ourselves to be touched deeply by them."
—Carter Heyward

Group Reading

The course begins with you, where you are and what brings you here. There is great emphasis placed on sharing your own life-experiences within a supportive environment. Doing so is, in itself, participating in an inclusive community where individual experiences are honored and heard. In such a community the body of Christ is formed and recognized, where all are known and loved. For without being truly known, you cannot be truly loved. The Scriptures point to this truth in emphasizing God's knowing us by name, knowing us in the womb, and God's presence with us wherever we go.

Read Psalm 139:1-18

We are deeply, intimately known by God and called to know God in return through our relationships with one another. So let us be as honest and as open to each other's experiences as we can be.

Group Discussion

- Are there questions about course format, organization, or leadership?

- Are there concerns about the confidentiality of what is shared during this class? What agreements can we make regarding how we will honor and share information heard here with those outside this class?

under Course Ethos, p. 377
- Review the guidelines for creating a community-oriented group. Any comments or questions about these?

see p. 317
Song "Walk With Me" (verses 1-3)

Group Discussion – Listening to Our Lives

1. What are your historical and geographical roots? (Where are you from, your family background, what sort of work have you done, etc.)

2. How does listening to each other foster your understanding of God's inclusive community–an inclusive church?

3. Why might it be important to create safe spaces for all people, of every sexual orientation, to actively participate in church and share their experiences?

4. Study the cover artwork by Jan Richardson entitled, *The Best Supper.* Why might it be labeled *best?* What does it mean to share a meal with others different from yourself?

5. In your own life, do you perceive connections between your faith and your sexuality?

6. What are your hopes and/or expectations for this course? In one phrase or sentence share those with the group.

Closing Song "Walk with Me" (verse 4)

Closing Prayer *(Read in unison)*

Creator God, you have made us as deeply relational beings. Help us to listen attentively to our lives, help us to discern the leaning of our hearts, help us to hear the pain and joy of others and to see the connections between others' experiences and our own. Amen.

A reminder: Select next week's facilitator!

Meeting 2
Spirituality and Sexuality

Facilitator Overview

As facilitator today:

— serve as timekeeper;

— facilitate discussions, making sure everyone who wants to has the opportunity to speak;

— lead (or ask someone to lead) the opening meditation, prayer, and songs (select tune for songs);

— designate next meeting's facilitator.

Overview

This session gives participants the opportunity to consider and re-think the dualism that presents sexuality and spirituality as separate and opposing aspects of our humanity.

Opening Prayer

Hallow this space with your presence, gracious God. In friend, in stranger, in earth, in sky, help me trace the contours of the sacred. Amen.

Song "For the Goodness of Our Bodies" p. 271 or
"A Hymn of Reconciliation" p. 271

Meditation

Watering Love
The center of the church is not love.
But at the center of the church is a seed, which is love.
Shall we water it?
Shall we tend to the promise of love in the center of the gift?
Or shall we continue to smother it,
To deny its existence for the sake of laws that bear no fruit
but crippling vine?
The center of the church is a seed, which is love.
We shall water it with our hands and hearts
and the testament of our lives together.
We shall not worry that the church will break to see such
loving growth.
The hands of God are large enough to hold the sprawling
green of love unbound.
— Dan Vera

Tools Everyone Needs

Shaping Sanctuary

pen or pencil

Optional:
journal or notebook

Purpose

To explore the theological implications of human sexuality;

To reflect on the connections between spirituality and sexuality.

Read Before Next Gathering

Toward an Integrated Spirituality, p. 9

Welcome One Another, p. 14

A Stranger in Our Midst, p. 35

Group Reading

Read Song of Solomon 1:9-17; 3:1-5; 8:5-7

Group Discussion

- How did you first learn of the Song of Solomon (Song of Songs) scriptures? How does it feel for the scriptures to use such sexual language?

- What does such language say about our bodily existence?

- How do we receive joy, awe, and pleasure?

- Can we, or should we, talk about sex in the church?

- Can you think of a time and place when you felt particularly close to God? Where was it? Why this place or time? What were the relationships involved? Were you in relationship to other people? To the environment?

- Chris Glaser argues that God became flesh in Jesus Christ, and through that embodiment we come to know God. Even when the body of Jesus of Nazareth left us, we were not left without an embodiment, as Paul conceptualized the church as the Body of Christ.

  - How do we know God through our bodies?

  - How do we know God through the body of Jesus?

  - How do we know God through the body of Christ (the church)?

- What about our sexuality calls us to be spiritual? What about our spirituality calls us to be sexual?

- If there are not separate spheres of spiritual and physical, then what does that mean for the way we live our day-to-day lives?

- Share a time when your compassion–the capacity to suffer with someone else–connected you with someone else and through your common suffering helped you understand the gospel message better.

Closing Prayer

God, who is known to us in the person of Jesus, help us to know our bodies, our sexuality and our sexual orientation as good. Help us use the power of touch to heal and not harm, the desire to connect to build up and not tear down, the passion of bodies to love rather than hate. Amen.

Meeting 3

Implications for Worship

Facilitator Overview

As facilitator today:

— serve as timekeeper;

— facilitate discussions, making sure everyone who wants to has the opportunity to speak;

— lead (or ask someone to lead) the opening meditation, songs and teach the body prayer;

— arrange for readers of the group reading;

— designate next meeting's facilitator.

Overview

In this session, a body prayer is used to help understand the embodied meanings behind the words we pray. It also uses discussion to allow participants to explore what it means to bring our whole lives to God and if, or how, our wholeness is addressed in worship.

Opening Prayer

Living memory. We cry out.
We are weary, Sore Sinew
Weary of painful struggle for some daybreak
for the simple light of a new day
when the too-long delayed justice may be ours.
We are angry, Great Passion
About racism and cruelty
unrelieved rage for long-time
rancor, which receives inadequate
resolve although much effort.
We are ready, Living Memory. Enable us
to hear what we need to hear. To dialogue
constructively. To do what we need to do.
To shatter the silences that bind us
and to act for change that shakes our
foundations for justice's cause
and for good.

— *Bobbi Patterson*

Tools Everyone Needs

Shaping Sanctuary

pen or pencil

Optional:
journal or notebook

Purpose

To explore the implications of our embodied existence for our worship time together;

To hear one closeted person's experience of the church;

To explore the meaning of bringing our whole lives to God.

Read Before Next Gathering

Chapter 3 on Ritualizing Our Lives

Justice liturgies, p. 192

Ritual of Celebrating Homecoming after Incarceration, p. 201

Ritual of Gathering Around One Who is Dying, p. 164

see p. 308

Song "We Are a Gentle, Angry People"

Group Reading

I was introduced to Brenda (not her real name) by long-time partners Cedric and Rupert. Brenda is a Minister of Music at a Central Methodist Episcopal (CME) church in the Southeast. For this article, I interviewed her over a series of meetings and email exchanges.

Just As She Is

I expected her to look different. But it turned out that Brenda looks just like so many Black-Churchgirls–well-kept, healthy, hair done, conservatively dressed, good jewelry. Even more, she looks like someone who can *play*, and *sing*, and *shout*, and *feel* the Holy Ghost! If she didn't tell you, you wouldn't have a clue that she were anything other than heterosexual.

It's probably the way she looks that keeps all the good, CME church folk from knowing. Brenda loves "good and God and life" and fills most every day with the work of Christ. She is a Minister of Music and, on at least five out of every seven days, she goes to Sunday School, Morning Service, 3:00 Service, Bible Study, choir rehearsal and more, that is, after her regular nine-to-five gig. Brenda is one of those people who just doesn't "feel right" unless she heads to church on *every* Sunday morning. She is, truly, a Churchgirl and she is "not ashamed of the Gospel."

So, how does Brenda work out this whole "Lesbian thing?" Well, the short answer is "by faith." The long answer is not so straightforward and only revealed itself through the living and telling of her story. Lesbian-Churchgirls don't often have opportunities to tell their stories. And for Black-Lesbian-Churchgirls, story-telling opportunities are even more rare.

This Churchgirl's first love was the daughter of a preacher. Both raised in the church, they knew that fornication was wrong, but it just didn't "click" that homosexual love fell into that category. All they knew was the time spent at Sunday School, Youth Choir, CYF and fund-raiser-fish-dinners had allowed them the time and space to want each other. The girls were never aware of a Word from the pulpit regarding the "sin" of homosexual desire and they had encountered no church directive to challenge their behavior. The church was nearly silent on sex, and in the silence, the girls became lovers.

The Churchgirl became a woman and packed her bags for a grown-up life in the big city. Her home church sent word and the big-city-church prepared a table for her. They made her feel at home. Singing, playing, directing the music. Brenda built a new home on the same old foundation of God. But now, with adult ears, she heard the sin-of-the-moment admonitions. "God made Adam and Eve, not Adam and Steve." There it was: Brenda was a sinner. But could it be true? Could her soul be unclean even while God's musical Word flowed through her? In her ministry, Brenda prepared the church for the worship experience. She enlivened the hearts of the people and the preacher and set the stage for the Word. And even as she served, ushers stood ready to assist when the power of God overcame Brenda and the time was ripe to get her *own* praise on. Her gift, music. The giver, God. Surely God was living in her.

The Churchgirl found love with another woman, and took pleasure reintroducing her beautiful lover to God. This beautiful woman got along splendidly with God; she began to call God's house her own. Now, as the scripture advised, they were equally yoked. But as happens to many a husband and wife, the yoke of Christ was not enough to keep betrayal at bay. So after a time, the lovers couldn't love anymore. Filled with pain and doubt, Brenda called out to God. "If this is not right, change me, oh God." Open to possibilities through Christ, Brenda let time lead her to a man. Friends before lovers, they had things in common and imagined the future. But it was not to be. Ending in malice and violence, the relationship left no evidence of a God-sanctioned grace for woman-with-man.

> "We long for a time when human sexuality, in spite of all its ambiguities, will be more integrated with our experience of the sacred and with the vision of God's shalom."
>
> —James Nelson

The Churchgirl never faltered. Through the ups and downs of love and loss, Brenda remained steadfast and faithful to her call. She organized special programs, arranged music, taught songs. She traveled to other congregations and took her ministerial "show" on the road. God blessed her with material success and gave her a spirit of discernment. She could recognize those who wore the clothes of Christ but came only to deceive. She saw through evangelists who proclaimed God's wrath for Gays by day and sought same-sex sex by night. She heard the personal stake in the preacher's silence when it was *his own* too-young daughter who was with child. She witnessed ill motives of titled-church-men as they sought entertainment from parishioners' desires.

She could have used it for ammunition. She could have called out all the hypocrites. But she remained faithful. Brenda trusted God to judge and she trusted God to speak to her soul. She received no new Word and the Lord had not changed her. She took comfort in God's inaction and continued to believe her life pleasing in God's sight.

As we met together, the Churchgirl reviewed her life and loves. In telling her story, Brenda realized that her heart is relationship-driven. She can see the beauty of women *and* the beauty of men. She can see herself either married to a man *or* fighting for the right to marry a woman. So, is Brenda really a Lesbian? Or is she a Bisexual woman? Or do these, or any labels, matter when we are talking about a Churchgirl? If labels are, in fact, important, it seems that Brenda would prefer to be labeled "Child of God." What Churchgirl-Brenda recognizes as most important is that true love *is* God and *of* God and that God lives in *anyone* who offers the spirit a home.

The Church does not honor her sexual orientation. They don't fully understand and embrace God's requirement to love *everyone*. But this Churchgirl finds the arms of God sufficient. Brenda has wondered, journeyed, and prayed. She *knows* that she is God's creation and God's creations are perfect.

— Marie Renfro-Collins

Group Discussion

• How is Brenda's experience like that of the "stranger" described in Bishop Egertson's sermon, *A Stranger in Our Midst?*

• How is the image of stranger an accurate and insightful image for speaking about LGBT persons' experience? Are there ways in which it might be limited or misleading?

• What does it mean for us to bring our whole lives to God? Including our sexual orientation? Including our anger or rage?

• If God's incarnation as human in the person of Jesus means our bodies and our sexuality are important–how should our worship reflect God's valuing of our human existence?

Group Activity

Learn the body prayer on p. 128 and pray it together using the body movements.

Group Discussion

- What does the experience of being "knuckle-to-knuckle" tell us about "trespasses?"

- What analogies can be drawn regarding the opening of fists to the forgiveness of linking fingers?

- How do exposed wrists speak to us of the vulnerability of "temptation?"

- How is the "kin-dom and the power" of God like holding hands with a neighbor?

- In the sermon, *The Stranger in Our Midst*, we are encouraged to think of LGBT persons as the loving father in the story of the prodigal son waiting to welcome home a church that has left its gospel home of inclusiveness to wander in a far away country of exclusion. How is this image helpful? How is it not?

Closing Prayer of Confession

O gracious and loving God,
who calls us to be your people in this age,
forgive us when we keep Christ in the past,
and the Gospel as letters on a page,
and the church as an organization
in which we may or may not participate.
Forgive us when fellowship and mission
is meant for and delivered to
those we already know and love
and we become a social club instead of your church.
Forgive us and have mercy upon us, O God.
Let your risen Christ reside here with us,
and the Gospel be the power of our lives,
and the church be a people and place
of showing your love wherever we may be.
In Jesus' name we pray. Amen.

— Church of the Redeemer

Closing Song "All Are Welcome"

see p. 276

Meeting 4

Meaningful Ritual

Tools Everyone Needs

Shaping Sanctuary

pen or pencil

Optional:
journal or notebook

Purpose

To open the meaning of traditional church rituals to participants;

To encourage and inspire participants to create and/or participate in meaningful rituals.

Read Before Next Gathering

Guidelines for Writing Liturgy, p. xvi

Chapter 5 Elements of Worship, p. 88, choose a couple of pieces that speak to you, note pieces with visual images, note ones that are easy for you to leave behind.

Facilitator Overview

As facilitator today:

— serve as timekeeper;

— facilitate discussions, making sure everyone who wants to has the opportunity to speak;

— lead (or ask someone to lead) the opening meditation, prayers and songs;

— designate next meeting's facilitator.

Overview

This session encourages participants to examine what rituals are in their day-to-day lives and to think of rituals that could be created to help them connect with God and one another.

Opening Meditation

Liturgy comes from a Greek word meaning the "work of the people."

> *The rituals that take place in the church are a kind of work, the soul's work....The word* liturgy *acts as a reminder that one of humankind's most important works is to praise the Creator together and to dwell with one another in prayerful manner.*

> — *Equal Rites*

Opening Prayer (read in unison)

O God,
we have heard the tradition
of the centuries.
Some of the words that have
condemned us to reject ourselves
and one another in your name.
We pray for the strength to say
"no more" to the wedges
that have kept us
separate from one another,
we pray so that we might be
reconciled with one another. Amen.

> — *Rosemary Ruether*

Song "We Limit Not the Truth of God"

see p. 275

Group Discussion

- What rituals have you experienced in the last week, inside or outside the church?

- In the readings for today, several people encountered times of tragedy, uncertainty, and joy and used rituals to carry them through their experiences. How do you imagine the participants of these rituals were empowered by participating in them?

- Was there a particularly difficult time in your own life when a ritual and the support of a loving community might have helped you?

- In the *Ritual of Letting Go*, there is a great deal of intimacy and risk involved in people sharing their pain during the pastor prayer. What allows people to trust one another enough to share their lives with others at this level? *see p. 57*

- What actions can you and your church take to create a "safe space" for people to bring their lives to God and the body of Christ?

Song "Freedom is Coming" p. 296, or
"Halle-halle-hallelujah" p. 298

Closing Prayer

See Bishop Wheatley's prayer on p. 93

Meeting 5

Creating Liturgy

Tools Everyone Needs

Shaping Sanctuary

pen or pencil

markers, crayons

large newsprint paper and flipchart

Optional:
journal or notebook

Purpose

To familiarize participants with the basic guidelines for writing liturgy and several prayer formats;

To inspire and empower participants to write their own prayers and liturgies.

Read Before Next Gathering

Sermons: *You Do Not Know, No Longer at Ease, & Discipleship After Sundown*

Facilitator Overview

As facilitator today:

— serve as timekeeper;

— facilitate discussions, making sure everyone who wants to has the opportunity to speak;

— lead (or ask someone to lead) the opening meditation, prayers and songs;

— find two readers for next week's readers' theater piece so that they can practice during the week;

— designate next meeting's facilitator.

Overview

This session uses a creative technique sometimes called "clustering" or "webbing" to brainstorm images and ideas from scripture passages and allows participants to create a collect.

Opening Prayer

Blessing God,
Whose caring hands cupped beneath the elements of the universe
    and–like a potter–fashioned the very vessels
    of our being
Reach out your hand in blessing on us this morning.

As you drew the lines of our palms
    and shaped the idiosyncrasies of our fingers
Teach us to reach out our hands to others in love
Help us not to raise the threatening fist
    but to warmly grasp the possibilities of new-found
    reconciliations.

Soften our touch, O God:
    for your creation suffers from warring and pollution
    and your people reach out for help and solace

Encourage and strengthen us with your wisdom
　　　Until we become like You
　　　　　fashioners of justice and love
　　　Hands open for peace and benediction
　　　Gathering blessing and flourishing life for all.
　　　　　Amen.

—Bobbi Patterson

Song "Song of the Soul" *(verses 1 and 2)*　　　　　　　*see p. 312*

Group Discussion

- From your reading this week, share which prayers, litanies, and liturgies you found meaningful to you.

- What images of God did these pieces evoke?

- What was the nature of humans and creation in these pieces?

- Which ones were least helpful to you and why?

Group Reading

Using Clustering to Write Liturgy

If you are stuck with just the germ of an idea or theme that you want to bring to a worship service, but are unable to broaden your initial idea, clustering can be a helpful writing technique to use. It can help loosen up your thinking, be more creative, and open you to images lying beneath your cognitive awareness. I have used it when working by myself, and also in groups when writing liturgy by committee.

Clustering is a simple writing tool with the following steps.

— Start with a blank page of paper and an idea.

— In the center of that page write a word or phrase (it can even be a verse of scripture).

— Draw a circle, oval or "balloon" shape around that word or phrase. (Gabriele Rico, who popularized this tool, refers to this encircled word or phrase as a "seed").

— Focus on that seed–keeping in mind the context for which you are writing.

— Take your time. Breathe. Relax.

— Focus on the seed.

— As other words, ideas, images, phrases or thoughts come to mind, write them in the blank areas of the page surrounding the seed.

— As you add a word or idea—consider the seed as the center hub and draw a line or spoke, like a string, out from that seed, connecting it to the new idea.

— If the new idea leads to another or different idea, add that newer thought further out from the center, also connecting it by a line to the previous word or idea (see following example on "Jesus Wept").

An extensive cluster can look like a spider's web—with lines running off from the center in all directions—and some of the spokes of the cluster becoming connected in unexpected and unpredictable ways. Some people refer to the technique as "webbing" for this reason. When I am well focused on a cluster or web process, a fully formed thought or beginning line of writing will rise up in my thinking. (That's what happened in the process of creating the example cluster on "Jesus Wept"—the following poem rose to the surface.)

Clustering is not magic; it is an acquired skill. I first learned about clustering in a seminary class where it was suggested as a way to open-up our thinking—to get past "writer's block" when starting a paper, reflection or sermon. The technique is described by Gabriele Lusser Rico in her books *Writing the Natural Way* and *Pain and Possibility: Writing Your Way through Personal Crisis*.

In *Pain and Possibility*, she explains, "The technique of clustering reflects the dynamically unpredictable processes of the human heart....The fact is that in the seeming randomness of a cluster, patterns do appear, in our apparently undetermined choices we discover self-references; in the irregularities of the clustering process we pick up meaningful recurrences that became strange attractors" (page 43).

There are two ways I have led groups to use clustering: to write liturgy and as scripture meditation.

Recently an "ad hoc" group at Dumbarton UMC was planning the worship service to celebrate our anniversary as a Reconciling Congregation. Each year's celebration had evolved a different theme, and the group was feeling a little stuck on a direction to take. I was enamored with a song, "Dazzling Bouquet" (p. 355). I had been introduced to at a planning retreat, and imagined there were possibilities of building the service around that song, or at least incorporating into the worship.

Unfortunately, no one had energy or focus at the end of a workday in the middle of the week. So I suggested that we try clustering around the themes: plants, seeds, flowers, etc. We already had a context for the worship—our Reconciling Congregation's anniversary celebration. So I invited the seven folks in the group to each take a word or related idea, write it on their blank page, focus on it and then cluster around it.

When everyone had quit writing a few minutes later, I invited individuals to share their clusters. I used newsprint and markers to record the images that were named: planting, growth, harvest, types of flora, plant attributes that are used to describe humans, Biblical images and scriptures that mention plants, flowers, manure and seeds (faith like a mustard seed, anyone?). Good! We had a beginning.

The clustering we shared was not complete liturgy, but it got us started. It also inspired one member of the group with confidence and creative empowerment to take home our newsprint. She formed our rough ideas into a Call to Worship, Confession-Pardon-Assurance and Acts of Response that included all the members of the congregation in creating several vases full of flowers that, after the celebration service were delivered to shut-ins by members of the church.

I have also used "clustering" in my senior high Sunday School class. One morning, as we were looking at a long and rather complicated Psalm, I invited the students to cluster the Psalm. All of them were familiar with the technique from school, where it is taught as an alternative to creating an outline. Specifically, I suggested that they each choose one verse or even a portion of a verse, focus on it, and cluster what comes out of that seed.

A few minutes later, we each shared marvelous and in-depth connections about our chosen portion of scripture. The webs touched on ways the youth had seen the concepts of the Bible enacted in their church, and where they saw God's love and caring through their families and friends. The same approach could be used with almost any age group, at a retreat setting or even during a worship service.

Even though clustering or webbing won't write liturgy for you, it is a handy tool when you want to do something more creative than relying on standard resources provided by the denomination or pre-printed materials that may not be the best fit for your setting.

Jesus wept – a cluster on the shortest verse in the Bible

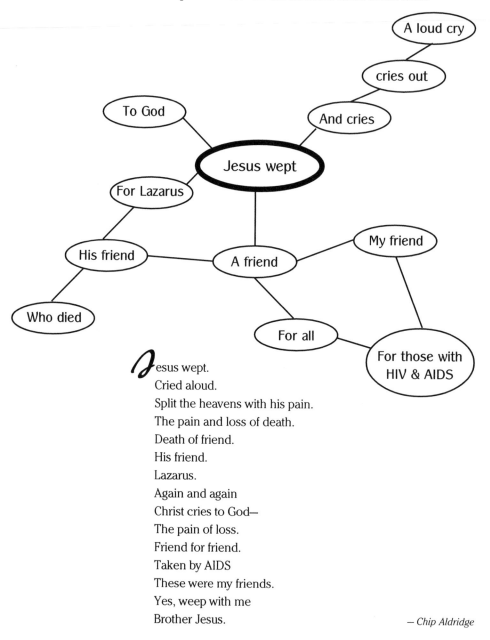

Jesus wept.
Cried aloud.
Split the heavens with his pain.
The pain and loss of death.
Death of friend.
His friend.
Lazarus.
Again and again
Christ cries to God—
The pain of loss.
Friend for friend.
Taken by AIDS
These were my friends.
Yes, weep with me
Brother Jesus.

— *Chip Aldridge*

Group Activity

Create a collect (brief, formal prayer used to draw the interests of people into one theme):

Using the guidelines for collects on p. xvii in the introduction, select one of the following opening images of God and construct a collect from that image. You may want to use the webbing/clustering technique to think creatively about the image of God you have chosen. Add a characteristic of God related to the name you choose below, the petition related to God's attribute, the intended result of the petition, and a final doxology. Use newsprint, crayons, markers, etc.

Spirit of New Beginnings	Sound of Silence
Wellspring of Wisdom	Christ the Healer
Carpenter of New Creation	Home of my Heart
Like a Mother Eagle	Hovering Dove
God of Wounded Hands	God of Earth and Air
God of the Exodus	Rabbi of the Poor
O Fathomless Well	God of queerness, mystery and surprises

Allow time for people to work on their collects, then share with each other how you found the process of creating a prayer. How was the formal structure of the collect restrictive or freeing?

Closing Song "Journey to Commitment" *see p. 304*

Closing Prayer *(unison)*

Gracious God, words are not enough to express our pain and joy and gratitude with life, and yet they are all we have. May we know the power of our words. Inspire us to write liturgies, powerful and real, that help us bring about social change. Amen.

Meeting 6

Visioning Our Lives and Our Church

Tools Everyone Needs

Shaping Sanctuary

pen or pencil

Optional:
journal or notebook

Purpose

If this is the last session, to bring closure to the class by envisioning actions to take as a result of the learning;

To envision how your life and church would differ if the incarnation were taken seriously.

Read Before Next Gathering

Shaping Sacred Space essay, p. 72

Creating a Community Banner, p. 79

Discuss your church's characteristics as they could be represented by a single fabric.

Facilitator Overview

As facilitator today:

— coordinate the room arrangement so that it facilitates the closing ritual;

— serve as timekeeper;

— facilitate discussions, making sure everyone who wants to has the opportunity to speak;

— lead (or ask someone to lead) the opening meditation, prayers, and songs;

— assign readers for readings;

— bring snacks;

— designate next meeting's facilitator, and the person responsible for gathering the necessary sewing supplies.

Overview

This class discusses three sermons and the story of a Transgendered woman as the basis for questions regarding the future of our church.

Opening Prayer

God of breath, may all our living exhale your love. May our breathing in and breathing out witness to your justice. May the things we buy, the food we eat, the choices we make, place us in right relation to all of creation. Amen.

Song "Freedom is Coming" p. 296

Meditation Read Micah 6:8

Group Reading

Transcendent Reality

I'm convinced that our Creator absolutely loves and delights in diversity. It's not too difficult to imagine why—just think of all the different types of plants, animals, terrain, and natural wonders on the earth, then consider all the billions of stars in the skies. Look, too, at the differences that abound even within humanity—skin color, hair and eye color, body shapes, facial features, levels of intelligence, varying talents, abilities, desires, strengths and weaknesses. How could anyone deny that God positively rejoices in diversity, dancing with delight at difference and uniqueness? It is creation's diversity that is its glory and its strength and that most fully reflects the character of its Creator. It's obvious to me that if the Christian church authentically cares about reflecting and embodying the characteristics of God, then it must genuinely welcome and embrace diversity and difference among its membership.

It is incumbent upon the institutional church, the Body of Christ, to act appropriately and responsibly with compassion, respect, acceptance and love toward all individuals (and that certainly includes LGBT people). If the church refuses to do so, it is acting heretically, not to mention diametrically opposite, the words and intentions of Jesus Christ, who said in Matthew 11:28, "Come unto me, *all* ye who are weary, and I will give you rest." Note that Jesus didn't say He would give rest only to some or to a privileged, exclusive few—He said *all*. That means you, me, and everyone else who wants to come to God, without limitation or barrier.

We need to learn to use the Bible as a textbook for our own liberation. Despite the often negative and discriminatory interpretations of the Bible that many of us learned while growing up, the scriptures are truly a liberating word of freedom for our souls. The love and acceptance of God is there in the Bible for anyone who desires a relationship with their Creator. I want to say this as emphatically as possible: don't ever let anyone take scripture out of context and use it to oppress you. William Sloane Coffin has remarked, "I am once again reminded that altogether too many Christians, even scholarly ones, use the Bible as a drunk does a lamp post—for support rather than for illumination." The Bible is a wonderful tool for us to use in our journey to God. We cannot allow the forces of negativity, bigotry, discrimination and oppression to halt that journey for us.

We also need to learn the differences between the concepts of freedom and independence with regard to being a Christian. Those terms are often used interchangeably, and I think that's a mistake. D.H. Lawrence once wrote that, "Men [sic] are not free when they are doing just what they like. The moment you can do just what you like, there is nothing you care about doing." We who are Christian often say we have "freedom in Christ," and so we do. However, the concept of freedom carries with it various limitations and responsibilities. We are not liberated to do just anything. We are liberated by Christ so that we might struggle against the oppression (of others and ourselves). Thus we have a responsibility to live our lives in a manner that will reflect the love of Jesus, who bought that freedom for us.

Independence, however, is quite another matter. We don't live in a social vacuum, and most of us don't live as hermits in caves. We are never truly independent. We all have bonds, links, and connections with others, the world around us, and certainly with our Creator. These are relationships that invariably color and influence our lives to varying degrees. What we do definitely affects others. For the most part, we are independent only to the extent that we have personal autonomy over the cognitive decisions we make. Yes, we have spiritual freedom in Christ, but we are not independent in the general sense of the word. We are all intricately involved with each other in various ways. What you and I do matters—our actions, energies and intentions affect everyone in some manner, and we need to live responsibly in the light of that knowledge.

Many of us have struggled with our own identities in relationship to God and to the church at one time or another. In the midst of those struggles, we need to remember to build each other up, not tear each other down. We who are minorities and allies must, as Benjamin Franklin once said, "hang together or we'll all hang separately." That's why it's so important for us to build strong bridges of love and respect between our various LGBT communities and the straight community, so that *all* who desire the liberating, life-giving presence and love of God may come to experience that joy and fulfillment for themselves. That's where God's love has led me–to a place where I am extremely proud and happy to be a Transgendered person; I want to share my pride and happiness, based in a recognition of God's love and acceptance for me, with others in all that I do.

I grew up despising, rejecting and running from the fact that I'm a differently-gendered person. My self-loathing almost destroyed me until the love of God eventually allowed me to learn that being Transgendered is indeed a blessing and a gift, not a curse. Despite the negativity of some religious groups, despite the unfounded fears of a misinformed society, and despite the presence of our own internalized phobias regarding "difference," God is calling and saying to each of us, "It's good to be who and what you are. Come home to me. I accept you completely. I want to give you dignity, respect, and, most of all, my eternal love. Together we can journey to new life–the abundant life I want for you."

— *Vanessa Sheridan*

Group Discussion

- What images of the church are offered by Vanessa's essay and the three sermons you read for today?

- What gifts could the church enjoy if it fully embraced the meaning of Christ's incarnation and our own embodiment?

- Consider where you started this study and what you now think about what it means to be embodied? What are some of the growing places in your thinking?

- In the sermon, "Discipleship after Sundown," Trey Hall states that Christ will not be tied down or restrained by our limitations. What does it mean to say that we try to restrain Christ? Have you ever felt yourself do this? Your church?

- Sid Hall, in his sermon, "No Longer At Ease," referred to some "big boulders" still lying around— some fear and prejudice– what boulders still block your path? Are there people who are helping you locate and lift them (as you are ready to move them)?

- Imagine Archbishop Romero standing in front of you, looking into your eyes and saying, "You are Jesus." How do you feel? How do you respond?

- Consider five ways that your daily habits–eating, buying, living– impact your relationships with others, your relatedness to creation and the environment.

- What aspects of your life are you willing to change to allow for new growth?

Gather around a
table (stand or sit as
you are able).

Light a candle.

Pass a snack around
the circle and offer it
to one another—it
can be bread, grapes,
candy (ice cream
gets a little messy).

Read the Readers'
theatre at right.

Closing Ritual

Voice 1:   Lying **sleepily** (pause) within is the **warm, mindless comfort** of the seed

Voice 2:   (spoken quietly) **Resting** in a sundrenched~

Voice 1:   sundrenched

Voice 2:   softening soil

Voice 1:   Then God bids a new morning to greet and stir her.
           And says to the root,

Voice 2:   "Come out!" and the seed says

Together: **"I will grow."**

Voice 1:   A tiny hand **emerges.**

Voice 2:   Your **root** holds all the energy~   of the **universe**

Voice 1:   energy

Voice 1:   An immense **energy** as **full** as the relentless ocean's **crash** (spoken loudly)

Together: **Against the shore.**

Voice 2:   (quietly) As **full** as a breast's desire to be suckled.

Voice 1:   And the seed says:

Together: **"I WILL grow."**

Voice 1:   The root **presses** through the dying case of the seed

Voice 2:   not hesitating

Together: **NOT HESITATING**

Voice 1:   **It must wound** its confinement,

Voice 2:   **It must wrestle** with its friend.

Voice 1:   Yet, a wound it is, as the pressing tears aside~

Voice 2:   tears aside

Go around the circle
and have each per-
son say one word of
a hope or vision of
growth they have for
themselves or the
group.

Voice 1:   what once was dear.
           Yet, a wound it is, a God wound,

Voice 2:   calling new life **out of the stillness,**

Together: (slowly) S E A R C H I N G in the dark soil
           with a tiny spark of light.

see p. 274

Sing "We Gather Round the Table" to the tune of Amazing Grace
          (*using upbeat tempo*).

Meeting 7

Making a Community Banner (optional)

Facilitator Overview

As facilitator today:

— coordinate the room arrangement and gathering of the banner supplies;

— lead (or ask someone with sewing experience to lead) the making of the banner;

— serve as timekeeper;

— facilitate discussions, making sure everyone who wants to has the opportunity to speak;

— lead (or ask someone to lead) the prayers and songs;

— designate next meeting's facilitator and who will be responsible for gathering the art supplies necessary.

Overview

To build community and a banner. If you have no sewing experience, this session may take some time and patience to complete. You may want to enlist the aid of someone who has some familiarity with sewing. The folks who have completed this activity suggests that those with no sewing experience can do it, but it does help to have at least one person around who is familiar with sewing supplies and techniques.

Opening Prayer

Weaver God,
who knit us together into the beautiful pattern of creation,
strengthen our ties to all of life,
fasten us securely to the fate of each other, and
weave us into the design of your kin-dom,
that we may pattern our lives after Christ
and quilt a new fabric of abundant living for all.
Amen.

Song "Weave Us Together"

see p. 321

Tools Everyone Needs

Shaping Sanctuary

Supplies for making the banner, see p. 79

Purpose

To build community by making a banner together;

To learn new sewing techniques,

To practice patience in piecework;

To offer a beautiful banner to the congregation as a symbol of the sanctuary being offered to all.

Read Before Next Gathering

Conducting a Art & Spirituality Workshop, p. 81

Group Discussion while Constructing Banner

Describe one of your own or your community's sacred spaces. What are the characteristics that make it sacred?

In his article, "Shaping Sacred Space," Philip Cox-Johnson argues that words on a banner can limit their meaning. Discuss your experience of the meaning of banners and what visual images have been important to you.

Closing Prayer

Be blessed, you who were born in the very image of God. Be blessed and be a blessing to others. Amen.

Meeting 8

Art & Spirituality
Workshop *(optional)*

Facilitator Overview

As facilitator today:

— make arrangements for room set-up according to workshop needs;

— coordinate the gathering and display of art supplies;

— serve as timekeeper;

— facilitate discussions, making sure everyone who wants to has the opportunity to speak;

— lead (or ask someone to lead) the meditation and prayer;

— assign readers in the closing litany.

Overview

Using lectio divina, participants will meditate on scripture passages and enter into a time of silence and creative, sacred "play," during which each will create a wind chime–a three-dimensional, auto-biographical journal page. Toward the end of the time together, participants will be offered the chance to discuss the creative process and will participate in a closing litany.

Opening Meditation

Follow instructions for workshop on p. 81

Tools Everyone Needs

Shaping Sanctuary

pen or pencil

Optional:
journal or notebook

Purpose

To have fun with arts and crafts;

To bring to life a scripture passage as it relates to your own life;

To facilitate individual and community insight and growth.

Acknowledgments

*O*n 1997, a ground-breaking curriculum, *Claiming the Promise*, was produced by a coalition of welcoming organizations in nine denominations. This in-depth Bible study on homosexuality is now in its third printing. The success of that collaboration led many of those involved to dream of another ecumenical publishing venture–the book you are now reading. Ecumenical work is not easy, and these small, sometimes fledgling, welcoming groups knew they faced considerable financial, organizational, and communication challenges to make this volume a reality. I am, therefore, particularly grateful for the small group of program coordinators who were determined that this dream would come true!

Similar vision (and a leap of faith) on the part of these welcoming groups also set in motion planning for "Witness Our Welcome" (WOW2000)–the historic, ecumenical gathering of *welcoming churches* and their allies in the U.S. and Canada (August, 2000, in Dekalb, Illinois). Two persons gave inspiring and energetic direction to the conference efforts: Ruth Garwood and conference coordinator, Mark Bowman. The cooperative preparation for this conference generated much of the excitement and impetus behind this worship resource.

The welcoming church movement program coordinators and others involved in these programs generously helped develop this resource: Michael Adee, Jan Bussert, Ron Coughlin, Bob Gibeling, Elizabeth Kaeton, Keith Kron, Amy Short and Jeff Zimmerman, and I offer a special word of thanks to Marilyn Alexander, Ann B. Day and Brenda Moulton. It is also fitting to acknowledge that numerous persons have served as coordinators of these programs over the years. The dedication they brought to the *welcoming church movement* is part of the spirit of this book.

Several welcoming programs provided critical support to the production of this volume. The Reconciling Congregation Program, with its long history, well-developed organizational structure and incredible staff (especially Betty Torrier, Dan Vera, Meg Carey and Lauren Porter), hosted the day-to-day details, financing and publishing efforts. The Open and Affirming Program of The UCC Coalition for LGBT Concerns offered a rich tradition of inclusive liturgy, music, and publishing resources. And the More Light Presbyterians brought more than ten years of experience in publishing the *More Light Update,* which offers prayers and meditations from diverse sources. In particular, the work of its long-time editor, Chris Glaser (now editor of the ecumenical journal, *Open Hands*) is commended.

I am indebted to all the contributors who so graciously shared their talents through writing and music. See the contributor section for information on these incredibly gifted folks, and look for more of their work when you have the chance.

For the beauty of this volume, I thank the two Jans. Designer Jan Graves and artist Jan Richardson.

For their assistance throughout this project and advice for staying within budget, I acknowledge Sheridan Press.

For their inspiring funding, which made initial development of this book possible, I offer deepest appreciation to the E. Rhodes and Leona B. Carpenter Foundation.

I am thankful to Susan Carini, Robert Ethridge and Bobbi Patterson for their support and advice. Appreciation also to the many other researchers, detectives, editors and readers, including: James Anderson, Chip Aldridge, and Karen Oliveto.

Finally, and most importantly, this book would not have been possible without the generous volunteer efforts of: Claudia Brogan, Lesley Brogan, Gilbert High, Steve Hilbun, Mary Callaway Logan, Marie Renfro-Collins, Jaye Turney, and Carl Wiltse. Thank you all.

Contributors

Harry Akers is a long-time Methodist who is presently an active member of Walnut Creek UMC in California. He is an ardent advocate for social justice and is well-loved in his congregation for his warmth and keen sense of humor. He has been married to his wife, Peg, for 63 years.

Mark Bowman, a founder and long-time executive director of the Reconciling Congregation Program, is now a consultant to non-profit organizations.

Claudia Brogan has worked and taught at universities in the Midwest and South for nearly eighteen years in the Human Resources and professional development arenas. She currently resides in North Carolina, where she walks her Norwegian Elkhound two miles a day and is studying Enneagram and Myers-Briggs typologies as a way of appreciating differing spiritual gifts.

Lesley Brogan's claim to fame is an unassisted triple play in softball a few summers ago. She has a B.S. in music therapy and a M.Div. from Candler School of Theology. She is awaiting ordination in the United Church of Christ. Lesley and her partner, Linda, are doing their best to raise their young son, John Brogan Ellis.

Gordon W. Brown is a United Methdodist Lay Speaker from the New York Conference, where he currently serves as Conference Coordinator for RCP. He also serves the connection as Secretary to the Conference Board of Church and Society where he frequently advocates for GLBT, national single-payer health care, and others, and serves as a liaison between the Conference and Exodus, a lifers' self-help and support group in a NYS Correctional Facility.

The Rev. Peter J.B. Carman is pastor of Lake Avenue Baptist Church, a welcome and affirming congregation (W&A), in Rochester, New York.

Community of Hope was commissioned in 1993 by the Oklahoma Conference of the UMC as a "base community" outreach ministry. In 1999 Community of Hope withdrew from the UMC in protest of the denominational ban against same-sex unions, and is now affiliated with the United Church of Christ.

With degrees in vocal performance and church music, **J. Philip Cox-Johnson** is currently a fiber artist and dyer, whose company, Gospel Colors, specializes in art for worship settings. He designs worship for local, national and international conferences for a variety of Christian denominations; leads workshops in church music, the use of symbols and colors in liturgy and worship; and provides hands-on workshops in surface design techniques with fabric and dyes. In addition to his work with Gospel Colors, he serves as director of music ministries at Rockbridge Christian Church in Columbia, Missouri.

The Reverend Ann B. Day is the Open and Affirming (ONA) Program Coordinator for The United Church of Christ Coalition for Lesbian, Gay, Bisexual, and Transgender Concerns.

The oldest gathering of United Methodist in the District of Columbia, **Dumbarton UMC** is loacted in the Georgetown neighborhood at 3133 Dumbarton Avenue, NW. Dumbarton UMC became a reconciling congregation February 22, 1987, and has found that a continuing journey of joy and hope has guided the community in other areas, such as accessibility.

The Rev. Paul Wennes Egertson, Ph.D., is Bishop of the Southern California West Synod, Evangelical Lutheran Church in America. He and his wife Shirley were married in 1956 and are the parents of six sons and six grandchildren. He has served as pastor of four Lutheran congregations in California and Nevada, as Director of the Center for Theological Study in the southwest, and as Assistant Professor of Religion at California Lutheran University in Thousand Oaks, California.

Thew Elliot is a music educator, writer, and performer in Washington, DC. His strong belief in the power of words and music to bring about social change guides his work within Dumbarton UMC, where he writes new texts, hymns, and simple songs for corporate worship. When he designs liturgies, his goal is "to free G-d from the traditional binds and symbols of hetero-patriarchy, and call the community into increasingly creative and responsible relationship with their Creator." Thew often produces original music for worship. Trained in piano and voice, he currently teaches at the Levine School of Music.

Dr. Thomas Farrington is a member and Pastoral Partner of Park Avenue Christian Church and professor at Berkeley College, Manhattan.

Muriel Follansbee is a retired college teacher of family and child development and a co-founder of the Sacramento chapter of P-FLAG in 1982. Her husband, Merrill Follansbee, who died in 1999, was a Presbyterian minister who served both the parish, Synod and Presbytery offices. Both Muriel and Merrill received tremendous affirmation from their gay son and from their many gay/lesbian friends and knew themselves to be blessed to be part of their lives.

Chris Glaser is the editor of *Open Hands* and the author of seven books, including *The Word Is Out–Daily Reflections on the Bible for Lesbians and Gay Men* and *Coming Out as Sacrament*. From his home in Atlanta, Chris travels widely, leading retreats and workshops, speaking and preaching.

Bob Gibeling became the first full-time employee, Program Executive, of Lutherans Concerned/North America in 1993. A native and resident of Atlanta, he is a member of the Lutheran Church of the Redeemer. With a MBA and 15 years in corporate communications and marketing, he uses his skills to promote full inclusion of Gay and Lesbian People in the Christian church.

A United Methodist pastor since 1979, **Dr. Sid Hall III** is the senior pastor of Trinity United Methodist Church, a Reconciling Congregation since 1992, in Austin, Texas. He is the author of *Christian Anti-Semitism and Paul's Theology* (Fortress Press, 1993), a member of the board of directors of the Reconciling Congregation Program, and a frequent speaker on Holocaust Studies, Anti-Jewish Theology in the Church, and Homophobia. His life-partner is Ronda Merrill Hall and their teenaged children are Rachel and David.

Trey Hall, a candidate for Ordained Ministry in The Northern Illinois Conference of The United Methodist Church and graduate of Candler School of Theology, Emory University ('00), is currently interim pastor of Thatcham and Kingsclere churches in the Newbury and Hungerford circuit of the British Methodist Church.

Judith Hanlon is the divorced mother of two young women and "pastor" of a congregation of single folk entitled, "Christian Singles Fellowship" (www.christianandsingle.com). The daughter of a Pentecostal minister and a musical mom, she attends Andover Newton Theological seminary and finds songwriting prayerful and creative. She worships in an Open and Affirming United Church of Christ congregation.

Youtha C. Hardman-Cromwell, PhD, is an elder in the Virginia Conference of the United Methodist Church. She has been a pastor of a local church, an administrator at Howard University School of Divinity, and is now appointed as Associate Director of the Practice in Ministry and Mission Program at Wesley Theological Seminary, where she coordinates the cross-cultural immersion requirement for the M.Div. degree program. Dr. Hardman-Cromwell leads spiritual retreats to Grenada, West Indies; presents "God's Trombones with Negro Spirituals" for churches and other organizations; and leads retreats, workshops and training events for religious organizations. She and her husband have four adult children and one grandchild.

Allen V. Harris is an ordained pastor in the Christian Church (Disciples of Christ). He recently resigned as Pastor of Park Avenue Christian Church in New York City after serving there for over ten years. Allen served as founding Developer of the Open & Affirming Ministries Program for the Gay, Lesbian and Affirming Disciples Alliance for nine years.

Gerry Hoyt is program manager for peer counseling for AIDS Survival Project in Atlanta, Georgia. He also serves on the Atlanta Episcopal Diocesan AIDS Task Force and is a member of Cathedral of St. Philip. His prayers have been used in Atlanta's ecumenical Pride Service and published in *Open Hands*.

The Reverend L. Annette Jones, D.Min., Ph.D., pastor of St. John's on the Lake First United Methodist Church in Miami Beach, Florida, recently moved to Florida from Houston, Texas, where she studied Tibetan Buddhism, taught at Rice University and the University of Houston, and had a private psychotherapy practice. She enjoys the fresh and playful spirit of creativity that emerges as she immerses herself in the present moment.

Timothy Kocher-Hillmer is a musician and bodyworker. A life-long Lutheran, he practices Tai Chi, chanting and meditation. Together with his partner Jim, Timothy writes songs and hymns, weaves ritual with play, and attempts to heal the earth by living simply and being open to the radical expansiveness of love.

Lee Krähenbühl is a folksinger, actor, director, and a professor in the Communications Department of Manchester College in North Manchester, Indiana. Lee co-pastors Skyridge Church of the Brethren, a publicly Open and Affirming congregation, with his partner, Debbie Eisenbise. Lee and Debbie live in Kalamazoo, Michigan, with their two-year-old daughter, Brooks.

Mary Krueger, Ph.D. is the Founding Director of the Bowling Green State University Women's Center, and has been teaching and studying sexuality and gender issues for twenty years. She is an educator, writer, feminist and mother (not necessarily in that order) and understands her spirituality most clearly through Unitarian Universalism. She once had a dream in which she heard herself say, "the things I believe in are justice, passion, the power of the written and spoken word, music, God, ice cream, and love."

Mark Liebenow is a member of Lakeshore Avenue American Baptist Congregation in Oakland California, a member of the Welcoming and Affirming Baptists. For the past ten years, he has written material for Lakeshore's worship services and edited their liturgical meditation books. His publications include: *And Everyone Shall Praise: Resources for Multicultural Worship* and *Prepare the Way*, both by Pilgrim Press.

Jorge Lockward is a native of the Dominican Republic and has served the United Methodist Church in several capacities, the current being as Coordinator of the Global Praise Program. He is a well-known workshop leader and liturgist in ecumenical circles and serves on the boards of Choristers Guild, The Hymn Society, Reformed Worship and the Reconciling Congregation Program.

Mary Callaway Logan is an artist, pastoral counselor, and United Methodist clergy. Her *Seeds of Light Studio* is a place for Spiritual Autobiography with Visual Expression groups. She is married to Kent, and has two daughters in college. Currently her art making is *assemblage*, collage in 3-dimensional form, and relies on biblical themes and nature.

The Rev. Helene Loper began as a Presbyterian and completed her M.Div at Columbia Theological Seminary in Atlanta. Because there was no room in the Presbyterian church (USA) where she could fulfill her calling to pastor, she transferred to Universal Fellowship of Metropolitan Community Churches (MCC) in 1990. She served seven years at Cornerstone MCC in

Mobile, Alabama, and is currently serving at LivingWaters MCC in Tuscaloosa, Alabama. She lives with Sheryl, her partner of nine years, and six cats.

Jan Lugibihl is a member of Oak Park Mennonite Church and is the director of a community center in Chicago. She is also a member of the Board of the Brethren Mennonite Council for Lesbian and Gay Concerns.

Dr. J. Mary Luti is the former associate dean of Andover Newton Theological School and taught in the department of History of Christianity. She is the author of numerous articles and *Teresa of Avila's Way*, a volume in the series, "The Way of the Christian Mystics." She is currently the senior minister of The First Church in Cambridge, Congregational (UCC).

Terryl & Marvin Marsh are members of the Association of Welcoming and Affirming Baptists.

George D. McClain is the former executive director of the Methodist Federation for Social Action. He is on faculty of the Doctor of Ministry Program at New York Theological Seminary and is a consultant to the New York Methodist Hospital. He lives on Staten Island with his wife of thirty-two years, the Reverend Tilda Norberg.

Kay McFarland is a retired clergywoman in the Christian Church (Disciples of Christ). She became a pastor in 1985 at the age of 53 after the death of a daughter from cystic fibrosis and her marriage ended after 30 years. She recently moved to Northern California to care for her infant granddaughter. Her family consists of 12 grand and great-grandchildren.

Marcia McFee is a consultant on worship and the arts and has preached, led worship and workshops at many Annual Conferences and general agency meetings of the United Methodist Church. She is a graduate of Saint Paul School of Theology and will begin work on her Ph.D. in liturgical studies and ethics this year at the Graduate Theological Union. Her new hands-on workbook, *The Worship Workshop*,

guides worship teams through evaluation, study and design of worship and can be ordered through worshipworkshop@aol.com.

Peter Meek, the Senior Minister at Hancock UCC in Lexington, MA, since 1980, is active in community and denominational affairs. He has published sermons in a variety of publications and is extremely proud of the way the large, many-minded congregation which he serves has been dealing with inclusiveness, including but not limited to Gay/Lesbian concerns.

Carolyn Henninger Oehler is the executive director of Scarritt-Bennett Center, Nashville, Tennessee. She has a long-time interest in inclusive language, imagery, and worship. Her recent studies have focused on religion and American culture.

Karen Oliveto is pastor of Bethany United Methodist Church, located in San Francisco. Karen has served in parish and campus ministries in rural and urban settings in New York and California. Karen served on the Reconciling Congregation Program Board of Directors for 6 years, serving as chair of the board for three years.

Bobbi Patterson is a faculty member in the Religion Department of Emory University and Director of the Theory Practice Learning Program of the Center for Teaching. Her current studies are in contemporary practices of spiritual formation and transformation, and how they relate to traditional practices of the early Christian monastic communities. She is especially interested in the interplay of embodiment, psychodynamics, symbol-making, and culture. An Episcopal priest, she lives with her husband in Decatur, Georgia, and enjoys yoga, kayaking, swimming, and hiking.

The Rev. Leslie Penrose was ordained in the UMC in 1989, and was appointed as the founding pastor of Community of Hope in 1993. After official complaints were filed against her in1999 for performing same-sex holy unions, She transferred her ordination from the United

Methodist Church to the United Church of Christ. She is also an adjunct professor at Phillips Theological Seminary, leads annual relationship-building trips to Central America, and feeds her spirit by two-step dancing every chance she gets.

Jennifer Pope is graduate of North Park Theological Seminary in Chicago and has had articles published in *The Covenant Companion* and *The Nature of Harmony*, a journal on issues of racism, reconciliation, and harmony.

Jan Powers lives and pastors (UCC) in Amherst, Massachusetts with her partner, Pam, Jan's son, Jordan, and three Pembroke Welsh Corgis. A "Jan-of-all-trades," her latest enthusiasm is for indigenous/contemporary worship.

Marie Renfro-Collins is a Black Churchgirl and Baptist preacher's kid. She is mother of two daughters and wife of one self-righteous man.

Jan L. Richardson serves as Artist-in-Residence at the San Pedro Spiritual Development, a retreat and conference center of the Catholic Diocese of Orlando. An ordained United Methodist minister in the Florida Conference, Jan graduated from Florida State University with bachelor's degrees in religion and creative writing and received a Master of Divinity degree from Candler School of Theology. She is the author of *Sacred Journeys: A Woman's Book of Daily Prayer, Night Visions: Searching the Shadows of Advent and Christmas*, and *In Wisdom's Path: Discovering the Sacred in Every Season.*

Ben Roe is active in Warren United Methodist Church, a small inner-city church in Denver, Colorado and maintains the World Wide Web site for the Reconciling Congregation Program and Open Hands. With a D.Min. from Claremont School of Theology, he has been an educator and counselor with a human sexuality ministry, but more recently does computer programming, education, and technical support. As a bisexual person, he and his partner

Maggie have been involved in many of the same movements for inclusion and justice.

Vanessa Sheridan is a transgendered Christian–a "recovering fundamentalist"–living in Minnesota. She is the author of two previously published books on transgender Christian spirituality and has recently finished the manuscript for a brand new book on transgender liberation theology. Vanessa is active as a speaker, preacher, writer, and educator, focusing on the connections/relationship between a transgendered status and Christianity.

Gloria Soliz has her M.Div. from the Pacific School of Religion and is a member of Bethany United Methodist Church in San Francisco. She has been a leader in the national Affirmation movement and in her local Reconciling Congregation Program.

Mike Stern is a poet/songwriter and resource leader for worship services, conferences, retreats and special events for all ages. His musical presentation express compassion, concern for social justice, peace and healing and evoke feelings of wonder at the beauty of creation and human diversity.

Maren C. Tirabassi is a bi-vocational pastor and writer. Her most recent book is a volume of poetry, *The Depth of Wells*, and she's looking forward to the publication of *Blessing New Voices*, and anthology of prayers by adolescents. She teaches the writing of poetry in prisons and schools and learns more than she teaches. She learns most from those with whom she lives–Don, Matt, Maria and her dog, Shade.

Betty Torrier is a tree-hugging, latte-carrying transplanted Seattlite on the staff at the national Reconciling Congregation Program office in Chicago. Her passions include implementing the intersection of spirituality and the arts for personal growth, group development and social justice.

Bob Treese is emeritus professor of practical theology, Boston University School of Theology. He now resides in St. Louis.

The Reverend, Dr. Eugene Turner is the Associate Stated Clerk for Ecumenical Relations of the General Assembly of the Presbyterian Church (USA). The husband of a school teacher, he is also the father of a daughter who is a school teacher and two sons, one an electrical engineer and the other a macro-biologist. He considers his greatest accomplishment to be his children.

Kelly Turney is a clergywoman and university administrator. She teaches on the subjects of discrimination, sexual harassment, clergy sexual misconduct, valuing diversity and spirituality in the workplace. She works with the Paul Rice Center for Spiritual Practice in Atlanta and serves on the national board for the Reconciling Congregation Program. Originally from Texas, she now lives in Decatur, Georgia, with her partner and two cats.

Dan Vera has been writing poetry for ten years. His work has been published in various regional poetry journals. Dan grew up in Texas and has lived in the Pacific Northwest and Colorado. He is the Outreach Coordinator for the Reconciling Congregation Program in Chicago, Illinois.

Melvin Wheatley is a retired United Methodist Bishop who with his wife of 60 years, Lucile, had three sons, one of whom was gay. They reside in Laguna Hills, California.

Carl Wiltse is Handbell Director at St. Mark Lutheran Church and Composer-in-Residence and Handbell Director at St. Mark's Episcopal Church, both in the Grand Rapids, Michigan area. Since retiring from teaching in 1993, Carl spends his time fulfilling commissions, singing, and participating in other music-related activities. Carl and his wife Pamela Bayes share their home with three loving, but slightly odd cats.

Miriam Therese Winter, a Medical Mission Sister, is a professor of liturgy, worship, spirituality, and feminist studies and director of the Women's Leadership Institute at Hartford Seminary in Connecticut. She has published a dozen books and 15 recordings of her hymns and songs. Available from www.mtwinter.hartsem.edu. Her latest recordings are *SpiritSong* and *Hymns Re-Imagined*, and prior to that, *EarthSong* and *WomanSong*.

Notes

Introduction

[1]James B. Nelson, *Embodiment: An Approach to Sexuality and Christian Theology* (Minneapolis: Augsburg Publishing House, 1978), 19.

[2]Kelly Brown Douglas, *Sexuality and the Black Church: A Womanist Perspective* (Maryknoll, New York: Orbis Books, 1999), 113.

[3]James B. Nelson, *Body Theology*, (Louisville: Westminster/John Knox Press, 1992), 22.

[4]Ibid., 21.

[5]Kelly Brown Douglas, *Sexuality and the Black Church: A Womanist Perspective* (Maryknoll, New York: Orbis Books, 1999), 115. Note, she quotes James B. Nelson, *Embodiment: An Approach to Sexuality and Christian Theology* (Minneapolis: Augsburg Publishing House, 1978), 18.

[6]Sallie McFague, Super, Natural Christians: How We Should Love Nature (Minneapolis: Fortress Press, 1997), 4.

[7]From the United Methodist Book of Worship. The United Methodist Publishing House, 369.

Chapter 1:
Embodied Theology: Sexuality, Inclusion and Worship

We know: From *A Sourcebook about Liturgy*, p. 95, Liturgy Training Publications. © 1994, Archdiocese of Chicago.

Integrating Sexuality: Reprinted with permission from *Open Hands*, Winter 1988.

[1]Matthew Fox, *Breakthrough: Meister Eckhart's Creation Spirituality in New Translation* (Garden City, NY: Image Books, 1980), 41.

[2]Ibid.

Spirituality and Sexuality:

[1]*Sexuality and the Sacred: Sources of Theological Reflection,* James Nelson and Sandra Longfellow, eds, (Louisville: Westminster/John Knox Press, 1994), 71.

[2]Toinette Eugene, "When Love Is Unfashionable: Ethical Implications of Black Spirituality and Sexuality" in *Sexuality and the Sacred,* 105

[3]Nelson and Longfellow, 71.

[4]Ibid., xiv.

[5]Joan Timmerman, *Sexuality and Spiritual Growth,* (New York: Crossroad, 1992) 7-8.

[6]Peter Gomes, *The Good Book* (New York: William Morrow and Company Inc., 1996), 14.

Toward an Integrated Spirituality: Reprinted with permission from *Open Hands*, Winter, 1988.

[1]James B. Nelson, *Between Two Gardens* (New York: Pilgrim Press, 1983), 5.

[2]Ibid.

[3]Beverly Wildung Harrison, *Making the Connections* (Boston: Beacon Press, 1985), 39.

[4]Ibid.

[5]Nelson, *Between Two Gardens*, 52.

[6]Ibid., 15.

[7]Susan Cady, Marian Ronan, and Hal Taussig, *Sophia* (San Francisco: Harper and Row, 1986), 80.

[8]Milenko Matanovic, *Lightworks* (Issaquah, Wash.: Lorian Press, 1985), 29.

[9]Virginia Ramey Mollenkott, "God-In-Here-And-Everywhere." *Daughters of Sarah*, March/April 1985, 6.

Chapter 2:
Proclaiming An Inclusive Community

Welcome One: Preached at: Bethany Christian United Parish, Worcester, MA, October 5, 1997, World Communion Sunday.

[1]Jennie L. Hendricks, *Memoirs of Jennie L. Hendricks and Henning V. Hendricks.* (Thoroughbred Press, 1973). 32-33.

[2]Fred B. Craddock, John H. Hayes, Carl R. Holliday, Gene M. Tucker. *Preaching Through the Christian Year A* (Valley Forge, Pennsylvania, 1992), 404.

Additional volumes providing background:

The Collegeville Bible Commentary. The Liturgical Press, 1989.

James M. Ward, *Thus Says the Lord: The Message of the Prophets* (Nashville, Abingdon Press, 1991).

Paul D. Hanson, *The People Called: The Growth of Community in the Bible* (NY, Harper and Row, 1986).

John Koenig, *New Testament Hospitality: Partnership With Strangers as Promise and Mission* by (Fortress Press, 1985).

Daniel Patte, *Paul's Faith and the Power of the Gospel: A Structural Introduction to the Pauline Letters* (Fortress Press, 1983).

No Longer at Ease: Preached at the 1999 Reconciling Congregation Convocation, Denton, TX.

[1]T.S. Eliot, *The Journey of the Magi* (1933).

You Do Not Know: Preached at Needham Congregational Church, Sunday, November 28, 1999.

(30) **It's A Question of Size**: From *Preach Out! Open and Affirming Sermons of the United Church of Christ*, ©1999 United Church Board for Homeland Ministries, Division of the American Missionary Association. Used by permission. Originally preached for Hancock United Church of Christ, Lexington, Massachusetts, February 21,1999.

Stranger in Our Midst: Keynote sermon at the Building An Inclusive Church Conference, Minneapolis, MN, April 17, 1999, ©1999 Via Media Services. All Rights Reserved. Permission is required to reproduce by any means more than one copy for personal use. Phone or FAX (805) 493-4565 or e-mail requests to VMServices@aol.com.

Discipleship After Sundown: This sermon was given on February 1, 2000, in the William R. Cannon Chapel of Emory University, Atlanta, GA.

[1]From the Christian Peacemaker Team website, www.prairienet.org/cpt/.

[2]Ibid.

Chapter 3:
Ritualizing Our Lives

The greatest: From *A Sourcebook about Liturgy* (Archdiocese of Chicago, Liturgy Training Publications, 1994) 177.

Ritual awakening: A version of this article was originally published in *Women's News and Narratives*, Spring 2000, Vol 8, No 1, published by Emory Women's Center. Used with permission.

[1]Kittredge Cherry and Zalmon Sherwood, ed. *Equal Rites* (Louisville, Westminster John Knox Press, 1995) xiii.

A Ritual: [1]Brian Andreas, *Mostly True: Collected Stories and Drawings* (Decorah, Iowa, StoryPeople Press), 43, 55.

Daniel's Story: [1]The phrase, "fierce tenderness," is from Mary E. Hunt's *Fierce Tenderness: A Feminist Theology of Friendship* (New York, Crossroad, 1991).

Chapter 4:
Creating Sacred Space

What matters: From *A Sourcebook about Liturgy*. © 1994 Liturgy Training Publications, 148.

Spirituality-Art Workshop: [1]From *Sensitive Chaos* by Schwenck, 128.

Chapter 5:
Body Parts: Elements of Worship

Be careful: "Amen" in *Assembly*, Volume 7:3, February 1981 and in "Liturgical Gestures, Words, Objects, edited by Eleanor Bernstein, csj., 1990. Published by the Notre Dame Center for Pastoral Liturgy. 1224 Hesburgh Library, Notre Dame, Indiana, 46556. Used with permission.

We are unique: From *Alive Now!* September/October 1991. Used with permission of author.

We believe in: Written for an Interfaith Pride Ser- (90) vice in Albany, NY, in 1991. Published in *More Light Update*, 1992. Used with permission.

I believe it: From *Touch Holiness*, edited by Ruth Duck and Maren Tirabassi, ©1990, Pilgrim Press. Used with permission.

I believe God's: Adapted from "The Credo" song in the musical HOME: The Parable of Beatrice and Neal, written by Tim McGinley. HOME was commissioned by the Reconciling Congregation Program in celebration of its 19th anniversary. It has toured the nation with fifteen performances to more than 2,000 persons.

As children: From the 3rd National Convocation of the Reconciling Congregation Program, 1993.

We embrace: From the National Coming Out Day Service, October 10, 1995 sponsored by GABLE, the Gay, Lesbian, and Bisexual caucus at Harvard Divinity School.

We will not: From Spirit of the Lakes UCC, 1993, Minneapolis, MN; adapted from *The Art of the Possible* by Dawna Markova.

Come on: From the 1999 *Leading the Dance: Living the Church Reimagined* conference sponsored by the Supportive Congregations Network / Brethren Mennonite Council for Lesbian and Gay Concerns, and the Church of the Brethren Womaen's Caucus.

Let us covenant: Adapted from the 5th national (95) convocation of the Reconciling Congregation Program, 1997.

Come from: From the third Sunday of Lent, 3/7/99.

Just a taste: From the 3rd National Convocation of the Reconciling Congregation Program, 1993.

God you call: From 1993, Minneapolis, Minnesota.

Blow through: From the twelfth anniversary of reconciling, 7/14/99.

Creating God: From the RCP Planning Retreat in Pawling, NY, September 6, 1998.

We are summoned: From 1992, Minneapolis, Minnesota.

Praise God: From accessibility materials for 1999 prepared by SEMAR, Inc. an agency of The Southeastern Jurisdiction of The United Methodist Church.

Come: From the United Church of Christ Coalition for Lesbian, Gay, Bisexual and Transgender Concerns National Gathering, 1999, Providence, RI.

We come together: From the 1999 *Leading the Dance: Living the Church Re-imagined* conference sponsored by the Supportive Congregations Network / Brethren Mennonite Council for Lesbian and Gay Concerns, and the Church of the Brethren Womaen's Caucus.

We come here: From the 1999 *Leading the Dance: Living the Church Re-imagined* conference sponsored by the Supportive Congregations Network / Brethren Mennonite Council for Lesbian and Gay Concerns, and the Church of the Brethren Womaen's Caucus.

We come to: From the 1999 *Leading the Dance: Living the Church Re-imagined* conference sponsored by the Supportive Congregations Network / Brethren Mennonite Council for Lesbian and Gay Concerns, and the Church of the Brethren Womaen's Caucus.

People of God: Adapted from the 5th national convocation of the Reconciling Congregation Program, 1997.

This call: Originally designed for opening worship for the Nebraska Annual Conference, © 1998 Peace by Peace Productions; permission granted for nonprofit use.

(105) **God like**: From "Remember Shiphrah and Puah" service, 7/6/97.

One God: See Sallie McFague's *Models of God: Theology for an Ecological, Nuclear Age* published by Fortress Press, 1987.

O gracious: From Cleveland Heights, Ohio.

Let us confess: From Toledo, Ohio.

God though: From Stewardship Sunday, 9/20/98.

God, you are: From the "Remembering Huldah" service, 7/13/97.

These stories: From the "Remembering Dorcas" service, 7/20/97.

In the very: From the 5th National Convocation of the Reconciling Congregation Program, 1997.

O God, deliver: From *Coming Out to God*, Prayer (110) 59. © 1990, permission granted for nonprofit use.

A prayer: From *More Light Prayer Book*, January 1991. Reprinted with permission.

Almighty: From the 1999 Disability Awareness Sunday materials prepared by SEMAR, Inc. an agency of The Southeastern Jurisdiction of The United Methodist Church.

I saw him: *Coming Out to God*, Day 32. © 1990 used with permission; permission granted for nonprofit use.

Forgive us: From Gay Pride Sunday, June 27, 1993, at The Riverside Church in NY, NY. Riverside is a member of the American Baptist Churches in the USA and the United Church of Christ.

Creating: From Pride Sunday Service, Park Avenue Christian Church, New York, New York, June 28, 1998.

In the many: From the Open and Affirming (ONA) Study Packet produced by the MA Conference, UCC, and the UCC Coalition for Lesbian, Gay, Bisexual, and Transgender Concerns, 1997. For information, call 508-856-9316. Used with permission.

We are: From *Open Hands*, Winter 1990, re-printed (115) with permission. Written by member of the Mid-Atlantic Affirmation for the 1988 interfaith Gay and Lesbian Pride service.

We are many: From the 5th national convocation of the Reconciling Congregation Program, 1997.

How quickly: From the 5th national convocation of the Reconciling Congregation Program, 1997.

Our God: From the 1999 *Leading the Dance: Living the Church Reimagined* conference sponsored by the Supportive Congregations Network / Brethren Mennonite Council for Lesbian and Gay Concerns, and the Church of the Brethren Womaen's Caucus.

It is not: From *Equal Rites: Lesbian and Gay Worship, Ceremonies and Celebrations*, edited by Kittredge Cherry & Zalmon Sherwood. © 1995 Westminster John Knox Press. Used by permission of Westminster John Knox Press.

Scripture urges: Adapted by Dan Vera from *Equal Rites: Lesbian and Gay Worship, Ceremonies and Celebrations*, edited by Kittredge Cherry & Zalmon Sherwood. © 1995 Westminster John Knox Press. Used by permission of Westminster John Knox Press.

Circle of Love: Prayer by Miriam Therese Winter, UM Book of Worship #488, © Medical Mission Sisters. Used with permission. Movements described by Jaye Turney.

(130) **We have good news and accept our**: From Chicago, IL.

Thank you Creator: From Chicago, IL.

Blessed are: From Pride Sunday Service, Park Avenue Christian Church, New York, New York, June 28, 1998.

Radiant God: From the 3rd National Convocation of the Reconciling Congregation Program, 1993.

O God, you are: From the 5th national convocation of the Reconciling Congregation Program, 1997.

(137) **O God, thank you**: From *More Light Prayer Book*, January 1991. Used with permission.

O God what: From *More Light Prayer Book*, January 1991. Used with permission.

God of all: From *Coming Out to God*, Day 35. © 1990 used with permission; permission granted for non-profit use.

God who revealed: From *More Light Update*, January 1994. Used with permission.

Spirit of Truth: From *More Light Update*, January, 1993. Used with permission.

Chapter 6:
Molding Occasional Services and Ritual Designs

The rugged: From *A Sourcebook about Liturgy*, © 1994 Liturgy Training Publications, 148.

World AIDS Day Service: Liturgy shaped by Andrea Bates, Thomas Farrington, and Allen Harris, Park Avenue Christian Church, New York City, December 1, 1999. Gathering by Father Ray Decker, Sacred Heart Parish Community, Olema, CA. Prayer of Unburdening by Marge Marsh, Church of the Covenant, Boston, MA. Prayers of the People by Allan W. Lee. Great Thanksgiving by Andrea Bates.

Jesus went: From *More Light Update*, January 1994. Taken from Un Llamado Ha Compasion: El Sida & La Communidad Hispana (A Call to Compassion: AIDS Ministry in the Hispanic Community).

(154) **Animal Blessing**: From Atlanta, GA; permission granted for non-profit use. Meister Eckhart found in *Earth Prayers: from Around the World, 365 Prayers, Poems and Invocations for Honoring the Earth* edited by Elizabeth Roberts and Elias Amidon,

SanFrancisco: HarperCollins, 1991. Prayer for the Animals adapted from Albert Schweitzer.

Blessing our Graduates: From Community of Hope for high school graduates.

Blessing mission: Designed to commission a mission team to Nicaragua.

Blessing journey: This blessing was offered on the last Sunday before a couple who had been founding companions with Community of Hope moved to another state.

Ritual of Betrothal: This Community of Hope ritual was developed for a couple not yet ready to make a life commitment.

Service gathering around: Prayer adapted from (164) the UCC Book of Worship, p. 364.

For the death of a church: Created for the closing service, June 20, 1999, of Grant Park-Aldersgate UMC in Atlanta, the first reconciling congregation in Georgia.

Prayer for One: From *Open Hands*, Winter, 1988. Re-printed with permission.

Service of Re-membering: This service was planned for Women's History Month in conjunction with the staff of the Emory Women's Center. *23rd Psalm* from Medicine Man, EMD/Capitol Records, 1990. Psalm 55 from in *Violence in the Family: a workshop curriculum for clergy and other helpers*, Cleveland: The Pilgrim Press, 1991. Forgiving litany adapted from prayers by the Reverend Caroline Sproul Fairless in Marie Fortune's *Violence in the Family*.

Jubilee Renewal: Service designed by Sarah Evans and J. Philip Cox-Johnson for Opening Worship Service of 1999 Reconciling Convocation, Texas. *Bring Many Names*, Brian Wren, © 1989 Hope Publishing Co., Chalice Hymnal. Blessing of Water adapted from WomanPrayer, WomanSong, by Miriam Therese Winter. Instructions for water ritual and the movements during the blessing written by Jaye Turney. *Go Down Moses* ©1989 United Methodist Publishing House, United Methodist Hymnal. Words of Meditation adapted from Thich Nhat Hanh found in *Earth Prayers*. *Water of Life* ©1995 Jaime Cortez, New Dawn Music, 5536 NE Hassalo, Portland, OR 97213. *As Water to the Thirsty* © Hope Publishing Co. Prayer of Thanksgiving adapted from United Methodist Book of Worship.

Jubilee Release: Litany of Lamentation adapted by Alicia Dean and Marcia McFee, Northaven UMC, Dallas, TX for the Reconciling Congregation Convocation Service, 1999. *Inspired by Love and An-*

ger, Iona Community, ©1997 Wild Goose Resource Group, GIA Publications *When Israel Camped in Sinai* © 1989 The United Methodist Publishing House.

Jubilee Reconcile: Prayers for the Church written by Philip Cox-Johnson. *Three Little Wolves*, Macmillan Publishers, 1993. Ubi Caritas, words: traditional; translation, Taize Community (France), Music Taize Community ©1991 GIA Publications. *We are the Body of Christ* by Jaime Cortex and Bob Hurd, New Dawn Music. *All Are Welcome*, GIA Publications, 1994.

Jubiliee Rejoice: Liturgy designed by William Bouton and Kelly Turney for the 1999 Reconciling Congregation Program Convocation. Bell Anthem available from A Minor Music Company, 932 Virginia, SE, Grand Rapids, MI 49506. *Revival in the Land*, words and music by Renee Morris ©1983 Great Sweetwater Publishing Co. Invitation to the Table written by Kelly Turney. Kyrie eleison, text: Ancient Greek, music: Russian Orthodox tradition, no copyright. Holy, Holy by William Loperena Puerto Rico. Sanctus by Jorge Lockward. Lord's Prayer adapted from the Prayer of Jesus, St. Hilda community in *Women Included: A Book of Services and Prayers*, 1991.

Ritual of Social Exorcism: From *Claiming All Things for God: Prayer, Discernment and Ritual for Social Change*, Nashville: Abingdon Press, 1998. Used with permission. See the book for more information regarding the power, use, and theology of this ritual.

Light One Candle: adapted from litanies from Euclid Avenue UMC in Oak Park, Illinois, University UMC in Madison, Wisconsin and Wheadon UMC in Evanston, Illinois, January, 2000. During the rituals, large, rainbow candles were blessed and sent to Sacramento for the public hearing again 67 clergypersons who allegedly violated church law by blessing the union of two women.

(200) **Sending Out**: Go Now in Peace, ©1976 Hinshaw Music, Inc.

Celebrating Homecoming: *This is a Day of New Beginnings* ©1984 Hope Publishing.

Naming Ritual after Separation: After divorcing her husband, Margaret no longer wanted to be identified by his name, but reclaiming her father's name didn't recognize all the 'becoming' of her life. So Margaret reached back into her own her-story and claimed a name for herself, a name which had been her grandmother's maiden name, and her mother's and her daughter's middle name. For Margaret, the claiming of the name Lee, was also a claiming of her place in a long line of strong women!

"I Am": Reprinted with permission from *Open Hands*, Fall, 1996. Hymn of Promise, © 1986 Hope Publishing Co.

Transition: In 1995, Mark Vickers died of AIDS. (206) He and his companion Brad had been founding members of Community of Hope and the first couple in the community to celebrate a Holy Union. The Community of Hope felt his loss deeply and found that as Brad healed enough to begin dating, many had a difficult time embracing this change. This ritual was designed to help speak out loud the commitment the Community knew they needed to make to Brad to allow him to become someone other than "Mark's companion."

Organizational visioning: From the Reconciling Congregation Visioning Retreat in Pawling, NY, September 6, 1998. Song of Praise, ©1983 GIA Publications, Inc. Sois La Semilla © The United Methodist Publishing House.

Called to Be: From the Reconciling Congregation Board of Directors Meeting, February 12, 2000.

Service of Vision: From the Reconciling Congregation Planning Retreat in Pawling, NY, September 6, 1998.

New staff: Here I Am, Lord ©1981 Daniel L. Schutte and NALR.

Chapter 7:
The Contour of Grace: Sacraments, Covenants and Pride Services

The very: From *A Sourcebook about Liturgy*, © 1994 Liturgy Training Publications, 92.

Sacrament of Baptism: From Chicago, Illinois.

You, O God: From the 5th national convocation (220) of the Reconciling Congregation Program, 1997.

From lonely: First offered during Advent, 1999 at Park Avenue Christian Church, New York City.

Here at: First offered at the Lessons & Carols Service, Park Avenue Christian Church, New York City, December 12, 1999.

The Lord: Written for Affirmation, Colorado, 1997.

Commissioning: From the United Church of Christ Coalition for Lesbian, Gay, Bisexual and Transgender Concerns National Gathering, 1999, Providence, RI.

O God: Pride Sunday Service, Park Avenue Christian Church, New York, New York, June 28, 1998.

Maundy Thursday: Adapted from Maundy Thursday services from Ruth Duck's *Bread for the Journey* and Lavon Baylor's *Gathered by Love*. "Remembering the Supper" in *Gathered by Love* (p 243, United Church Press). Excerpt from Roberta Bondi on pp 134-144.

(232) **We who**: Excerpt from prayer with families, in *An Improbable Gift of Blessing–Prayers and Affirmations to Nurture the Spirit* by Maren Tirabassi and Grant, United Church Press, 1998, used with permission.

Celebration of Same-Gender: In Madison, WI. From *Open Hands*, Winter 1988. Used with permission.

Loving Spirit: From the National Coming Out Day Service, October 9, 1998 co-sponsored by GABLE, the gay, lesbian, and bisexual caucus at Harvard Divinity School and HUUMS, Harvard Unitarian Universalist Ministry for Students.

Prayers of the People: From the "Journey with God" Ecumenical Pride Service, Atlanta, GA, June, 1998.

Evening Prayer: From the Thanksgiving Service of the Pride Interfaith Coalition at Harvard University, November 19, 1998.

(240) **Prayers of the Community**: From the Thanksgiving Service of the Pride Interfaith Coalition at Harvard University, November 19, 1998.

Litany of Joys: From An Interfaith Service in Celebration of National Coming Out Day, October 15, 1999 co-sponsored by GABLE, the gay, lesbian, and bisexual caucus at Harvard Divinity School and HUUMS, the Harvard Unitarian Universalist Ministry for Students.

For those who fear: National Coming Out Day Service, October 10, 1995 sponsored by GABLE, the gay, lesbian, and bisexual caucus at Harvard Divinity School.

Coming Out: From *Open Hands*, Winter, 1988. Used with permission.

Chapter 8:
Voices of Wisdom

Celebrating: From *A Sourcebook about Liturgy*,© 1994 Liturgy Training Publications, 84.

Interpreting Psalms: Reprinted with permission from the *More Light Psalter*, January 1995.

Psalm 30: From the 1999 *Leading the Dance: Living the Church Re-imagined* conference sponsored by the Supportive Congregations Network / Breth-

ren Mennonite Council for Lesbian and Gay Concerns, and the Church of the Brethren Womaen's Caucus.

Psalm 150: From the 1999 *Leading the Dance: Living the Church Re-imagined* conference sponsored by the Supportive Congregations Network / Brethren Mennonite Council for Lesbian and Gay Concerns, and the Church of the Brethren Womaen's Caucus.

Psalm of Discipleship: WomanWord, Crossroad (251) Publication Co. © 1990 Medical Mission Sisters; used with permission.

Prophetic Voices: Adapted by Betti Torrier from *Our Passion for Justice: Images of Power. Sexuality, and Liberation* by Carter Heyward, Pilgrim Press, 1984.

Overheard: From the "Remembering Huldah" service, July 13, 1997, Washington, DC.

Ever-Present Grace: Reprinted with permission from the *More light Psalter*, January 1995.

We are the They: Originally created for "That All (255) May Worship, That All May Serve: Making Our Communities of Faith Accessible," March 4, 1997, Saint Paul School of Theology, © 1997 Peace by Peace Productions.

Good News: From Faith United Church of Christ in Iowa City, Iowa. The quotations and ideas about Mary and John are from John J. McNeill, *Taking A Chance on God: Liberating Theology for Gays, Lesbians, and Their Lovers, Families, and Friends* (Beacon Press, 1988). The quotations and ideas about same-sex unions in the early church are from John Boswell, *Same-Sex Unions in Pre-modern Europe* (Villard Books, 1994). The quotation about Our Whole Lives is from Pamela M. Wilson's *Our Whole Lives Sexuality Education for Grades 7-9* (Unitarian Universalist Association and United Church Board for Homeland Ministries, 1999) ix.

Chapter 9:
Musical Shapes: Congregational Singing

The Lord: From *A Sourcebook about Liturgy*. © 1994, Liturgy Training Publications, 147.

For the Goodness of Our Bodies: by Ruth Duck © The Pilgrim Press. Used with permission.

Lazarus: Text by Peter Carman © 1997, The Asso- (272) ciation of Welcoming & Affirming Baptists. Permission is granted for unlimited use by its membership and for one-time use in worship by others, provided the following acknowledgment is included: by Peter Carman © 1997 the Association of Welcoming & Affirming Baptists. Used by permission.

O Spirit, Spring: words © 1998 by The Pilgrim Press, Cleveland, OH 44115. All rights reserved. Used with permission.

We Gather: words by Jane Parker Huber © 1982. Used by permission.

Chapter 10:
Songs Beyond the Basics

A new: From *A Sourcebook about Liturgy*. © 1994, Liturgy Training Publications, 172.

Chapter 11:
Selected Worship Resources

Worship: From Equal Rites, Kittredge Cherry & Zalmon Sherwood, ed. © 1995 Westminster John Knox Press, xix.

Chapter 12:
Study Guide

Study Guide: Adapted from Michael Schut's guide in *Simpler Living, Compassionate Life*, Living the Good News, 1999.

Guidelines for Groups: From three sources: Cecile Andrews' *The Simplicity Circle: Learning Voluntary Simplicity Through a Learning for Life Study Circle*, 1994; *The Circle of Simplicity: Return to the Good Life* published by HarperCollins, 1997 and *Simpler Living, Compassionate Life*, edited and compiled by Michael Schut published by Living the Good News for Earth Ministry.

(381) **It takes a**: From Carter Heyward's Touching Our Strength: The Erotic as Power and the Love of God. © HarperSanFrancisco, 100.

Hallow this space: From Jan Richardson's *Sacred Journeys: A Woman's Book of Daily Prayer*. © 1995 Upper Room Books, 310.

We know God: From Chris Glaser's "Our Spirituality: How Sexual Expression and Sexual Oppression Shape It" in *Open Hands*, Vol 8, No 1, Summer 1992, 5.

The root: From Carter Heyward's *Touching Our Strength: The Erotic as Power and the Love of God*. © HarperSanFrancisco, 141.

We long: From James B. Nelson's *Body Theology*. © 1992 John Knox Press, 16.

(390) **The rituals**: From *Equal Rites*. Kittredge Cherry & Zalmon Sherwood, ed. © 1995 Westminster John Knox Press, xiii.

O God: Adapted from *Sexism and God Talk*. ©Beacon Press, 1993.

The technique of clustering: From Gabriele Lusser Rico's *Pain and Possibility: Writing Your Way through Personal Crisis*. © 1991 Jeremy Tarcher. See also *Writing the Natural Way*. © 1983 Jeremy Tarcher.

Create a collect: Adapted from a Barbara Day (397) Miller Workshop, October, 1999, Atlanta, GA.

Index

(Indexed Scriptures appear at the end of each letter section)

Liturgical movement, 123-129, 185
Liturgical visuals, 79
Lockward, Jorge, 280
Logan, Mary Callaway, 56, 69, 81, 250
Loper, Helene H., 167
Lugibihl, Jan, 94-95, 101-102, 117, 249
"Lullabye," 306
Luti, J. Mary, 26

Lamentations, 144
    4:15-21, 183
    5, 181
    8:5-8, 250
Leviticus 11, 44
    25:9-10, 177
Luke 9:28-36, 134
    13:10-17, 61

M

Marriage, 235. *See also* Covenant ceremony
Marsh, Terryl and Marvin, 199
Maundy Thursday, 229
McClain, George, 194, 371
McFarland, Kay L., 247
McFee, Marcia, 105, 122-126, 129, 256
McGinley, Tim, 91
Meek, Peter, 30
Memorial, 14, 145, 151, 167
Mennonite, vii, 52, 372
Metropolitan Community Church, 259, 373
Midwife, 105
Miller, Jane Ramseyer, 327, 348, 360, 362
"Mine is the Church," 355
Miriam, 108, 135, 221
Moon, 14, 150, 381; new, 136
More Light Presbyterians, vii, 374
More Light Update, 149
"Mothering God, You Gave Me Birth," 360
Movement. *See* Liturgical movement
Music, xv, 59, 61, 69, 71, 94, 101, 112, 126, 152, 154,
    164, 171, 191, 234, 263, 266-369, 375

Mark 1:29-39, 47
    13:24-37, 26
Matthew 4:23, 148
    5, 244; 5:3-12, 167
    11:28, 399
    13:3-10, 208
    15:21-28, 95, 118, 134
    25:31-46, 14, 35
Micah 4:7, 120
    6:8, 398, 318, 368

N

Name changing, 203, 204-207
Nature, xi, 69, 130, 154, 216, 270

O

Oasis, vii, 69, 130, 154, 216, 270
Oehler, Carolyn Henninger, 9
Offertories, 130
Oliveto, Karen, 141, 143, 204-205, 270

"On My Honor," 356
Open and Affirming, vii, 16-19, 26, 96, 257, 260-261,
    264, 374
Open Hands, 37, 115, 371
"O Spirit, Spring of Hidden Power," 274
"Ours is the Journey," 358

P

Pain, vi, xii, 2, 23, 25, 57, 58-65, 67, 77, 92, 114-115,
    127, 132, 137, 139, 146, 149, 151, 164-168, 170-
    176, 182, 195, 214, 224, 231, 234, 238, 247, 251,
    254, 256, 262, 272, 382, 387, 391, 396-397
Parents of LGBT, xviii, 32, 57, 115, 137-139, 146, 172,
    182, 184, 187
Park Avenue UCC, 130, 147, 228
Parker, Rebecca, 243
Passages, 375
Patterson, Bobbi, 96, 131-133, 151, 174, 385, 393
Penrose, Leslie, 56, 66, 153, 157-163, 175-176, 201-
    207, 215
Pentecost, 14, 44, 93, 98, 381
Ph.D. rituals, 159-160
Pope, Jennifer, 137
Powers, Jan, 335, 342
Prayer forms, xvi-xvii
Prayers, x, xv, 47, 64, 65, 111, 113, 123, 127-128, 130-
    139, 144, 145, 147-149, 151, 154-155, 163-165,
    170, 178, 180, 191, 193-194, 203, 211, 217, 219-
    220, 228-229, 234-235, 238-242, 265, 370-371,
    380, 382-387, 389-390, 397-398, 403-404
Presbyterian, vii, 259, 371, 374
Price, Ann Freeman, 290, 291, 364
Pride, 237-243
Pride Interfaith Coalition (Harvard), 240
Puah, 416

Psalms 19, 98
    23, 171, 246
    30, 249
    37:1-13, 248
    42, 246
    43, 246
    55:4-8, 171
    60, 243
    62, 106; 62:5-12, 114
    65, 208
    69, 246
    104, 178
    121, 145
    139, 60, 243; 139:1-18, 381
    150, 249

Q

Quaker, 210, 374
"Questions Still Unresolved," 273

R

Racism, ix, xi, 11, 37, 40, 132, 138, 214, 252, 261, 38?
Readings, contemporary, 59, 70, 81, 145, 171, 231,
    232, 250-264, 381, 384, 386, 393, 398;
    scripture, 59, 158, 244, 171, 177, 194, 249, 264,
    384